Digital Platforms, Competition Law, and Regulation

Comparative Perspectives

Edited by
Kalpana Tyagi
Anselm Kamperman Sanders
and
Caroline Cauffman

•HART•
OXFORD • LONDON • NEW YORK • NEW DELHI • SYDNEY

HART PUBLISHING

Bloomsbury Publishing Plc

Kemp House, Chawley Park, Cumnor Hill, Oxford, OX2 9PH, UK

1385 Broadway, New York, NY 10018, USA

Bloomsbury Publishing Ireland Limited, 29 Earlsfort Terrace, Dublin 2, D02 AY28, Ireland

First published in Great Britain 2024

First published in hardback, 2024

Paperback edition, 2025

A catalogue record for this book is available from the British Library.

A catalogue record for this book is available from the Library of Congress.

Library of Congress Control Number: 2023949481

ISBN: PB: 978-1-50996-937-1
ePDF: 978-1-50996-940-1
ePub: 978-1-50996-939-5

Typeset by Compuscript Ltd, Shannon

DIGITAL PLATFORMS, COMPETITION LAW, AND REGULATION

This open access book offers a comparative and inter-disciplinary perspective on the unique competition law challenges presented by the converged digital markets.

Following the digitalisation of even the most traditional bricks-and-mortar sectors of the economy, a well-functioning internal market can only be guaranteed by ensuring the competitiveness of the digital markets. What role do intellectual property law and competition law play in this digital world? How can a more economic analysis strengthen innovation policies to achieve a truly competitive digital single market?

The book provides a rigorous discussion of the many reasons why the regulatory responses, not just in Europe but in other jurisdictions too, may fall short. It addresses an array of procedural, substantive and other issues that are generating intense debate across the antitrust community. This includes the scope and objectives of digital regulation, whether the application of ex-ante rules would result in fragmentation and inconsistencies, and whether such regulatory regimes are an appropriate tool for substantive assessment. The book explores whether the application of these rules would effectively tackle the contestability-related concerns in the platform markets, whether they can be applied without undermining other rights such as privacy, and whether they are appropriate for this digital age as well as the new digital era ahead of us.

Part 1 offers a detailed inter-disciplinary perspective on the most recent legislative solutions in the European Union, namely, the Digital Services Act, the Digital Markets Act, and the Data Act. Part 2 offers competition and regulatory responses to these ever-emerging digital challenges by the UK, US, Latin American, Indian and Chinese regulators.

PREFACE

The uptake of the digital economy has substantially and irreversibly changed our social and economic behaviour. Digitisation and digitalisation of the economy has transitioned everything from how we connect and communicate, to how we search for and consume digital and physical goods and services. In the early stages of the digital economy, competition authorities erred on the side of lenient enforcement. However, as the platform economies started to mature, consistent and conjoint signs of anti-competitive behaviour by the digital conglomerates have begun to emerge.

This book offers an informed view from across five jurisdictions, namely the European Union, the United Kingdom, the United States, Latin America, India and China on the issue of competition and regulation in the platform economy.

The book is divided into two parts.

The first part presents EU-centered regulatory responses to the emerging digital challenges. The EU Digital Markets Act, Digital Services Act, and the Data Act remain the key focus of discussion in part I of the book.

While the top stories about antitrust enforcement in digital markets often heard about in media and specialised outlets focus on the European Union, competition agencies in other regions of the world are also pro-actively eyeing the regulation of digital platforms. Though regulatory responses may be slow to come by, the competition authorities in these jurisdictions have played a vital role in regulating competition in these emerging markets. Part II of this book accordingly maps the competition and regulatory responses to the ever-emerging digital challenges by the UK, Latin American, US, Indian, and Chinese regulators.

A common thread that weaves all these contributions together is a detailed insight into the practices and experiences of these jurisdictions that led to an informed belief in the need for regulation of the digital platforms. These contributions evaluate whether the current competition and regulatory framework is sufficient to address novel challenges posed by the platform economy. Further, as the discussion on the regulating digital platforms shifts from 'why' and 'whether' one such measure is required to 'how' such legislation should be implemented, these contributions address the normative dimension of the design of one such regulatory framework. The book concludes with a reflection on whether the time is now ripe to move from a monocentric to a more multi-faceted and polycentric view on competition and regulation in the digital markets.

CONTENTS

LIST OF CONTRIBUTORS

Manuel Abarca is an associate lawyer at Estudio Lewin Abogados based in Santiago, Chile. He is also Professor of Competition, Data and Regulation in Digital Markets at Universidad Diego Portales.

Oles Andriychuk is Professor at Newcastle University Law School and Visiting Senior Researcher, V Kavolis Transdisciplinary Research Institute, Vytautas Magnus University, Kaunas, Lithuania. He specialises in digital competition law and policy, focusing currently on a comparative analysis of the EU Digital Markets Act and the UK Digital Markets, Competition and Consumers Bill. He directs an independent academic Digital Markets Research Hub (www.youtube.com/@digital.markets) – a small channel on YouTube discussing the latest developments in regulating competition in digital markets. He also coordinates a new tailored LLM in Competition Law and the Digital Economy offered by Newcastle Law School.

Pratiksha Ashok is a PhD Researcher at the UC Louvain, Belgium. Pratiksha has a double degree in Business Administration and Law, Masters in Corporate and Commercial Laws, and a Master in Corporate Law. Her PhD research is on consumer protection in the collaborative economy, under the PROSECO Project (Platform Regulations and Operations in the Sharing Economy).

Rosa L Baum's legal practice primarily consists of antitrust and competition law, securities litigation and enforcement, and commercial litigation. She holds a bachelor's degree from Colorado College, a master's in public policy from the Harvard Kennedy School, and a law degree from Harvard Law School.

Caroline Cauffman is Associate Professor of Private, Competition and Consumer Law at Maastricht University, the Netherlands, a Visiting Professor at the University of Hasselt, Belgium, a member of the Flying Faculty at the China-EU School of Law, an assessor at the Belgian competition authority, and a lawyer.

Margherita Corrado is a PhD Candidate in Legal Studies (curriculum in Business and Social Law) at Bocconi University, Italy, where she also works as a teaching assistant in Intellectual Property and Competition Law related courses. She was a Visiting Researcher first at the Max Planck Institute for Innovation and Competition (Munich) in 2021, and then in 2023 at the University of Helsinki (Finland). Prior to starting her PhD, she pursued an LLM in Intellectual Property and Technology Law at Washington University School of Law in Saint Louis (USA) while studying for her master's degree in Law and as part of a special double-degree program.

She also gained some professional experience in boutique law firms specialising in IP and Competition Law and she was recently admitted to the Italian Bar.

Federico Ghezzi is Professor of Business Law at Bocconi University in Milan. His main fields of research are competition law, company law and their intersection. In addition, Federico focuses on the optimal design and effectiveness of European and Italian competition law investigative and decisional powers.

Allen P Grunes is an antitrust lawyer who advises clients on mergers and acquisitions in a range of industries and represents clients before the US antitrust agencies. He previously spent more than a decade at the USDOJ Antitrust Division. He is co-author of *Big Data and Competition Policy* (Oxford University Press 2016). He serves on the Advisory Boards of the American Antitrust Institute and the Institute for Consumer Antitrust Studies at Loyola University Chicago School of Law. He holds a bachelor's degree from Dartmouth College, a law degree from Rutgers University, and a master of laws degree from New York University.

Subhashish Gupta is professor of Economics at IIM, Bangalore. His interests are in industrial organisation, regulation, antitrust, economics of organisations, and telecommunications. He has served as a consultant to the World Bank, the ADB, TERI, the Government of India, the Competition Commission of India, AICTE, and 24/7 Customer. He has taught managerial economics, game theory, industrial organisation, regulation, and advanced microeconomics to PGP, PGPPM, EPGP, PGPPM, EEP, and FPM students. He was previously chair of the Economics Area and Admissions Chair for IIM Bangalore.

Juan David Gutiérrez is an associate professor at Universidad de los Andes (Colombia). He holds a PhD in Public Policy and an MSc in Public Policy from the University of Oxford and a Master of Law and Economics (LLM) jointly awarded by the University of Bologna and Erasmus University Rotterdam.

Birgit van Houtert is Assistant Professor of Private International Law, Maastricht University, the Netherlands.

Qian Li is a PhD candidate at the Faculty of Law, at Maastricht University. Her main research interests include law and economics, competition and regulation, and commercial law. Her PhD dissertation tackles concerns caused by AI-enabled price discrimination from a comparative law and economic perspective.

Mariateresa Maggiolino is associate professor of economic law at Bocconi University in Milan, where she also is the director of the integrated master of arts in law. Her main fields of research are antitrust law, data law, IP law, and banking law.

Joanna Mazur is assistant professor at the Faculty of Management at the University of Warsaw, analyst at DELab UW and Center of Antitrust and Regulatory Studies (ORCID: 0000-0002-0417-5743).

Sneha Mehta is a qualified attorney from India and a dedicated legal professional specialising in IP, media, and entertainment law. With an LLM qualification in Advanced Masters in IP and Knowledge Management from Maastricht Faculty of Law, Sneha served as a senior executive legal at Endemol Shine India before relocating to Amsterdam, Netherlands. Currently, she works as an IP paralegal in a law firm in Amsterdam.

Niels Philipsen is Professor of Shifts in Private and Public Regulation at Erasmus University Rotterdam and Vice-Director of the METRO research institute at Maastricht University, the Netherlands. He is also Adjunct Professor at the School of Law and Economics at CUPL in Beijing, China. His main research interests include law and economics, competition and regulation, torts and insurance, and environmental law.

Anselm Kamperman Sanders is Professor of Intellectual Property Law at Maastricht University, the Netherlands. He is Director of the Advanced Masters Intellectual Property Law and Knowledge Management (IPKM LLM/MSc), and Academic Director of the Institute for Globalization and International Regulation (IGIR) at Maastricht University, the Netherlands. He sits as deputy judge in the Court of Appeal, The Hague, which has exclusive jurisdiction over patent disputes.

Kalpana Tyagi is Assistant Professor of Intellectual Property and Competition Law at Maastricht University. She holds a multidisciplinary PhD (*summa cum laude*) from the Max Planck Institute for Innovation and Competition, Munich. She has also worked as a research policy analyst at International Telecommunications Union, Geneva. Thereafter, she worked at the University of Århus, Denmark, whereby she developed the Center for Law & Digitalization with focus on emerging technologies such as AI and blockchain technology.

Mehmet B Unver, PhD, lecturer in law at University of Hertfordshire, specialises in IT/communications law, copyright, and competition law with a focus on digital markets, data protection, AI ethics, and governance. His research interests lie in governance of emerging technologies from a multidisciplinary perspective, including issues concerning transparency, trust, and ethics as well as economic regulation of digital markets.

Laura Zoboli is Assistant Professor in Commercial Law at the University of Brescia and Scientific Coordinator of the Centre for Antitrust and Regulatory Studies at the University of Warsaw. She obtained her PhD from Bocconi University, has held a Marie Curie Fellowship at the University of Turin, and served as a visiting researcher at the Max Planck Institute for Innovation and Competition and the Berkman Klein Center at Harvard University.

TABLE OF CASES

European Union

Court of Justice

General Court

European Commission

Argentina

Chile

China

Colombia

Germany

Mexico

The Netherlands

Poland

India

Italy

United Kingdom

United States of America

TABLE OF LEGISLATION

European Commission

China

France

International Treaties

India

United States of America

Reports

Chile

Colombia

Mexico

Peru

1

Introduction: Regulating Digital Platforms

Shall We, Shall We Not?

KALPANA TYAGI

1. Introduction

The invisible hand of innovation sustains the comforts of modern day life. Digital intermediaries, such as search engines, social media, and professional networking platforms, are a key player in the digital ecosystem. When the internet was still in its infancy, jurisdictions worldwide, including the EU as well as the US, decided to offer them an immunity. This immunity offered intermediaries an assurance that they would not be held liable for allegedly infringing content available on their platforms. The approach had its positive effects, as various platforms emerged and flourished over time.

As the platform economy progressed, and notably with the rise of the big data, and complex algorithms that could now make meaningful interpretations and insights from data generated by the platforms, the platforms saw increasing value in the data gathered (and the information available therein). As platforms collected data and used this information to offer targeted advertisements, policy-makers too took account of this evolving aspect of the platform economy. The evolution of the intermediaries, coupled with convergence in the telecommunications sector, presented new challenges for policy-makers. Convergence in the telecommunications sector refers to the fact that a given device may perform multiple functions that were earlier performed by distinct devices. It also meant that devices could now communicate with each other. Consider for example the convergence between the telecommunications and the media sector. One of the immediate fallouts of convergence was heightened mergers and acquisitions in the converged telecoms sector, whereby the deregulation of the sector meant that the fixed-line telephone operators and the Mobile Network Operators (MNOs) faced intense competition in the market. A natural response to this intense competition was consolidation in the sector. The telecom mergers were subject to intense scrutiny by competition authorities worldwide. The European Commission, in particular, reviewed many

4-to-3 telecom mergers across Member States in the EU. Most of these mergers, with the exception of the proposed TeliaSonera and Telenor merger in Denmark, and the H3G UK and Telefónica merger in the UK, received the Commission's conditional approval.[1] The merger between AT&T and Time Warner, first prohibited by the US Department of Justice, but then subsequently unconditionally cleared by a US district court, well illustrates the ever evolving business models, and the correspondingly augmented and robust approach of the telecom and content-driven firms seeking to re-invent themselves, and innovatively conduct business in the digital age.[2] The telecommunications, media, and the fixed landline players (that had earlier enjoyed incumbency advantages, and positions of dominance, prior to the introduction of sector-specific regulation) thus responded to the Schumpeterian 'wave of creative destruction' called digitisation, digitalisation, and convergence, with digital transformation and mergers and acquisitions (hereafter referred to as mergers). There was, however, yet another field that experienced immense innovation – this was the fast-emerging platform economy, which although quite similar, and also dependent upon the telecoms infrastructure, was still somewhat dissimilar from the converged telecommunications sector. In this platform economy, also known as multi-sided platforms (MSPs), platforms create value by facilitating 'direct interaction between' customers and participants who are situated on the different sides of the market.[3] In other words, they solve the coordination problem between different sides of the market, and facilitate transactions that may otherwise not take place. There are some novel features of the MSPs – qualities that one does not quite see in the converged telecommunications sector. These characteristics include, amongst others, the economics of 'free', the role of user generated content (UGC), the role of big data and algorithms, and the winner-takes-all nature of these markets. Like the traditional telecommunications sector, these big data-driven MSPs also rode high on the wave of mergers. Notable mergers in the early phases include Google's foresighted and not-so-expensive acquisition[4] of its now highly valuable and well-integrated assets such as Waze, Doubleclick, YouTube, and ITA; Microsoft's acquisition of Azure and LinkedIn; and Facebook's (now Meta) acquisition of Instagram and WhatsApp. These acquisitions were a great value add to the portfolio of these firms. In addition to the role of mergers, perhaps even more central to the platform economy are the sector-specific features

[1] K Tyagi, 'Four-to-Three Telecom Mergers: Substantial Issues in EU Merger Control in the Mobile Telecommunications Sector' (2018) 49 *IIC*, link.springer.com/article/10.1007/s40319-018-0677-3.

[2] K Tyagi, 'Implications of the AT&T/Time Warner Decision for Vertical Integration and Media Business Models in the age of digitization' (2018) 1(2) *Competition Policy International* 1(2) www.researchgate.net/publication/327106444_IMPLICATIONS_OF_THE_ATTTIME_WARNER_DECISION_FOR_VERTICAL_INTEGRATION_AND_MEDIA_BUSINESS_MODELS_IN_THE_AGE_OF_DIGITIZATION.

[3] A Hagiu, 'Strategic Decisions for Multisided Platforms' MIT Sloan Management Review (19 December 2013), sloanreview.mit.edu/article/strategic-decisions-for-multisided-platforms.

[4] Consider for example, YouTube, today one of Google's most treasured assets, which was acquired by Google in 2006 for $1.65 billion. The Associated Press, 'Google buys YouTube for $1.65 billion', *NBC News* (9 October 2006), www.nbcnews.com/id/wbna15196982.

that makes them patently distinct from the other sectors of the economy. Section 2, thus, accordingly, brings to light these atypical features of the platform economy. Sections 2 and 3 also establish the inter-linkages amongst contributions from the authors in this volume and how they offer an insight, first, on the novel competition law concerns that frequently emerge in the digital economy, and second, what are the distinct regulatory responses to the contestability challenges therein. This book reflects the discussion and developments in the field up to August 2023.

2. The Economics of the Platform Economy

This section outlines the key economic aspects that make the multi-sided platform (MSP) economy distinct from the other more traditional sectors of the economy. A definition of these economic principles is important, as the European Commission's Sector Inquiry Report[5] (in the EU), as well as the Monopolokommission's Industry 4.0 report[6] (in Germany), the Furman Report (in the UK),[7] and the Stigler Report[8] (at the University of Chicago in the US), all identify a common set of industry-specific factors and dynamics of the platform economy that make it distinct from the other sectors of the economy. These studies also suggest that it is on account of these special features that the digital economy needs a more nuanced approach to competition and regulation.

The Industrial Organization (IO) literature reveals that the digital economy benefits from certain distinct industry-specific factors, such as direct and indirect network effects, single homing, and high switching costs that make it prone to tipping.[9] In the platform economy, these sector-specific features result in 'an imbalance in bargaining power [between the platform, the users, and the sellers on these platforms]'.[10] The relative bargaining power between the press publishers, and the digital intermediaries is one such notable example. Digital platforms gain traction as they offer content. One such content is news. In order to address

[5] European Commission Press Release, 'Antitrust: Commission publishes final report on consumer Internet of Things sector inquiry' (20 January 2022) ec.europa.eu/commission/presscorner/detail/en/ip_22_402.

[6] Bundesministerium für Wirtschaft und Klimaschutz, 'Ein neuer Wettbewerbsrahmen für die Digitalwirtschaft' (9 September 2019) www.bmwk.de/Redaktion/DE/Artikel/Wirtschaft/kommission-wettbewerbsrecht-4-0.html.

[7] HM Treasury, 'Unlocking digital competition, Report of the Digital Competition Expert Panel' (Furman Report) (13 March 2019), www.gov.uk/government/publications/unlocking-digital-competition-report-of-the-digital-competition-expert-panel.

[8] The Stigler Center: Digital Platforms Committee, 'Stigler Committee on Digital Platforms: Final Report' (16 September 2019) www.chicagobooth.edu/research/stigler/news-and-media/committee-on-digital-platforms-final-report ('Stigler Committee on Digital Platforms: Final Report').

[9] J Haucap and T Stühmeier, 'Competition and antitrust in Internet markets' in JM Bauer and M Latzer (eds), *Handbook on the Economics of the Internet* (Elgaronline 2016) 183–210, https://www.elgaronline.com/view/9780857939845.00017.xml.

[10] European Commission, Proposal for a regulation of the European Parliament and of the Council on promoting fairness and transparency for business users of online intermediation services, COM (2018) 238 final, 2018/0112.

this resulting imbalance of power, the 2019 Copyright in the Digital Single Market Directive (CDSM) created a new neighbouring 'press publishers' right' for EU-based press publishers.[11] The entrenched position of digital platforms can be gauged from the fact that despite this neighbouring intellectual property (IP) right being offered to the press publishers, this could not entirely solve the problem of the press publishing industry. The French Competition Authority (FCA) had to subsequently intervene, based on the provisions in EU competition law, and the French competition law, namely 'abuse of economic dependence' for effective enforcement of this related right.[12] On the other side of the Atlantic, and as Grunes and Baum discuss in chapter twelve, the proposed Journalism Competition and Protection Act (JCPA), seeks to balance the disequilibrium between the digital platforms and news publishers, as it identifies how the platforms, such as Google and Facebook are accused of '"free-riding" off the news … [driving] … journalism into financial collapse'.[13] To facilitate a more balanced outcome, the JCPA 'carves out an exemption allowing news publishers to collectively bargain with digital platforms'.[14] Chapter thirteen by Tyagi further elaborates on the instances of abuse of economic dependence in the platform economy, and how they are treated under the national competition law provisions in the EU.[15]

The impetus to this digital revolution and the rise of the MSPs was first offered by digitisation, digitalisation, digital transformation, and convergence.[16] Therefore, in order to understand the dynamics of the platform economy, one must first understand the factors that shape it, and help it evolve into the form seen today. These peculiarities are in turn, leveraged on by firms in the form of corporate strategy, and business model innovation. Notable strategic responses, as discussed below, include digital nudging, economics of 'free', 'open early – close later', and platform envelopment.

2.1. Digitisation, Digitalisation, and Digital Transformation

Digitisation and digitalisation are some of the most fundamental and basic enablers of the rise of the multi-sided platform economy (in other words, digital

[11] Article 15, Protection of press publications concerning online uses, Directive (EU) 2019/790 of the European Parliament and of Council of 17 April 2019 on copyright and related rights in the Digital Single Market and amending Directives 96/9/EC and 2001/29/EC [2019] OJ L130/92.

[12] For a critical analysis of the FCA's decision, see K Tyagi, 'Interim Measures for Press Publishers in France: Copyright and Competition at the *Carrefour* of Creativity & Innovation' (2021) *Research Gate* www.researchgate.net/publication/359692187_Interim_Measures_for_Press_Publishers_in_France_Copyright_and_Competition_at_the_Carrefour_of_Creativity_Innovation.

[13] B Wofford, 'Facebook Freeloads Off Newspapers. This Plan Might Stop It', *Wired* (30 September 2022), www.wired.com/story/facebook-freeloads-off-newspapers-this-plan-might-stop-it. See A Grunes and R Baum (ch 12 in this volume) 236.

[14] Grunes and Baum (n 13) 236.

[15] See K Tyagi (ch 13 in this volume).

[16] See section 1 above on convergence and how it offered an impetus to mergers in the telecommunications sector.

transformation of the economy). The expressions, though closely intertwined, carry distinct connotations. This sub-section, accordingly, elucidates these technical terms, in order to establish the correlation between them.

2.1.1. Digitisation

Digitisation means that the content that may be available in the form of a hard copy (such as a book, a video cassette, or a phonogram) or as an analogous signal is converted into a digital format. This digital format takes a binary form (that is, in the form of '0'and '1').[17] Digitisation is an age-old phenomenon that can be traced at least to the advent of the scanner. Invented by the French Scientist, Edouard Belin in 1913, the scanning technology was based on the Pantelegraph technology, which dates even further back in time. Giovanni Caselli invented Pantelegraph in the 1860s.[18]

The question is what makes the current trend of digitisation distinct from the earlier attempts to digitise? It is the phenomenon called 'mass digitisation' that offered digitisation the impact that one sees today.[19] Whereas small scale digitisation, such as by libraries or even an individual, may help create personal collections and infringe copyright-protected content on a small scale (and thereby, contribute to piracy), technology-enabled mass digitisation at an industrial scale have had a more widespread and global impact. As Gupta and Mehta articulate in chapter eight, digitisation meant that the cost of making an additional marginal copy of the work plummeted close to zero.[20] These falling marginal costs led to large-scale piracy of all types of digital content, but most notably music and books.[21] A global consensus facilitated by the World Intellectual Property Organisation (WIPO) led to the two internet treaties, namely, the WIPO Performances and Phonograms Treaty (WPPT) and the WIPO Copyright Treaty (WCT).[22] Whereas the WCT deals with copyright, the WPPT deals with the rights neighbouring upon copyright (a distinction that is more pronounced in *droit d'auteur* tradition, ie the continental Europe's civil law tradition, vis-à-vis the common law countries, such as the UK, Australia, and the US). At the EU level, these internet treaties were implemented via the 2001 Information Society Directive.[23]

[17] KT Hanna, 'Definition: Digitization', *TechTarget: WhatIs.com*, www.techtarget.com/whatis/definition/digitization, accessed 1 July 2023.

[18] Scantopdf, 'The History of the Office Scanner', scantopdf.com/blog/the-history-of-the-office-scanner, accessed 16 August 2023.

[19] K Coyle, 'Mass Digitization of Books' (2006) 32(6) *Journal of Academic Librarianship* 641, doi.org/10.1016/j.acalib.2006.08.002.

[20] See S Gupta and S Mehta (ch 8 in this volume) 141–143.

[21] See Gupta and Mehta (n 20) 142.

[22] See Gupta and Mehta (n 20) 142.

[23] Directive 2001/29/EC of the European Parliament and of the Council of 22 May 2001 on the harmonisation of certain aspects of copyright and related rights in the information society [2001] OJ L167/10.

From the perspective of the platform economy, two large-scale industrial digitisation efforts merit mention. The first is the Google Book Project, and the second is the Amazon book project, whereby books were digitised *en masse*. This mass scale digitisation could, in part, be facilitated through significant improvements in the scanning technology – first, the newly invented photographic process to create digital images of hard copies, and second, the optical content recognition (OCR) technology.[24] While Google's stated aim for digitising millions of books was to 'offer a searchable index to the books on library shelves',[25] and Amazon used the technological innovation to enhance its 'Search Inside the Book capability' to help readers identify relevant books to purchase,[26] this digitisation of content also contributed to digitalisation, a phenomenon that we turn to next.

2.1.2. *Digitalisation*

Digitalisation, unlike digitisation, is process-driven, meaning it affects how a value chain operates. According to Gartner, digitalisation may be defined as the process of using 'digital technologies' for business model transition and offering additional value-generating opportunities.[27] Consider for example, the digitalisation of the retail sector. The emergence of e-Retail has affected many levels of the retail value chain – these range from the supply chain (logistics) [upstream market] to the emergence of online shopping websites [downstream in the value chain]. A critical discussion on the Italian *Amazon* decision and the Fulfilment by Amazon (FBA)[28] service, as discussed in chapter two by Ghezzi and Maggiolino, illustrates some of the novel competition law issues that result from the digitalisation of retail. The Latin America competition authorities – which have largely responded to the wave of digitalisation through case law – also offer an interesting insight. It emerges that the legislators' silence on competition concerns in the Latin American and the Caribbean (LAC) digital markets has been effectively addressed by their antitrust agencies pursuing a detailed case-by-case approach.[29] Gutiérrez and Abarca (chapter nine) undertook an empirical study to fathom the decisions of the '29 national competition authorities in 23 LAC countries' between 2015 and 2022, and found that over 50 per cent of these cases, and/or reports concerned digital markets.[30] Even within the digital markets, maximum attention of the LAC agencies was given to the ride hailing apps, e-commerce, and over-the-top media services (OTT).[31] In chapter eleven, Li and Philipsen discuss the *Liu Quan* case,

[24] Coyle (n 19) 642.
[25] Coyle (n 19) 645.
[26] Coyle (n 19) 645.
[27] Gartner, 'Gartner Glossary: Digitalization', https://www.gartner.com/en/information-technology/glossary/digitalization, accessed 16 August 2023.
[28] See section 3 for a discussion on the *Amazon* case.
[29] See JD Gutiérrez and M Abarca (ch 9 in this volume) 159–176.
[30] Gutiérrez and Abarca (n 29); see in particular Table 9.1 on p166 and appendix on pp 175–176.
[31] Gutiérrez and Abarca (n 29) 165, 174.

decided under the Chinese tort law, to offer guidance on how discriminatory treatment in the digital markets, such as AI-related price discrimination, may be treated under the Chinese Anti-Monopoly Law (AML).[32]

These contributions succinctly discuss how different competition agencies have quickly responded to digitalisation, while the legislature may follow up and respond to these market changes with a lag.

2.1.3. *Digital Transformation*

Digitisation and digitalisation are enablers of digital transformation. As the word digital transformation indicates, it is a transition by an organisation to become more agile and digitally enabled. Whereas digital firms such as Amazon commenced their business in the digital space, and then integrated backwards to produce, sell, and manage physical goods, a normal bricks and mortar firm may be required to undertake a series of steps across the entire value chain to go digital. The evolutionary process of going digital by a traditional bricks and mortar firm is referred to as digital transformation.[33]

2.2. Network Effects and Tipping

Network effects are a key feature of the platform economy. This means that the value of a network is the square of the number of its users. Put simply, if the number of users is 'n', then the value of the network is 'n^2'. This may be referred to as a 'direct network effect'. A typical example of a direct network effect is the traditional fixed-line telephone and now, mobile phones. The greater the number of people who own a telephone, the larger is the value of the network for the other users in the network.

Network effects may also be indirect (or cross-side effects). Indirect network effects means that the value of the network increases multi-fold for the users on one side of the market, as more and more users join the other side of the market.[34] In the platform economy, indirect network effects have a vital role to play to influence and shape the conditions of competition in these markets. Examples include Google Android, Google Advertising Ecosystem, and Microsoft Windows.

Network effects bring with them an accompanying phenomenon called 'tipping'. This has significant implications for how competition plays out in the platform

[32] Q Li and NJ Philipsen (ch 11 in this volume).

[33] J Bloomberg, 'Digitization, Digitalization, And Digital Transformation: Confuse Them At Your Peril (29 April 2018) https://www.forbes.com/sites/jasonbloomberg/2018/04/29/digitization-digitalization-and-digital-transformation-confuse-them-at-your-peril/?sh=7a130a2c2f2c (accessed 16 August 2023).

[34] NL Johnson, 'What are Network Effects', *Applico*, www.applicoinc.com/blog/network-effects, accessed 1 July 2023.

economy. The nature of the platform economy is such that the competition is 'for' the market, and not 'in' the market. This means that once the market tips to one player, this dominant player may then effectively serve the entire market. When the digital economy was still in its infancy, competition authorities adopted a non-interventionist approach. It was widely believed that the dynamic nature of these markets meant that monopoly would be short-lived, and it was in fact a reward for innovation. In other words, the Schumpeterian wave of creative destruction would ensure that the monopoly power was transient, and as soon as a better offering became available on the market, the incumbent monopolist was quickly displaced by this new, more efficient and innovative entrant.[35] Monopoly rent was not the result of rent-seeking behaviour by the incumbent; rather, it was the result of their fortitude, foresight, and innovation. Examples abound in the early stages of the internet where this argument seemed to hold water. Early on, the market for search engines was highly competitive, and players such as AltaVista and Yahoo! amongst others, fiercely competed with Google in the online search market. However, once the markets tipped to Google, little meaningful competition, if any, was seen in the search market. In both the EU, as well as the US, Google's search engine enjoys a market share of 90 per cent. As neatly articulated in an ongoing antitrust lawsuit in the US district court of Colorado:

> Close to 90 percent of all internet searches done in the United States use Google. No competing search engine has more than 7 percent of the market, and, over the past decade, no new entrant in the general search market in the United States has accounted for more than 1 percent of internet searches in a given year.[36]

Network effects, and the accompanying tipping of the platform markets, has thus raised significant competition law concerns. These concerns include insurmountable barriers to market entry and limited contestability of the digital markets.

2.3. The Economics of 'Free', Digital Nudges, and Dark Patterns

Platforms offer us information, and/or direct us towards relevant websites for free. When users enter a search word on Google, they receive search results. While this information may apparently seem free (at least devoid of any monetary costs), it has substantial non-cost elements therein. From an economic perspective, these platforms solve the transaction costs problem, and facilitate transactions that may

[35] JA Schumpeter, *Capitalism, Socialism and Democracy* (first published 1927, Harper & Row 1942).

[36] Complaint at para 4, State of Colorado et al v Google LLC, No 1:2020cv03715 (DDC filed 17th December 2020), as referred to by A Bonatti and others, 'More Competitive Search Through Regulation' Candid Issue Lab (20 May 2021) 2, issuelab.org/resource/more-competitive-search-through-regulation.html, accessed 1 July 2023.

otherwise not take place.[37] By charging one side of the platform a higher price, and offering the other side of the platform access to information and content for free, platforms facilitate a transaction. This can be seen as a positive welfare and enabling effect of these MSPs.

These MSPs are not a new phenomenon. Consider, for example, the case of newspapers that have for long offered to their subscribers, newspapers well below cost. These newspapers and magazines cross-subsidised the readers by attracting advertisers to pay for advertising. Likewise, consider the case of dating clubs that offer an attractive platform for people to come together and seek a suitable match. If these practices have existed for long, and these MSPs facilitate welfare-enhancing transactions, then what or where is the problem? In other words, why is there a competition law (or any other legal, such as privacy or data protection) concern at all? The concern arises as MSPs gather data from us, and derive disproportionately higher value from the data thus gathered. They extract value from this data by gathering insights about the user's tastes and preferences, and accordingly, offer a more targeted and personalised recommendation. In its Online Platforms and Digital Advertising Study, the Competition and Markets Authority for instance found that in the UK, in the year 2019 alone, the digital advertising costs equalled around £14 billion, which approximates around £500 per household.[38] In a nutshell, even though a user does not pay for the use of the platform, the data gathered therein has substantial value for the other side of the platform (namely the advertisers). While platforms subsidise the users, and offer them (apparently) free access to content and information, they charge supra-normal prices from the advertisers. In the UK alone, this market is valued at £14 billion annually.

Further, the platforms do not offer this access to content and information in a neutral manner. Platforms' architecture nudges users to make choices and take actions that may diverge from their real tastes and preferences. This is referred to as a 'dark pattern'. Although the use of nudges, and capturing consumer interest through attractive interfaces may not be illegal per se, the manipulative and unexplainable tactic to drive 'consumers into buying products and services', that they may otherwise not watch, or use or purchase is certainly undesirable.[39] Even though some of these services (such as the content on YouTube) may be available for free, nudging consumers into watching such content is not only socially sub-optimal, it also contributes to, and adds to the platform's market power, as it leads to more views and targeted advertising. This overall leads to a vicious circle of enduring dominance of the platforms. To illustrate with an example, see Ashok's discussion on Uber in chapter seven, where the author describes how Uber Eats 'provides

[37] DS Evans and R Schmalensee, 'The Antitrust Analysis of Multi-Sided Platforms' in R Blair and D Sokol (eds), *Oxford Handbook on International Antitrust Economics* (Oxford University Press 2015) 405–07.

[38] Competition and Markets Authority, 'Online Platforms and Digital Advertising Study' (3 July 2019) 8, https://www.gov.uk/cma-cases/online-platforms-and-digital-advertising-market-study.

[39] Stigler Committee on Digital Platforms: Final Report (n 8) 12.

rankings [without revealing] the main parameters used' to offer these ratings.[40] These ratings are an important input for the consumer to make an informed choice. If the consumer is not informed of the criteria for these ratings, this brings forth consumer protection and competition law concerns. While Ashok evaluates the consumer protection framework, Andriychuk, in chapter three, explores the different polycentric benchmarks that an effective *ex ante* approach may pursue to take 'different aspects of digital competition' into account.[41] In chapter thirteen, Tyagi contemplates whether the time is now ripe to transition the competition law discourse from monocentric to, in the words of Professor Lianos, a more 'polycentric' one.

2.4. Open Early – Close Later

'Open early – close later' is one of the frequently deployed strategies in the converged telecoms sector, as well as the platform economy. According to Shapiro and Varian, in network-driven industries, firms may first seek to reach a critical mass (in other words, tip the markets) by deploying an 'open policy' that encourages complementary firms to rely on them, and develop complementary products and services. However, once dominance of the incumbent firm is established, it has incentives to offer less favourable terms or even completely refuse to interconnect with the competitors.[42] This issue, for instance, was recently very well-elucidated upon by the EU General Court in the *Google Shopping* case.[43] At the start, Google was very open ('open early') as it displayed organic search results based on their relevance and similarity. However, as the markets tipped to Google as the dominant search engine, it began to replace the organic search results with its 'own specialised results' ('close later'). The moment for this transition of strategy was the point in time when the platform had gained a position of supra-dominance, and there was neither any meaningful competitor nor a real threat of viable market entry in a timely manner. In other words, 'when a platform faces limited competitive constraints, opportunistic behaviour can become profitable', as the users do not have any meaningful alternative to turn to.[44] In the *Google Shopping* case, the GC identified this 'change of conduct on the part of the dominant operator [Google]' as an indicator of competition 'off' the merits.[45] As Baum discusses in chapter twelve, in an early investigation in the US, the Federal Trade Commission (FTC)

[40] See P Ashok (ch 7 in this volume) 126.

[41] See O Andriychuk (ch 3 in this volume) 46, 53, 59.

[42] C Shapiro and HR Varian, *Information Rules: A Strategic Guide to the Network Economy* (Harvard Business School Press, 1999).

[43] F Bostoen, 'The General Court's *Google Shopping* Judgment Finetuning the Legal Qualifications and Tests for Platform Abuse' (2022) 13(2) *Journal of European Competition Law & Practice* 83.

[44] Bostoen (n 43) 83.

[45] Case T-612/17 *Google LLC, formerly Google Inc. and Alphabet Inc. v. Commission* EU:T:2021:763, paras 181, 183.

investigated whether Google 'was anti-competitively promoting its own vertical properties through alterations of its search results page'.[46] Balancing between Type I (false positive) and Type II (false negative) errors, the FTC accepted a handful of voluntary commitments including the discontinuance of scrapping by Google, and removing restrictions that prevented advertisers from multi-homing. With experience in hindsight, Baum views this as 'arguably "misread[ing] the evidence that was in front of them"'.[47] This is further elaborated in chapter thirteen by Tyagi, by drawing a distinction between Type I and Type II errors, and the time may now seem ripe to develop a coherent framework for an *ex ante* regulation of digital platforms, such as the one envisioned in the EU's Digital Markets Act. Unlike the EU, which has taken a hard law approach to address the issues in the platform economy, China has resorted to traditional competition law tools, and pursued a soft law approach. In chapter eleven, Li and Philipsen look at two principal practices – first, how the Chinese competition authorities have addressed artificial intelligence (AI) related price discrimination, and second, how the Chinese Guidelines on the Platform Economy promotes fair competition in the platform economy.[48] As a soft law approach, such as use of guidelines, offers more flexibility, agility, and minimises the possibility of strong fallouts from a Type I error, Chinese soft law approach offers an interesting benchmark to compare a soft law approach vis-à-vis a hard law approach in the digital markets.

2.5. Platform Envelopment

In digital markets, platforms often use their position of strength [the origin market] to enter the targeted market.[49] Factors that may determine the vitality of envelopment include '[either] demand side [or] … supply side commonality'.[50] This envelopment may be referred to as 'market envelopment'.[51] However, as the practice is frequently deployed in the platform markets, it is also generally, and more commonly, known as 'platform envelopment'. Condorelli and Padilla study 'platform envelopment strategies' whereby the dominant platform 'leverages data obtained from the shared user relationships', and define three commonly deployed tying strategies – namely, bundling, virtual bundling, and self-preferencing.[52] Platform envelopment offers a 'complementary theory' on how the platform

[46] Grunes and Baum (n 13) 223.

[47] See Grunes and Baum (n 13) 223, quoting L Nylen, 'How Washington Fumbled the Future', *Politico* (16 March 2021), www.politico.com/news/2021/03/16/google-files-ftc-antitrust-investigation-475573.

[48] Li and Philipsen (n 32).

[49] K Tyagi, *Promoting Competition in Innovation through Merger Control in the ICT Sector: A Comparative and Interdisciplinary Study* (Springer 2019) 37.

[50] Tyagi (n 49) 37.

[51] Tyagi (n 49) 37. TR Eisenmann, G Parker and MW Van Alstyne, 'Platform Envelopment' (27 July 2010) Harvard Business School Working Paper 07-104, doi.org/10.1002/smj.935, 3.

[52] D Condorelli and J Padilla, 'Harnessing Platform Envelopment in the Digital World' (2020) 16(2) *Journal of Competition Law and Economics* 1, 11–13,doi.org/10.1093/joclec/nhaa006.

markets may tip towards certain digital conglomerates 'not through Schumpeterian innovation … but rather through the leveraging of market power, user base' and envelopment.[53] The European Commission's 2019 Report, too, expressed concerns about 'platform envelopment', as this offers an unfair advantage to 'established platforms with a strong user base and [access] to complementary profil[-ing]' to enter related markets.[54] In case of Google for instance, Google has successfully deployed the platform envelopment strategy to enter the mobile operating services market [the target market] by using its position in the online search market, the Google Search [the source market].[55] The buck does not stop here. It functions like a continuous loop of platform envelopment, and the platform expands in related markets to develop an ecosystem of services.

3. How Do the Contributions in this Volume Complement Our Understanding of Competition and Regulation of the Digital Platforms?

As section 2 elaborates, the atypical nature of the platform economy caught the attention of the regulators early on. The EU was quick to respond to these emerging digital challenges. As a starting point, it is important to clarify that EU competition law, and more broadly speaking, competition law in general does not prohibit dominance. Dominance, in fact, may be the dividend that a monopolist deserves following the introduction of a successful product or service to the market. Further, the nature of the platform markets is such that these platforms tend to tip to a certain dominant standard. In *Microsoft/Skype*, the Commission unconditionally permitted a merger-to-monopoly. What EU competition law casts on these dominant platforms is a special responsibility to not to engage in conduct that is *de hors* competition on the merits. What is competition on the merits? In other words, what is that fine line of conduct that an undertaking may not transgress and thereby, risk engaging in anti-competitive conduct? In *Amazon Marketplace and Amazon Buy Box*, the Commission opined:

> Competition on the merits may, by definition, lead to the departure from the market or the marginalisation of competitors that are less efficient and so less attractive to consumers from the point of view of, among other things, price, choice, quality or innovation.[56]

Competition that is 'not' on the merits is a competition law concern. In the *Google Shopping* case, for instance, the General Court opined that a dominant undertaking

[53] Condorelli and Padilla (n 52) 10.

[54] J Crémer, Y-A de Montjoye, and H Schweitzer, 'Competition Policy for the Digital Era: Final Report' (2019) European Commission, 108, op.europa.eu/en/publication-detail/-/publication/21dc175c-7b76-11e9-9f05-01aa75ed71a1/language-en.

[55] Condorelli and Padilla (n 52) 34.

[56] Case AT. 40462 – *Amazon Marketplace* and AT. 40703 – *Amazon Buy Box* (2022) 942, at para 161.

has 'a special responsibility' to not cause obstruction to 'genuine, undistorted competition on the internal market'.[57]

3.1. The Role of the National Competition Authorities

The national competition authorities have played an important role in throwing light on, and developing case law regarding the digital platforms, and fine-tuning the criteria to determine conduct that may be deemed abusive. Consider for example, the case of *Amazon Buy Box*, as discussed in chapter two by Ghezzi and Maggiolino. Amazon enjoys an advantage in terms of size that offers it the economies of scale and scope to gather large volumes of data. Some scholars argue that data are abundantly available, and thus like air and water, which are free and abundantly available to all. On the other hand, data has also been compared to resources such as oil, meaning that they are difficult to gather, collect, and process in order to develop meaningful insights. In *Amazon Marketplace and Amazon Buy Box*, the Commission opined on the situation whereby data can be a source of competitive advantage:

> In view of Amazon's market power, the size and volume of the affected markets and number of online resellers concerned, as well as the volume, the variety, velocity and overall value of the data involved, the Commission preliminarily concluded that Amazon's Data-use Conduct was capable of distorting the competitive process in online retail markets by generating a structural competitive advantage for Amazon Retail. In turn, this structural advantage would typically materialise via increased risks and costs of its online retail competitors for winning transactions and/or their partial foreclosure from the sale of highest-demand products, thereby depriving them of scale and marginalising them.[58]

The commitments offered by Amazon in the *Amazon Marketplace* and *Amazon Buy Box* cases in December 2022, are applicable to all of the European Union, with the exception of Italy.[59] This is in light of the fact that the Italian Competition Authority (ICA) in December 2021 had fined Amazon and imposed a set of behavioural commitments on the world's leading e-commerce service provider. The decision is discussed at length in chapter two by Ghezzi and Maggiolino. The ICA's 2021 decision was also very instructive for the Commission to reach its preliminary assessment in *Amazon Marketplace and Amazon Buy Box*. The ICA has, generally, played a very important role in unearthing and fining conduct by the digital players. In a short span of two years, that is between 2020 and 2022, the ICA initiated several investigations under the competition and consumer protection

[57] Case T-612/17 *Google and Alphabet v Commission (Google Shopping)* EU:T:2021:763, paras 150–54. See also reference to and the discussion of the cases *Intel v Commission*, *Post Danmark*, and *TeliaSonera Sverige* therein.

[58] Case AT. 40462 – *Amazon Marketplace* and AT. 40703 – *Amazon Buy Box*, at para 171.

[59] Case AT. 40462 – *Amazon Marketplace* and AT. 40703 – *Amazon Buy Box*, at para 237.

law against these digital gatekeepers.[60] In the Amazon e-book distribution case, the Commission identified that Amazon was 'an unavoidable trading partner [for EEA-based] E-book Suppliers'.[61]

The *Google Advertising Display* case, initially opened up by the ICA, prematurely closed as the Commission had taken cognisance of Google's conduct in the market for advertising display.[62] In other words, the preliminary view formed by the ICA offered some insights and inputs that then led to the Commission's initiation of investigations against Google as well as Amazon. Ghezzi and Maggiolino thus offer a good backdrop and a case study to evaluate the role of national competition authorities (NCAs) in identifying and assessing competition law concerns early on in the platform markets. The authors also establish that even when competition authorities may be able to identify harm, it remains difficult to clearly outline and name these harms. In the *Amazon* case referred to above, the ICA fined Amazon for preferential treatment towards commercial customers that used its logistics service, known as Fulfilment by Amazon (FBA).[63] The complexity and the novelty of the legal issues therein may explain the ICA's silence on the conceptualisation of Amazon's behaviour. While alluding to 'Amazon's conduct as a case of self-preferencing', the ICA did not take pains to develop its case by meeting the EU General Court's requirements as specified in the *Google Shopping* case.[64] This challenge rears its ugly head as the harms presented by the digital economy do not neatly fit into one clearly defined area of law. They often transcend and transgress into different disciplines of law. Does this mean that we are moving towards a touchpoint of reflection, whereby phenomena such as digitalisation, platformisation, and the rise of the internet of things (IoT) call for a re-alignment of the current narrowly defined price and efficiency-driven approach to competition policy?

3.2. Polycentric Nature of Competition in the Digital Markets

Convergence in the digital economy has also contributed to the convergence of traditionally distinct areas of law. Privacy and data protection, for instance, have became increasingly central to the big data debate. However, the notion of privacy varies, as not everyone shares the 'same raw intuition about privacy'.[65] Common to all is our 'jurified intention of privacy', one that 'reflects our knowledge of, and

[60] See F Ghezzi and M Maggiolino (ch 2 in this volume) 25–41.

[61] Case AT. 40153 – *E-book MFNs and related matters (Amazon)*, Article 9 Regulation 1/2003 (4 May 2017), at para 157.

[62] See Ghezzi and Maggiolino (n 60) 25.

[63] See Ghezzi and Maggiolino (n 60) 27–29.

[64] See Ghezzi and Maggiolino (n 60) 30–33.

[65] JQ Whittman, 'The Two Western Cultures of Privacy – Dignity v. Liberty' (2004) 113(6) *The Yale Law Journal* 1160, www.jstor.org/stable/4135723.

commitment to, the basic legal [and] cultural values'.[66] While we all desire privacy, our actual online behaviour digresses from our desire for privacy in the online environment. This dichotomy is referred to as the 'privacy paradox'. What can possibly better explain this paradox? An empirical survey on user behaviour tried to unearth the reasons for this 'privacy paradox'. The authors found that rather than the attraction of targeted and focused advertising, it is users' resignation to the fact that they do not have much control over digital firms, and online marketers as regards what they learn about them, and have therefore, come to accept it as a given in the digital world.[67] This 'privacy paradox', in turn, is well-exploited by the digital platforms through the use of nudges. While making such [privacy] paradoxical responses to the digital nudges, we leave a digital footprint.[68] These troves of data are extremely valuable for the firms, as they offer meaningful insights about user behaviour. Platforms process this data to make meaningful interpretations, and offer targeted advertising. As this requires processing of personal data, as per Article 2 of the General Data Protection Regulation (GDPR), the data protection regulation is triggered. Article 4(1) of the GDPR suggests that any information relating to 'an identifiable natural person is one who can be identified, directly or indirectly, in particular by reference to an identifier' falls under its preview. Targeted advertising, and the use of data therein, has over time, offered platforms such as Google, a position of distinct competitive advantage. While a position of competitive advantage, and a position of monopoly is not a problem per se, an abuse of such a position, in other words competition *off* the merits, is. This in turn triggers competition law concerns, as the cases involving Google, Amazon, and Facebook (now Meta) indicate. In light of these resulting legal overlaps, as early as 2016, the European Data Protection Supervisor observed that the rise of the data economy amalgamates the issue of reduction in consumer welfare (a competition law concern), lack of transparency and intelligible information (a consumer law concern), and data portability (a data protection law concern) as common concerns for policy-makers.[69] The overlapping nature of these distinct legal fields, at the EU level at least, is also reflected in the emerging High-Level Institutional Frameworks, whereby the EU legislator is increasingly taking due account of this

[66] Whittman (n 65) 1160–61.

[67] See reference to the study by J Turow, M Hennessy, and NA Draper, 'The Tradeoff Fallacy – How Marketers are Misrepresenting American Consumers and Opening them up to Exploitation' *Anneberg School for Communication* (2015), repository.upenn.edu/cgi/viewcontent.cgi?article=1554&context=asc_papers in Condorelli and Padilla (n 52).

[68] S Barth and MDT de Jong, 'The privacy paradox – Investigating discrepancies between expressed privacy concerns and actual online behaviour – A systematic literature review' (2017) 34(7) *Telematics and Informatics* 1038, www.sciencedirect.com/science/article/pii/S0736585317302022.

[69] Preliminary Opinion of the European Data Protection Supervisor, 'Privacy and competitiveness in the age of big data: The interplay between data protection, competition law and consumer protection in the Digital Economy' (March 2014), edps.europa.eu/data-protection/our-work/publications/opinions/privacy-and-competitiveness-age-big-data_en.

intersection between different legal disciplines.[70] As Andriychuk rightly questions in chapter three, it emerges that the 'exclusivity claim' of price-based neoclassical approach of competition law and economics is put to challenge in the digital economy.[71] To correctly fathom and address issues in the digital economy, the narrative seems to be in a 'transition from mono- to polycentricity … [one that] is non-linear and very gradual'.[72] Referring back to our discussion on zero-price economics and the privacy paradox of the platform economy, it emerges, and as Andriychuk points out 'the interests of end users are very difficult to define by using the traditional law and economics toolkit' as they do not completely capture the issues at hand.[73]

Moreover, competition law in particular is generally activated only after the harm has occurred. Furthermore, even where *ex ante* action (such as is the case with merger control) is possible, our current understanding and well-developed legal framework may limit enforcement possibilities therein. A fully fledged investigation in competition law may take a long investigation period and resources, as it requires that the entire *ex post* competition law enforcement process be followed. This process calls for the following three steps: first, the definition of the relevant market; second, finding that the allegedly abusive firm is dominant in the relevant market; and third, that the dominant firm has abused its market power, its position of dominance. Even when the Commission uses its settlement provisions, such as under Article 9 of the Regulation 1/2003 instead of the regular long drawn out investigations, the time taken to reach a settlement may still be anywhere between one to two years. Consider for example two settlement decisions concerning the converged information and communication technology (ICT) sector. In the *Amazon* case, the Commission took over two years before it could squeeze some settlement and agreement with Amazon.[74] The *Amazon E-book Distribution* case was perhaps the quickest to settle as the parties reached an agreement in just one year.[75] Moreover, such a settlement, even though binding, it in no way contributes to a material assessment of the conduct, and whether such a conduct may be deemed as an infringement of competition law.[76] Competition law investigations are often lengthy, and take time to materialise. On average, it takes around three years from the time the Commission initiates investigation to the date when the

[70] B Beems, 'The DMA in the broader regulatory landscape of the EU: An Institutional Perspective' (2022) *European Competition Journal* 25.

[71] Andriychuk (n 41) 45.

[72] Andriychuk (n 41) 46–47. See also I Lianos, 'Polycentric Competition Law' (2018) 70(1) *Current Legal Problems*, doi.org/10.1093/clp/cuy008.

[73] Andriychuk (n 41) 53–54.

[74] Case AT. 40462 – *Amazon Marketplace* and AT. 40703 – *Amazon Buy Box.*

[75] Case AT. 40153 – *E-book MFNs and related matters (Amazon)*, Article 9 Regulation 1/2003 (4 May 2017).

[76] Recital 13, Council Regulation (EC) No 1/2003 of 16 December 2003 on the implementation of the rules on competition laid down in Article 81 and 82 of the Treaty OJ L 1 (Regulation 1/2003).

Commission reaches its infringement decision.[77] The outlier in this case is the *Google Search (Shopping)* case that took close to a decade to materialise, whereby the Commission took well over eight years to reach a finding of infringement, followed by another three year long protracted period of proceedings before the General Court.[78] As the detailed discussion about the ongoing, and complete, antitrust investigations against the large digital market players indicate, these investigations are painfully long, and the remedies have limited effect, if any. The limited effectiveness of the remedies may be explained on the grounds that the markets have already tipped onto a standard by the time an infringement (or even a settlement) decision is reached, and remedies enter force. As the current legal framework may not suffice to address the problems raised by the MSP economy in a timely manner, there emerges an evident need for a well-rounded regulatory framework. An *ex ante* regulatory framework eliminates the need for the well-established pre-requisites in law. This is where an *ex ante* regulatory framework, such as the EU's Digital Markets Act, steps in to 'complement [and not] overshadow' the *ex post* competition law enforcement.[79] The atypical characteristics of the platform economy have given rise to a *de facto* 'global consensus [for] ex-ante (economic) regulation of digital markets'.[80] In this regulatory race, the EU has taken a clear lead, with its Digital Services Act package (comprising of the Digital Markets Act (DMA) and the Digital Services Act (DSA)). In chapter ten Unver compares the regulatory approach across three jurisdictions, namely, the EU, US, and UK. He studies the approach pursed in these jurisdictions from 'the context' of the policy, 'the criteria' that is used for the designation of the behaviour that needs to be addressed, and the design of the remedial framework (in other words, the toolbox) to correct the behaviour.[81] Unver offers an economic rationale for digital platform regulation, namely how market failures in the platform economy may be more effectively corrected *ex ante* through regulation.[82] The choice of legal basis for the DMA in the EU is notable as it identifies the cross-border nature of the digital markets.

3.3. Choice of Legal Basis

The legal basis of the DMA is Article 114 Treaty on the Functioning of the European Union (TFEU), and not Article 103 TFEU. The choice of the legal basis can be justified as the platform economy is borderless, and affects the entire internal

[77] F Bostoen, 'Understanding the Digital Markets Act' (2023) 68(2) *The Antitrust Bulletin* 8, doi.org/10.1177/0003603X231162998.

[78] Case T-612/17 *Google LLC and Alphabet Inc v European Commission*, confirming the Commission's decision in Case AT.39740 *Google Search (Shopping)*.

[79] Andriychuk (n 41) 55.

[80] MB Unver (ch 10 in this volume) 182.

[81] Unver (n 80) 177–201.

[82] Unver (n 80) 177–181.

market[83] (and even global markets). This choice is expected to facilitate a uniform and consistent application of the DMA. Copyright law, for instance, has an important role to play in shaping the dynamics of competition in the digital markets. The EU copyright law – which has largely been harmonised through directives – is a case in point with which to draw parallels, and determine how the choice of legal basis for the DMA may ultimately determine its effectiveness. As directives are binding only as regards the results to be achieved, leaving upon Member States the discretion as regards 'the choice of form and methods',[84] and in light of the territorial nature of copyright[85] (harmonised largely through Directives at the EU level), the digital single market to this day, regrettably, remains fragmented and divided along national boundaries. As Houtert brings to light in chapter four,[86] in light of the territorial nature of copyright, and the licensing agreements therein, online content service providers such as Netflix and YouTube offer differentiated access to content to users situated across different EU Member States.[87] Houtert takes the 'Anne Frank diaries' as a case in point. The Ann Frank diaries are in the public domain in most of the Member States. However, in the Netherlands, they continue to benefit from copyright protection. When the Swiss-based Ann Frank Fonds pursued a legal action against two Dutch-based and one Belgian non-profit organisation (NGO), it thoughtfully chose the Amsterdam district court to litigate the dispute.[88] The decision of the Amsterdam district court is interesting as it throws light on the paradox that exists between the so-called borderless nature of the digital markets, and how geo-blocking may continue to divide the markets along national lines. The district court was of the opinion that as the defendants had taken 'all reasonable efforts [such as] geo-blocking and an "access check" … to prevent internet users from the Netherlands from accessing the website', this may be interpreted to mean that geo-blocking accompanied by access check are robust instruments 'to prevent being sued [across national courts]'.[89] The 2015 Digital Single Market Strategy identified geo-blocking as a key cause of the fragmentation of the Internal Market, and accordingly, the Commission proceeded to adopt the 2018 Geo-blocking Regulation.[90] However, copyright-related geo-blocking, as the *Anne Frank* case illustrates, remains an issue that can only be resolved via the 'unification of EU copyright law [such as through the] EU Copyright Code, and a pan-EU licensing model'.[91] Houtert further establishes how the situation has been exacerbated following another harmonisation

[83] G Colangelo, 'DMA Begins' (2023) 11(1) *Journal of Antitrust Enforcement* 5, academic.oup.com/antitrust/advance-article-abstract/doi/10.1093/jaenfo/jnac033/6978883?redirectedFrom=fulltext.
[84] Article 288 TFEU.
[85] R Polčák, 'Territoriality of Copyright Law' in P Szczepanik and others (eds), *Digital Peripheries: The Online Circulation of Audiovisual Content from the Small Market Perspective* (Springer 2020).
[86] B van Houtert (ch 4 in this volume).
[87] Houtert (n 86) 66, 78–79.
[88] Houtert (n 86) 66–67.
[89] Houtert (n 86) 79.
[90] Houtert (n 86) 73–77.
[91] Houtert (n 86) 75–76.

attempt (again via a Directive), namely Article 17 Copyright in the Digital Single Market (CDSM), which in turn creates situations whereby online content sharing service providers (OCSSPs), such as Facebook, YouTube and others, may have incentives to 'geo-block a livestream [to prevent copyright infringement] in Member States [where these platforms may not have the relevant licence]'.[92] Houtert's discussion offers a fine-drawn and subtle input on, and substantiates the choice of legal basis for, the DMA and the DSA. In addition, it may be useful to add that the *bpost* and the *Nordzucker* decisions also influenced the final version of the DMA, as the DMA now clearly also includes the principle of *ne bis in idem*.[93] As per the well-established Roman civil law principle of *ne bis in idem*, simultaneous legal actions can not be initiated based on the same grounds. The principle is also clearly enunciated in Article 50 of the Charter of Fundamental Rights which has the status of primary law following the Lisbon Treaty entering force.[94]

3.4. Measuring the Efficiency and Effectiveness of Regulatory Measures

The rise of the internet, and the accompanying digitalisation, caused 'a paradigm shift in the social and economic behaviour'[95] of the platform users. Notable amongst them is the rise of user generated content (UGC), and the accompanying intermediary liability. With the rise of the UGC, a clear distinction emerged in the classification of 'active' and 'passive' intermediaries. Active intermediaries are those that actively 'engage with the content that they 'host' on their platforms, which [in turn] means higher responsibility for that content'.[96] In addition, in light of the increased sophistication of the complex and advance algorithms, the platforms can now gather rich insights, and make meaningful interpretations about their users' behaviour, tastes, and preferences. The platforms today are no longer as dumb as they were initially believed to be. Users both benefit from as well as contribute to the growth of these platforms. This means that the platforms today not only facilitate transactions, they also benefit from the activities that take place on their platform by gathering content, data, and making meaningful interpretations therefrom. Facebook, for instance, has a daily active user base of 2 billion users worldwide, and 2.96 billion monthly active users worldwide in 2022.[97] Not only do these large platforms have a large user base, their users also spend large and substantial amount of time on these apps, for a diverse range of

[92] Houtert (n 86) 78.
[93] Colangelo (n 83) DMA, Recital 86.
[94] R Schütze, *European Union Law* (3rd edn, Oxford University Press 2021).
[95] Gupta and Mehta (n 20) 148.
[96] Gupta and Mehta (n 20) 150.
[97] Meta Investor Relations, 'Meta Reports Fourth Quarter and Full Year 2022 Results' (1 February 2023).

activities – such as seeking information, communicating with their peers, and for entertainment. As per the Australian Competition and Consumer Commission's (ACCC) Report, for example, in Australia, in the year 2022 alone, an average adult user spent 17.2 hours per month on Facebook, and 9.9 hours on Instagram per month.[98] Both Instagram and Facebook are owned by the Meta group. In addition, such a user may also be using and spending substantial time on other social platforms. Further, these platforms are not stand-alone products. They are often part of a well-integrated ecosystem.

What does all this mean for advertising and marketing? It means that in order to gain customer's attention and have a higher user engagement, businesses must advertise on these platforms, which are a part of an integrated platform. This offers the platforms access to superior and well-curated information.

In the German *Facebook* case, the Bundeskartellamt (BKartA) found that Facebook was dominant in the market for social networking; a finding that was subsequently upheld by the Oberlandesgericht (OLG) Düsseldorf, the Düsseldorf Higher Regional Court, and the Bundesgerichtshof (BGH, the German Federal Court of Justice).[99] The BKartA was of the opinion that Facebook processed users' personal data by combining data from distinct sources, and profiled users within the meaning of Article 4 GDPR.[100] As per Article 6(1) GDPR, data may be processed provided that the processor has a legitimate ground to process this data, which may include consent of the data subject. The OLG Düsseldorf refrained from considering whether Facebook's conduct was GDPR compliant, as it was of the opinion that there existed no casual relationship between Facebook's dominance and a violation of the GDPR. It nonetheless referred the case to the Court of Justice of the European Union (CJEU) to discuss whether the conduct should be deemed to constitute processing of 'sensitive personal data' as per Article 9(1) GDPR.[101] As per the BKartA, a decision subsequently upheld by the OLG Düsseldorf as well as the BGH, Facebook's contractual undertaking with its users along with its data policy, were 'business terms [under] § 19 GWB [Gesetz gegen Wettbewerbsbeschränkungen]'.[102] According to the BKartA, the 'normative causality' between dominance, conduct and effect were sufficient to constitute abuse under § 19(1) GWB (Konditionenmissbrauch).[103] The OLG Düsseldorf differed from the BKartA, as in the opinion of the former, 'conduct causality' cannot be

[98] Australian Competition and Consumer Commission (March 2023) 'Analysis of and reference to Sensor Tower Data in Australian Competition & Consumer Commission, Digital Platforms Services Inquiry, Interim Report 6: Report on Social Media Services', 9, www.accc.gov.au/about-us/publications/serial-publications/digital-platform-services-inquiry-2020-2025/digital-platform-services-inquiry-march-2023-interim-report.

[99] BKartA, B6-22/16, OLG Düsseldorf VI-Kart 1/19 and BGH, KVR 69/19.

[100] PG Picht and C Akeret, 'Back to Stage One? – AG Rantos' Opinion in the Meta (Facebook) Case' (2023) 9, papers.ssrn.com/sol3/papers.cfm?abstract_id=4414591. See also references therein.

[101] Picht and Akeret (n 100) 9.

[102] Picht and Akeret (n 100) 17–19.

[103] Picht and Akeret (n 100) 17.

assumed, rather it must be established in case of an exploitative abuse.[104] The BGH, on the other hand, further refined and fine-tuned the BKartA's arguments while agreeing and suggesting that in case of two-sided markets, where one sees both exclusionary and exploitative conduct, one need not apply a stricter standard (than the one required under § 19(2) (1) GWB, applicable in case of exclusionary abuse, whereby one can assume 'normative causality').[105] The case is currently pending before the CJEU for preliminary reference. Advocate General Rantos has already offered his opinion in the case.[106] The German *Facebook* case is but one notable, and also one of the first examples, as to how processing user's personal data for profiling purposes can be deemed as an anti-competitive conduct. This line of argument is also reflected in the decisions of the LAC competition authorities. In chapter nine, Gutiérrez and Abarca, for instance, discern the decisions of the Chilean, Columbian, and Mexican competition authorities in the proposed Walmart/Cornershop/Uber mergers.[107] Notably, the Chilean competition authority's preliminary observations about 'exploitative risks regarding the use of user's data' draws a nice parallel to the German *Facebook* case.[108]

If data and algorithms are so central to a sustained competitive advantage, then can a mandated data sharing scheme, or the Commission's proposed data spaces foster competition across digital markets? In chapter six Corrado and Zoboli discuss how data can be an important barrier to market entry. The authors systematically evaluate the European data strategy, and the Commission's strategy on Common European Data Spaces.[109] As different sectors of the economy may present distinct data-related issues, the authors take the proposed European Health Data Space, and evaluate them against the larger Business-to-Business (B2B) Data Sharing framework in the EU. Corrado and Zoboli evaluate how cross-sectoral data sharing such as the Health Data Spaces may promote innovation. The authors also offer safeguards that must be taken into consideration to ensure that these data spaces do not become platform for collusion amongst competitors. While data are the fuel of the digital economy that lubricates the wheel of innovation, casting a duty to share data is a complex task. Equity and more equitable opportunities for innovation may call for data sharing; however, such a condition must be imposed cautiously. Opportunities to voluntarily share data may offer an opportunity for market players to collude.[110] There are two related competition law concerns in case of mandated or voluntary data sharing: first, competitors

[104] Picht and Akeret (n 100) 17–18.
[105] Picht and Akeret (n 100) 17.
[106] Opinion of the Advocate General Rantos in Case C-252/21 (20 September 2022), eur-lex.europa.eu/legal-content/en/TXT/?uri=CELEX:62021CC0252.
[107] Gutiérrez and Abarca (n 29) 168–174.
[108] Gutiérrez and Abarca (n 29) 165, 172.
[109] M Corrado and L Zoboli (ch 6 in this volume).
[110] I Graef and J Prüfer, 'Governance of Data Sharing: A Law and Economics Perspective' (2021) Center for Economic Research Discussion Paper, 10, research.tilburguniversity.edu/en/publications/governance-of-data-sharing-a-law-amp-economics-proposal.

may come to know each other's strategies and strategic advantages, and thereby, enhance incentives to collude; and second, when such data sharing is restricted to a handful of market players (such as in the case of a data sharing arrangement or data pooling), it may create opportunities to the advantage of these players.[111] Accordingly, interdisciplinary scholarly insights indicate that it may be advisable to exchange only 'raw user information', as this will exclude commercially sensitive information.[112] While GDPR may not prohibit processing of personal data, it does introduce a 'new right to data portability for data subjects, which facilitates the exchange and re-use of personal data'.[113] It is important to add here that the right to data portability is distinct from the right to erasure, and invoking the former does not automatically invoke the latter.[114] This means that even if a dominant firm were to facilitate portability under the GDPR, it will still have a data advantage.[115]

Access to data, databases and algorithms may also be a pre-requisite for effective legal enforcement in the digital markets. In chapter five, Mazur critically evaluates how, and under what circumstances can the Commission and the Digital Services Coordinator respectively request such information, and what legal provisions under the DMA and DSA offer such a possibility.[116]

[111] Graef and Prüfer (n 110) 3. See also the references therein.
[112] Graef and Prüfer (n 110) 4.
[113] Graef and Prüfer (n 110) 11–12.
[114] Graef et al (2018).
[115] Graef and Prüfer (n 110) 3.
[116] J Mazur (ch 5 in this volume).

PART I

Digitalisation and the EU's Regulatory Response

2

The Notion of Abuse

Cues from the Italian FBA Amazon *Case*

FEDERICO GHEZZI AND MARIATERESA MAGGIOLINO

1. Introduction

Over the course of 2020 to 2022, the Italian Competition Authority (ICA) frequently investigated and fined digital ecosystems for their anticompetitive conduct. Not only did it open several cases under consumer protection law,[1] but it also initiated four major cases under EU competition law. In particular, although it was obliged to close one of these cases because the European Commission had meanwhile opened a proceeding on the same issue,[2] the ICA ended the other three investigations with prohibition decisions and significant fines.[3] Among them, the *FBA Amazon* case stands out for, among other things, its *legal ambiguity*, which we will discuss here.

On the one hand, it is clear that the ICA condemned Amazon for making Prime and other Amazon services accessible exclusively to commercial customers who delivered their goods using Amazon's logistics service – called Fulfillment by Amazon (FBA) – in lieu of other independent logistics service providers. On the other hand, it is unclear how the ICA conceptualised such behaviour. It *explicitly* qualified Amazon's conduct as a case of 'self-preferencing', although it did not build this charge by meeting the liability conditions that the European General Court affirmed in *Google Shopping*.[4] At the same time, the Amazon

[1] ICA, 10-01-2018, *WhatsApp-clausole vessatorie*, 3/2018; 10-12-2020, *Amazon-Vendita online Emergenza sanitaria*, 49/2020; 9-2-2021, *Facebook-Raccolta Utilizzo dati degli utenti*, 8/2021; 7-9-2021, *I Cloud Apple/Clausole vessatorie*, in 38/2021; 9-11-2021, *I cloud*, 47/2021, 16-11-2021, *Google Drive-Sweep 2017*, 47/2021; 22-3-2022, *Google Drive-clausole vessatorie*, 13/2022.

[2] ICA, 12-10-2021, *Google nel mercato italiano del display advertising*, 43/2021.

[3] ICA, 27-4-2021, *Google/Compatibilità App Enel per Italia con sistema Android Auto*, 20/2021; 16-11-2021, *Vendita prodotti Apple e Beats su Amazon Market Place*, 47/2021; 31-11-2021, *FBA Amazon*, 49/2021.

[4] Case AT.39740 *Google Search (shopping)* (27 June 2017), confirmed Case T-612/17 *Google LLC and Alphabet Inc v European Commission* EU:T:2021:763.

decision is replete with words and expressions evoking a 'tying' case. First, the ICA frequently refers to the company's different product combinations as well as the idea that Amazon's business clients did not spontaneously choose such pairings. Second, the ICA used the adjective 'essential' to describe Prime and the other Amazon services, dealing with them *as if* they were essential facilities. Indeed, the remedy of making Prime and those services accessible on FRAND (fair, reasonable, and non-discriminatory) terms to anyone who meets certain quality requirements is reminiscent of the duty to share that is usually adopted in essential facility cases. Finally, there is room to argue that because it focused on the effects of the company's practice, the ICA overlooked the form that the practice took – and the class of exclusionary practices to which it could belong. The ICA determined that Amazon's conduct produced an exclusionary effect and was likely to worsen consumer welfare, not only in the Italian market for intermediation services on marketplaces (the primary, monopolised market), but also by reinforcing Amazon's market dominance generally for logistic services for e-commerce operators (the secondary market). Moreover, as Amazon could not put forward any business justification for such behaviour, the ICA concluded that the conduct did not lead to any efficiency gain or innovation capable of offsetting the anticompetitive effects.

From here – or, at least, *from the ICA's reluctance to pigeonhole Amazon's conduct into a single class of practices and write the decision accordingly* – a general theoretical question can be raised: if one believes – as we do – that the effects-based approach would be the most appropriate to assess monopolistic practices, why does it matter whether Amazon's conduct is a case of tying, a case of essential facility, or a case of self-preferencing? More explicitly, if a dominant firm is said to be abusing its power when its conduct is likely to exclude rivals in an anticompetitive way without producing any efficiency or innovation gain in return, why does the form of that conduct – or the class of practices to which such behaviour is said to belong – matter? Or should one believe that qualifying a practice as self-preferencing sorts things out, because such a qualification traces the conduct to a family of practices – discriminatory practices – that differs from that of exclusionary practices?

In this chapter we examine these issues in light of the idea that, under a true effects-based approach, practices that take different forms but that, in light of the specific circumstances of the case, are likely to produce the same effects, should have an equal chance of being considered abusive. More specifically, we ask whether, when faced with a practice attributable to a class of conduct such as tie-ins or refusals to deal, competition authorities and private plaintiffs can prove its illegality without satisfying the liability conditions traditionally associated with that class of conduct, but instead demonstrating that those practices are exclusionary and have produced – or could produce – more anticompetitive than pro-competitive effects.

In so doing, we do not intend to reiterate the well-established idea that the notion of abuse is open-ended, so there may be practices, such as AstraZeneca's notorious conduct,[5] that are abusive even though they are included neither among those listed in Article 102 of the Treaty on the Functioning of the European Union (TFEU) nor among those typified by the European Commission and the European Union courts. Neither does this chapter emphasise the well-established notion that dominant firms can carry out specific harmful economic strategies through an array of (pricing and non-pricing) practices. Instead, in this chapter we argue that, among the EU Court requirements that make different classes of exclusionary conduct abusive, there are some that are necessary – the requirements that relate to the effects of these practices – and others that point to certain factual circumstances that can be substituted for other factual circumstances depending on the scenarios under consideration.

In the remainder of the chapter, section 2 briefly describes the facts of the *FBA Amazon* case. Section 3 highlights the passages of the decision in which the ICA gives Amazon's conduct different legal characterisations, and we analyse the effects of this approach and what makes it legitimate. In section 4 we then discuss and refute a first interpretative hypothesis that qualifying Amazon's conduct as self-preferencing is independent of any other possible qualification of Amazon's conduct as exclusionary and anticompetitive. In section 5 this is countered with the second interpretative hypothesis that the different classes of exclusionary conduct which the ICA identified in Amazon's behaviour – ie tying in, refusal to deal, and possibly self-preferencing – are autonomous legal characterisations independent of one another. We repudiates this conjecture, and finally in section 6 we focus on the interpretative hypothesis that indeed legitimises the *FBA Amazon* decision: the only legal characterisation that matters in considering exclusionary conduct abusive is the one based on its actual and potential effects. In section 7 the role that requirements such as coercion and essentiality should play if the notion of abuse were truly effects-based is analysed. Section 8 concludes.

2. The Facts

In December 2021, the ICA fined Amazon €1,128,596,146 for violating Article 102 TFEU – ie for abusing its dominant position in the Italian market for intermediation services on marketplaces (the primary, monopolised market).

First, the ICA found that Amazon used its power to push the sellers active on its platform (hereinafter, 'the sellers') to adopt its own logistics service, FBA, instead of the logistics services offered by competing e-commerce operators in the market (the secondary, competitive market). In particular, the ICA noted that Amazon nudged[6] sellers to opt for FBA by offering 'non-replicable features

[5] *Astra Zeneca/Novartis* Case No COMP/M.1806 (26 July 2000).
[6] *FBA Amazon* (n 3), para 701.

of its platform' conditional on the use of FBA and,[7] hence, not accessible to sellers that finally chose to use other logistic operators. These features were: (i) the use of the Prime label, which in turn allowed sellers both to participate in special events such as Black Friday, Cyber Monday, and Prime Day and to increase the likelihood of being selected for the Buy Box; and (ii) the possibility of avoiding the strict performance indicators that Amazon applied to monitor and punish the bad performance of sellers using logistic operators other than FBA. These features were deemed 'non-replicable'[8] because they were game changing: they could increase sellers' visibility on the platform and thus boost their sales (as well as Amazon's revenues).[9]

Second, the ICA found that such conduct produced two structural effects that affected the market performances of – and, thus, consumer welfare in – both the primary, monopolised market and the secondary, competitive market. Namely, Amazon leveraged its power in the primary market to: (i) exclude other logistics operators (even integrated ones) from the secondary market,[10] given that many sellers were induced to use FBA over other logistics operators; and (ii) exclude other online marketplaces from the primary market,[11] because the costs for sellers of multi-homing – that is, of having a different logistics operator like FBA for each marketplace other than Amazon – would be prohibitively high.[12] After swelling its presence in both markets, Amazon had then positioned itself to increase prices and decrease the quality, variety, and degree of innovation of its supply.[13] In other words, according to the ICA, underlying Amazon's strategy was a classic and straightforward theory of harm: using market power in the primary, monopolised market to strengthen its structural positions in both the primary and secondary markets and then worsen Amazon's offer (not only in terms of prices,[14] but also in relation to the other variables on which consumer welfare depends) without losing customers.

Third, according to the ICA, Amazon was not able to put forward any objective justification for its conduct: it was not successful in indicating the efficiencies resulting *from the link* between FBA and the above non-replicable features of its own platform.[15] Nor – and granted that this should not have been the point – was it capable of showing why FBA was the best logistics service among the many offered, or why services other than FBA were not good enough.[16] It is true that such a link could be justified by maintaining that it was necessary to protect the

[7] ibid, paras 68586.
[8] ibid, para 696.
[9] ibid, para 737.
[10] ibid, paras 728 and 810.
[11] ibid, 728, 841, and 848.
[12] ibid, paras 836–37.
[13] ibid, paras 805–06.
[14] ibid, para 811.
[15] ibid, paras 703 and 725–26.
[16] ibid, paras 720–22.

quality of the 'package-service' that Amazon offers to its end users (consumers), which is made of two 'component-services': the purchase of a given product on the platform and its quick and certain delivery. However, as the imposed behavioural remedies exemplify, linking the above features to FBA is not the least anticompetitive way to protect the quality of the package-service. Indeed, such a result could have been achieved by imposing objective quality standards on any seller that wanted to deliver its products purchased on www.amazon.it through a logistic services provider other than FBA.[17]

As mentioned, the chapter takes these facts as given and focuses on their legal characterisation to discuss why this should matter.

3. How Many Legal Characterisations were Found in Amazon's Practice?

Words matter. The terms and phrases that antitrust authorities use to characterise the conduct they scrutinise are crucial not only because they serve to explain the actions of the authorities and thus increase the transparency and accountability of their intervention, but also – and perhaps primarily –because they serve to establish the *model situation* on which the authorities challenge firms.

As is well-known, at least in civil law systems, legal norms are conceived as abstract facts – model situations, indeed – to which legislators associate one or more consequences according to the scheme 'if A, then B'.

Therefore, for the sake of legal certainty, precisely specifying the model situation in dispute achieves multiple crucial objectives. First, it serves to crystallise the facts that the authorities are required to prove in order to demonstrate the unlawfulness of the conduct under scrutiny, as well as the facts on which firms must focus in order to show the non-injurious nature of that conduct. Second, it allows us to understand whether the invoked legal norm can find application and thus whether the legal consequences it provides for can unfold. Finally, accurate identification of the model situation allows the reviewing court to check who among the authorities and firms has proved their theory, be it the theory of harm or a defence.

However, even a casual reader of the Italian *Amazon* decision would stumble upon three different ways of referring to Amazon's conduct as *exclusionary* and *anticompetitive*. Indeed, the decision's words and expressions would equally fit a tying case, an essential facility case, and a self-preferencing case. Consider, for example, that in, back-to-back sections, the ICA was able to state:

- '[Amazon's] abusive conduct consists in *having coupled* with FBA a set of features indispensable for the success of [the sellers] on the platform … In

[17] ibid, para 725.

this way, on its marketplace, Amazon *has artificially combined* two distinct services … in order to create *an illicit incentive* to purchase FBA, in the absence of alternative ways of accessing the same features and their benefits'.[18]

- 'The visibility and benefits associated with the set of features above identified *has essential nature* for the success of the seller's activity on www.amazon.it'.[19]
- 'Amazon has been able to exploit its *super-dominant* position among marketplaces to increase demand for its logistics service from third-party sellers at the expense of competing services in the secondary non-monopolized market. This allows the firm's conduct to qualify as *self-preferencing*.'[20]

Furthermore, the ICA remarked throughout that Amazon *discriminated* between two categories of commercial customers: those who employed FBA and those who did not. In particular, the ICA focused on the discriminatory nature of Amazon's conduct when it clarified that 'Amazon operates its marketplace *without providing a system* for evaluating the logistics services on *clear, ex ante defined and non-discriminatory standards*'[21] and when – while addressing Amazon's self-preferencing – it stated that 'in the absence of a valid objective justification, *the difference in treatment* between the logistics service provided by the dominant firm and competing services that might be equally efficient constitutes, as confirmed by the ruling in the *Google Search (Shopping)* case, a practice unrelated to merit-based competition and therefore constitutes a violation of Article 102 TFEU'.[22] Emblematically, even at the very beginning of the decision, the ICA seemed to classify self-preferencing as a discriminatory practice by noting that Amazon's conduct is rooted in 'Amazon's ability to discriminate on the basis of whether or not Amazon's marketplace sellers subscribe to its FBA logistics service ("self-preferencing")'.[23]

Finally, as mentioned in section 2, the ICA focused on the effects of Amazon's conduct to show that it was *abusive* because it was exclusionary in both markets, capable of worsening consumer welfare there, and unable either to produce efficiency gains and innovation or to have any objective justification.[24]

However the *FBA Amazon* decision stands out for its abundance of qualifying words that do not make it clear what model situation the ICA actually held against Amazon. In other words, how did Amazon violate Article 102? To answer this question, a first hypothesis must be investigated: that Amazon violated Article 102 because it engaged in self-preferencing, understood as a discriminatory practice different from exploitative and exclusionary abuses.

[18] ibid, paras 713 and 824 (emphasis added).
[19] ibid, paras 714 and 715 (emphasis added).
[20] ibid, para 716 (emphasis added).
[21] ibid, para 718 (emphasis added).
[22] ibid, para 723 (emphasis added).
[23] ibid, para 3.
[24] ibid, paras 801–48.

4. Is Self-preferencing an Autonomous Model Situation?

As is well-known, the model situation included in Article 102 consists of two elements: the dominant position of the investigated firm – the structural element – and the abusive conduct of that firm – the behavioural element.

It is well-established in literature and case law that that Article 102 prohibits two different *families* of conduct:[25] exploitative and exclusionary abuses. Therefore, nobody has ever surmised that the conditions under which a practice is exploitative are equivalent (or fungible) to the conditions under which a practice is exclusionary and anticompetitive – exploitative and exclusionary practices have long been viewed as *two autonomous legal characterisations, independent one of another*, although a same practice may be exploitative and exclusionary at the same time.[26] Due to this classification, scholars have also deemed discriminatory practices to be a subset of either exploitative practices or exclusionary practices.

However, the advent of the digital economy, the uproar raised by self-preferencing cases,[27] and the fact that they may be framed as discriminatory practices,[28] as the ICA somehow did in the *FBA Amazon* case, leads one to wonder whether the notion of abuse is not indeed tripartite – ie whether discriminatory practices should represent *a stand-alone legal characterisation* different from those of exploitative and exclusionary practices. In other words, one could wonder if the model situation corresponding to discriminatory practices should be kept separate from the distinctive model situations applying to exploitative and exclusionary practices.[29]

[25] G Monti, 'The General Court's Google Shopping Judgment and the Scope of Article 102 TFEU', papers.ssrn.com/sol3/papers.cfm?abstract_id=3963336.

[26] A Jones and B Sufrin, *EU Competition Law* (OUP 2009) 364.

[27] P Ibanez Colomo, 'Self-preferencing: Yet Another Epithet in Need of Limiting Principles' (2020) 43 *World Comp* 417; P Bougette, O Budzinski and F Marty, *Self-preferencing and Competitive Damages: A Focus on Exploitative Abuses* (2022) Gredeg WE No 2022-01; E Deutscher, 'Google Shopping and the Quest for a Legal Test for Self-preferencing Under Article 102 TFEU' (2021) 6 *European Papers* 3; I Graef, 'Differentiated Treatment in Platform-to-Business Relations: EU Competition Law and Economic Dependence' (2019) 38 *Yearbook of European Law* 452; L Hornkohl, 'Article 102 TFEU, Equal Treatment and Discrimination after Google Shopping' (2022) 13 *Journal of European Competition Law and Practice* 99; A Licastro, 'Il self-preferencing come illecito antitrust?' [2021] *Il diritto dell'economia* 401; A Portuese, *'Please, Help Yourself': Toward a Taxonomy of Self-preferencing*, Information Technology & Innovation Foundation, 25 October 2021.

[28] N Petit, 'Theories of Self-Preferencing under Article 102 TFEU: A Reply to Bo Vesterdorf' (2015) 1(3) *Competition Law & Policy Debate* 4. To be sure, scholars have also framed self-preferencing as: (i) a refusal to deal case – see P Ibanez Colomo, 'Indispensability and Abuse of Dominance: From Commercial Solvents to Slovak Telekom and Google Shopping' (2019) 10(9) *Journal of European Competition Law and Practice* 532; (ii) as a tying case – see E Iacobucci and F Ducci, 'The Google Search Case in Europe: Tying and the Single Monopoly Profit Theorem in Two-sided Markets' (2019) 47 *European Journal of Law and Economics* 15; and (iii) as a margin squeeze case – see F Bostoen, 'Online Platforms and Vertical Integration: The Return of Margin Squeeze?' (2018) 6(3) *Journal of Antitrust Enforcement* 355.

[29] See also, though before the advent of self-preferencing, R O' Donoghue and J Padilla, *The Law and Economics of Article 102 TFEU* (Hart Publishing 2013) 245.

We believe that the prohibition of exploitative and exclusionary practices exists to realise two different policy goals. Unfair prices and trading conditions, which directly harm consumers and the counterparties of dominant firms, are forbidden so as to advance *fairness* and an *equal distribution of wealth*. Exclusionary practices, on the other hand, which harm rivals and, in so doing, consumers and their welfare/well-being, are forbidden so as to protect the competitive structure of markets, because in market economies competitive markets are expected to produce economic growth and prosperity for the good of all, including consumers.[30] By the same token, we believe that if EU institutions wanted to ensure that dominant firms treat their commercial partners equally, discriminatory practices would be prosecuted as stand-alone infringements, precisely because they impose different conditions on those partners' equivalent transactions. If this were the case, ensuring *equal treatment* would indeed be an autonomous policy goal different from those underlying the prohibition of exploitative and exclusionary practices.

However, in dealing with a secondary-line injury case, the *MEO* judgment ruled out this option.[31] There, the Court of Justice made clear that not every dominant firm applying dissimilar conditions to equivalent transactions causes an injury that EU competition law must prevent.[32] Rather, to apply Article 102, competition authorities and private plaintiffs must demonstrate, on a case-by-case basis and in light of the relevant circumstances, that the dissimilar conditions applied to equivalent transactions caused a competitive disadvantage.[33] True, in *MEO*, the Court did not explain what constitutes a competitive disadvantage. In particular, it did not classify discriminatory practices as exclusionary conduct: it did not state that the competitive disadvantage must consist in exclusion, although a discriminatory behaviour that affects the competitive structure of the market and produces overwhelming anticompetitive effects clearly causes a competitive disadvantage that EU competition law must prosecute.[34] However, in *MEO* the Court clearly stated that a dominant firm – even a dominant firm that is not vertically integrated – does not violate Article 102 if the different treatment that it imposes on its customers and suppliers does not put them at a competitive disadvantage.

Conversely, in the most recent *Google Shopping* ruling, the General Court held that dominant firms must obey the general principle of equal treatment.[35] Nevertheless, the Court also established that Article 102 TFEU applies to self-preferencing only if the conduct at hand is capable of producing exclusionary

[30] Case C-377/20 *Servizio Elettrico Nazionale* (*SEN*) EU:C:2022:379.

[31] Case C-525/16 *MEO v Autoridade da Concorrência* EU:C:2018:270.

[32] ibid, para 25.

[33] ibid, para 37.

[34] G Colangelo, 'Antitrust Unchained? The Case against Self-preferencing and the Zeitgeist in EU Competition Law' (2022) ICLE Working Paper No 2022-09-22 (who, by reading *MEO* in light of *Intel* and its effects-based approach, fills the gap between discriminatory and exclusionary practices).

[35] *MEO* (n 31), para 160.

effects as well as a recognisable anticompetitive impact.[36] Hence, one could raise doubts about the internal consistency of *Google Shopping*: if the principle of equal treatment applies, why should competitive harm ever matter, and why should it consist in the harm specifically produced by exclusionary conduct that is anti-competitive? On the other hand, if this is the competitive harm that must be appreciated in order to apply Article 102, why should discriminatory practices – or, at the very least, self-preferencing practices – ever qualify as a separate family of abusive practice, distinct from and in addition to exclusionary and anticompetitive behaviour?

We believe that at present – ie in the absence of further rulings that would bring order to the matter – the argument that discriminatory conduct represents a third distinct case of abuse of dominance should be rejected. The self-preferencing hypothesis should represent only one of the different forms of exclusionary and anticompetitive practices that dominant firms may hold in order to alter the competitive structure of the market and, in so doing, harm consumers and their welfare.

Moreover – and for our point of interest here – we reject the first reconstructive hypothesis formulated above: we consider that, beyond the words used, in the *FBA Amazon* case the ICA did not charge Amazon with having engaged in merely discriminatory conduct and thereby evading the obligation of parity of treatment. Rather, we believe that the ICA alleged that Amazon violated Article 102 by engaging in exclusionary and anticompetitive conduct that, like all conduct qualifying in these terms, fits the profile of discrimination. Indeed, on closer inspection, all exclusionary behaviour – whether an exclusive contract, a tying practice, or a refusal to contract – implies differential treatment that, if the conduct examined is indeed capable of excluding discriminated rivals and reducing consumer welfare, results in a clear competitive disadvantage.

This conclusion, however, is only partial. Having established that discriminatory practices – or, at the very least, self-preferencing practices – are a kind of exclusionary and anticompetitive practice, we want to ask whether self-preferencing itself should not be considered a model situation in its own right and therefore distinct from those of tying practices and refusal to deal.

5. What would be the Effect if the Existing Classes of Exclusionary Conduct were Autonomous Model Situations?

If cases of tie-ins, refusals to deal, discrimination, and self-preferencing amounted to autonomous legal characterisations – ie to model situations independent of one another – the criteria which the Commission and the EU Courts have progressively

[36] ibid, paras 166 and 175.

established over time to ascertain the anticompetitive nature of such practices ought to be regarded as the requisite abstract components shaping the aforementioned scenarios encapsulated within Article 102. Consequently, these very criteria should also be recognised as the elements upon which both the Commission and private litigants must construct their respective contentions.

More expressly, consider that under the *Microsoft* ruling of the Court of First Instance (CFI), tie-ins are anticompetitive when: (i) the firm in question possesses a dominant position in the tying market; (ii) the tie exists between two separate products; (iii) consumers suffer coercion; (iv) there is a reasonable likelihood of foreclosure in the tied market; and (v) the dominant firm's conduct lacks objective justification.[37] Likewise, under *Oscar Bronner*, refusals to deal that prevent the emergence of new business relationships are anticompetitive when: (i) the claimed resource is essential; (ii) the refusal is likely to have a negative effect on competition; and (iii) the conduct does not have any objective justification.[38] Finally, in *Google Shopping*, the General Court established the company's self-preferencing behaviour as anticompetitive due to: (i) the universal vocation and openness of Google's search engine; (ii) the features of the Google's general results page, which *were deemed akin to* those of an essential facility; (iii) Google's super-dominant or ultra-dominant position, which enabled the firm to act as a gateway to the internet; (iv) a market characterised by very high barriers to entry; (v) the idea that Google's conduct was abnormal, rather than necessary and rational – in sum, it transgressed the scope of competition on the merits.[39]

If these classes of exclusionary practices amounted to different and autonomous model situations, the ICA would have had to trace Amazon's conduct back to *one* of those model situations and then satisfy the specific conditions (*and not others*) that make that class of conduct (*and not another one*) unlawful.

However, the ICA did not do so. Moreover, the ICA did not show that Amazon's commercial clients suffered coercion, which is one of the requirements of the tie-in model situation. The ICA showed that Amazon nudged its commercial clients to opt for FBA. However, being induced to decide (ie to use FBA for logistic services) does not mean losing the freedom to make another decision (ie to use FBA's rivals instead), as it is in cases of technological and contractual tying, in which it is technological incompatibility and/or a mandatory contractual clause that deprive consumers of the ability to choose alternative products to those tied.

Likewise, the ICA did not demonstrate that Prime and the other Amazon's services combined with FBA were 'essential' within the meaning of the essential facility doctrine. The ICA also did not show that there were 'technical, legal or even economic obstacles' that made it impossible, or even unreasonably difficult,

[37] Case T-201/04 *Microsoft Corp v Commission* EU:T:2007:289.

[38] Case C-7/97 *Oscar Bronner* EU:C:1998:569.

[39] Case T-612/17 *Google LLC, formerly Google Inc and Alphabet Inc. v European Commission* EU:T:2021:763.

to duplicate Prime or Amazon's other services.[40] The ICA proved that Amazon's commercial clients that had access to Prime and the company's other services saw their sales increase, because those platforms' features were game changers. However, demonstrating the (enormous) value of these resources is not the same as demonstrating that resources fungible to those of Amazon would not have been *economically viable* for Amazon's rivals that decided to undertake the same investments as Amazon.

Similarly, while the ICA did not verify that the facts of the *FBA Amazon* case met the requirements that the General Court set forth in *Google Shopping*, the Authority maintained that Amazon's conduct was nonetheless a case of self-preferencing because Amazon applied unequal and unjustified preferential treatment to use of its own services, pursuing a leveraging strategy and hence falling outside the scope of competition on the merits.[41]

In sum, the ICA did not set its decision by tracing Amazon's conduct back to one of the aforementioned classes of conduct and did not prove that all the conditions of unlawfulness specific to the 'chosen' class were met. One could therefore conclude that the ICA not only did not develop its reasoning in an orderly manner, but it also did not prove its case (!).

However, in one of the most significant passages of the *FBA Amazon* decision, the ICA wrote that 'the qualification of conduct as abusive does not depend on whether it falls within "a given classification", but on the identification of the substantive characters used to qualify the abusive nature of the conduct, which may vary according to the conduct under consideration and the specific circumstances of the case'.[42]

Indeed, in relation to exclusionary and anticompetitive practices, Article 102 admits a single model situation that is based on the effects that dominant firms' practices are capable of producing and that is alternative to the many model situations corresponding to the specific practices, such as tie-ins and refusals to deal, with which the case law is familiar.

6. The Effects-based Notion of Abuse as the Only Model Situation for Exclusionary and Anticompetitive Practices

Regarding the family of *exclusionary abuses*, the Court of Justice has maintained:

> It is in no way the purpose of Article 102 TFEU to prevent an undertaking from acquiring, on its own merits, the dominant position on a market. Nor does that provision seek to ensure that competitors less efficient than the undertaking with the dominant

[40] *Oscar Bronner* (n 38), paras 44–46.
[41] ibid, paras 236, 504, 506, 716, 723, and 810.
[42] *FBA Amazon* (n 3), paras 711–12.

> position should remain on the market. Thus, not every exclusionary effect is necessarily detrimental to competition. Competition on the merits may, by definition, lead to the departure from the market or the marginalization of competitors that are less efficient and so less attractive to consumers from the point of view of, among other things, price, choice, quality or innovation.[43]

In other words, the Court of Justice is crystal clear that Article 102 is by no means intended to dis-incentivise the efficiency gains and the innovations that dominant firms may realise on the basis of their own merits, nor to ensure that less efficient competitors remain on the market.[44] As said earlier, Article 102 prohibits exclusionary practices because, by using their significant market power to harm the competitive structure of the market, dominant firms prevent the market from delivering beneficial results in terms of price, output, quality, variety, and innovation.

Therefore, unless antitrust decision-makers decide to prosecute a dominant firm for the exploitative nature of its practices, under Article 102 dominant firms are decidedly allowed to engage in practices that *do not exclude* rivals – as is the case, for example, when a firm signs one-year exclusive contract with a small distributor. Moreover, under Article 102, dominant firms can even adopt practices that exclude actual rivals, marginalise them in a niche of the relevant market, or prevent potential rivals from entering it, if these exclusionary effects are *not anti-competitive* – ie if they are the natural consequence of competition on the merits, as happens, for example, when a pricing practice leads to the exclusion of rivals that are not as efficient as the dominant firm. Finally, under Article 102, firms are even free to engage in practices that produce exclusionary and anticompetitive effects if indeed these practices can be objectively justified because they produce countervailing effects in terms of price, choice (also called 'variety'), quality, and innovation that benefit consumers.

Thus, the constituent elements of exclusionary and anticompetitive practices are three: (i) their likely exclusionary effects; (ii) their likely anticompetitive effects that are not offset by likely efficiency and innovation gains; and (iii) the absence of additional and different objective justifications for such practices. Specifically, while those who challenge the unlawful nature of the conduct at hand must prove its actual or potential exclusionary and anticompetitive effects, those who argue for the lawful nature of that conduct must prove the preponderance of its actual or potential pro-competitive effects and/or the occurrence of other objective justifications.

This confirms and exemplifies that under Article 102 the illegality of exclusionary and anticompetitive practices does not depend on the *form* these practices take,[45] but on their *effects* – even potential ones. In other words, when tracing

[43] Case C-413/14 P *Intel* EU:C:2017:632, paras 133–34.
[44] *SEN* (n 30), paras 84–86.
[45] ibid, para 72.

dominant firms' real-world exclusionary practices back to the normative hypothesis included in Article 102 – ie back to the notion of abuse – antitrust decision-makers should not focus on the form of the practices at hand, but on their impact on market structure, if any, and on the effects they produce on the five variables (price, output, quality, variety, innovation) on which consumer welfare depends. As a consequence, on the one hand, practices likely to produce the same exclusionary and anticompetitive effects should have the same chance (likelihood?) of prohibition, regardless of their different forms; on the other hand, practices having the same form but producing different effects should have a different chance of being prohibited on the basis of the (potential/actual) effects at hand.

Therefore, returning to the *FBA Amazon* case, one could argue that such an effects-based notion of abuse *is the only legal characterisation* that should matter *for exclusionary practices* and, hence, the only model situation to which antitrust decision-makers should adjudicate exclusionary conduct occurring in the real world. In other words, the relevant abstract elements composing the notion of abuse applicable to exclusionary conduct should be the effects that the legislator wants to avert by enforcing Article 102 – namely that dominant firms use their conduct to undermine the competitive structure of the market without producing any pro-competitive effect in return.

However, if this interpretation is correct – ie if the effects-based notion of abuse were the only model situation applicable to exclusionary conduct – one should ask what the role of the aforementioned classes of exclusionary conduct and the associated lists of conditions would be.

7. The Importance of Focusing on (Alternative) Facts Showing the Illegality of a Practice

More than 20 years ago, the ICA was required to assess an exchange of information that took place in the market for motor vehicle liability policies (RCA).[46] The exchanges among firms were private and frequent and involved the vast majority of the insurance companies active in the market. The information was related to personalised past and present pricing and was not accessible to consumers. However, the market for automobile liability insurance policies *was not an oligopoly*. As a result, it could have been concluded that the behaviour at hand was lawful, because it did not meet all the liability conditions hitherto developed by case law to discern the illegality of information exchanges. However, the ICA decided otherwise, pointing out that the market for motor vehicle liability policies *was highly regulated*. The ICA clarified that information exchanges that occur in oligopolistic markets risk being anticompetitive because they increase

[46] ICA, 28-7-00, *RC Auto*, in 30/2000.

transparency *in contexts that are already highly transparent in themselves*. Thus, if a market is made very transparent by regulation, the latter is a factual circumstance that can be considered, *in place of* the number of competitors, to conclude that the information exchange in question increases transparency *in a context that is already itself very transparent*.

From a theoretical point of view, the ICA did not consider the oligopolistic market structure a condition of liability without which it would have failed to demonstrate the illegality of the information exchange. The ICA qualified the oligopolistic market structure as a factual circumstance from which possible anticompetitive effects could be inferred and which, consequently, could be replaced by another factual circumstance that would legitimise the same inference.

Likewise, the question arises whether it would be correct and possible to apply the same approach to the list of conditions – say also requirements – associated with exclusionary practices. Consider, for example, the conditions that make a tying practice unlawful. Beyond the circumstances of the firm's dominance and those peculiar to any exclusionary and anticompetitive practice – the exclusionary and anticompetitive effects in the absence of any objective justification – the case law hinges on the existence of a link between the two distinct products and on consumer coercion.

When verified, the first condition serves to exclude that: (i) tied products are not the equivalent of a right shoe and a left shoe – they do not correspond to two inseparable components of a single product; or (ii) the dominant firm's behaviour does not mark the advent of a new product capable of supplanting the goods that previously circulated separately from one another – as happened when, in the 1970s and 1980s, IBM assembled into a single machine several hardware components that until then were sold separately.[47] However, this consideration – or, more precisely, the amount of truth and accuracy this consideration contains – would not be lost by asking plaintiffs to merely focus on the exclusionary and anticompetitive effects of the dominant firm's practice. The above scenarios of the two inseparable products and of the revolutionary innovation should, however, be considered while discussing the objective justification of the practice and its prevailing pro-competitive effects.

As for consumer coercion, this factual element can also be absorbed into the discussion that takes place – and must always take place – while analysing the exclusionary and anticompetitive impact of the practices under consideration. More explicitly, the coercion of consumers – or, more generally, the coercion experienced by tie-in buyers – indicates that exclusion is highly likely because the individuals targeted by the tie-in product cannot choose the products of the dominant firm's competitors. However, depending on the scenario at hand, other factual

[47] *Transamerica Computer Company, Inc v IBM*, 698 F.2d 1377 (9th Cir 1983); *Memorex Corp v IBM*, 636 F.2d 1188 (9th Cir 1980); *California Computer Products, Inc and Century Data System, Inc, v IBM*, 613 F.2d 727 (9th Cir 1979).

elements – from super-dominance to cognitive biases[48] – may show that exclusion is equally very likely precisely because the individuals targeted by the tie-in product are prevented from choosing otherwise. In assessing bundle rebates, the Commission already accepts the occurrence of exclusionary effect *in the absence of a legal obligation* to choose the bundle *but in the presence of an economic incentive* to do so.[49] In other words, the Commission already accepts that the exclusion relevant to the application of Article 102 TFEU can arise not from a legal obligation but from another factual circumstance. As a result, it is unclear why consumer coercion should be the only factual circumstance relevant to finding tying abusive if one can show that such a practice is exclusionary, produces more anticompetitive than pro-competitive effects, and admits of no other objective justification.

A similar consideration should also take place with respect to the requirement of essentiality that needs to be verified in order to consider unlawful a refusal to deal that prevents the beginning of a new business relationship. With respect to this scenario, indeed, the essentiality requirement tells that exclusion will be highly probable precisely because rivals cannot carry out their business activities without access to the essential resource at hand. However, as *Google Shopping* shows, other factual circumstances can lead to the same conclusion.[50] In the (presumed) impossibility of demonstrating the essential nature of Google Search, the Commission nonetheless pointed out that other elements – ranging from the universal functionality of the search engine to the super-dominance of Google – made plausible the idea that Google's rivals interested in competing in secondary markets would have found it unreasonably difficult to vertically integrate upstream and substitute Google Search with their own search engines.[51]

Hence, we agree that the notion of self-preferencing was developed in relation to practices that could not qualify as tying or refusal to share essential resources.[52]

[48] CMA, 'Online Choice Architecture How digital design can harm competition and consumers' Discussion Paper (CMA 2022).

[49] 'Communication from the Commission – Guidance on the Commission's enforcement priorities in applying Article 82 of the EC Treaty to abusive exclusionary conduct by dominant undertakings' [2009] OJ C45/7, paras 47–62.

[50] Here we do not wish to deny that the requirement of essentiality was identified to defend both the dominant firm's freedom to contract and its property rights; nor do we wish to refute the idea that too easy a sharing of proprietary resources might reduce the incentives to innovate and compete for the dominant firm and its rivals. We take the view that, precisely because of what has just been said, the requirement of essentiality depends on the degree of exclusion – a very high degree of exclusion – that antitrust authorities are willing to tolerate before considering the dominant firm's refusal to deal as unlawful. What we want to argue in this chapter is that other factual circumstances, alternatives to the essentiality requirement, might nonetheless affect the degree of exclusion authorities are willing to tolerate before assessing as unlawful the conduct of the dominant firm, whatever form this conduct involving a proprietary resource takes.

[51] Undoubtedly, one might posit that the factors which the Commission employed in lieu of essentiality within the Google Shopping decision were inadequate substitutes for the latter. However, such an assertion does not inherently establish the invalidity of the intellectual process by which an actual circumstance is deliberated upon as a replacement for another.

[52] P Akman, 'The Theory of Abuse in Google Search: A Positive and Normative Assessment under EU Competition Law' (2016) 2 *Journal of Law, Technology and Policy* 301.

Nonetheless, we do not find that this way of proceeding should necessarily be considered a strategy that the Commission and national authorities should use to escape the strictness of the model situations provided for in Article 102, since we believe that Article 102 should include only two model situations: that of exploitative practices and that of exclusionary practices. In other words, the criticism that self-preferencing would be a contrivance can find acceptance to the extent that the existing types of exclusionary and anticompetitive conduct are considered autonomous legal characterisations and, consequently, to the extent that all the conditions attached to them are deemed strictly necessary for applying Article 102 TFEU. Otherwise, if what matters for prohibiting the exclusionary behaviours of dominant firms is only the actual and potential effects they produce, self-preferencing represents, on par with all other possible forms of exclusionary and anticompetitive practices, only one of the possible ways of describing behaviours that harm the competitive structure of the market and produce prevalent anticompetitive effects.

8. Concluding Remarks

In light of what has been written so far, one might wonder why we have chosen to engage in this discussion. Some might think that our intent is to demonstrate the merits of the *FBA Amazon* case. Others might believe that we prefer a loose application of Article 102 TFEU, especially in these times when big tech companies have become the preferred target of antitrust authorities and agencies.

None of this.

We are not animated by an attempt to save an otherwise shaky decision, because all decisions encompass light and shadow, and because even an unfounded decision would not cast doubt on the quality of an independent authority like the ICA. Nor do we want to take sides for or against digital giants, for two reasons: first, because we believe that preconceived positions against these companies are deeply unfair because these companies – like all others – can sometimes do good and sometimes bad; second, and above all, because the task of antitrust law is not to defend or attack a certain group of companies, but to evaluate from time to time the specific facts that have happened in a given scenario regardless of the company involved.

Internal consistency is instead the main reason that the different categories of exclusionary practices with which the case law is familiar should not be deemed proper legal qualifications. If Article 102 has to be interpreted in light of the effects-based approach, the differences among classes of exclusionary conduct should not exist.

After all, empirically speaking, Amazon's conduct is not the only example of monopolistic conduct that may fall under different, equally grounded categories of exclusionary behaviours, although, in practice, foreclosure of competitors and strengthening of dominant market power are the sole phenomena these practices generate in the market. Consider, for instance, the case of a multi-product monopolist realising both a durable good and, in competition with third parties, its spare parts. Suppose it launches a new version of the durable product that is compatible only with an updated version of such spare parts, offered by the same dominant firm, and not with the previous versions of spare parts. Independent producers of those spare parts that are excluded from the after-market because of such incompatibility could try to attack the new version of the durable good by claiming that (i) the innovation is a sham, because its only *raison d'etre* is that of excluding dominant firms' competitors from the secondary market for spare parts; (ii) the new durable good consists in tech-tying, that deprives consumers of the freedom to choose the spare parts that should work with the durable good; and (iii) the new mechanical interface between the new durable good and its spare parts is an essential facility that the monopolist must share with its competitors in order to guarantee interoperability and their follow-on innovation.

In all three cases, the factual constitutive elements and the effects of the material practice at hand are the same. Thus, under a true effects-based approach aimed at identifying whether a certain conduct effectively deviates from 'normal' competition and is likely to undermine the competitive structure of the market, the chances of prohibiting the above three descriptions of the same conduct should be the same.

However, under the current case law, those three descriptions amount to three separate legal characterisations. Therefore, the liability conditions governing sham innovation, tech tie-ins, and refusals to deal are not the same, to the point that every attorney could order the three claims from the hardest to be met (sham innovation) to the easiest (tech-tying) to succeed.

Hence, as this example shows, the need to prove different liability conditions for each category of exclusionary practices undermines the goal of the effects-based approach implied – ie it avoids practices that materialise in the same way and have the same effects being subject to different assessments and thus having different probabilities of being prohibited.

Of course, some might observe that designating exclusionary and anticompetitive effects in the absence of objective justification as the only constituent elements of the abuse case applying to exclusionary and anticompetitive practices might detract from the certainty of the system. And this is because the presence of the aforementioned lists of conditions, which are different for each type of exclusionary conduct, would have the merit of limiting the discretionary power of antitrust authorities while ensuring that companies under investigation can effectively organise their defences. However, it should be noted that even a legal characterisation of the effects-based notion of abuse carries the burden of proving the aforementioned three constituent elements. Consequently, legal certainty would not be lost. More simply, then, antitrust authorities and firms should centre their investigations and defences on the factual circumstances that, from time to time, make exclusion and prevailing anticompetitive effects possible, while simultaneously precluding potential objective justifications.

3

The Digital Markets Act

Tailoring the Tailors

OLES ANDRIYCHUK*

1. Introduction

The Digital Markets Act (DMA) is an EU regulation in the field of the digital economy, aiming to recalibrate paradigmatically the relationships between the enforcers of EU competition law and its main actors.[1] The proposal was submitted by the European Commission to the European Parliament in December 2020 within the ordinary legislative procedure (OLP).[2] It was introduced following a detailed public consultation,[3] commissioned expert reports,[4] and very intense academic discussion,[5] which aimed to articulate within the epistemic community

* The usual disclaimer applies.

[1] Regulation (EU) 2022/1925 of the European Parliament and of the Council of 14 September 2022 on contestable and fair markets in the digital sector and amending Directives (EU) 2019/1937 and (EU) 2020/1828 (Digital Markets Act), Brussels, 11 July 2022, PE-CONS 17/22.

[2] Proposal for Regulation of the European Parliament and of the Council on Contestable and Fair Markets in the Digital Sector (Digital Markets Act), Brussels (15 December 2020) COM(2020) 842; final 2020/0374 (COD).

[3] Commission's Factual summary of the contributions received in the context of the open public consultation on the New Competition Tool, 15 December 2020.

[4] J Crémer, Y-Alexandre de Montjoye, and H Schweitzer, 'Competition Policy for the Digital Era', European Commission Report (2019). See also J Furman and others, 'Unlocking Digital Competition', Report of the Digital Competition Expert Panel (2019); I Brown, 'Interoperability as a Tool for Competition Regulation', Open Forum Academy Report (2020); C Busch and others, 'Uncovering Blindspots in the Policy Debate on Platform Power', Final Report by the Expert Group for the Observatory on the Online Platform Economy (2021).

[5] H Schweitzer, 'The Art to Make Gatekeeper Positions Contestable and the Challenge to Know What Is Fair: A Discussion of the Digital Markets Act Proposal' (2021) 28(3) *ZEuP* 1; P Ibáñez Colomo, 'Protecting the "Law" in Competition Law' (2021) 11(7) *Journal of European Competition Law & Practice* 333; G Monti, 'The Digital Markets Act: Improving Its Institutional Design' (2021) *European Competition and Regulatory Law Review* 90; F Jenny, 'Changing the Way We Think: Competition, Platforms and Ecosystems' (2021) *Journal of Antitrust Enforcement* 1; D Geradin, 'What Is a Digital Gatekeeper? Which Platforms Should Be Captured by the EC Proposal for a Digital Market Act?', SSRN (18 February 2021); M Jacobides and I Lianos, 'Ecosystems and Competition Law in Theory and Practice', UCL Centre for Law, Economics and Society Research Paper Series, No 1 (2021); A de Streel

of EU competition law all eventual pros and cons of the reform. The new rules will primarily concern the main digital market players. They will be designated formally with the status of *gatekeepers*. The gatekeepers will be assigned a wide range of obligations aiming to improve *fairness* and *contestability* in *core platform services*: (a) online intermediation services (such as e-commerce market places or online software applications services); (b) online search engines; (c) online social networking services; (d) video-sharing platform services; (e) number-independent interpersonal communication services (messaging services); (f) operating systems; (g) web browsers; (h) virtual assistants; (i) cloud computing services; (j) advertising services, including any advertising networks, advertising exchanges, and any other advertising intermediation services provided by a provider of any of the core platform services (CPS) listed in points (a) to (i).[6]

The reform will have a prolific spillover effect on the whole spectrum of industries functioning in online markets and on the overall architecture of the digital economy. The interests, positions, arguments, and narratives accompanying the legislative process are very diverse, the stakes are very high, and the implications for the field of digital competition law, economics, and policy are potentially *tectonic*.[7]

The purpose of this chapter is twofold. After mapping out in section 2 the economic and societal context necessitating and predetermining the adoption of such extraordinarily proactive competition rules, the chapter articulates seven distinctive features of the emerging paradigm of EU digital competition law (section 3). It then explains how these seven distinctive features are encapsulated and are supposed to function in the DMA (section 4). Section 5 concludes the chapter.

2. The Great Transformation

It becomes a truism to claim that competition policy requires readjustment. The traditional mechanisms, nurtured by the orthodox application of neoclassical law and economics price theory, are not capable to comprehend fully and to remedy effectively the challenges (and also opportunities) emerging in the rapidly developing digital economy. Among the main shortcomings requiring improvement are procedural, temporal, and normative constraints, limiting the capability of the

and others, 'Making the Digital Markets Act More Resilient and Effective', CERRE Recommendations Paper (May 2021); N Petit, 'The Proposed Digital Markets Act (DMA): A Legal and Policy Review' (2021) 12(7) *Journal of European Competition Law and Practice* 529; A Komninos, 'Legal, Institutional and Policy Implications of the Introduction of a New Competition Tool' (2021) 19(1) *Concurrences* 1.

[6] Art 2(2) DMA.

[7] P Ibáñez Colomo, 'New Times for Competition Policy in Europe: The Challenge of Digital Markets' (2021) 12(7) *Journal of European Competition Law & Practice* 491.

enforcers of the general *ex post* competition rules to protect competition in the internal market. The very narrative of the protection of competition also appears to be construed too narrowly. Competition policy is in the process of incorporating into its predominantly protective rationale (*ex post*, responding to an instance of individual infringement) the proactive (*ex ante*, responding to more systemic market challenges without constraining itself to instances of individual infringements) one.

This trend goes hand-in-hand with the growing pleas for a greater openness of the discipline to a broader set of societal values and interests, which can be shaped by competition policy, triggering thereby a host of 'competition and regulatory' movements. This situation has direct implications on the discussion about the normative foundations of competition law, economics, and policy. Law and economics – the approach that in the past appeared to be accepted consensually as the main (if not the only) methodological and normative measurement of rational, predictable, efficient, consumer- and innovation-oriented competition policy – is in decline.

What is in decline is in fact not neoclassical law and economics as such. The community of competition lawyers and economists is getting more critical and more sceptical about the instrumentalised and reductionist ersatz version of competition law and economics, claiming its axiomatic ability to discover the only right answer to the wide spectrum of incommensurable competition problems. In other words, what is in decline is not competition law and economics, but only the *exclusivity claim*, made by competition law and economics.

For decades, competition policy was perceived as a universalist discipline. Such universalism had at least three important interdependent dimensions: (i) the universalism of metrics; (ii) the universalism of goals; and (iii) the universalism of agenda.

The *universalism of metrics* concerns a pervasive use of mathematical formulas to understand and explain the conduct of undertakings and consumers. This vision is embedded in a categorical conviction that market processes are fully rational and fully measurable. As the relationships are complex, the mathematics underpinning it is equally complex. The inherently societal phenomenon of economic competition has been transferred from the domain of social sciences to the domain of natural sciences and scientific positivism more specifically. This approach can be called 'axiomatic competition policy'. The mathematical formulas were assigned with natural sciences-style causality.[8] Economic conduct and economic interests were attributed deterministic features akin to the laws of buoyancy, inertia or gravitation.[9]

[8] A warning against the scientific determinism in law has been raised by one of the greatest legal minds: H Kelsen, 'Causality and Imputation' (1950) 61(1) *Ethics* 1.

[9] O Andriychuk, 'Between Microeconomics and Geopolitics: On the Reasonable Application of Competition Law' (2022) 85(3) *Modern Law Review* 599.

As the laws of nature are uncontroversially universal, the assumption is that competition policy ought to be universal too.[10] This logical conclusion has underpinned the normative aspect of *the universality – the welfare-focused universalism of goals of competition policy*.

If all polities pursue the same universal goal/s of competition policy, using the same universal methods of competition economics, all national competition laws should be designed in the same universalistic fashion, reflecting the objective interests of scientifically provable, rational economic reality, thereby unifying *the universalistic agenda* of the global competition community.

The holism, universalism, and globalism of competition law, economics, and policy were perceived as their mutually invigorating features. This distilled, purified, and inward-oriented approach to economic competition is based on the doctrinal foundations of competition law and economics.

The new period of competition policy has different preconditions and different distinctive features. It is characterised by a greater methodological and normative openness of the field, coinciding with a new fragmentation of the international agenda. Competition *law*, *economics*, and *policy* are in the transition from mono- to polycentricity. Such a transition is non-linear and very gradual.

Competition *economics* is becoming polycentric in the sense of being more open to the co-existence of different methods, metrics, and approaches, abandoning thereby the *exclusivity* modality of neoclassical microeconomics. In the same vein, the field is in transition from a single-goal vision to the plurality of goals. Competition *economics* will have to recalibrate its holistic approach to consumer welfare as we are entering a polycentric modality[11] that goes beyond single metrics, thus accommodating itself to the condition of multifaceted indeterminacy and moderate relativism.

The polycentricity of competition *law* implies that several legitimate internal goals may be articulated with no *a priori* hierarchical primacy of one over the other. It will also have to re-gain the skills of balancing and interaction with other societal interests that are protected and promoted by other areas of law. This greater openness implies greater indeterminacy. Contrary to the underlying assumption of the monocentric approach, the condition of indeterminacy is not a shortcoming or a pathology in the realm of law. A rich jurisprudential literature exists, dealing with this inherent feature of law.[12] A greater engagement with these rich legal philosophical sources will be accompanying the transition.

[10] M Horwitz, 'Law and Economics: Science or Politics?' (1980) 8(4) *Hofstra Law Review* 905: 'For more than one hundred and fifty years, the slogan, "law is a science" has dominated American legal thought. The economic analysis of law is only the most recent claimant to draw upon the prestige of the natural sciences in the effort to create a system of legal thought that is objective, neutral, and apolitical'.

[11] I Lianos, 'Polycentric Competition Law' (2018) 71(1) *Current Legal Problems* 161.

[12] HLA Hart, 'The Concept of Law' (Clarendon Press 1994) v; R Dworkin, 'Law's Empire' (Harvard University Press 1986) vii: '[O]ur law consists in the best justification of our legal practices as a whole, … in the narrative story that makes of these practices the best they can be'.

The third dimension of polycentricity implies a transition from a global 'Bretton Woods' vision of competition *policy* to a period of new pragmatism. All the obvious instances of international cooperation between competition agencies will remain and mature, but they will not necessarily be underpinned by the ethos of a syncretic ideological fusion of all national approaches, interests, visions, and positions into a single universalistic competition project. The holistic universalism of competition policy is also in decline because of a greater realisation that some of the members of the global competition community were playing by the rules selectively, applying the principles of the universal competition law, economics, and policy mainly to situations benefiting their own industrial / trade / political agenda and disregarding the principles in cases where the universalistic rationale of competition was not compatible with the national interests. Competition rules and the competition philosophy were applied *promiscuously*. The universalist principles were complemented with non-transparent selective instances of public–private partnership, subsidisation, and aid, as well as broader strategic economic planning. The situation when some polities take the rules seriously and others do not always do so, cannot be a foundation for a longstanding trust. While most use the façade of the same language, the meaning inferred is different and context dependent. The ethos of universalist is being replaced by the new pragmatic national competition policies, calibrating their domestic competition rules in accordance with their interests, ideologies, theories, and needs.

The following section conceptualises the key distinctive features of this new approach.

3. EU Digital Competition Law

The overarching goal of the DMA is to offer a new set of competition rules, which would allow a more effective pursuance of EU competition policy in the area of the digital economy.[13] Among the main interrelated features of this new digital competition rules are the following:

(1) Complementing a protective/restorative modality of traditional *ex post* competition rules with the elements of a proactive one.
(2) De-pathologising or acknowledging the inevitability of the condition of legal and economic indeterminacy and of the method of legal and economic interpretation.

[13] Opinions stating that 'DMA pursues a different but complementary objective to competition law' (F Chirico, 'Digital Markets Act: A Regulatory Perspective' (2021) 12(7) *Journal of European Competition Law & Practice* 496) are not in conflict with the view submitted by this chapter. The DMA is different to the traditional *ex post* competition law. It is, however, a necessary (and so far missing) component of competition policy *sensu lato*, consisting of the complementary preventive and proactive dimensions.

(3) Selectivity and bespokeness of addressees of the obligations, and the asymmetric scope of the obligations themselves.
(4) Intentional vagueness of the rules, which are designed in a way necessitating later refinement.
(5) Dialogical fine-tuning, tailoring the substance of the obligations by means of an informal interaction between the enforcers and the addressees of the rules, allowing the concrete meaning of specific obligations on each specific addressee to be defined.
(6) Abandonment of the single-metric methodology of efficiency, certainty, and internal coherence; the tolerance of a more polyvalent meaning of competition; protection and enhancement of the different dimensions and incarnations of the competitive process and other traditional competition-centric goals.
(7) Greater openness for interaction with other important societal values – economic as well as non-economic; greater policy-making engagement (ie 'competition and …' movements).

More specifically, the implications of these seven factors are discussed in detail below.

3.1. Proactive Competition

For decades competition policy was tuned to its preventive mode. Almost all known mechanisms of competition law are designed primarily to protect rather than promote competition. The protective approach may be associated both with non-interventionist (attempts to minimise Type I errors), as well as with interventionist (attempts to minimise Type II errors) modes. The disagreement between these two normative approaches would be framed in terms of how much protection – greater or lesser – is actually needed.

The new proactive approach complements the function of the protection of competition with the function of its further development and design by allowing to nurture and shape its specific features. This endeavour can never be associated with the premise of an absolute scientific certainty. As the reliance on such absolute certainty is in decline even for a protective *ex post* mode, competition policy is becoming liberated from its formalistic constraints – becoming more pragmatic and prone to communication with other societal interests.

The idea about the proactive competition policy is underpinned by a broader epistemic revision of our perception of the markets. Such a revision has two fundamental components: *descriptive* and *prescriptive*.

The *descriptive* component concerns a better understanding of the very phenomenon of economic competition. The situation in the markets is spontaneous, diverse, and unique. It is not exhausted by the binary good/bad mode, which tolerates public intervention only in case of the latter. The real-life competitive process is a spectrum of endless shades and grades of colour. None – apart from the extreme and unrealistic poles (perfect competition vs perfect monopoly) – is unequivocally and categorically better than the other *a priori*. The idea of the markets' spontaneity is much closer to the notion of their non-calculability than to the notion of non-intervention. Markets can be shaped – channelling their newly discovered spirit of entrepreneurship in directions beneficial for society.

The *prescriptive* element concerns the conceptual separation of the spontaneity of the markets and the imperative of non-intervention. The idea that markets can never be understood in their totality does not automatically imply that these markets should be left unregulated. Nurturing markets can be done both by not intervening as well as by targeted interventions. As long as such regulatory interventions do not make an epistemic claim of their ability to understand the markets in full, they themselves become components of the invisible market processes. *Without* an intervention, markets are spontaneously unique in their *ad hoc* constellation. *With* such a regulatory intervention, markets become spontaneously unique in another *ad hoc* constellation. In other words, the spontaneous order of competition is primarily an imperative for non-calculation, not necessarily for non-intervention.

3.2. Interpretive Turn

Competition policy cannot exist in isolation. The same open-ended provisions of EU primary competition rules mean different things in different periods as the law is inherently interpretive.

Legal interpretivism does not negate the importance of scientific certainty. It only denies its holistic and categorical exclusivism. The elements of indeterminacy and relativism allow only for *some* context-dependent interpretation.[14] They do not substitute certainty with indeterminacy. The arguments will continue to be shaped in the categorical intra-disciplinary language of economics and in the categorical intra-disciplinary language of law, but both languages are becoming more open to interpretation.

The transition from the condition of absolute certainty to the condition of relative indeterminacy is unnoticeable at the level of the legal and economic rules. They may remain the same or may change. What is decisive is not the text, but the context, the reading of the text, and the epistemic approach to it. If no monocentric scientifically provable truth about competition (or about its foundational elements such as, for example, market definition)[15] exists, several competing accounts,

[14] S Makris, 'Openness and Integrity in Antitrust' (2021) 17(1) *Journal of Competition Law & Economics* 3.

[15] M Eben, 'The Antitrust Market Does Not Exist: Pursuit of Objectivity in a Purposive Process' (2021) 17(3) *Journal of Competition Law & Economics* 587: 'There is, after all, no such thing as an 'antitrust market' (or any other market, for that matter). Markets are merely analytical tools'.

interpreting the same rules, facts, and theories, may be simultaneously correct. The stakeholders will continue competing with each other to offer an interpretation of the rules, which would be accepted by the decisionmaker in each case. In a polycentric enforcement universe, the decision-making process is not perceived as a box-ticking machinery, merely validating the correct answers.

It is often possible that two or more alternative interpretations of specific legal rules, economic theories and factual circumstances may simultaneously meet the standards of economic, legal, and factual correctness. In these cases – and it is usually these cases which matter most – the decision cannot be deduced automatically via a logical syllogism. The case would require some form of discretion. This question of judiciary discretion is at the core of the foundational topics in legal theoretical literature. It is very likely that the interpretive turn of the discipline will trigger a greater interest among competition lawyers in their theoretical *alma mater.*

3.3. Asymmetric Scope

The DMA is designed to be applied only to a very narrow group of undertakings with the strategic position in the digital markets: gatekeepers. Defining the scope of the addressees of the rules is an endeavour requiring a surgical precision. A perfectly correct calibration of gatekeepers implies a situation where all undertakings that have an entrenched strategic position in a specific market are captured by the definition. At the same time, the definition should not extend to the 'second tier' of the biggest market players. This category comprises the undertakings, which are the most plausible new entrants in the gatekeepers' markets.

Capturing those who should not be captured would not only harm these undertakings. It would also harm substantially inter-platform competition in these markets inasmuch as it would prevent a meaningful possibility for potential competitors to challenge the gatekeepers. Defining the quantitative and qualitative thresholds too narrowly would allow some of the *de facto* gatekeepers not to be covered by the DMA. Defining them too widely would designate as gatekeepers those which are in fact the main real and potential challengers of the *status quo*.

It is important in this context to note that the structure of the DMA is binary. This implies that those falling within its scope are not differentiated in terms of their size and actual market power. Conversely, those meeting all but one criterion would not be subject to the rules at all. This feature is not new and is present in the rationale of unilateral conduct as such. However, in light of the *ex ante* proactive mission of digital competition law, its importance is increasing. Under the logic of Article 102, an incorrect definition of dominance would have negative implications mainly for a specific market and often an even narrower impact on a specific relationship within a specific market. Under the logic of the DMA, incorrect designation of gatekeepers would have significant implication on the entire digital market. In the former situation, the mistake would merely affect a specific anticompetitive conduct. In the latter situation, the mistake would have much more systemic outcomes.

The binary mode in *ex ante* digital rules also means that the rules are designed primarily to tackle the structural imperfections of the markets rather than being focused only on protecting and promoting the interests of business and end users. Should the latter be the case, a more proportional correlation between the power of the gatekeeper and its obligations would be more suitable. This approach is being used in the Digital Services Act. The Digital Services Act indeed aims primarily to protect the markets vertically. The DMA's focus goes beyond this primary goal, expanding also horizontally.

Finally, the asymmetric scope of the DMA is not exhausted by the designation of its addressees. It is also one of the distinctive features of the obligations themselves. To a large extent, the obligations of each gatekeeper will be correlated to the markets in which it operates and to the business models it uses and to the products and services it offers in those markets.

3.4. Opacity by Design

The individualisation of legal rules, aiming to offer the most effective regulatory remedy to each systemic challenge to competition in digital markets, is complemented and reinforced by the opacity and all-inclusiveness of the rules themselves. The asymmetry of the DMA, in other words, does not stop at the level of designating gatekeepers. It also expands to the level of the substantive scope of the rules.

There are at least three reasons for the rules to be intentionally designed in opaque terms. First, this feature allows them to be futureproof. The markets evolve rapidly, and broader, more generalist rules are more likely to be interpreted purposefully. Second, the narrower the rules, the easier it is for compliance teams to draft measures, but these may meet the letter of the law without complying with its spirit. Third, and most importantly, the idea of intentionally opaque, all-inclusive rules may help the enforcers to overcome the procedural trap in which the mechanism of *ex post* competition rules is stuck.

Many cases are either lost or not even initiated in the first place on purely formal, procedural grounds, immaterial to the substance of rules.[16] If the stakes are high and even the strongest enforcers operate with finite resources, outperforming the best legal teams in courtroom is a challenge in itself. This challenge would become even greater in light of a more interpretive turn and a more proactive approach to designing competition policy.

[16] Some authors (eg C Caffarra, 'The Big Global Regulation Experiment', presentation at the Strathclyde Centre for Internet Law and Policy monthly webinar series, 5 March 2021, available at www.youtube.com/watch?v=4sPS-uY322E) propose looking deeper into the role and function of the judiciary in this excessive emphasis on the procedural casuistic.

By making the substantive obligations very wide and virtually impossible to comply with, the Commission, essentially, hedges its future procedural position in courts. The standard of proof of the DMA in other words is fairly low. If necessary, an instance of non-compliance would be demonstrated relatively easily – particularly in contrast with similar infringements under *ex post* rules. This format would allow the Commission to focus on pursuing the strategic policy objectives rather than spending most of its resources on endless formalities.

This feature is intentionally present in the DMA. The title of Article 6 DMA ('Obligations susceptible to being further specified') does not infer complacency or freeloading by the drafters, putting together a compilation of all known abuses in digital markets. These obligations are designed to be further specified case-by-case. It is not a juristic bug, but rather a smart juristic feature of the DMA.

3.5. Dialogical Relationship

The asymmetric scope and the opacity by design do not imply that the purpose of the enforcers is to make the gatekeepers liable. It is not the substantive scope of the obligations, which constitutes the main originality of the DMA, and it is not the mere possibility of imposing high pecuniary, behavioural, or structural remedies, which makes this proposal so innovative. These elements are important. The end goal, however, is the ability to control. The real power of the DMA is not in the obligations it imposes, but in the obligations that it *does not* impose. Having the ability to interpret the scope of obligations in a much wider way than they are currently interpreted allows the Commission to design the agenda in its communication with gatekeepers. The idea is to create formal legal preconditions, which will act as a bargaining chip, encouraging individual dialogue between the parties.

One of the implications of the de-axiomatisation of competition policy is that there is no condition in the markets, which can be consensually seen as the best or even as the optimal for the economy. All markets – and the digital markets in particular – are in a situation of a continuous flux. They are simultaneously the goals and the means to other goals.

The digital power of the gatekeepers is unprecedented. They design our economic choices, preferences, and conduct. They can transfer their omnipotent power from the domain of economics to the domain of politics with one click. This possibility does not necessarily have to materialise in reality. The very capability of doing so suffices.[17] This explains that while the words in the regulatory dialogue will concern the substance of concrete obligations of Article 6 DMA, the broader context underpinning the dialogue may go far beyond this.

[17] L Zingales, 'Towards a Political Theory of the Firm' (2017) 31(3) *Journal of Economic Perspectives* 113.

This feature of the DMA may explain why the Commission appears to be reluctant to share its enforcement competences with the national competition authorities (NCAs) despite all the obvious synergies and improvements. Such a delegation would dissolve the power of the Commission not to prescribe and prohibit, but rather to immunise and leverage, inflating the entire mechanism of the regulatory dialogue. As the effectiveness of leniency is inflated if the whistle-blowers' immunity is not expanded from public to private enforcement, the effectiveness of the dialogue would be inflated if the promise of the Commission to turn a blind eye on a specific type of conduct or market feature could be 'improved' by any of the 27 NCAs.

3.6. Polycentric Benchmarks

Another systemic feature of the new *ex ante* approach is its simultaneous involvement in shaping of different aspects of digital competition.

First, it protects and promotes competition through the prism of the benefits to end users. While due to such features of the digital economy as zero price and privacy paradox, the interests of end users are very difficult to define by using the traditional law and economics toolkit, many of those interests appear to be of no or little relevance for the enforcers. Yet, it is evident that the final goal of any policy should ultimately be beneficial to the interests of end users, even if the focus of the policy is placed on the rights of business users and horizontal competitors.

Second, it protects and promotes horizontal (between business users) and vertical (between business users and platforms' downstream subsidiaries) competition within each online platform. This is the most explicit and relatively easy to shape dimension of competition. Most of the provisions of the DMA are designed for calibrating this dimension of competition.

The *third* important aspect is related to competition between online platforms. It consists of two structurally very similar but normatively very different dimensions: inter-ecosystem competition and non-ecosystem inter-platform competition.

Inter-ecosystem competition implies a mutual expansion of each gatekeeper to the area of other core platform service (CPS). Schematically, this can be seen as a situation where all incumbents are simultaneously challengers in all other CPSs. This situation is relatively easy to achieve as the incumbents are the only digital undertakings that are capable of leveraging their competences and data from one CPS to the other. If assessed through the prism of the previous paradigm, such a format would be capable of satisfying all the traditional parameters of effective competition. The problem with this situation concerns the broader societal interests of not tolerating a two-tiered system of competition. While nominally, competition between semi-closed ecosystems would deliver most of the economic benefits associated with competition on the merits, the barriers to entry for newcomers would be even higher – and thus the problem would be of a more normative, ideological nature than the functional aspects of such format of competition. Also, it may cement further the systemic status of several strategic gatekeepers, making any external entry highly unlikely.

The non-ecosystem inter-platform competition mirrors the strengths and weaknesses of the inter-ecosystem competitions. Contrary to the previous one, it is a very societally desirable format as it would imply new entries by non-gatekeepers. Contrary to the previous one, it is almost impossible to achieve in practice, as such new entries by non-gatekeepers are almost impossible in the circumstances, where all or most of the digital markets are systemically mono- or oligopolised.

3.7. Societal Engagement

Finally, a higher level of openness implies that some other societal policies (eg privacy, sustainability, industrial policy) may be pursued by digital competition law. Equally, these policies may also contribute to achieving competition-centred goals. The axiomatic approach to competition policy implies the presence of a condition in the market that would be characterised as procompetitive. In this sense, the role of enforcement was focused at discovering and protecting this imaginary condition. Even if unachievable in practice, it was seen as an important theoretical construct, legitimising enforcement – this being the only criterion for distinguishing between good and bad competition policy.

Such a perception implied the purity of the discipline. Any interaction with other economic and non-economic goals was seen as polluting the purity of competition policy. Digital competition policy is more interactive and pragmatic in this respect, less inward-oriented and more scientifically purified. Such an openness is not unlimited and is steered by certain internal epistemic protocols. The main disciplinary boundaries are the rigid, formalised languages of economics and law. Becoming more open to interpretation, these languages did not become all-inclusive, preserving dialectically[18] an elastic balance between openness and integrity.[19]

The transition from the inward-oriented closeness to a more interactive, polycentric vision of competition policy as one of many societal instruments, is a two-way street. On one hand, competition becomes influenced by other societal interests. On the other hand, those societal interests also become more open

[18] O Andriychuk, 'Dialectical Antitrust: An Alternative Insight into the Methodology of the EC Competition Law Analysis' (2010) 31(4) *European Competition Law Review* 156.

[19] S Makris, 'Openness and Integrity in Antitrust' (2021) 17(1) *Journal of Competition Law & Economics* 2: '[R]easonable disagreements cannot be fully eradicated because they are ignited by two opposing yet complementary endogenous forces of antitrust: openness and integrity … A careful look at antitrust systems shows that openness is not only inevitable but also desirable. Without openness, antitrust could become a formulaic and ineffective field of law … Yet, excessive openness can destabilize the Rule of Law or incite the instrumentalization of antirust. In other words, integrity requires openness, but the latter, if excessive, can undermine the integrity of the law'.

to the influence of competition-oriented normative perspectives. The area needs a robust conceptual toolkit to be developed for a better understanding of the unprecedented challenges as well as opportunities that are emerging for competition policy in general. The development in the area of the digital economy in many respects catalyses these processes.

4. The DMA: Epitomising the Broader Trend

After section 3 highlighted seven distinctive features of new digital competition rules, this section checks the DMA against these seven elements.

4.1. Proactive Competition

A more proactive approach to shaping digital competition in the internal market can be identified in the very rationale of the DMA. By being an *ex ante* regulation, it inherently addresses the instances of systemic market failures, not individual infringements. This implies that the purpose of the rules is less protective and restorative, and more proactive and procompetitive. This can be also seen as manifested explicitly in one of the two main goals of the DMA, as well as its full title: contestability. While in many cases the proposal refers to protection of contestability, in some it explicitly refers to its more proactive modality.

The main procedural novelties introduced by the Regulation are equally explicit about the extended goal of the enforcer, going far beyond its role as a mere guardian. Empowering the Commission with many additional competences and duties would be simply unnecessary if the goals were limited exclusively to the protective mode.

In terms of substantive obligations of the gatekeepers, most of them are designed not only to protect various formats of inter- and intra-platform competition, but also to promote it.

The DMA complements, and by no means substitutes or overshadows, the current *ex post* modality. A greater proactive role is not a recalibration of enforcement priorities, but rather an expansion of the enforcement capacities. After all, the protective and proactive functions of (digital) competition law are dialectically interdependent.[20] Drawing a categorical line between them, or limiting competition policy only to its protective mode, is an artificial and reductionist construct requiring a critical re-examination.

[20] O Andriychuk, 'Dialectical Antitrust: An Alternative Insight into the Methodology of the EC Competition Law Analysis' (2010) 31(4) *European Competition Law Review* 155.

4.2. Interpretive Turn

The main epistemic mechanisms for understanding competition policy are developed in competition law and in competition economics. The new proactive modality of digital competition policy implies a more interpretive use of its legal and economic arms. The phenomenon of economic competition can never be determined in its totality. It is inherently embedded into the logic of relative indeterminacy.

At first glance, the DMA may trigger a cognitive dissonance with the established epistemic features of competition law and competition economics. Both arms of competition policy are traditionally characterised by an undisputable virtue: legal and economic certainty. Such a dissonance is illusionary. The very phenomenon of economic competition is underpinned by the metaphor of the invisible hand of the spontaneous market processes. Equally, in the domain of jurisprudence, the questions of indeterminacy of law and legal interpretation are at the centre of the theoretical discussions. Not only are both economics and law capable of dealing with the conditions of indeterminacy and interpretation, but these issues are at the core of their theoretical and practical characteristics. Both inherited a rich legacy and operate sophisticated apparatus allowing the effective internalisation of the new epistemic reality to the theoretical and practical domains of competition policy.

The Commission is assigned by the DMA with a significant interpretive discretion. The DMA is full of adjectives and value judgements. Adjectives in law are gateways to interpretation, as they are inherently dependent on the individual context. Their further refinement and limitation in judicial practice is a lengthy process.

The Act is drafted in a manner making a substantial limitation of the competence of the enforcer by legal precedents very unlikely in a short- and medium-term perspective. Essentially, this feature reflects and mirrors the abovementioned procedural trap (long proceedings, distinction between liability *qua* penalty and liability *qua* compliance, *de facto* the interim measure effect of the case before the last instance judgment enters into force) with the difference that the most likely victim of that trap would be not the enforcer but rather the gatekeepers.

Each of the DMA obligations – even those which are supposed to be self-executing – have various context-dependent meanings. They also trigger various follow-on non-axiomatic situations in the markets. Such a condition of a relative indeterminacy and polysemy implies the impossibility of finding (or even imagining) a monovalent answer to each specific challenge. The game does not have an end.

4.3. Asymmetric Scope

Designation of gatekeepers is a binary process. Undertakings meeting three cumulative quantitative criteria will become gatekeepers. Those not meeting at least one criterion – and even by a little – will normally not be the subject of the rules at all.

The central question concerns establishing criteria for defining the strategic goals of the proactive modality of digital competition law. If the goal concerns exclusively the objectives of fairness and contestability, then there is no evident formal ground for disagreeing with the use of the DMA as a strategic leverage of established systemic market players non-active in the EEA market (even regardless of their eventual intentions of entering the EEA market).

A more interpretive and instrumental interpretation of the DMA may imply that its purpose goes beyond the requirements of fairness and contestability. In doing so it should question whether, and if so, why such implications are desirable for the European Union. In any event, discussion is needed at least on the layer analysing the likelihood of such consequences. The eventual problematisation of these consequences shifts the discussion to the last two identified features of the DMA: its polycentric enforcement and its societal engagement.

The polycentric enforcement implies the analysis of the goals of the DMA from a broader (but intra-competition) perspective. The societal engagement implies the analysis of the interaction of the DMA with a narrower (but extra-competition) perspective. In other words, the polycentricity of digital competition law implies a plurality of goals and narratives within the area of competition policy, whereas the societal engagement implies the interaction of digital competition law with other legitimate societal interests (both in the sense of being influenced by these interests and in the sense of shaping these interests).

The increase of quantitative thresholds indicates a greater regulatory polarisation between the biggest and the rest. The binary structure of gatekeeper designation inherently implies the existence of this delineation. With regard to the proactive shaping of digital competition such an increase may epitomise a belief that the greatest competition with the existing incumbent may be offered by their immediate pursuers. A romanticised ethos of the garage style start-up entrepreneurship is gradually transforming these days into an urban myth. Keeping such undertakings outside the scope of the DMA for as long as possible would increase the probability of challenging the *status quo*.

4.4. Opacity by Design

Opacity by design is the central legal feature of the DMA. The traditional *ex ante* / *ex post* differentiation of competition rules implies broad and open to interpretation *ex post* principles, which in instances of systemic market failures may be complemented by *ex ante* rules. Such a complementarity implies stricter and much wider obligations. To mitigate the disbalance and to increase certainty, there is an expectation that all *ex ante* obligations must be clear and unequivocal, leaving no or very narrow room for interpretation. The system is usually designed in such a way that all the addressees understand what precisely they have to comply with. The obligations of the DMA are fundamentally different. They are imprecise, vague and wide.

At least with regard to the obligations of Article 6(1) DMA, it is clear that the vagueness is intentional, and it is manifested in the name of the article. Pursuant to Article 7(7) DMA, the gatekeepers may ask for specification 'to determine whether the measures that the gatekeeper intends to implement or has implemented under Article 6 are effective in achieving the objective of the relevant obligation in the specific circumstances'.[21] This implies an explicit encouragement of a regulatory dialogue. If the dialogue is constructive, the individually calibrated measures may be seen as the version of obligations of Article 6(1) DMA tailored specifically for the gatekeeper. This laser-focus also means that the binding effect of the obligations would begin from the moment of the calibration (*ex nunc*). If the dialogue is not initiated or if the consensus is not reached, the binding effect – and, evidently, the liability for non-compliance – begin from the moment of establishing the status of gatekeeper (*ex tunc*).

This reconfiguration of power in the 'enforcer–incumbent' bargaining process is complemented by another important dimension: the scope of obligations. There is a long list of very wide and far-reaching obligations, most of which are made intentionally opaque. Non-compliance with these obligations would lead to high pecuniary liability, complemented with the possible imposing of behavioural or structural remedies. Remarkably, the enforcer would be able to impose *any* behavioural and/or structural remedy. The requirement of the proportionality of the remedy to the committed infringement appears to be precisely as elastic and open to interpretation as the new modality of digital competition policy is expected to be. Also, it is symptomatic that the wording of this provision changes the tonality from 'non-compliance' to 'infringement'.

4.5. Dialogical Relationship

The idea of a dialogical, individualised approach to enforcement is not new. Its embryonic rationale is reflected in various mechanisms of non-judicial dispute resolution. In the context of EU competition law enforcement, the most developed one is the mechanism of commitments.[22] It allows the enforcer 'to meet the concerns' identified during the investigation. Of course, it is not as proactive as the DMA. It is limited rather to the restorative dimension of the alleged infringement. Also, it is limited to the specific infringement; thus it is *ipso facto* context-specific rather than systematic. Finally, the shape of commitments is initially designed by alleged infringers, and not by the enforcers. However, even such a reduced form of a regulatory dialogue may be seen as an attempt to go beyond an individual infringement, and look at broader issues of market tailoring.[23]

[21] Art 7(7) DMA.

[22] Council Regulation (EC) No 1/2003 of 16 December 2002 on the implementation of the rules on competition laid down in Articles 81 and 82 of the Treaty [2003] OJ L1/1.

[23] Opinion of AG Pitruzzella in Case C-132/19 P, *Groupe Canal+ v Commission* EU:C:2020:355, para 68: '[T]he Commission and the national authorities should not be allowed to succumb to the

The new modality expands the scope of the dialogue. By being *ex ante*, it does not limit it to a specific instance of violation of law. Furthermore, it does not limit it to a specific obligation. Finally, the narrative-shaping privilege of first drafting of the proposed outcomes is assigned to the Commission, not to the gatekeepers.

Formally, the 'regulatory dialogue' covers all (and only) the 11 provisions of Article 6(1) DMA. The substantive scope of the activities addressed by Article 6(1) DMA implies that *de facto* the dialogue will concern the whole spectrum of businesses undertaken by a specific gatekeeper. Unlike the mechanism of commitments, the regulatory dialogue is not necessarily context-, fact- or conduct-constrained. The dialogue is not limited to a recovery of a specific aspect of competition, harmed by the infringement. Neither it is limited by a requirement to check the compatibility of its outcomes against the opinions of third parties affected by conduct. Due to genuine interdependencies of various processes and factors in the digital economy, the dialogue may be launched having in mind a set of specific practices, but nothing can prevent its further evolution into a continuum of a much broader agenda. The issues that the enforcer wants to discuss may indeed be discussed within its broad framework. Finally, unlike the mechanism of commitments as known in Regulation 1/2003, the mechanism of the regulatory dialogue is indeed dialogical. There is scope for both parties to articulate their positions, views, and interests. Because the scope of the dialogue concerns the future more than past conduct, it can be also characterised by a greater plasticity and adaptability.

Such a strategic potential of the format of the regulatory dialogue explains why the Commission is so keen to keep the enforcement of the DMA exclusively within its competence. The dialogue may go far beyond the formal agenda of the meeting. Furthermore, as the balance of the bargaining power in the dialogue is shifted to the Commission, not the gatekeeper, the real purpose of the dialogue may well go far beyond calibrating each specific shade and nuance of each specific adjective in each specific obligation of Article 6(1) DMA. The Commission may use it as a leverage in shaping the new proactive, strategic vision of digital competition policy (if not beyond). This is one of a very few possible explanations (and from the normative perspectives, advocated by this chapter, also justifications) for maintaining such an exclusive competence.

Another possible limitation of the effectiveness of the regulatory dialogue may come from private enforcement of the DMA. Not only may it lead to fragmentation,[24] but also it could diminish the Commission's 'carrot' power (ie the benefit it could offer, in contrast to the 'stick' of punishment). This concern

temptation to regulate, using decisions on commitments not so much as a remedy for anticompetitive conduct, but rather to impose a given form on economic relations in the market'. For a detailed analysis of this issue in general and the Opinion of AG Pitruzzella in particular, see N Dunne, 'Challenging Competition Commitment Decisions: Groupe Canal+' (2021) 58(4) *Common Market Law Review* 1229.

[24] A Komninos, 'The Digital Markets Act and Private Enforcement: Proposals for an Optimal System of Enforcement' in *Eleanor Fox Liber Amicorum – Antitrust Ambassador to the World* (Concurrences, 2022 forthcoming.

may explain the logic for dividing obligations of the gatekeepers into two groups: Article 5 covers self-executing obligations, which are thus sufficiently clear, precise, and concrete to have horizontal direct effect; and Article 6 covers those which require further specification, and supposedly not concrete enough to having direct effect. This logic would support a thesis of the regulatory dialogue using a 'carrot' and 'stick' bargaining instrument for shaping the strategic proactive digital competition policy. An important – and very sensitive – avenue for avoiding fragmentation (and thereby for strengthening centralisation) would be to design a mechanism granting 'rule of precedence' for public enforcement and to limit 'the role of private enforcement only to "follow-on" cases for a reasonable period'.[25] Clearly, the fact that the DMA does not mention a private enforcement mechanism does not imply that it will not be used by the affected parties in national proceedings. A more secure way would be to design a specific mechanism for enforcing the provisions of the DMA by private entities. This would channel the process, establish the necessary safeguards and prevent the abovementioned shortcomings. Such an avenue is possible inasmuch as the DMA is secondary EU legislation, 'it is open to EU legislation to introduce limitations on competence and, thus, on the direct effect of the legal rules it contains'.[26]

4.6. Polycentric Benchmarks

A fundamental question, which has to be addressed when applying the DMA, is a definition of the goal/s the regulation aims to achieve, and an establishment of parameters for evaluating the effectiveness of the DMA performance. Calibrating the taxonomy of the goals in the polycentric period of competition law is an endeavour of a paramount strategic importance. The goals may be classified by different criteria. Some may be seen as being internal while others as external to the phenomenon of economic competition. The internal goals are addressed in this subsection; the external goals are covered in the following one.

The DMA is a regulation aiming to protect and promote competition in the digital markets. Competition in the markets implies a focus on the structural, systemic aspects of the model. By definition, this approach is deductive, top-down. It is less interested in the welfare effects and benefits for consumers. The role of and the impact of the DMA on consumers (called in the Regulation 'end users') is rather indirect and instrumental. In the long run, fair and competitive markets are pro-consumer. This is tautological. However, the benefits for consumers are neither in the heart of the DMA rationale nor in the parameters of assessing its functioning.[27] The well-known privacy paradox (discussed above) is omnipresent.

[25] ibid, 12.
[26] ibid, 11.
[27] Some parliamentary amendments (eg Amendment 129 (Amendments by individual MEPs)) propose a higher articulation of the interests of consumers.

Consumers are generally satisfied with what they are offered at the moment. There will always be room for incremental improvements and adjustments, but there are other instruments in Internet governance that should be used for this purpose. The omnipresence of the privacy paradox implies that this behavioural phenomenon is not exhausted with how consumers treat their privacy. It can be easily expanded *mutatis mutandis* to the ways how consumers (we) treat algorithmic tailoring of their newsfeeds, search results, rankings, reviews, and reports. Digital consumers are happy with living in echo-chambers – they are happy to be fed by the previous choices and preferences of themselves and those from their echo-chambers. The unprecedented growth of the gatekeepers would not be possible without a critical mass of satisfaction with their services. Arguably, consumers are not necessarily happy with competition. They are not necessarily impressed by the variety of choices. Many (most?) are happy with single homing, and perceive most of the core platform services as defined by the DMA more as appliances and infrastructure, the duplication of which gives little in terms of improvement and much more in terms of confusion and dissatisfaction. The bottom line of this observation is a fairly paternalistic note that the real interests of end users are not always identical to the vision of such interests held by end users themselves.

This situation may explain why the main focus of the substantive provisions of the DMA is placed on intra-platform competition. The gatekeepers are seen essentially as unavoidable trading partners as the holders of critical infrastructure.[28] The main task of most of the substantive obligations of the DMA is to impel the gatekeepers to act responsibly vis-à-vis their business and end users. The idea of triggering intra-platform competition without necessarily challenging the systemic status of the incumbent is the most obvious and the most reasonable tactical format. The value in the digital economy is also created beyond the gatekeepers – going far beyond the CPSs. It would be myopic to reduce the opportunities of digital competition exclusively to the consumer side. It would be equally myopic to reduce them exclusively to the inter-platform dimension. The lion's share of the improvements, capable to be delivered by the DMA, concern the proper calibration of the intra-platform competition.

The challenges and opportunities of the digital economy, however, are not exhausted by the task of shaping the intra-platform dimension of competition. It is precisely competition between platforms that matters most strategically. It is the main systemic layer that defines how and by whom the digital value is created and accumulated. Furthermore, with a degree of stylisation the reluctance of end users to use the traditional benefits offered to them by competition may be extrapolated to business users as well. Many of them – including all of the most successful

[28] Amendment 128 (Amendments by individual MEPs) proposes to define digital services as 'essential facilities for the digital economy by providing access to critical infrastructures'. This terminology of 'essential facility' appears to be not the most suitable as it coincides with the term as used in applying Art 102 TFEU. Such terminological confusion is not necessary.

users – enjoy an established position within a specific CPS provider. They have a reliable reputation, meaningful market share, and trajectory of growth, and defined channels of communication with their gatekeepers upstream and end users downstream. Finally, numerous improvements in intra-platform competition would hedge them against various exploitative practices by the gatekeepers.

Against this background, having upstream CPS new entrants reshuffling the existing state of affairs may lead to fragmentation and reconfigure the situation in those markets. Competition would be improved by the traditional natural force of creative destruction, but neither end users nor business users – let alone the gatekeepers – would be welcoming the new business circle.

In light of these factors, as well as taking into account the natural systemic zero-sum features of the digital markets, the possibility for triggering effective (or any) inter-platform competition does not appear to be very plausible without proactive regulatory measures. Even if it were possible, the most plausible new entrants would be gatekeepers of other CPSs, controlling other relevant product and/or geographic markets. If such inter-ecosystem competition is desirable at all is a question to which each jurisdiction may have a different answer. On one hand, there is no traditional competition-related value that the inter-ecosystem competition would be not capable of delivering. On the other hand, an effective inter-ecosystem competition would make the main strategic perspectives of the domestic digital economy less ambitious. Regardless of the answer to this question, the discussion on the ways of promoting non-ecosystem inter-platform competition goes beyond the scope of the polycentric enforcement of competition rules, expanding the boundaries of the discipline to the issue of its interaction with external societal values.

4.7. Societal Engagement

The new modality of digital competition law implies its greater openness to other societal values and interests. One of the main external interests relevant to the DMA is the emergence and scaling up of new digital markets operators capable of competing locally and globally with the entrenched gatekeepers. This interest goes beyond competition policy – even if taken from the polycentric perspective – but competition policy remains the main instrument contributing to achieving this goal.

The global digital race is to a large extent a zero-sum winner-takes-most endeavour. Having stakes at the highest upstream level is of a paramount importance for each polity with the skills and capabilities to contribute to shaping the global digital agenda for the decades to come. The tactical focus of the DMA is correctly placed on the intra-platform competition. Its overall strategic *raison d'être*, however, is embedded in the non-ecosystem inter-platform competition.

5. Conclusion

This chapter is not arguing for a need to recalibrate competition policy along the elaborated seven theses. It conceptualises the existing condition, proposing merely a greater acknowledgement of this objective situation and its epistemic thematisation. Neither does it argue for a vulgar abandoning of the traditional metrics of competition law and competition economics, replacing these cornerstones of competition policy with the principles of political necessity. It only pleads for abandoning the absolutist belief in an absolute methodological and normative correctness of the legal and economic answers, presented deterministically as if they were natural rather than social phenomena.

The new period is not a transition from one monocentric approach to another. No other method can replace law and economics and become a new exclusive professional language for the discipline. Due to its remarkable universal ability to reduce all societal values, rights, interests, and policies to a single price theory metric, law and economics will remain the main method of analysis in competition policy. Its decline concerns only losing its exclusive status. No other legal or economic method is capable of offering an alternative universalist agenda.

The new reality appears to be a condition of asynchronous co-existence of several legal and economic theories, underpinning the discipline, with law and economics remaining the leading, but no longer the exclusive, approach. It is important for the epistemic community of competition law to develop a more variative attitude to the condition of relative indeterminacy, and the overlapping co-existence of incommensurable (and occasionally conflicting) goals, methods, and interests, as well as to a much more intense dynamic of interaction between competition and other societal values. This new condition is inherently postmodern.

The dynamically changing reality necessitates a fundamental change in our perception of the very nature of competition policy. This policy was designed, nurtured, and dogmatised as a theoretical construct, as a closed system with no or minimal considerations about an external dimension. The purification of competition policy and its artificial insulation from any other legitimate societal policy or interest is myopic and harmful. Such economic formulas, models, assumptions, and methodologies are all perfectly sound and robust *in abstracto* – but only *in abstracto*.

Postmodernism, unlike many critical theories, is an ideologically neutral concept – a theory which relativises the absolute beliefs and reliance on the omnipotence of human mind to comprehend and to rein in the scientifically discoverable reality, and does not intend to offer an alternative political agenda. Postmodern competition policy does make any radical claims vis-à-vis its predecessor law and economics. It mainly focuses on adapting competition policy to the new reality without compromising on the core principles of competition as such. It does relativise the holistic beliefs in the universal competition policy, but it does not promote economic protectionism or nationalism. By no means should it be read as a refutation of neoclassical economics and the reliance on legal precedents – the two wings of modernist competition policy. Such a refutation would lead to cacophony, protectionism, and arbitrariness. Yet, the postmodern reality requires greater flexibility of the theory of economic competition. Structurally, the DMA encapsulates all these new features. It remains to be seen to what extent this potential will be materialised in practice.

4

Assessing Geo-blocking as a Tool to Prevent the Risk of Being Sued in EU Member States for Cross-border Copyright Infringements

A Plea for the 'Directed Activities' Approach to Jurisdiction

BIRGIT VAN HOUTERT

1. Introduction

Did you know that if you post content online, such as a blog post, you can easily be sued before the courts of multiple EU Member States for copyright infringement? It will be costly and time consuming to face a lawsuit brought in a Member State which is not the Member State in which you are domiciled. You may therefore consider blocking access to content for internet users of certain Member States. The technology of 'geo-blocking' blocks or limits access to online content or online interfaces, such as websites and application, for the internet users of a certain state or states. This technology generally identifies the geographical location of the internet user by the user's Internet Protocol (IP) address.

The divergence of copyright protection between EU Member States can also be regarded as a reason to geo-block content for users of Member States in which this content is protected by copyright, as will be illustrated by the *Anne Frank* case below.[1] In spite of the existence of EU law related to copyright, copyright

[1] For more factors that may play a role in preventing a lawsuit being brought in certain Member States for cross-border copyright infringements, see B van Houtert, 'Geo-blocking as a tool to prevent being sued in EU Member States for cross-border copyright infringements?', blog post published on 31 May 2022, available at: www.maastrichtuniversity.nl/blog/2022/05/geo-blocking-tool-prevent-being-sued-eu-member-states-cross-border-copyright.

protection has not been fully harmonised.[2] Whether a work is protected by copyright may therefore vary between Member States.[3] Copyright licence agreements are often territorially limited, which can also be a reason to geo-block copyright protected content for users of Member States.[4] For example, online content service providers, such as Netflix and YouTube, frequently block access of content for users of certain states if the copyright licence agreement for this content does not include these states. The following case provides an illustration of the use of geo-blocking with respect to copyright protected content.

At the end of 2021, two Dutch-based non-profit foundations and a Belgian non-profit association published their academic research on the website www.annefrankmanuscripten.org. This website contains manuscripts, namely diaries, written by the world-renowned Anne Frank, which are source documents related to their research. While the copyright on Anne Frank's works has expired in many countries, it has not yet expired in the Netherlands.[5] Therefore, the research institutes used the technology of geo-blocking to block access to their website for internet users located in the Netherlands. In addition, the website contains an 'access check' which requires users who access this website to declare that they are not accessing from specified countries such as the Netherlands. The Dutch foundations and Belgian association were nevertheless sued before the Dutch District Court of Amsterdam for copyright infringement by the Swiss-based non-profit foundation 'Anne Frank Fonds' which inherited the copyright in Anne Frank's work.[6]

With respect to the liability for copyright infringing activities in the Netherlands, the District Court of Amsterdam ruled in the *Anne Frank* case that the defendants could not be held liable in the Netherlands based on the following two-fold reasoning. First, the defendants had taken all reasonable efforts to prevent internet users from the Netherlands from accessing the website because they were using geo-blocking and an 'access check' in the case of users from the

[2] See A Kur, T Dreier, and S Luginbuehl, *European Property Law: Text, Cases and Materials* (2nd edn, Edward Elgar Publishing 2019) 399. 'The EU copyright law [currently] consists of 13 directives and 2 regulations, harmonising the essential rights of authors, performers, producers and broadcasters.' See digital-strategy.ec.europa.eu/en/policies/copyright-legislation.

[3] For instance, the national copyright laws of Member States have different rules on the protection of moral rights. See B van Houtert, *Jurisdiction in Cross-border Copyright Infringement Cases: Rethinking the Approach of the Court of Justice of the European Union* (ProefschriftMaken 2020), paras 5.1.2, 6.2.2.1. Available at: cris.maastrichtuniversity.nl/en/publications/jurisdiction-in-cross-border-copyright-infringement-cases-rethink.

[4] G Mazziotti, 'Is Geo-blocking a Real Cause for Concern in Europe?', European University Institute Working Papers Law 2015/43, p 1.

[5] The District Court of Amsterdam has indicated that the copyright of the 'Anne Frank Fonds' regarding Anne Frank's work expires on 1 January 2037 in the Netherlands. See District Court of Amsterdam (The Netherlands), *Anne Frank Fonds v Anne Frank Stichting, Koninklijke Nederlandse Akademie van Wetenschappen* ECLI:NL:RBAMS:2015:9312, para 4.3.3.

[6] District Court of Amsterdam (The Netherlands), 1 February 2022, *Anne Frank Fonds v Anne Frank Stichting, Koninklijke Nederlandse Akademie van Wetenschappen, Vereniging voor Onderzoek en Ontsluiting van Historische Teksten* ECLI:NL:RBAMS:2022:328.

Netherlands trying to access the website via, for instance, a virtual private network (VPN) connection.[7] Hence, the defendants were not committing copyright infringing activities in the Netherlands; the requirement of communication to the public laid down in Article 3 of the Directive 2001/29/EC on the harmonisation of certain aspects of copyright and related rights in the information society ('the InfoSoc Directive') had therefore not been fulfilled.[8] Second, the District Court emphasised that even if a large number of users from the Netherlands were able to access the website in spite of the use of geo-blocking and the 'access check', it would be questionable whether the copyright infringement claim could have been granted since copyrights are not absolute.[9] As indicated by recitals 3 and 31 of the InfoSoc Directive and the ruling *YouTube and Cyando* of the Court of Justice of the European Union (CJEU),[10] particularly in the online context it is important to strike a fair balance between the interests of copyright holders, on the one hand, and the interests and fundamental rights of users of protected content such as the freedom of science, on the other hand.[11]

In the *Anne Frank* case, the use of geo-blocking to block access for internet users in the Netherlands could thus not prevent the defendants being sued in the Netherlands. Furthermore, the role of geo-blocking seems to be marginalised by the second part of the District Court's reasoning with respect to the liability for copyright infringing activities in the Netherlands as described above.

This chapter will assess the use of geo-blocking as a tool to prevent a company or individual that posts online content, or provides goods or services online being sued in EU Member States for cross-border copyright infringements.[12] This topic will be assessed from various perspectives, namely private international law; EU law, in particular the EU Geo-blocking Regulation;[13] copyright protection; the right to information; and cross-border trade. The remainder of this chapter is divided into four sections, followed by conclusions. Section 2 will set out the broad EU approach to the jurisdiction of Member States' courts in cross-border copyright infringement cases. In view of this broad approach to jurisdiction, the

[7] *Anne Frank* case (n 6), para 4.2. A virtual private network (VPN) connection enables internet users to pretend to be in another location rather than their real location by providing a different IP address. The user can therefore bypass location-based internet restrictions a result of geo-blocking. With respect to the legality of the use of VPNs to bypass geo-blocking measures and whether this practice amounts to an infringement of copyrights, see A Marsoof, 'Geo-blocking and Virtual Private Networks: A Comparative Discourse in Copyright Law', WIPO-WTO Colloquium Papers 2017.

[8] *Anne Frank* case (n 6), para 4.2. Directive 2001/29/EC of the European Parliament and of the Council of 22 May 2001 on the harmonisation of certain aspects of copyright and related rights in the information society [2001] OJ L167/10 ('the InfoSoc Directive').

[9] *Anne Frank* case (n 6), para 4.3.

[10] Joined Cases C-682/18 and 683/18 *Frank Peterson v Google LLC and Others and Elsevier Inc v Cyando AG* EU:C:2021:503.

[11] *Anne Frank* case (n 6), para 4.3.

[12] The author of this chapter has based this chapter on her dissertation (see n 3 above) and her blog post (see n 1 above).

[13] See n 33 below and accompanying text.

effectiveness of geo-blocking as a tool to prevent an online provider of content, goods, or services being sued for copyright infringement in Member States will be scrutinised. Section 3 will examine the influence of the Geo-blocking Regulation on the use of geo-blocking as a tool to prevent an online provider of content, goods, or services being sued for copyright infringement in EU Member States. Therefore, the legal limitations on the use of geo-blocking stipulated in the Geo-blocking Regulation will be assessed. Section 4 will illustrate the possible use of geo-blocking in practice and its negative effects on copyright protection, the right to information, and cross-border trade. Section 5 will argue in favour of a private international law-based solution that reduces the need to use geo-blocking, which would keep the internet more open.

2. The Use of Geo-blocking in View of the Broad EU Approach to Jurisdiction in Cross-border Copyright Infringements

From a private international law perspective, the first question that arises in a cross-border copyright infringement case is whether the court seised will have jurisdiction to assess the case. An EU Member State court therefore has to consider the applicability of the Regulation (EU) No 1215/2012 on jurisdiction and the recognition and enforcement of judgments in civil and commercial matters, also referred to as Brussels I bis.[14] According to the general jurisdiction rule in Article 4 Brussels I bis, the courts of the Member State in which the alleged copyright infringer is domiciled have jurisdiction with respect to the entire cross-border copyright infringement dispute.[15] Potential copyright infringers can thus, on the basis of Article 4 Brussels I bis, always be sued before the courts of the Member State in which they are domiciled in spite of geo-blocking access to potential infringing content for internet users of that Member State.

Article 8(1) Brussels I bis provides a jurisdiction rule that could play a role in a cross-border copyright infringement case that involves more than one defendant and where the defendants are domiciled in different Member States. The alleged copyright infringer can then also be sued before the courts of the Member State in which their co-defendant is domiciled provided that the claims are so closely connected that it is expedient to hear and determine them together to avoid the

[14] Regulation (EU) No 1215/2012 of the European Parliament and of the Council of 12 December 2012 on jurisdiction and the recognition and enforcement of judgments in civil and commercial matters [2012] OJ L351/1, referred to as 'Brussels I bis'.

[15] Art 63(1) Brussels I bis stipulates that a company or other legal person is domiciled at the place where it has its statutory seat, central administration, or principal place of business. In this chapter 'the place of establishment' will be used to denote the place of domicile of legal persons.

risk of irreconcilable judgments resulting from separate proceedings.[16] In view of Article 8(1) Brussels I bis, geo-blocking potential infringing content may thus not be efficient where one of the defendants is domiciled in the Member State to which the access has been blocked. As illustrated by the *Anne Frank* case in the introduction, the Belgian association could nonetheless be sued before the Dutch court because its co-defendants were established in the Netherlands.

Besides the general jurisdiction rule of Article 4 Brussels Ibis, Article 7(2) Brussels I bis contains an additional special jurisdiction rule for cross-border cases related to tort, such as copyright infringements. Article 7(2) Brussels I bis provides jurisdiction to the courts for the place where the harmful event occurred or may occur. In the case *Handelskwekerij GJ Bier v Mines de Potasse d'Alsace SA*, the CJEU ruled that the latter jurisdiction rule includes two jurisdiction grounds: namely the place where the event giving rise to the damage occurred, known as the *Handlungsort*, and the place where the damage occurred or may occur, known as the *Erfolgort*.[17]

With respect to an online copyright infringement case, the CJEU has interpreted the *Handlungsort* under Article 7(2) Brussels I bis as the place where the alleged copyright infringer has its seat since that is where the alleged infringer took and carried out the decision to place the allegedly copyright infringing content online on a particular website.[18] The latter jurisdiction ground will therefore coincide with the general jurisdiction ground in Article 4 Brussels I bis. The jurisdiction ground of the *Handlungsort* will thus also provide jurisdiction to courts of the Member State in which the alleged copyright infringer is domiciled in spite of the use of geo-blocking to disable access to the allegedly infringing content for internet users of the latter state.

In three cross-border copyright infringement cases *Pinckney*, *Hi Hotel*, and *Pez Hejduk*, the CJEU broadly interpreted 'the place where the damage occurred or may occur' (ie the *Erfolgsort*) by conferring jurisdiction on the courts of the Member State in which the damage is likely to occur.[19] The jurisdiction of the latter courts is limited to the damage that occurred within the Member State of the court seised.[20] The rulings *Pinckney*, *Hi Hotel*, and *Pez Hejduk* indicate that the latter

[16] See the CJEU's interpretation of the requirements in Art 8(1) Brussels I bis in the following cross-border patent infringement case: Case C-539/03 *Roche Nederland BV and Others v Frederick Primus and Milton Goldenberg* EU:C:2006:458. With respect to an infringement of Community designs, see the joined Cases C-24/16 and C-25/16, *Nintendo Co Ltd v BigBen Interactive SA* EU:C:2017:724, paras 38–67.

[17] Case C-21/76 *Handelskwekerij GJ Bier v Mines de Potasse d'Alsace SA* EU:C:1976:166, paras 24–25.

[18] Case C-441/13 *Pez Hejduk v EnergieAgentur. NRW GmbH* EU:C:2015:28, paras 24–26. See also Case C-523/10 *Wintersteiger AG v Products 4U Sondermaschinenbau GmbH* EU:C:2012:220, para 36, involving an alleged online national trademark infringement, in which the CJEU rejected the place of the server as jurisdiction ground in view of the objective of foreseeability.

[19] Case C-170/12 *Peter Pinckney v KDG Mediatech AG* EU:C:2013:635, para 43; Case C-387/12 *Hi Hotel HCF SARL v Uwe Spoering* EU:C:2014:215, para 35; Case C-441/13 *Pez Hejduk*, para 34.

[20] Case C-170/12 *Pinckney*, paras 44–46; Case C-387/12 *Hi Hotel*, paras 38-39; Case C-441/13 *Pez Hejduk*, paras 36–37. In Case C-68/93 *Fiona Shevill and Others v Press Alliance SA* EU:C:1995:61,

'likelihood of damage' criterion will easily be satisfied.[21] Even if another person – ie a third party[22] – has put copyright infringing content or goods online, or for sale in a Member State, without the knowledge of the initial copyright infringer, the initial infringer can be sued before the courts of each Member State where the damage may occur.[23] With respect to online copyright infringements, the CJEU ruled that the courts of Member States can obtain jurisdiction based on the mere accessibility of copyright infringing goods or content via the website in the Member State of the court seised.[24]

Since the jurisdiction of these latter courts is territorially limited to the damage caused within the Member State of the court seised, the copyright holder may file a copyright infringement claim in each Member State. The alleged copyright infringer may therefore unexpectedly be sued simultaneously in all Member States for copyright infringement. Considering the paramount principle of predictability underlying the jurisdiction rules of the Brussels I bis Regulation, the CJEU's broad 'likelihood of damage' approach (including the accessibility approach) regarding cross-border copyright infringements has been criticised by various scholars.[25]

In view of the accessibility approach to jurisdiction, geo-blocking could be considered as a tool to prevent the risk of being sued for copyright infringement before the courts of other Member States than the Member State of domicile, or the Member State in which the co-defendant is domiciled. However, the question can be asked whether courts could nevertheless obtain jurisdiction based on the accessibility approach since internet users may circumvent geo-blocking by accessing the website via a VPN connection, or other means to circumvent geo-blocking. With respect to the liability for copyright infringement, the Dutch District Court in the *Anne Frank* case held that the defendants took all reasonable

paras 28–33, the CJEU established the 'mosaic principle' under Art 7(2) Brussels I bis that 'at the place where the damage was sustained, a claim can only be brought for damage sustained in the forum state, not for the world-wide damage'. See P Mankowski, 'Special Jurisdiction Article 7' in U Magnus and P Mankowski (eds), *European Commentaries on Private International Law: Brussels Ibis Regulation* (Dr Otto Schmidt KG 2016) 278. See also joined Cases C-509/09 and C-161/10 *eDate Advertising GmbH v X and Olivier Martinez and Robert Martinez v MGN Ltd* EU:C:2011:685, para 51.

[21] Van Houtert (n 3), para 5.2.4.1.

[22] With respect to the concept of 'third party' in the *Pinckney* case, see the Opinion of Advocate General N Jääskinen issued on 13 June 2013 in Case C-170/12 *Peter Pinckney v KDG Mediatech AG* EU:C:2013:400, paras 37–38.

[23] Case C-170/12 *Pinckney*, paras 44, 47; Case C-387/12 *Hi Hotel*, para 37. With respect to the third party-based approach to jurisdiction in cross-border copyright infringement cases, see also van Houtert (n 3), paras 3.5 and 5.2.3.

[24] Case C-170/12 *Pinckney*, para 44; Case C-441/13 *Pez Hejduk*, para 34.

[25] See, *inter alia*, van Houtert (n 3), para 5.2.4.1; R Matulionyte, 'Enforcing Copyright Infringements Online: In Search of Balanced International Private Law Rules' (2015) 6 *Journal of Intellectual Property, Information, Technology and E-Commerce Law* 132, 133–34; P Peter and C Kopp, 'Die internationale Zuständigkeit für Immaterialgüterrechtsverletzungen im Internet nach den EuGH-Entscheidungen *Hejduk* und *Pinckney*' (2016) 65 *Gewerblicher Rechtsschutz und Urheberrecht Internationaler Teil* 232, 235. See also Opinion of Advocate General N Jääskinen issued on 13 June 2013 in the case C-170/12 *Pinckney*, para 68.

efforts to prevent internet users from the Netherlands from accessing the website by means of geo-blocking and an 'access check' in case users from the Netherlands tried to access the website via, for instance, a VPN connection.[26] By analogy, the *Anne Frank* judgment could indicate that the mere use of geo-blocking would not be sufficient but an additional 'access check' would be required to prevent the risk of being sued before a court of a different Member State on the basis of the online accessibility of alleged copyright infringements.

In the context of a request for rectification and removal of defamatory content online, the CJEU ruled that 'in light of the ubiquitous nature of the information and content placed online on a website and the fact that the scope of their distribution is, in principle, universal' the latter request is 'a single and indivisible application and can, consequently, only be made before a court with jurisdiction to rule on the entirety of an application for compensation for damage'.[27] The latter ruling seems to indicate that the CJEU considers the internet as borderless which cannot be territorially divided by geo-blocking.[28] With respect to a court order to disable access to online defamatory content, Advocate General Szpunar nonetheless pointed out that geo-blocking can be considered as a valuable tool to disable access to this content in spite of the argument that 'the geo-blocking of the illegal information could be easily circumvented by a proxy server or by other means'.[29]

In view of the CJEU's third party-based approach to jurisdiction, as explained earlier, the effectiveness of geo-blocking as a tool to prevent jurisdiction in cross-border copyright infringement cases can also be questioned. If you block copyright protected content for internet users of a certain Member State but another person puts this content online, users of the latter state will still be able to access the infringing content. On the basis of the third party-based approach to jurisdiction, courts of the latter state would be able to obtain jurisdiction in spite of the fact that the defendant had blocked the access for users of this state. For instance, if the defendant blocked online access to allegedly copyright infringing photographs for users of a particular Member State but a third party published these photographs in photobooks and offered them online for sale, or even only in bookshops in that particular Member State,[30] the defendant could be sued in that Member State.

[26] *Anne Frank* case (n 6), para 4.3.

[27] Case C-194/16 *Bolagsupplysningen OÜ and Ingrid Ilsjan v Svensk Handel AB* EU:C:2017:766, para 48.

[28] M Trimble, 'Copyright and Geo-blocking: The Consequences of Eliminating Geo-blocking' (2019) *Journal of Science & Technology Law-Boston University* 476, 482–83. See also DJB Svantesson, 'European Union Claims of Jurisdiction over the Internet – An Analysis of Three Recent Key Developments' (2018) 9 *Journal of Intellectual Property, Information Technology and E-Commerce Law* 113, 122.

[29] Opinion of Advocate General M Szpunar issued on 4 June 2019 in Case C-18/18 *Eva Glawischnig-Piesczek v Facebook Ireland Ltd* EU:C:2019:458, paras 100–01.

[30] See, for instance, Case C-387/12 *Hi Hotel*, para 37. With respect to the third party based approach to jurisdiction, see van Houtert (n 3), paras 3.5 and 5.2.3.

In sum, the effectiveness of geo-blocking as a tool to *prevent* being sued for cross-border copyright infringements in Member States is limited by the broad EU approach to jurisdiction in cross-border copyright infringement cases. Geo-blocking potential copyright infringing content can never prevent being sued before the courts of the Member State in which you are domiciled, or in the case of co-defendants you may be sued in one of the Member States in which they are domiciled. Based on the broad CJEU's 'likelihood of damage' approach to jurisdiction, geo-blocking can also not prevent the online provider of content, goods, or services being sued in a particular Member State or multiple Member States. It could be argued that the possibility to circumvent geo-blocking via a VPN connection, or other means, entails the likelihood that damage may occur in the Member State in which access for internet users has been blocked. Moreover, based on the third party-based approach to jurisdiction, courts can obtain jurisdiction based on the mere accessibility of copyright infringing content that has been put online by a third party even if the defendant had blocked this content for internet users of that Member State. To conclude, geo-blocking can nonetheless be used as a tool to *reduce* the risk of being sued before the courts of a certain Member State or Member States based on the 'accessibility' approach to jurisdiction.[31]

In view of the broad EU approach to jurisdiction in cross-border copyright infringement cases, Table 4.1 shows in a summarised manner that geo-blocking cannot prevent but can merely reduce the risk of being sued in a certain Member State or Member States. Section III will explain the legal limitations imposed by the Geo-blocking Regulation on the use of geo-blocking as a tool to reduce the risk of the online provider of content, goods, or services being sued in Member States for copyright infringements.

Table 4.1 Can geo-blocking prevent the risk of being sued for copyright infringement?

Jurisdiction grounds in cross-border copyright infringement cases under Brussels I bis and the CJEU's rulings	**Can geo-blocking be regarded as an effective tool to prevent an online provider of content, goods, or services being sued before the courts of a Member State?**
Article 4 courts of the Member State in which the defendant is domiciled	No
Article 8(1) courts of the Member State in which the co-defendant is domiciled	No See District Court of Amsterdam (the Netherlands), 1 February 2022, ECLI:NL:RBAMS:2022:328 (*Anne Frank*)

(continued)

[31] Van Houtert (n 1).

Table 4.1 ***(Continued)***

Jurisdiction grounds in cross-border copyright infringement cases under Brussels I bis and the CJEU's rulings		**Can geo-blocking be regarded as an effective tool to prevent an online provider of content, goods, or services being sued before the courts of a Member State?**
Article 7(2) courts of the place in which the harmful event occurred or may occur	*Handlungsort:* the place in which the event giving rise to damage occurred *Pez Hejduk:* the place in which the defendant is domiciled	No
	Erfolgsort: the place in which damage occurred or may occur *Pinckney, Hi Hotel, Pez Hejduk*: the place in which the damage may likely occur The 'likelihood of damage' approach to jurisdiction includes: – the accessibility approach – the third party-based approach to jurisdiction	Geo-blocking can *reduce* the risk of being sued in a certain Member State or Member States

3. The Influence of the Geo-blocking Regulation

In 2015, the European Commission launched the Digital Single Market Strategy plan which aims to address unjustified geo-blocking that is causing 'consumer dissatisfaction and fragmentation of the Internal Market'.[32] As a result, Regulation (EU) 2018/302 on addressing unjustified geo-blocking and other forms of discrimination based on customers' nationality, place of residence, or place of establishment within the internal market ('the Geo-blocking Regulation') came into force in December 2018.[33] The main prohibition against geo-blocking is laid

[32] Communication from the Commission to the European Parliament, the Council, the European Economic and Social Committee and the Committee of the Regions, A Digital Single Market Strategy for Europe, Brussels 6 May 2015, COM(2015) 192 final, p 6.

[33] Regulation (EU) 2018/302 of the European Parliament and of the Council of 28 February 2018 on addressing unjustified geo-blocking and other forms of discrimination based on customers' nationality,

down in Article 3(1) of this Regulation: 'A trader shall not, through the use of technological measures or otherwise, block or limit a customer's access to the trader's online interface for reasons related to the customer's nationality, place of residence or place of establishment'.[34] Article 3(2) specifies that a trader is not allowed to redirect a customer, without the customer's express consent, to another version of the trader's online interface that uses another language or layout, based on the customer's nationality, place of residence, or place of establishment. As clarified in Article 3(3), the prohibition on geo-blocking will not apply if it is necessary in order to comply with EU law.[35] Furthermore, Articles 4 and 5 Geo-blocking Regulation prohibit the use of different general conditions of access to goods or services, and different conditions for payment, for discriminatory reasons based on the customer's nationality or place of residence, or establishment in the EU.

The Geo-blocking Regulation concerns the relationship between traders and customers. This Regulation broadly defines a trader as any natural or legal person who is acting, including through any other person acting on behalf of the trader, in the European Union for purposes relating to the trade, business, craft, or profession of the trader.[36] A customer has also been broadly defined as a consumer who is 'a national of, or has his or her place of residence in, a Member State, or an undertaking which has its place of establishment in a Member State, and receives a service or purchases a good, or seeks to do so, within the Union, for the sole purpose of end use'.[37] The Geo-blocking Regulation can thus even be applicable with respect to business-to-business relationships, for instance, if a company purchases computers for its employees from an online electronics shop.

Certain services are excluded from the scope of the Geo-blocking Regulation. This Regulation does not apply to the activities referred to in Article 2(2) of the Directive 2006/123/EC on services in the internal market ('the Service Directive') such as non-economic services of general interest; transport services; audiovisual services; gambling services; healthcare services; and certain social services.[38] Audiovisual services often involve copyright protected content. These services include online video and film distribution, and broadcasting of

place of residence or place of establishment within the internal market and amending Regulations (EC) No 2006/2004 and (EU) 2017/2394 and Directive 2009/22/EC [2018] OJ L60I/1 ('the Geo-blocking Regulation').

[34] For the definition of an online interface see Art 2(16) Geo-blocking Regulation.

[35] Art 4(5) Geo-blocking Regulation illustrates that with respect to the sale of books, the prohibition under the Geo-blocking Regulation 'shall not prevent traders from applying different prices to customers in certain territories in so far as they are required to do so under the laws of Member States in accordance with Union law'.

[36] Art 2(18) Geo-blocking Regulation.

[37] Art 2(13) Geo-blocking Regulation. See also Art 2(12) Geo-blocking Regulation for the definition of consumer.

[38] Art 1(3) Geo-blocking Regulation. Directive 2006/123/EC of the European Parliament and of the Council of 12 December 2006 on services in the internal market (2006) OJ L376/36 ('the Service Directive').

audiovisual content.[39] Another exclusion has been laid down in Article 4(1)(b) Geo-blocking Regulation. The latter provision stipulates the prohibition on using different general conditions of access to goods or services for discriminatory reasons; however, an exception is made for electronically supplied services 'the main feature of which is the provision of access to and use of copyright protected works or other protected subject matter, including the selling of copyright protected works or protected subject matter in an intangible form'. These services concern the online distribution of music, games, e-books, and software.[40] Traders offering these services can thus use geo-location technologies to apply different general conditions of access, such as prices and delivery conditions, based on the customer's place of residence or establishment. However, the traders are nevertheless bound by the prohibition to geo-block access to their online interface for discriminatory reasons, as laid down in Article 3 Geo-blocking Regulation.[41] An internet user may thus access an online interface that offers non-audiovisual electronically supplied services, 'mainly for information purposes (such as for price-comparison purpose), since a cross-border transaction will be lawfully made only if the service provider has cleared copyright for the territory of the user'.[42]

Article 1(5) Geo-blocking Regulation stipulates that this Regulation does not affect the rules applicable in the field of copyright and neighbouring rights, notably the rules provided for in the InfoSoc Directive. Article 9(2) Geo-blocking Regulation also states that the extension of the Regulation to the aforementioned excluded services will only be possible provided that traders have the 'requisite rights' to make copyright protected work accessible in all Member States.[43] Nonetheless, the Commission's report on the first short-time review of the Regulation indicates the possible negative consequences of such an extension for consumers, service providers, the industry related to the creation and production of copyright protected works, and the 'related welfare impacts' in relation to cultural diversity.[44] Scholars argue that the elimination of copyright related geo-blocking requires a unification of EU copyright law, as an EU Copyright Code, and

[39] A Broocks and others, 'Geo-blocking: A literature review and new evidence in online audio-visual services', JRC Digital Economy Working Paper 2020-01, p 2, available at joint-research-centre.ec.europa.eu/system/files/2020-11/jrc120267.pdf.

[40] ibid.

[41] See recital 8 in the preamble of the Geo-blocking Regulation.

[42] TE Synodinou, 'Geo-blocking in EU Copyright Law: Challenges and Perspectives' (2020) 2 *GRUR International Journal of European and International IP Law* 135, 146.

[43] See recital 37 and Art 9 Geo-blocking Regulation.

[44] Report from the Commission to the European Parliament, the Council, the European Economic and Social Committee and the Committee of the Regions on the first short-term review of the Geo-blocking Regulation, 30 November 2020, COM(2020) 766 final, pp 1, 11. The latter report refers to the accompanying Commission Staff Working Document, Part 2/2, Brussels 30.11.2020, SWD(2020) 294 final, section 3.1.5.4. which is, *inter alia*, based on R Procee and others, 'Study on the impacts of the extension of the scope of the Regulation to audiovisual and non-audiovisual services giving access to copyright protected content'. With regard to the consequences of the elimination of geo-blocking, see Trimble (n 28) 497–500. See also Broocks and others (n 39) 7.

a pan-EU licensing model.[45] It has nevertheless been asserted that this solution will not be feasible from a political perspective.[46]

As explained in section 2, geo-blocking could be considered as a tool to reduce the risk of being sued in multiple Member States on the basis of the accessibility approach to jurisdiction regarding cross-border copyright infringements. Article 1(6) of the Geo-blocking Regulation stipulates that this Regulation does not affect EU Private International Law. However, as a result of the Geo-blocking Regulation, traders operating in the EU are often no longer able to use geo-blocking as a tool to reduce the risk of being sued in multiple EU Member States for cross-border copyright infringements.[47] The prohibition on geo-blocking has therefore increased the unpredictability for many traders as regards in which Member States they may be sued. Based on the accessibility approach to jurisdiction they could even be sued in all Member States for providing online services or goods that allegedly infringe copyrights. Small trading companies, in particular, may therefore decide not to provide online goods and services to customers in the EU.[48] This will not facilitate cross-border trade.

Considering the aforementioned excluded services and the definitions of trader and customer in the Geo-blocking Regulation, section 4 will illustrate in which cases it is still possible to use geo-blocking as a tool to reduce the risk of being sued before the courts of a particular Member State, or Member States, other than the Member State in which the defendant or co-defendant is domiciled. In addition, the negative effects of geo-blocking on copyright protection, the right to information, and cross-border trade will be pointed out.

4. The Use of Geo-blocking in Practice and its Negative Effects

Non-profit providers of information constitute a category that is allowed to use geo-blocking as such providers are not considered to be traders under the Geo-blocking Regulation. This category includes, for instance, providers of online encyclopedias, open access scientific repositories, and bloggers who provide non-commercial content. As explained in section 2, they can nevertheless not prevent the possibility that they may be sued in the Member State in which they, or their co-defendants, are established or domiciled. Yet, in view of the broad 'likelihood of damage' approach to jurisdiction, non-profit providers of information can use

[45] J Hoffman, 'Crossing Borders in the Digital Market: A Proposal to End Copyright Territoriality and Geo-blocking in the European Union' (2017) 49 *The George Washington International Law Review* 143, 147–48; Synodinou (n 42) 146.

[46] Mazziotti (n 4) 13.

[47] Van Houtert (n 3), para 4.5.3.

[48] Van Houtert (n 3), para 4.4.1.

geo-blocking to reduce the risk of being sued in a particular Member State, or multiple Member States.

However, if providers of information block their content for users of Member States, this will impede the cross-border flow of information to the detriment of education and innovation.[49] The right to information has generally been considered as a fundamental right, *inter alia*, laid down in Article 11 of Charter of Fundamental Rights (CFR) of the European Union of 2000.[50] The CJEU has provided a number of rulings 'in favour of freedom of expression and access to information at the expense of the interests of rights holders'.[51] With respect to liability for cross-border copyright infringements, the Dutch District Court's reasoning in the *Anne Frank* case seems to indicate that regardless of whether the defendant made use of the tool of geo-blocking, in the online context it is particularly important to strike a fair balance between the interests of copyright holders, on the one hand, and the interests and fundamental rights of users of protected content such as the freedom of science, on the other hand.[52] The latter ruling fits the 'trend of focusing on strengthening the exceptions and limitations to copyright and emphasizing users' rights and access'.[53] Section 5 will propose the adoption of an approach to jurisdiction in cross-border copyright infringement cases that provides more predictability than the broad 'likelihood of damage' approach to jurisdiction and could reduce the need to geo-block for providers of information. The proposed approach also considers the principle of balancing the interests of copyright holders, on the one hand, and users of information, on the other hand.

As indicated in section 3, audiovisual services are excluded from the prohibition to geo-block access for users of Member States. With respect to these services, traders can therefore use geo-blocking as a tool to reduce the risk of being sued in certain Member States for copyright infringements.[54] Particularly in view of

[49] Van Houtert (n 3), para 5.2.4.3. PK Yu argues that geo-blocking 'has serious ramifications for access to information and knowledge in both developed and developing countries'. See PK Yu, 'A Hater's Guide to Geo-blocking' (2019) 25 *Journal of Science & Technology Law – Boston University* 503, 504.

[50] Charter of Fundamental Rights of the European Union proclaimed on 7 December 2000 by the European Parliament, the Council of Ministers and the European Commission, entered into force on 1 December 2009 [2000] OJ C364/1. See also Art 10 European Convention for the Protection of Human Rights and Fundamental Freedoms, adopted in Rome on 4 November 1950, entered into force on 3 September 1953, which 'guarantees the freedom of expression which includes the freedom to receive and impart information'. See also S Mendis, *Copyright, the Freedom of Expression and the Right to Information. Exploring a Potential Public Interest Exception to Copyright in Europe* (Nomos 2011) 29.

[51] A McWhirter, 'Communication to the public online: protecting copyright or breaking the Internet?' (2020) 15 *Journal of Intellectual Property Law & Practice* 390, 390. See also the CJEU's case law mentioned by McWhirter (n 1).

[52] *Anne Frank* case (n 6), para 4.3.

[53] Trimble (n 28) 497. Trimble refers to A McDonald and others,'403 Forbidden: A Global View of CDN Geoblocking' ACM IMC.

[54] As stated in Recital 8 in the preamble of the Geo-blocking Regulation, 'audiovisual services, including services the principle purpose of which is the provision of access to broadcast of sports events and which are provided on the basis of exclusive territorial licenses, are excluded from the scope of this Regulation'.

copyright licence agreements, online content service providers like Netflix and YouTube often limit access to audiovisual services, such as streaming of particular movies, for customers of certain Member States. Considering the broad responsibility for the use of copyright protected content, laid down in Article 17 of the Directive (EU) 2019/790 on Copyright and Related Rights in the Digital Single Market,[55] online content-sharing service providers may use geo-blocking as a tool to reduce the risk of being sued in multiple Member States. Social media platforms, like Facebook and Instagram, may therefore geo-block a livestream for users of certain Member States.

However, geo-blocking of access to audiovisual services for internet users in several Member States will reduce the cross-border flow of information and may even be detrimental to freedom of expression.[56] In addition, geo-blocking increases the risk of online copyright piracy, which has a detrimental effect on copyright protection and reduces the revenues of copyright holders.[57] Researchers have pointed out that consumers often resort to using illegal websites to watch films that are blocked, even though they would be willing to pay.[58] As mentioned in section 3, traders providing non-audiovisual electronically supplied services that contain copyright protected content, such as music and e-books, are not allowed to geo-block access to their online interfaces but they can use geolocation technologies to employ different general conditions of access to their services for reasons related to a customer's nationality, place of residence, or place of establishment. The use of these technologies can nonetheless entail the same detrimental effects as geo-blocking of audiovisual services.

According to the Geo-blocking Regulation, traders providing only goods and services to traders that are not end users, such as retailers, are allowed to use geo-blocking. In view of the accessibility approach to jurisdiction, geo-blocking can be used by these traders to reduce the risk of being sued in a certain Member State or Member States for cross-border copyright infringements. The latter will, however, impede the proper functioning of the Single Market that aims to remove hurdles for consumers and businesses.[59] On 10 March 2020, the European Commission published its report 'Identifying and addressing barriers to the Single Market', which states that retailers are facing 'territorial supply constraints imposed by

[55] Directive (EU) 2019/790 of the European Parliament and the Council of 17 April 2019 on copyright and related rights in the Digital Single Market and amending Directives 96/9/EC and 2001/29/EC [2019] OJ L130/92.

[56] Van Houtert (n 1). PK Yu points out that 'geoblocking harms society by raising privacy and free speech concerns'. See Yu (n 49) 509.

[57] Hoffman (n 45) 145–46, 148, 152–53. See also Mazziotti (n 4) 1, 11.

[58] Hoffman (n 45) 153 refers to P Dootson and N Suzor, 'The Game of Clones and the Australia Tax: Divergent Views About Copyright Business Models and the Willingness of Australian Consumers to Infringe' (2015) 38 *UNSW Law Journal* 206, 226–27.

[59] Communication from the Commission to the European Parliament, the Council, the European Economic and Social Committee and the Committee of the Regions, Identifying and addressing barriers to the Single Market, Brussels, 10 March 2020, COM(2020) 93 final, at 1.

suppliers directing retailers to buy nationally'.[60] 'These practices, which may infringe competition law, can fragment the single market with the detriment to consumers as well as businesses.'[61]

Furthermore, if traders operate outside the EU, the use of geo-blocking access for users of all Member States will significantly reduce the risk that they may be sued in multiple Member States for alleged copyright infringements. It will, however, be detrimental for cross-border trade.[62] As argued in the previous section, small trading companies in particular might decide not provide online goods and services to customers in the EU to reduce the risk of being sued in multiple Member States, which will not facilitate online trade.

Table 4.2 shows in a summarised manner which online providers of content, goods, or services are legally allowed to geo-block and its negative effects.

Table 4.2 Geo-blocking in practice and its negative effects

Who is legally allowed to geo-block services or content	**Negative effects due to geo-blocking**
Traders that offer services and goods to traders that are not end users, for instance, suppliers to retailers	– Geo-blocking may infringe competition law – Fragmentation of the single market, with the detriment to consumers as well as businesses (European Commission report, 'Identifying and addressing barriers to the Single Market', 10 March 2020)
Traders operating outside the EU	– Impedes cross-border trade
– Providers of audiovisual services, for instance, Netflix, YouTube – Providers of non-audiovisual electronically supplied services that contain copyright protected content are not allowed to block or limit access to online interfaces, but they can use geolocation technologies to employ different general conditions for discriminatory reasons, for instance, Spotify, Storytel	– Increases online copyright piracy – Impedes the cross-border flow of information and may even be detrimental to the right to freedom of expression
Non-profit providers of information, for instance, providers of online encyclopedias, open access scientific repositories, and bloggers providing non-commercial content	– Impedes the cross-border flow of information to the detriment of education and innovation

[60] ibid, 7.
[61] ibid, 7.
[62] See also van Houtert (n 3), para 5.2.4.3.

5. A Plea for the 'Directed Activities' Approach to Jurisdiction to Reduce the Need to Geo-Block

The author of this chapter has advocated in her PhD dissertation for the adoption of the 'directed activities' approach under Article 7(2) Brussels I bis regarding cross-border copyright infringement cases.[63] Based on the 'directed activities' approach, the court of a Member State will have jurisdiction provided that the defendant objectively intended to direct its copyright infringing activities or content to that Member State.[64] With respect to alleged copyright infringements via the internet, the following non-exhaustive factors may play a role to decide to which state activities have been directed: use of a specific language; use of a country code top-level domain name; and 'geographical areas to which the seller is willing to dispatch the product'.[65] The scope of the court's jurisdiction on the basis of the 'directed activities' approach will generally be limited to the damage caused within the Member State of that court.[66] Yet, the author of this chapter has argued that the courts of the Member State in which the damage has been 'flagrant substantial' in relation to the entire damage caused by an ubiquitous copyright infringement dispute should obtain full jurisdiction.[67]

Compared to the current 'likelihood of damage' approach to jurisdiction, the 'directed activities' approach to jurisdiction will provide more predictability

[63] For the full argumentation in favour of the 'directed activities' approach to jurisdiction in cross-border copyright infringement cases, see van Houtert (n 3), in particular para 6.1 (for references to case law and scholars); para 7.5.3 (on the targeting approach to jurisdiction established by scholars and several courts of states of the United of America); and para 8.2.

[64] van Houtert (n 3), paras 6.1, 6.1.1, and 6.1.3 (demonstrates the 'directed activities'-based escape clause proposed by the CLIP group, see n 67 below). See, *inter alia*, S Depreeuw and J-B Hubin, 'Of availability, targeting and accessibility: online copyright infringements and jurisdiction in the EU' (2014) 9 *Journal of Intellectual Property Law & Practice* 750, 764; M Husovec, 'Comment on "Pinckney": Council Regulation (EC) No 44/2001 of 22 December 2000 on Jurisdiction and the Enforcement of Judgments in Civil and Commercial Matters, Art 5(3) – Peter Pinckney v. KDG Mediatech AG' (2014) 44 *International Review of Intellectual Property and Competition Law* 370, 373. See also Opinion of Advocate General Jääskinen in Case C-170/12 *Pinckney*, paras 59–66.

[65] Case C-324/09 *L'Oréal SA and Others v eBay International AG and Others* EU:C:2011:474, para 65. Van Houtert (n 3), para 4.5.3 and 6.1.2. In Case C-585/08 and C-144/09 *Peter Pammer v Reederei Karl Schlüter GmbH & Co KG and Hotel Alpenhof GesmbH v Olivier Heller* EU:C:2010:740, para 83, the CJEU provided a non-exhaustive list of factors to determine whether activities are directed to a Member State as stipulated in the jurisdiction rule in Art 17(1)(c) Brussels I bis related to consumer contracts.

[66] With respect to the mosaic approach, see section 2.

[67] Van Houtert (n 3), para 8.3.2.2.1. This proposed combined approach to jurisdiction is an adapted version of Arts 2:202 and 2:203(2)(b) Principles on Conflict of Laws related to Intellectual Property, the so-called 'CLIP Principles'. See for the final text of these Principles of 1 December 2011, www.ip.mpg.de/en/research/research-news/principles-on-conflict-of-laws-in-intellectual-property-clip.html. The concept of ubiquitous infringements can be defined as 'concurrent multi-territorial infringements evoked by a single act of operation'. See S Chaen, T Kono, and D Yokomizo, 'Jurisdiction in Intellectual Property Cases: The Transparency Proposal' in J Basedow, T Kono, and A Metzger (eds), *Intellectual Property in the Global Arena. Jurisdiction, Applicable Law, and the Recognition of Judgments in Europe, Japan and the US* (Mohr Siebeck 2010) 78, 98. For instance, copyright infringing content disseminated via the internet.

regarding in which Member State or Member States potential copyright infringers may be sued.[68] Under the latter approach, a court cannot obtain jurisdiction based on the mere accessibility of the website involved, or on the basis of copyright infringing activities committed by third parties without the consent of the defendant. Adopting the 'directed activities' approach to jurisdiction would also entail consistency in the case law of the CJEU related to the requirement of targeting the public of a Member State to localise online infringing activities in that state in order to determine whether the alleged infringer is liable.[69]

Geo-blocking of access to content or online interfaces for users of a certain Member State can be considered as a factor to indicate that the defendant did not intend to direct its copyright infringing activities or content to that Member State. Yet, the use of geo-blocking will not be a decisive factor since the assessment involves all circumstances of the case that indicate that the defendant objectively directed its activities to a particular Member State.[70] Trimble has pointed out that 'where courts in the EU consider targeting, it does not appear at this time that an absence of geoblocking alone would lead to the conclusion that a defendant had directed his activities to a member state'.[71] With respect to a claim of geo-blocking for a website concerning a Benelux trademark infringement, the Dutch Court of Appeal in The Hague rejected this claim since the website involved had not been directed to the Netherlands.[72]

Courts have even 'questioned the accuracy of geoblocking, not least because geoblocking can be circumvented'.[73] As argued in section 2, the decision of the District Court in the *Anne Frank* case also leaves room for the interpretation that geo-blocking may not be a sufficient tool to prevent the online content provider being sued in a certain Member State. Furthermore, the CJEU's statement that the internet is borderless and cannot be territorially divided seems to indicate that geo-blocking may not be considered as a legal tool to block content for users in a particular Member State.[74]

The 'directed activities' approach to jurisdiction will also provide traders that are prohibited from geo-blocking the opportunity to prevent the possibility of being sued in a certain Member State or Member States other than the Member

[68] Van Houtert (n 3), para 6.1.4.1. See also Matulionyte (n 25) 136. M Szpunar refers to the predictability of the court's jurisdiction in cross-border European Union trade mark infringement cases based on the targeting approach. See Opinion of Advocate General M Szpunar issued on 28 March 2019 in Case C-172/18 *AMS Neve Ltd and Others v Heritage Audio SL and Pedro Rodriguez Arribas* EU:C:2019:276, paras 83–84.

[69] Opinion of AG Jääskinen in Case C-170/12 *Pinckney*, paras 61–64. See also van Houtert (n 3), para 3.2.2; Case C-324/09 *L'Oréal and Others*, paras 61–67; Case C-5/11 *Donner* EU:C:2012:370, paras 27–30; Case C-173/11 *Football Dataco and Others v Sportrader*, paras 37–39.

[70] With respect to the 'directed activities' approach to jurisdiction, see van Houtert (n 3), para 6.1.

[71] Trimble (n 28) 494.

[72] Court of Appeals of The Hague (The Netherlands), 14 September 2021, *Rat Pack DE v Ratpac US*, ECLI:NL:GHDHA:2021:1953.

[73] Trimble (n 28) 482.

[74] Case C-194/16 *Bolagsupplysningen OÜ*, para 48. See also section 2.

State in which they or their co-defendants are established. With respect to the jurisdiction rule of Article 17(1) Brussels Ibis related to cross-border consumer disputes, the Geo-blocking Regulation clearly states that 'the mere fact a trader complies with this Regulation should not be construed as implying that a trader directs activities to the consumer's Member State'.[75] Thus, if traders do not block or limit access to their online interfaces that does not imply that their activities are directed to all Member States.[76] As stated above, traders can indicate that their online activities are directed to a certain Member State by using, for instance, a particular language; a country code top-level domain name; delivery location(s). The Geo-blocking Regulation stipulates that traders are not obliged to provide cross-border delivery of goods.[77] Traders may also apply territorial limitations on after-sales customer assistance or after-sales services offered by the trader to the customer; limiting these services or assistance to a specific Member State may also be an indication that the trader has directed activities to that Member State.[78]

Furthermore, it has been argued that the prohibition on geo-blocking copyright protected content will have a negative effect on cultural and linguistic diversity.[79] The use of a particular language as a factor to indicate 'directed activities' may help to maintain this diversity in the EU.

The 'directed activities' approach to jurisdiction is also beneficial to online providers of content and services that are allowed to geo-block such as non-profit providers of information. As argued in section 2, in view of the CJEU's broad 'likelihood of damage' approach, geo-blocking can *reduce* the risk of being sued in a certain Member State or Member States. While the 'directed activities' approach to jurisdiction reduces the importance of geo-blocking, it will provide other tools that could *prevent* being sued in a certain Member State or Member States. Online providers of services and content can use a particular language, or country code top-level domain name of a certain Member State to prevent being sued in other Member States with the exception of the Member State in which they, or their co-defendants, are domiciled or established. Reducing the use of geo-blocking by online providers of information and traders would keep the internet more open, which is beneficial for online trade, the cross-border flow of information, and freedom of expression.[80]

In addition, the 'directed activities' approach will be beneficial to traders providing non-audiovisual electronically supplied services that contain copyright protected content since they can apply different conditions based on the customer's

[75] See Recital 13 and Art 1(6) Geo-blocking Regulation. With respect to the interaction between the Geo-blocking Regulation and EU private international law related to consumer disputes, see M Campo Comba, 'The New Geo-Blocking Regulation: General Overview and Private International Law Aspects' (2018) 3 *Nederlands Internationaal Privaatrecht* 512.

[76] Recital 13 in the preamble and Art 1(6) Geo-blocking Regulation. See van Houtert (n 3), para 4.5.3.

[77] See Recital 23 Geo-blocking Regulation.

[78] See Recital 28 Geo-blocking Regulation. See van Houtert (n 3), para 4.5.3.

[79] Mazziotti (n 4) 7, 11–15. See also Trimble (n 28) 499–500.

[80] Van Houtert (n 1).

nationality, place of residence, or establishment in the EU. As explained in section 3, these traders are not allowed to geo-block. Based on the CJEU's broad 'likelihood of damage' approach, these traders may therefore be sued in all Member States for cross-border copyright infringements. According to the 'directed activities' approach, the fact that traders employ different conditions for customers of different Member States could nevertheless indicate that their services are directed to certain Member States.

From a broad perspective, the proposed combined approach to jurisdiction involving the 'directed activities' criterion and the 'flagrant substantial damage in relation to the entire damage' criterion will likely balance the interests between copyright holders, on the one hand, and users of information and traders, on the other hand.[81] The principle of balancing the interests between copyright holders and stakeholders, such as users of information and traders, originally belongs to the field of copyright law. Yet, the author of this chapter has employed this principle to rethink the CJEU's approach to jurisdiction in cross-border copyright infringement cases which is in line with the trend of instrumentalisation of private international law.[82]

As pointed out by the District Court in the *Anne Frank* case, copyrights are not absolute.[83] According to the case law of the CJEU and Article 17(2) CFR, intellectual property is protected as a right to property.[84] Yet, Article 17(1) and Article 52 CFR indicate that 'fundamental rights generally do not have an absolute character and need to be weighed against other fundamental rights and public interests'.[85]

Section 4 mentioned that the CJEU has regularly included the fundamental right of information in this balancing act. While the CJEU considers the freedom of trade as a general principle of EU law, 'the interests of traders can also be considered as legitimate interests that may restrict the right to property such as copyrights'.[86] As argued in this section, the 'directed activities' approach would provide predictability to online providers of information and traders regarding in which Member States they may be sued. Moreover, this approach would reduce the

[81] Van Houtert (n 3), para 8.3.2.2.1.

[82] With respect to the argumentation to use the principle of balancing the interests related to copyrights in the context of private international law, see van Houtert (n 3), para 4.4 and the assessments in chs 5–8. For more information on the 'instrumentalisation of private international law', see, *inter alia*, Th M de Boer, 'De vermaatschappelijking van het international privaatrecht' (1980) 55 *Nederlands Juristenblad* 785; J Meeusen, 'Instrumentalisation of Private International Law in the European Union: Towards a European Conflicts Revolution?' (2007) 9 *European Journal of Migration and Law* 287; V Van Den Eeckhout, 'The Instrumentalisation of Private International Law: Quo Vadis? Rethinking the "Neutrality" of Private International Law in an Era of Globalisation and Europeanisation of Private International Law' (2013), available at papers.ssrn.com/sol3/papers.cfm?abstract_id=2338375.

[83] See section 1 above.

[84] See Case C-347/03 *Regione autonoma Friuli-Venezia Giulia and Agenzia regionale v Ministero delle Politiche Agricole e Forestali* EU:C:2005:285, para 120.

[85] Van Houtert (n 3), para 4.4.2.4.1. Van Houtert refers to T Tridimas, *The General Principles of EU Law* (2nd edn, Oxford University Press 2006) 311.

[86] See, *inter alia*, Case C-280/93 *Federal Republic of Germany v Council of the European Union* EU:C:1994:367, para 78; Case C-44/79 *Liselotte Hauer v Land Rheinland-Pfalz* EU:C:1979:290, paras 31–32.

need to use the tool of geo-blocking which would keep the internet more open for the cross-border flow of information and trade.

From the perspective of copyright holders, the 'directed activities' approach will likely reduce the number of Member States in which copyright holders can bring their case compared to the broad 'likelihood of damage' approach to jurisdiction. Yet, the proposed 'flagrant substantial damage in relation to the entire damage' approach to jurisdiction in ubiquitous copyright infringement cases may provide copyright holders the additional possibility of suing the alleged copyright infringer for the entire damage in a Member State which is not the Member State in which the infringer is domiciled. Particularly where the infringer acted in a so-called 'copyright haven', the latter approach will likely increase the possibility of efficient redress and therefore enhance copyright protection.[87] Furthermore, a decrease of geo-blocking will reduce the temptation of online copyright piracy for internet users.

This section has shown that private international law is more than just an area of law that coordinates private legal relationships involving a cross-border character. Private international law can be used as a tool to enhance public goals such as the facilitation of cross-border trade and to protect fundamental rights such as copyright, the right to information, and freedom of expression.

6. Conclusion

Section 2 has argued that the effectiveness of the use of geo-blocking as a tool to prevent being sued in EU Member States for cross-border copyright infringements is limited by the broad EU approach to jurisdiction with respect to cross-border copyright infringement cases. Section 3 has demonstrated that the possibility to use geo-blocking as a tool can also be limited by the Geo-blocking Regulation, which generally prohibits traders from geo-blocking access to their online interfaces. Hence, traders may face unexpected legal action in all Member States for alleged online copyright infringements. Small trading companies, in particular, might therefore even block their online interfaces for customers in all EU Member States to prevent the risk of being sued in multiple Member States, which will be detrimental for cross-border trade.

Section 5 argued that the 'directed activities' approach to jurisdiction in cross-border copyright infringement cases would provide more predictability to

Geiger and Schönherr pointed out that 'intellectual property rights need to be weighed against other competing fundamental rights and freedoms, such as the freedom of expression or freedom to conduct business'. See C Geiger and F Schönherr, 'The Information Society Directive' in IA Stamatoudi and PLC Torremans (eds), *EU Copyright Law: A Commentary* (Edward Elgar Publishing 2014) 452.

[87] Van Houtert (n 3), paras 2.2.2.2 and 8.3.2.2.1. A 'copyright haven can be defined to mean countries or jurisdiction in which certain copyright protections are not respected or are enforced in a lax fashion'. See Y Kang, 'Is Copyright Haven A True Haven? Legal and Economic Analyses of Copyright Haven' (2003) 31 *Korean Journal of International and Comparative Law* 95, 100.

potential copyright infringers as regards in which Member States they may be sued. It will provide traders that are prohibited from geo-blocking the opportunity to prevent being sued in multiple Member States by indicating that their activities are directed to a particular Member State or Member States. Compared to the current broad 'likelihood of damage' approach to jurisdiction, even online providers of services and content that are allowed to use geo-blocking would be better able to prevent being sued in a certain Member State or Member States for cross-border copyright infringements. Moreover, the 'directed activities' approach diminishes the importance of geo-blocking since Member States' courts would not be able to obtain jurisdiction based on the mere online accessibility of alleged copyright infringing content. This approach could therefore reduce the need to geo-block, which would keep the internet more open for the cross-border flow of information, freedom of expression, and cross-border trade, and would decrease online copyright piracy.

5

Access to Data, Databases, and Algorithms in the Digital Markets Act and the Digital Services Act

JOANNA MAZUR*

1. Introduction

While the role of access to data and algorithms in shaping competition, for example as an entry barrier in digital markets,[1] is still debated in scholarly literature, it is becoming more and more evident that there are circumstances in which it is necessary to ensure the possibility of examining data, databases,[2] and algorithms used in digital services. The motivation for ensuring access to data, databases, and algorithms may arise from various grounds, such as an attempt to strengthen the competition on digital markets, or the need to ensure that conduct is not anti-competitive. The question which this chapter aims to answer is how the Digital Markets Act (DMA)[3] and the Digital Services Act (DSA)[4] approach the need of ensuring such access for the purpose of enforcing law in the digital markets. Moreover, the chapter provides a comparison between these legal acts and the enforcement tools that the Commission uses based on the European Union (EU) competition law, and the requests for information which are allowed on the basis of EU competition law.

* This research was funded under the National Science Centre (Poland) grant OPUS, number: 2018/31/B/HS5/01192. Joanna Mazur is supported by the Foundation for Polish Science (FNP).

[1] For an EU-oriented perspective on the catalogue of challenges arising for competition law in relation to the use of big datasets and artificial intelligence (AI), see eg CS Hutchinson, 'Potential Abuses of Dominance by Big Tech through their Use of Big Data and AI' (2022) 10(3) *Journal of Antitrust Enforcement* 443.

[2] As the relationship between data and databases is not clarified in the legal acts analysed below, I refer either to databases or to data, depending on which of these terms is used in the relevant provision.

[3] Regulation (EU) 2022/1925 of the European Parliament and of the Council of 14 September 2022 on contestable and fair markets in the digital sector and amending Directives (EU) 2019/1937 and (EU) 2020/1828 (Digital Markets Act) [2022] OJ L265/1 (DMA).

[4] Regulation (EU) 2022/2065 of the European Parliament and of the Council of 19 October 2022 on a Single Market for Digital Services and amending Directive 2000/31/EC (Digital Services Act) [2022] OJ L 277/1 (DSA).

The chapter is structured as follows: section 2 presents the results of the analysis concerning the possibilities and limitations of the approach towards access to data, databases, and algorithms for the purpose of the enforcement of the DMA and DSA. Section 3 answers the question to what extent do these solutions broaden the scope of access to data, databases, and algorithms compared to already existing solutions which enable the Commission to access any information relevant to investigated cases in the area of competition law. Section 4 concludes. The research is based on the method of formal-dogmatic legal analysis and on desk research of the relevant literature and documents.

2. Access to Data, Databases, and Algorithms for the Purposes of Enforcement in the DMA and DSA

This section provides a detailed overview of the regulatory framework governing access to data, databases, and algorithms in the DMA and DSA. For each of the legal acts, the following questions are addressed: (1) What kind of uses of technology are covered by the provisions concerning the access (defined by the types of services provided or by the types of technologies used)? (2) Access to which of the following is guaranteed by the relevant provisions: data, datasets, or algorithms? (3) Who can request access? (4) In what kind of circumstances can access be requested? (5) What are the possible consequences of not providing the required access?

2.1. Digital Markets Act

The DMA focuses on the regulation of core platform services providers and, in particular, gatekeepers, understood – on the basis of Article 2(1) – as undertakings providing core platform services, designated pursuant to Article 3 (see further below). The catalogue of core platform services is defined in Article 2(2), and includes online intermediation services; online search engines; online social networking services; video-sharing platform services; number-independent interpersonal communications services; operating systems; web browsers; virtual assistants; cloud computing services; and online advertising services.[5] In order to be designated as a gatekeeper, a core platform service provider needs to fulfil the conditions enumerated in Article 3, namely: it must have a significant impact on the internal market; provide a core platform service which is an important gateway for business users to reach end users; and enjoy an entrenched and durable

[5] For the examples, see A de Streel and P Larouche, 'The European Digital Markets Act proposal: How to improve a regulatory revolution' (2021) 2 *Concurrences* 46, 48.

position in its operations (or it must be foreseeable that it will enjoy such a position in the near future). Article 3(2) includes quantitative indicators under which a core platform service provider is presumed to satisfy the respective requirements and, therefore, fit into the definition of a gatekeeper.[6] However, the Commission also designates as gatekeepers the providers of core platform services that meet each of the requirements of Article 3(1), but do not satisfy each of the quantitative thresholds adopted in Article 3(2).[7]

In terms of provisions concerning ensuring access to algorithms and data, the DMA refers to undertakings and associations of undertakings and not solely to the providers of core platform services or gatekeepers. The use of this broad category in this regard stems from the fact that the undertakings to which the request for information is addressed may not yet be designated as gatekeepers. For example, if the undertaking provides services identified as core platform services and therefore may fall into the category of gatekeeper – but it is not designated as such – access to its algorithms and datasets could be requested by the Commission. Moreover, it is important to note that the DMA is technologically neutral, in the sense that it is applicable to service providers independent of the technology they use.[8]

The most important provision of the DMA in regard to access to information for the purposes of the enforcement of this Act is Article 21, which allows the Commission to, in a manner of simple request or by decision, ask undertakings and associations of undertakings to 'provide all necessary information'. In its second sentence, Article 21(2) directly refers to requests to access any data[9] and algorithms of undertakings,[10] as well as information about testing and explanations

[6] According to Art 3(6) DMA: 'The Commission is empowered to adopt delegated acts in accordance with Article 49 to supplement this Regulation by specifying the methodology for determining whether the quantitative thresholds laid down in paragraph 2 of this Article are met, and to regularly adjust that methodology to market and technological developments, where necessary.'

[7] See F Chirico, 'Digital Markets Act: A Regulatory Perspective' (2021) 12(7) *Journal of European Competition Law & Practice* 493, 493.

[8] In contrast to, eg, the proposed AI Act which scope is defined in accordance with the technologies which will fit into the adopted definition of artificial intelligence (see Commission, 'Proposal for a Proposal for a Regulation of the European Parliament and of the Council Laying Down Harmonised Rules on Artificial Intelligence (Artificial Intelligence Act) and Amending Certain Union Legislative Acts', eur-lex.europa.eu/legal-content/EN/TXT/?uri=CELEX%3A52021PC0206).

[9] It was the Council's version of the proposal that included a change from the word 'data-bases', used initially, to the word 'data': Council, 'Proposal for a Regulation of the European Parliament and of the Council on Contestable and Fair Markets in the Digital Sector (Digital Markets Act) – General Approach' ('Council – General Approach'), data.consilium.europa.eu/doc/document/ST-13801-2021-INIT/en/pdf. Data is defined as 'any digital representation of acts, facts or information and any compilation of such acts, facts or information, including in the form of sound, visual or audiovisual recording': Art 2(24) DMA.

[10] It was the Parliament's amendment 176 that included a proposal to add 'information about testings': European Parliament, 'Digital Markets Act. Amendments Adopted by the European Parliament on 15 December 2021 on the Proposal for a Regulation of the European Parliament and of the Council on Contestable and Fair Markets in the Digital Sector (Digital Markets Act)', www.europarl.europa.eu/doceo/document/TA-9-2021-0499_EN.html.

on algorithms and data as specific types of information that can be requested by the Commission.

As Article 21(1) refers first to 'information' and then separately to 'access to any data and algorithms', it may be interpreted as differentiating between the two. Neither the term 'information' nor the term 'algorithm' are defined in the DMA. This could be interpreted as an element offering higher level of flexibility regarding the understanding of what should be covered by these terms. This is especially relevant for the term 'algorithm', as its meaning is not well established in law. Thus, I argue that lack of the relevant definition may limit the effectiveness of this provision, as the undertakings may, for example, provide general descriptions of the algorithms but refuse to allow access to the source code. The distinction between access to an algorithm and to the source code can be hugely significant for the scope of access to the software, as illustrated by a case concerning a request based on the Polish Freedom of Information Act to receive access to an algorithm used in an automated decision-making system used in the judiciary. The Polish court decided that the algorithm should be subject to the right to access information. However, it distinguished the algorithm from the source code, which was not automatically included in the term 'algorithm'. As a result, the Ministry of Justice published a PDF file that described the algorithm used in the system, not the source code itself.[11]

The division between 'information' on the one hand and 'data' and 'algorithms' on the other is also problematic because Article 21(2) refers to simple requests concerning information from undertakings and associations of undertakings and does not explicitly mention data and algorithms. The reference to 'information' in Article 21(2) might be thus interpreted as not including data and algorithms. However, the definition of 'data' in the DMA, namely, 'representation of acts, facts or information (*sic!*) and any compilation of such acts, facts or information' which have a digital form, suggests that at least some types of data can be also covered by the term 'information'.[12]

A distinction between data and algorithms and information is, however, further supported by the content of Article 21(3), which defines two types of decision that can be issued by the Commission requesting access to the relevant information. The first type concerns information.[13] The second type refers to the decisions which require an undertaking to provide access to its data, algorithms, and information about testing. These decisions should state the purpose of the request and fix the time limit to provide the access, and information about the penalties for

[11] For the judgment, in Polish, see III OSK 836/21 (Naczelny Sąd Administracyjny). For the file with the algorithm, see Ministerstwo Sprawiedliwości, 'Algorytm Na Podstawie Dokumentacji Analitycznej. Aktualizacja Do Wersji 1.12 SLPS', www.gov.pl/web/sprawiedliwosc/algorytm.

[12] Art 2(24) DMA.

[13] According to Art 21(3) DMA, such a decision should include 'the legal basis and purpose of the request, specify what information is required and fix the time limit within which the information is to be provided'.

not complying with the request. Moreover, such decisions may impose periodic penalty payments. It also seems that only this type of decision should indicate that the undertaking has the right to judicial review of the decision by the Court of Justice of the European Union.[14]

On the one hand, this way of using the terms 'information' and 'data' does not provide enough clarity regarding the meaning and the difference between the scope of these terms. Especially taking into account the difficulties concerning the enforcement of existing regulations in regard to big tech companies,[15] one can expect that the lack of precision and clarity will result in the gatekeepers questioning the status of the information that they are supposed to provide. On the other hand, what is interesting in this regard is the fact that the DMA obliges the undertakings to provide 'explanations' regarding any data, algorithms of undertakings, and information about testing. The possibility for the Commission to request, for example, both the algorithm and its explanation could facilitate the process of receiving adequate information and confronting the explanation provided by the undertaking with the independent analysis performed by the Commission.

What seems problematic is that information collected on the basis of, among others, Article 21 (and Article 23, on which see below), can be used only for the enforcement of the DMA.[16] First, this begs the question whether it would be possible for the Commission to use the algorithms or data in other types of proceedings, if they should be perceived as something different from information. Second, it raises concerns about situations in which the Commission would identify anti-competitive behaviour or other type of infringement that is not covered by the DMA. Then, in light of the DMA provisions, it seems necessary for the Commission or national competition authorities (NCAs) to collect the relevant information again.

In addition to the possibility of requiring access to algorithms and data by the Commission that the DMA foresees in Article 21, Article 23 broadens the scope of the access to include auditors or experts appointed by the Commission and the NCA of the Member State, enforcing the rules referred to in Article 1(6)[17] in whose territory the inspection is to be conducted. While, based on Article 21, the Commission appears to be allowed to require the relevant information at any time, even before opening a market investigation or a proceeding,[18] Article 23

[14] Which does not mean that only this type of decision is subjected to judicial revision, but – merely – that this type of decision is to include information about such a possibility.

[15] See M Cox and K Haar, 'Platform Failures How short-term rental platforms like Airbnb fail to cooperate with cities and the need for strong regulations to protect housing' (2020), left.eu/content/uploads/2020/12/Platform-Failures-Airbnb-1.pdf.

[16] However, Art 36 foresees certain exceptions in this regard, eg: 'The information collected pursuant to Article 14 shall be used for the purposes of this Regulation, Regulation (EC) No 139/2004 and national merger rules': Art 36(2) DMA.

[17] As Art 1(6) DMA enumerates the powers linked to the enforcement of competition law, this category mostly entails national competition authorities.

[18] Such an interpretation is confirmed by the Council's proposal to add a provision on the significance of information requests for determining the status of an undertaking as a gatekeeper in Art 3(3): Council – General Approach.

concerns all necessary inspections of an undertaking or association of undertakings.[19] During inspections, officials and other accompanying persons authorised by the Commission may require access to and explanation of, among others, the undertaking's IT system, algorithms, and data handling, as well as recording or documenting the explanations given by any technical means.[20] Such an inspection should be ordered by the Commission's decision which, among other things,[21] specifies the date of the inspection. The fact that an inspection would have to take place after informing the undertaking of its date may limit the effectiveness of this tool.

The DMA foresees financial penalties for not complying with the obligations included in Articles 21 and 23. Four types of behaviour may result in fines not exceeding 1 per cent of the total turnover in the preceding financial year; however, only if the behaviour is intentional or characterised by negligence. The fines, imposed by the Commission, concern: (1) failure to provide access to data, algorithms, or information about testing (in relation to Article 21); (2) failure to supply the information requested within the time limit fixed (in relation to Article 21) or supplying incorrect, incomplete, or misleading information or explanations (in relation to Article 21); (3) failure or refusal to provide complete information on facts relating to the subject-matter and purpose of an inspection (in relation to Article 23); (4) refusal to submit to an inspection (in relation to Article 23).[22] Additionally, there is a possibility for the Commission to impose periodic penalty payments (not exceeding 5 per cent of the average daily turnover in the preceding financial year per day). These penalty payments may be used to force the undertakings to provide correct and complete information (in relation to Article 21); ensure access to data, algorithms, and their explanation (in relation to Article 21); and submit to an inspection (in relation to Article 23).[23]

2.2. Digital Services Act

The most important provisions of the DSA in regard to the issue of access to data, datasets, and algorithms, are Article 69 and Article 72, which refer, respectively, to the power of conducting inspections and the monitoring actions that can be taken by the Commission.

[19] Thus, the article resembles the solutions known from EU's competition law: with regard to the Commission, Art 20 of Council Regulation (EC) No 1/2003 of 16 December 2002 on the implementation of the rules on competition laid down in Articles 81 and 82 of the Treaty [2003] OJ L1/1, and in regard to the national competent authorities, Art 6 of Directive (EU) 2019/1 of the European Parliament and of the Council of 11 December 2018 to empower the competition authorities of the Member States to be more effective enforcers and to ensure the proper functioning of the internal market (ECN+ directive) [2019] OJ L11/3.

[20] Art 23(2)(d) DMA.

[21] Art 23(6) DMA.

[22] For the full catalogue, see Art 30 DMA.

[23] For the full catalogue, see Art 31 DMA.

Article 72 of the DSA concerns access to, and explanations relating to, algorithms and databases. Its scope covers the monitoring of the implementation of and compliance with the DSA by the providers of very large online platforms (VLOPs) and very large online search engines. This limits the possibility of accessing the algorithms and databases only to the providers of services which provide a given service to a number of average monthly active recipients in the EU equal to or higher than 45 million and which are designated as VLOPs or very large online search engines in accordance with the DSA's provisions.[24] The DSA foresees the possibility for the Commission to appoint independent external experts and auditors as well as experts and auditors from competent national authorities that would assist the Commission in its enforcement-related activities.

Doubts about the interpretation of this provision are similar to those concerning the DMA. For example, there is no definition of 'algorithm' or 'database', and there is no clarity on the question whether algorithms and databases should be treated as belonging to the category of 'information' or if they should be treated as separate subjects of the Commission's request to access a particular type of data. These doubts have huge significance for the scope of the solutions proposed in the DSA, as its Article 67 refers to requests for information. It does not explicitly mention algorithms and databases, but provides the Commission with the ability to require the provision of information relating to infringement from VLOPs and very large online search engines and any other natural or legal persons who may be in possession of information relevant for a particular investigation.[25] If algorithms and databases are to be treated differently than any other kind of information, then the Commission's abilities to request this type of data could be based only on Article 72 of DSA, and, to a limited extent, in the context of inspections – but not on Article 67.

On the basis of the provisions on the power to conduct inspections (Article 69), the Commission can require an explanation on and access to,[26] among other things, algorithms and data handling.[27] Inspections are limited to the premises of VLOPs or very large online search engines, and any other persons who could have information on violations of the DSA provisions. In this case, the assistance of external experts or auditors as well as of Digital Services Coordinator or other competent national authorities of the Member State in the territory of which the inspection is conducted is allowed.[28]

[24] Art 33 DSA.

[25] Similarly to the DMA, there is a possibility of issuing simple requests and decisions concerning required information: Art 67 DMA.

[26] The Commission's proposal did not include 'access', which – considering the similarity between the provision on the inspections in the DMA and DSA – was surprising. The Council proposed significant amendments to Art 69, including the addition of 'access' in relation to, among others, algorithms, and data handling. Thus, the final version of the DSA includes both access and explanation on algorithms.

[27] Art 69(2)(d) DSA.

[28] Art 69(3) DSA.

In terms of fines which are foreseen in the DSA, the most relevant for the infringement of requests for access to or explanation on the algorithms appears to be the general inclusion of fines for intentional or negligent infringement of the relevant provisions of the DSA by VLOPs and very large online search engines. The fines are supposed to not exceed 6 per cent of the undertaking's total turnover in the preceding financial year.[29] Moreover, fines not exceeding 1 per cent of the total annual income or worldwide turnover in the preceding financial year[30] can be imposed, among others, in the case of supplying incorrect, incomplete, or misleading information in response to a simple request or request by a decision pursuant to Article 67. However, as it is not clear whether algorithms and databases fall into the category of information, it is also problematic to unequivocally claim that this provision could be used in reference to such an infringement of the regulation. The fines are, nevertheless, also foreseen in a case of failing to comply with the measures adopted by the Commission pursuant to Article 72[31] and in a case of a refusal to submit to an inspection.[32]

That means that if there were problems concerning the provision of access to algorithms or datasets, it is possible to impose fines on the basis of Article 74. However, Article 76 – concerning periodic penalties – includes specific solutions which refer to a refusal to submit to an inspection pursuant to Article 69 and a failure to comply with the measures adopted by the Commission pursuant to Article 67, which strengthens the division between information and algorithms. Such a division may be problematic because Article 72 is not included in the categories of infringements that may result with periodic penalties, whereas 'supply [of] correct and complete information in response to a decision requiring information pursuant to Article 67' is.[33]

In addition to the provisions analysed above, the DSA also includes solutions that refer to access to data that will be used to monitor and assess compliance with the DSA (Article 40). They are focused on VLOPs and very large online search engines, which should provide the Digital Services Coordinator (DSC) of the establishment[34] or the Commission, 'at their reasoned request and within a reasonable period specified in that request, access to data that are necessary to monitor and assess compliance with this Regulation'.[35] Article 40(3) foresees

[29] Art 74(1) DSA.
[30] Art 74(2) DSA.
[31] Art 74(2)(e) DSA.
[32] Art 74(2)(d) DSA.
[33] Art 76 DSA.
[34] This term describes: 'the Digital Services Coordinator of the Member State where the main establishment of a provider of an intermediary service is located or its legal representative resides or is established': Art 3(n) DSA.
[35] Art 40(1) DSA.

the obligation for the providers of VLOPs and very large online search engines to explain the design, logic, the functioning and the testing of their algorithmic systems, including their recommender systems to the Commission or to the DSC of the establishment.

Similarly, as in the provisions analysed above, the problem is the scope of information that VLOPs and very large online search engines are obliged to provide. As Article 40(1) refers to access to data, and Article 40(3) refers to the explanation of the design, the logic, the functioning, and the testing of their algorithmic systems, including their recommender systems, it is not clear whether Article 40 covers also access to algorithms or only their explanation. If the guaranteed access concerns merely data, then its relation to Article 72 – which concerns access to, and explanations relating to, algorithms and databases – is not clear.

What is different in Article 40, is its personal scope: upon a reasoned request from the DSC of the establishment, data must be provided to vetted researchers for the purpose of research on risks connected to the operation of these types of platforms.[36] The DSA defines the conditions which must be fulfilled by the researchers in order to be granted a status of 'vetted researchers',[37] and regulates various scenarios concerning access to data.[38] More details are to be developed by the Commission, which has the obligation to adopt delegated acts supplementing the DSA by laying down the technical conditions under which providers of VLOPs or of very large online search engines are to share data and the purposes for which the data may be used.[39]

The importance of Article 40 may be limited by the fact that specific conditions concerning this access should take into account, among others, the protection of the platforms' trade secrets.[40] VLOPs can evoke the protection of confidential information – including trade secrets – as a reason for requiring an amendment of the request to access data.[41] In such a case the undertaking is obliged to propose

[36] Art 40(4)–(12) DSA. The European Parliament also proposed to broadening the scope of the provision to vetted not-for-profit bodies, organisations or associations, see Amendment 342, European Parliament, 'Digital Services Act. Amendments Adopted by the European Parliament on 20 January 2022 on the Proposal for a Regulation of the European Parliament and of the Council on a Single Market For Digital Services (Digital Services Act) and Amending Directive 2000/31/EC', www.europarl.europa.eu/doceo/document/TA-9-2022-0014_EN.pdf. However, the final version of DSA does not include all these types of bodies, but does include the researchers affiliated with, eg, not-for-profit bodies, organisations and associations.

[37] Art 40(8) DSA.

[38] For example, the need to amend the request if the providers of VLOPs or of very large online search engines are unable to give access to the data requested because they do not have access to the data or because giving access to the data will lead to significant vulnerabilities in the security of their service or the protection of confidential information, in particular trade secrets, see Art 40(5)–(6) DSA.

[39] Art 40(13) DSA.

[40] Art 40(2) and Art 40(13) DSA.

[41] Art 40(5) DSA.

some other manner of fulfilling the request, which should be analysed by the DSC of the establishment. The DSC of the establishment is subsequently obliged to decide upon the request to amend the initial application. This solution seems to be quite complicated, and the feasibility of receiving any data on this basis will probably be very limited.

3. How Do the Proposed Solutions Change the Approach to Access to Information in the Context of Digital Markets?

The analysis of the provisions on access to information, data, datasets, and algorithms of the DMA and DSA confirms the general similarity between the organisation of enforcement in these legal acts to the enforcement of EU's competition law.[42] The analysed provisions to a great extent resemble the rules on requesting information in the Council Regulation (EC) No 1/2003 of 16 December 2002 on the implementation of the rules on competition laid down in Articles 81 and 82 of the Treaty ('Council Regulation 1/2003'). This is illustrated by Table 5.1, which compares the relevant provisions from these legal acts.[43]

Table 5.1 Comparison of solutions on access to information, algorithms, datasets, and data in the Digital Markets Act, the Digital Services Act, and Council Regulation 1/2003

	Digital Markets Act (DMA)	**Digital Services Act (DSA)**	**Council Regulation 1/2003**
Scope of the provisions on access	Undertakings and associations of undertakings.	Providers of VLOPs and very large online search engines.	Undertakings and associations of undertakings.
Purposes	To carry out Commission's duties under the DMA.	To monitor the implementation and compliance with the DSA.	To carry out the duties assigned to it by this Regulation.

(continued)

[42] See, eg, 'The DMA proposal entrusts the Commission with the exclusive authority to apply its provisions and puts in place enforcement procedures that mirror the ones the Commission relies on in the context of its Article 101 and 102 TFEU enforcement.' P Van Cleynenbreugel, 'The Commission's digital services and markets act proposals: First step towards tougher and more directly enforced EU rules?' (2021) 28(5) *Maastricht Journal of European and Comparative Law* 667, 678.

[43] Council Regulation 1/2003 (n 19).

Table 5.1 *(Continued)*

	Digital Markets Act (DMA)	Digital Services Act (DSA)	Council Regulation 1/2003
Access for whom and to what? For the purposes of the enforcement of the given legal act	*Commission:* – information; data, algorithms, and information about testing as well as explanation on algorithms, data, and information about testing; – inspections: access to and explanation on, among others, IT systems, algorithm, and data handling. *Auditors and experts, and national competent authority of the Member State, enforcing the rules referred to in Article 1(6) in whose territory the inspection is to be conducted:* – inspections: access and explanation of, among others, IT systems, algorithm, and data handling.	*Commission:* – information from providers of VLOPs and very large online search engine, as well as any other natural or legal person acting for purposes related to their trade, business, craft or profession that may be reasonably aware of information relating to the suspected infringement, including organisations performing the audits; – access to and explanations on algorithms and databases; – inspections: access to and explanation on algorithms and data handling; – data that are necessary to monitor and assess compliance with this Regulation and explanation of the design, logic, the functioning and the testing of algorithmic systems, including recommender systems.	*Commission:* all necessary information.

(continued)

Table 5.1 ***(Continued)***

	Digital Markets Act (DMA)	Digital Services Act (DSA)	Council Regulation 1/2003
		External experts, auditors, Digital Services Coordinator (DSC) or other competent national authorities of the Member State in the territory of which the inspection is conducted: – inspections: among other things, access to explanation on algorithms and data handling. *DSC of establishment:* – access to data that are necessary to monitor and assess compliance with this Regulation and explanation of the design, logic the functioning and the testing of algorithmic systems, including recommender systems. *Vetted researchers:* – access to data that are necessary for research on risks connected to the operation of VLOPs (limited by, among other things, the confidentiality of information).	

(continued)

Table 5.1 ***(Continued)***

	Digital Markets Act (DMA)	Digital Services Act (DSA)	Council Regulation 1/2003
Conditions under which the relevant authority may access information	Issuing simple request or decision (information). Issuing simple request or decision (algorithms and data). Inspections.	Issuing simple request or decision (information). Unspecified (access to, and explanations on algorithms and databases). Inspections. Upon reasoned request and within a reasonable period specified in the request (data that are necessary to monitor and assess compliance with this Regulation).	Issuing simple request or by decision.
Penalties	Fines (intentional or negligent behaviour).	Fines (intentional or negligent behaviour).	Fines.

According to Article 18 of Council Regulation 1/2003, the Commission may 'by simple request or by decision, require undertakings and associations of undertakings to provide all necessary information', which – in its essence – is identical to the content of Article 21 of the DMA and Article 67 of the DSA. Article 20 of Council Regulation 1/2003, concerning inspections, provides the overall framework for Article 23 of the DMA and Article 69 of the DSA. As according to these provisions of Council Regulation 1/2003, it is possible to request access to algorithms,[44] the question is what do the new legal acts change in terms of broadening the regulatory toolbox of measures that support the enforcement of law of digital markets by allowing access to algorithms, data, and datasets? Thus, in this section, the most significant differences between the approach to access to information which was adopted in Council Regulation 1/2003, and the approach that is present in the DMA and DSA, and problems which arise from the regulatory strategy selected in these new legal acts are indicated.

What is crucial in the analysed legal acts is the terminology used. While they mention access to algorithms and datasets directly, one can wonder if this is the right solution. Only the term 'data' is defined in the analysed legal acts, while the term 'algorithms' and 'datasets', are not defined. This blurs the scope of allowed access, for example, in terms of understanding what an algorithm is and whether

[44] See Bundeskartellamt and Autorité de la concurrence, 'Algorithms and Competition' 65–67, www.autoritedelaconcurrence.fr/sites/default/files/algorithms-and-competition.pdf.

it is possible to access the source code if only the term algorithm is mentioned in the given regulation. Moreover, elements of the provisions which concern access to algorithms, data, and datasets are separated from the provisions on access to information, which may cause problems if algorithms, data, and datasets are not directly mentioned in a particular context. Thus, I argue that it would be more efficient to provide a broad definition of 'information' with an open catalogue of examples such as algorithms, data, and datasets.

In terms of the scope of these legal acts, the DMA is focused on enterprises which can be designated as gatekeepers and on establishing a set of obligations that they are supposed to fulfil. The access of the Commission to algorithms and data is a necessary tool to enable the assessment, first, of whether a given service provider is a gatekeeper, and, second, of whether it follows the obligations included in the DMA. The DMA equips the Commission with the powers similar to the ones it has in the area of enforcement of Articles 101 and 102 of the Treaty on the Functioning of the European Union (TFEU),[45] but in regard to the examination of specific types of behaviour in the specific sector.[46] In the case of the DSA, the possibility of accessing algorithms and datasets is limited to situations in which the Commission monitors whether VLOPs follow the rules of this Act.

This shows that the general focus of all the legal acts analysed above is to ensure that access to data, databases, and algorithms for the purpose of their enforcement will be guaranteed only for selected authorities: for the DMA, this will be the Commission; and for the DSA, this will be the Commission and DSC of the establishment (with the exception of the DSA's Article 40 and its focus on vetted researchers). The role of other authorities – in particular, the national ones – is limited. The question which appears is whether providing – mostly the Commission – with such powers, will result in more efficient and speedier[47] control over the practices of big tech companies – the need for which inspired the proposal of these new legal acts in the first place. On the one hand, qualifying certain types of gatekeepers' and very large online platforms' behaviour as falling under regulation could be perceived as a step towards identifying anti-competitive behaviour and addressing it. On the other hand, taking into consideration the growing workload for the Commission, one may suspect that the practical difficulties regarding enforcement will not be resolved by providing mainly the Commission with the possibility of investigating big tech companies.[48]

[45] Consolidated version of the Treaty on the Functioning of the European Union [2012] OJ L326/47.

[46] Thus, the DMA can be called 'sector-specific competition law': see N Petit, 'The Proposed Digital Markets Act (DMA): A Legal and Policy Review' (2021) 12(7) *Journal of European Competition Law & Practice* 529, 529.

[47] For underscoring speed of enforcement as motivations for the adoption of the DMA, see L Cabral and others, 'The EU Digital Markets Act: A Report from a Panel of Economic Experts' (2021) European Commission: Joint Research Centre (JRC122910) 10 publications.jrc.ec.europa.eu/repository/bitstream/JRC122910/jrc122910_external_study_report_-_the_eu_digital_markets_acts.pdf.

[48] For a critical approach to investing all the enforcement powers in the Commission, see, eg, Rupprecht Podszun, who argues for the support of private enforcement in regard to the gatekeepers

4. Conclusions

The analysis of the DMA and DSA illustrates the fundamental difficulties EU law faces in light of the ongoing digital transition. The first challenge is the question of the terminology applied to the digital world: using specific terms (data, databases, algorithms) instead of establishing them as examples of a broader category of information may create interpretational doubts regarding the rules governing access to such types of information. Moreover, it is not clear if under the term 'algorithm' one should also include the source code. The fact that the DMA and DSA refer to algorithms and do not mention source code, seems to indicate that there might be a difference between the meanings of these terms, but the lack of definitions makes it impossible to develop comparisons the results of which would apply to these legal acts.

Second, the legal acts show that the EU is keen to adopt regulatory solutions which to a great extent replicate the ones already existing in the area of competition law, namely providing the Commission with a power to enforce the proposed regulations and, in order to enable such enforcement, the power to request necessary information. Such a regulatory strategy leaves us with the question whether the Commission will be able to efficiently use the powers it is about to acquire, and, on a more general note, whether such a focus on solutions strongly inspired by the ones developed in the context of the traditional economy will prove adequate for combating challenges linked to the digital one.

Third, in addition to these provisions, which directly concern the issue of access to algorithms and data for the purposes of the act's enforcement, the DMA proposal also envisages obligations on gatekeepers to provide access to certain data.[49] The provisions concerning this issue[50] significantly differ from the ones analysed above, as their purpose is not to enable any institutions or bodies to scrutinise the algorithms or data, but rather to provide companies with the ability to examine certain types of data collected by the gatekeepers about the issues directly linked to these companies. They include provisions on ensuring the effective portability of data generated through the activity of an end user;[51] provisions obliging

('Yet, if lawmakers believe in the power of competition and private parties, they, should open a forum so that private enforcement can enter the competition for enforcement. This requires another "Courage"-moment in European law, giving real effect to the DMA by introducing legislation for private enforcement in the field. Otherwise, the European Commission turns into a gatekeeper for the regulation of digital markets.' R Podszun, 'Private Enforcement and Gatekeeper Regulation: Strengthening the Rights of Private Parties in the Digital Markets Act' (2022) 13(4) *Journal of European Competition Law & Practice* 254, 267).

[49] Measures which would support changes of the structure of digital markets by forcing the undertakings to share their data are to a certain extent present in the legal acts analysed, but in regard to algorithms or source code they are not present at all.

[50] For their analysis, see S Vezzoso, 'The dawn of pro-competition data regulation for gatekeepers in the EU' (2021) 17(2) *European Competition Journal* 391.

[51] Art 6(9) DMA.

the gatekeepers to provide business users or third parties authorised by a business user 'access to, and use of, aggregated and non-aggregated data, including personal data, that is provided for or generated in the context of the use of the relevant core platform services or services provided together with, or in support of, the relevant core platform services by those business users and the end users engaging with the products or services provided by those business users';[52] the provision on 'access on fair, reasonable and non-discriminatory terms to ranking, query, click and view data in relation to free and paid search generated by end users on its online search engines';[53] and the right to receive data guaranteed to the advertisers and publishers, as well as third parties authorised by advertisers and publishers.[54]

The presence of these provisions shows that access to datasets, information, and algorithms is perceived from two perspectives. On the one hand, DMA and DSA include provisions which include necessary measures to ensure the enforcement of these legal acts. On the other hand, other provisions approach access to data as a way of influencing how digital markets are shaped. Hopefully, the latter type of provisions will have an impact on the manner in which digital markets work,[55] since the analysis of the provisions that are supposed to guarantee the effectiveness of the enforcement of DMA and DSA presented above shows that it is not clear whether they will improve the existing solutions.

[52] Art 6(10) DMA.

[53] Art 6(11) DMA.

[54] Art 6(8) DMA states that they should be guaranteed, upon their request and free of charge, 'access to the performance measuring tools of the gatekeeper and the data necessary for advertisers and publishers to carry out their own independent verification of the advertisements inventory, including aggregated and non-aggregated data.' Art 6(8) DMA.

[55] 'This could be a game changer. The combination of Art 6(a), (h) and (i) creates a compulsory access and use regime benefitting the business users, stopping just short of a property right, to the data generated by the business user and its end users on the platform.' B Lundqvist, 'The Proposed Digital Markets Act and Access to Data: A Revolution, or Not?' (2021) 52 *IIC* 239, 240.

PART II

Global Responses to Digitalisation

6

Are Data Spaces a 'Silver Bullet' for the EU Data Economy?

MARGHERITA CORRADO AND LAURA ZOBOLI*

1. Introduction

The ongoing technological progress has led to an exponential growth in the volume of data collected, processed, and used by companies in all industrial and commercial sectors. If used in an innovative and pro-competitive way, data sharing and re-use become crucial to harness the potential of data for innovation. They can also help to significantly reduce market entry barriers for start-ups and for small and medium-sized enterprises (SMEs), which usually have the know-how to process data but lack the financial resources to collect them.[1]

At the same time, however, firms may exploit data sharing to engage in anti-competitive conduct.[2] For instance, they may share competitively sensitive information, such as marketing and pricing strategies, output levels, and new product developments. Therefore, whatever form of collaboration is used to share data, stakeholders should be able to determine *ex ante* which types of data they can share and which they cannot. This also applies to the European common data spaces, ie the new data sharing frameworks announced by the European data strategy,[3] which represent the focus of the present chapter. Indeed, while many studies have examined the application of competition law to the data economy, few of them have explored the competition law challenges relating to data spaces.[4]

* The authors acknowledge the support of the National Science Centre, Poland (decision UMO-2018/31/B/HS5/01192). Although there was a joint conception of the chapter overall, Margherita Corrado drafted sections 3 and 4, while Laura Zoboli drafted sections 2 and 5. Sections 1 and 6 were drafted jointly.

[1] FTC, 'Data Innovation, and Potential Competition in Digital Markets – Looking Beyond Short-Term Price Effects in Merger Analysis' (CPI Antitrust Cronicle 2018).

[2] B Lundqvist, 'Data Collaboration, Pooling and Hoarding under Competition Law' (2018) *SSRN Electronic Journal*, www.ssrn.com/abstract=3278578.

[3] European Commission, 'A European Strategy for Data' (Communication) COM(2020) 66 Final ('European Data Strategy').

[4] Publications Office of the European Union, *Sharing Data (Anti-)Competitively Will European Data Holders Need to Change Their Ways under the Proposed New Data Legislation?* (Publications Office 2022) data.europa.eu/doi/10.2830/913446.

Since there is no fixed definition of data spaces, they can be understood as an ongoing initiative at EU level aimed at promoting the availability of 'large pools of data in [specific] sectors and domains [of public interest], combined with the technical tools and infrastructures necessary to use and exchange data, as well as appropriate governance mechanisms'.[5] In practical terms, in order to increase data flow within and across sectors of particular relevance, the EU institutions announced the development of sectoral data spaces in identified areas of public interest. As part of this initiative, the Commission released a Staff Working Document on Common European Data Spaces,[6] providing an overview of data spaces in general, as well as a proposal for a Regulation on the European Health Data Space,[7] which focuses on the features and structure of the health data space only.

Although data spaces are sector-specific, they share common features, which will be discussed in section 3; therefore, even if the proposals for the other data spaces announced have not yet been released, some information on their governance mechanisms can be inferred from policy documents published by the EU on data spaces in general.[8] Above all, what we do know is that data spaces mirror in part the mechanisms for sharing private data already undertaken within the ongoing privately driven initiatives. For these reasons, it is essential to move from current B2B data sharing mechanisms to identify potential risks – and in particular anticompetitive risks – that could arise from data exchange among actors involved in the data spaces initiative.

Against this backdrop, the chapter, after developing an overview for the B2B data sharing phenomenon in the EU (section 2), discusses the recent European data strategy and the main EU legislative initiatives on data sharing agreements that lead to the proposal of data spaces (section 3). Then, based on the recently released Staff Working Document on Data Spaces, it provides an overview of the features and structure of such domain-specific data spaces. In this context, it seeks to explore what data spaces are, why they are innovative, what are the main shortcomings and whether they truly represent a 'silver bullet' for the EU data economy, ie whether they are the appropriate solution to existing data sharing obstacles. To answer this question, the chapter (section 4) critically evaluates the European Health Data Space proposal. Section 5 discusses why data spaces can be a vehicle for collusion. In doing so, the section first provides for an assessment of data sharing agreements from a competition law perspective. Then, starting with the anticompetitive risks that data sharing agreements – mainly in the form of data

[5] ibid, 21.

[6] European Commission, 'Commission Staff Working Document on Common European Data Spaces' SWD(2022) 45 final ('Staff Working Document on Data Spaces').

[7] European Commission, 'Proposal for a Regulation of the European Parliament and of the Council on the European Health Data Space' COM(2022) 197 final ('EHDS Proposal').

[8] In addition to the policy documents, starting from 2021 the EU has launched a series of preparatory actions in the various sectors. See, for example, European Commission, 'Digital Europe Programme (DIGITAL) Call for proposals – Preparatory actions for Data Spaces' (2021).

spaces – may raise, it focuses on the main innovations introduced by the newly published guidelines on Horizontal Cooperation Agreements[9] on information exchange, which is the key for the success of data spaces.

2. A Framework of B2B Data Sharing Agreements

Business-to-business data sharing is the process whereby a company makes its own data available to another company that is interested in these data for its own business purposes, and this is typically implemented by means of civil contracts.[10] If two players that operate at same level of the production or distribution chain enter into a B2B data sharing agreement, then we have a horizontal agreement. If these players are at different levels in the value chain, then we have a vertical agreement. A company that shares data may either do so willingly or – rarely – as a result of a specific legal obligation. For instance, French law no 2016-1321[11] obliges commercial companies to open up categories of data of public interest, such as data generated in the context of procurement or commercial data for the development of official statistics.[12]

When we deal with data sharing, we consider data not only as an *output* – ie as a product generated through a process – but also as an *input*, capable of generating and/or improving processes, products and services.[13] If we consider a company that holds a certain set of data and another company that has access to and re-uses the same set, the value that the first company assigns to its data may be independent of the value acknowledged by the second company.[14] In addition, data holders may reap additional rewards for sharing data whose value they have already exploited.[15]

[9] European Commission, 'Guidelines on the applicability of Article 101 of the Treaty on the Functioning of the European Union to horizontal cooperation agreements' (Communication) (2022).

[10] European Commission. Directorate General for Communications Networks, Content and Technology and everis Benelux, *Study on Data Sharing between Companies in Europe: Executive Summary* (Publications Office 2018), data.europa.eu/doi/10.2759/634327.

[11] Loi no 2016-1321 du 7 octobre 2016 pour une République numérique, JO République Française no 0235 of 7 October 2016.

[12] European Commission, 'Staff Working Document on the free flow of data and emerging issues of the European data economy, accompanying the document Communication Building a European Data Economy' COM(2017) 9 final 32.

[13] M Maggiolino, *I big data e il diritto antitrust* (Egea 2018) 21.

[14] DD Sokol and R Comerford, 'Does Antitrust Have a Role to Play in Regulating Big Data?' in RD Blair and D Sokol (eds), *The Cambridge Handbook of Antitrust, Intellectual Property, and High Tech* (Cambridge University Press 2017). In fact, the ability to create additional value by using the same data for other purposes is noted as one of the defining aspects of the data economy – on this point see G Cattaneo and others, 'How the Power of Data Will Drive EU Economy. First Report On Policy Conclusions' (2018).

[15] F Mezzanotte, 'Access to Data: The Role of Consent and the Licensing Scheme' in RS Lohsse, R Schulze, and D Staudenmayer (eds), *Trading Data in the Digital Economy: Legal Concepts and Tools* (Nomos/Hart 2017).

When data are shared bilaterally or multilaterally by companies involved in the agreement, it is usually referred to as 'data pooling'.[16] In particular, Lundqvist defines data pooling or pools as agreements whereby firms 'share their digitalized information regarding a given market, in reference to a given service or generally in an industry, or within an e-ecosystem'.[17] There is no an all-embracing model for data pools, as they can be configured in different forms. First, it depends on the type of data being shared: some may refer to consumers or users' data; while others may relate to a technology, product, or distribution information based on specific proprietary pool technology.[18] There are also data pools that include public data, such as health data pools created to conduct research in digital health markets.[19]

The EU recognises the innovation and value generated by increased access and re-use of private datasets. At the same time, it acknowledges that currently there are many obstacles to data sharing among private players, including lack of trust, lack of data control over shared data, and requirements set by cross-setting regulations, including privacy rules. Therefore, in the last few years the EU has concentrated its efforts to issue a set of guidelines, reports, and legislative proposals aimed at encouraging data sharing and pooling, providing, *inter alia*, the creation of safe and secure environments where companies can easily share and access data.

To increase the availability, use, and demand for data and data-driven products and services the Commission has adopted a 'comprehensive approach'[20] that takes into consideration the needs of both the public and private sectors. In this section we will discuss those provisions in the proposals that impact on data sharing between private parties.

As a first step, the Commission has approved a series of ambitious regulatory projects as part of its digital and data strategies, namely the Digital Services Act (DSA),[21] the Digital Markets Act (DMA),[22] and the Data Governance Act

[16] J Cremer and others, 'Competition Policy For The Digital Era' (European Commission 2019), ec.europa.eu/competition/publications/reports/kd0419345enn.pdf.

[17] B Lundqvist, 'Competition And Data Pools' (2018) 7 *Journal of European Consumer and Market Law* 146.

[18] ibid 149. See also N Zingales, 'Data Collaboratives, Competition Law and the Governance of EU Data Spaces' (31 July 2021), available at ssrn.com/abstract=3897051 or dx.doi.org/10.2139/ssrn.3897051.

[19] Zingales (n 18) 9.

[20] European Data Strategy, 26.

[21] European Commission, 'Proposal for a Regulation on the European Parliament and of the Council on a Single Market For Digital Services (Digital Services Act) and amending Directive 2000/31/EC' COM(2020) 825. The political agreement on the proposal was reached on 23 April 2022. See 'Digital Services Act: Commission Welcomes Political Agreement on Rules Ensuring a Safe and Accountable Online Environment' (2022), ec.europa.eu/commission/presscorner/detail/en/ip_22_2545.

[22] European Commission, 'Proposal for a Regulation on the European Parliament and of the Council on Contestable and Fair Markets in the Digital Sector (Digital Markets Act)' COM/2020/842 final (2020). The political agreement on the proposal was reached on 25 March 2022. See European Commission, 'Digital Services Act: Commission Welcomes Political Agreement on Rules Ensuring a Safe and Accountable Online Environment' (2022), ec.europa.eu/commission/presscorner/detail/en/ip_22_2545.

(DGA),[23] with the intent to create thriving and inclusive European digital and data markets.[24]

In particular, the DSA introduces a common set of rules on intermediaries' obligations and accountability across the single market. The DMA imposes a number of data sharing obligations on large online platforms that act as gatekeepers[25] to reduce their exclusive control over the data they collect and, therefore, to decrease their leverage in the market for platform services.[26] These obligations 'seek to eliminate market distortions within the platform, including self-reporting and information asymmetries between the platform and its commercial users; as well as distortions between competing platforms'.[27]

The DGA includes measures to increase trust in data sharing, as the lack thereof is currently a major obstacle and results in high costs; new rules on neutrality to allow novel data intermediaries to function as trustworthy organisers of data sharing; tools to give players the control over the use of data they generate by making it easier and safer for companies and individuals to voluntarily make their data available for the wider common good under clear conditions.[28]

As second step, the Commission released on February 2022 a new horizontal legislative proposal that completes the EU legislative framework within the data realm, namely the Data Act.[29] Its objective is to introduce new measures to create an equitable data economy by ensuring access to and use of data and enhancing B2B and B2G (business-to-government) sharing mechanisms.[30] From the public consultation conducted between June and September 2021 it emerged that engaging in data sharing practices with other companies is a common practice among stakeholders.[31] However, the latter encounter many difficulties, including technical issues (data interoperability and transfer mechanisms), barriers to data access (ie denied access for competition concerns), prohibitive prices, and abuse of contractual imbalance.[32] Therefore, the consultation revealed the need to provide

[23] Council and Parliament Regulation (EC) 2022/868 of 30 May 2022 on European Data Governance and Amending Regulation (EU) 2018/1724 (Data Governance Act) [2022] OJ L 152/1.

[24] L Zoboli, 'Fueling the European Digital Economy: A Regulatory Assessment of B2B Data Sharing' (2020) 31 *European Business Law Review* 665.

[25] A gatekeeper is a provider of core platform that: has a significant impact on the internal market; operates a core platform service which serves as an important gateway for business users to reach end users; and enjoys an entrenched and durable position in its operations or it is foreseeable that it will enjoy such a position in the near future.

[26] L Cabral and others, 'The EU Digital Markets Act' (JRC Publications Repository, 2022), publications.jrc.ec.europa.eu/repository/handle/JRC122910.

[27] ibid, 23.

[28] European Commission, 'Commission Proposes Measures to Boost Data Sharing and Support European Data Spaces' (2020), ec.europa.eu/commission/presscorner/detail/en/ip_20_2102.

[29] European Commission, 'Proposal for a Regulation of the European Parliament and of the Council on harmonised rules on fair access and use of data' COM(2022) 68 final ('the Data Act'). This chapter was drafted when the Data Act was still a proposal but, before its final publication, the regulation successfully passed the trialogue process and was approved by Parliament. The finalised text is accessible at https://www.europarl.europa.eu/doceo/document/A-9-2023-0031-AM-027-027_EN.pdf.

[30] 'Public Consultation on the Data Act' (*Shaping Europe's digital future*, 2022), digital-strategy.ec.europa.eu/en/consultations/public-consultation-data-act.

[31] ibid.

[32] ibid.

greater certainty to stakeholders through the establishment of fair, transparent, and non-discriminatory conditions for accessing and sharing data, even if they are exchanged for public purposes.

To this end, the Data Act provides opportunities for data re-use, as well as measures to remove barriers to data sharing, promote a fair and equitable access to data, and enhance interoperability.[33] The main provisions include: measures to increase legal certainty for consumers and businesses that access and use data from the use of connected products and related services; general rules applicable to data holders obliged to make data available; measures to address unfair contractual terms regulating the access to and use of data; and essential requirements for operators of data spaces to facilitate interoperability of data, data sharing mechanisms, and services.[34]

The DGA and the Data Act are based on the European Data Strategy of February 2020, which has the ultimate goal of creating a single European data space, ie a genuine single market for data, which is open to data from across the world.[35]

3. The Last Step for Data Sharing: The European Data Spaces

As the last step of the EU Data Strategy, the Commission provides for the introduction of common and interoperable data spaces in specific strategic areas and domains of public interest where the use of data will have a systemic impact on both the ecosystem and the citizens.[36]

At a structural level, data spaces involve 'a data relationship between trusted partners who adhere to the same high-level standards and guidelines in relation to data storage and sharing [of their data]'.[37] The aim of data spaces is to accelerate the digital transformation in the identified fields by overcoming legal and technical barriers to the voluntary sharing of data by organisations and addressing the issue of lack of trust through the development of common rules for use of data that are fair, practical, and clear.[38] In addition, data spaces seek to create

[33] Data Act, *Explanatory Memorandum*, 1 ff, eur-lex.europa.eu/legal-content/EN/TXT/?uri=COM%3A2022%3A68%3AFIN.

[34] 'Press Corner' (European Commission – European Commission, 2022) ec.europa.eu/commission/presscorner/detail/en/qanda_22_1114.

[35] 'A European Strategy For Data' (*Shaping Europe's digital future*, 2022), digital-strategy.ec.europa.eu/en/policies/strategy-data.

[36] Zoboli (n 24) 671. See also 'Commission Welcomes Political Agreement To Boost Data Sharing And Support European Data Spaces' (*European Commission – European Commission*, 2022) ec.europa.eu/commission/presscorner/detail/en/ip_21_6428.

[37] 'Data Spaces' (*GaiaX A Federated Secure Data Infrastructure*), gaia-x.eu/what-is-gaia-x/deliverables/dataspaces.

[38] Staff Working Document on Data Spaces, 16.

an environment in which market participants feel empowered to share more data for use within the economy and society, while retaining control over the data they themselves generate. By making available large pools of good-quality and interoperable data in identified sectors, the resulting system of cross-sector and sectoral data spaces, combined with the necessary infrastructure for data use and exchange and appropriate governance mechanisms, should contribute increasing movement of data across Member States and across sectors.[39]

The European Data Strategy announced the creation of 10 sectoral data spaces: (i) industrial (manufacturing) data space; (ii) Green Deal data space, (iv) health data space; (v) financial data space; (vi) energy data space; (vii) mobility data space; (viii) data space for public administration; (ix) skills data space; and (x) European Open Science Cloud. This non-exhaustive list has been later expanded with the inclusion of (xi) a data space in the media sector; and (xii) a data space for cultural heritage.[40]

Beyond the specificities of each sector, data spaces share a number of common features that can be summarised as follows:

– *Interoperability and Interconnection:* Data spaces shall be developed in connection with other data spaces operating in different sectors. For example, the Green Deal data space[41] will work in synergy with data from other sectoral data spaces, including the European data space for smart circular applications.[42] Interoperability should be implemented, *inter alia*, through the development of appropriate and common standards at the EU level in compliance with sector requirements.[43] To this end, the Data Act proposal explicitly provides that the Commission may adopt specific guidelines laying down interoperability specifications for the functioning of data spaces, such as architectural models and technical standards implementing legal rules and arrangements between parties that foster data sharing, such as regarding rights to access and technical translation of consent or permission.[44] In addition, the Data Act provides essential interoperability requirements for data spaces that operators

[39] ibid, 21. On the opportunities and challenges of data spaces see Simon Scerri and others, 'Common European Data Spaces: Challenges and Opportunities', *Data Spaces Design, Deployment and Future Directions* (Springer 2022).

[40] Staff Working Document on Common European Data Spaces, 1.

[41] The Green Deal data space aims to interconnect currently fragmented and dispersed data from various ecosystems, both private and public sector, to support the objectives of the 2019 European Green Deal. See 'Information Session on a Preparatory Action for the Common European Green Deal Data Space under the Digital Europe Programme (DIGITAL)' (*Shaping Europe's digital future*, 2022), digital-strategy.ec.europa.eu/en/events/information-session-preparatory-action-common-european-green-deal-data-space-under-digital-europe.

[42] Within the framework of the Common European Green Deal data space, the European Strategy for Data mentions an action for the creation of a common European data space for Smart Circular Applications in order to make available the most relevant data for enabling circular value creation along supply chains.

[43] Staff Working Document on Common European Data Spaces, 43.

[44] Data Act, Art 33.

must comply with. Among these, Article 33 includes the need for adequate and consistent description of data and datasets, in particular with regard to their quality, structure, the method by which the data are collected, as well as the technical means to access them. This would facilitate the recipient's access to and re-use of data.

Through Article 33 on data access and use and interoperability, the Data Act aims to contribute to the development of common data spaces. However, the vagueness of some provisions introduced by the Data Act risks hindering rather than promoting the creation of data spaces. As pointed out by the Max Planck Institute in its position paper, the Data Act introduces requirements for data spaces operators, but does not define them.[45] We know that, generally speaking, participants in data spaces include data providers, users and intermediaries.[46] The notion of 'operators' could therefore refer to all or only some of these actors. Moreover, the Data Act makes no reference to interoperability across data spaces.[47] It is therefore important to specify whether the requirements set for operators also apply to interoperability across sectors and, in the latter case, how they would fit in with the features of each data space.

- *Technical Data Infrastructure and Governance Framework:* Data spaces will be based on common technical infrastructures to facilitate coordination and ensure fair data pooling and sharing among actors.[48] In addition, common elements across sectors will be implemented through the establishment of a horizontal governance structure that encompasses a set of administrative and contractual rules establishing rights to access, process, use, and share data in a trustworthy and transparent manner.[49] Such common elements will then be complemented with sector-specific rules.[50] In addition, according to the DGA, a European Data Innovation Board will be established in the form of an expert group tasked with assisting the Commission in the development of data spaces, among other tasks.[51]
- *Data control:* Data holders will have control over the data they generate and share, whether in return for payment or for free.[52] In particular, data owners have control over who accesses their data, for what purpose, and under what

[45] J Drexl and others, 'Position Statement of the Max Planck Institute for Innovation and Competition of 25 May 2022 on the Commission's Proposal of 23 February 2022 for a Regulation on Harmonised Rules on Fair Access to and Use of Data (Data Act)' [2022] *SSRN Electronic Journal* 81.

[46] 'Data Spaces' (*GaiaX A Federated Secure Data Infrastructure*) gaia-x.eu/what-is-gaia-x/deliverables/dataspaces.

[47] Drexl and others (n 45) 83.

[48] Staff Working Document on Data Spaces, 4.

[49] J Bodenkamp, 'Common European Data Spaces and The Data Economy' (3 November 2022).

[50] Governance frameworks must also comply with the relevant EU legislation (eg the GDPR, ePrivacy Directive, Platform to Business Regulation).

[51] Data Governance Act, Art 26. In particular they are commissioned to propose guidelines on data spaces and, more generally, to advise the Commission on security requirements, access procedures and cross-industry standards for data sharing.

[52] Staff Working Document on Data Spaces, 3.

conditions.[53] Due to increased trust, both businesses and individuals will have greater incentives to share data, thereby fostering the creation of an interconnected and competitive European data economy.[54]

- *Openness:* participation to an open number of organisations and individuals that respect EU rules and values. Openness would also foster competition 'between different product and service providers requiring data sharing thereby avoiding any potential competition lock-in due to manufacturers' specific protocols'.[55] This is particularly relevant for the repair sector. Indeed, currently manufacturers and designers often exercise *de facto* control over data generated by the use of a product or related service, thereby creating lock-in effects and hindering the market entry of after-sales service providers.[56]
- *Compliance with European rules and cross-sectoral measures:* Data spaces are to operate in full compliance with existing rules on personal data protection provided for in the General Data Protection Regulation (GDPR).[57] This means in practice that, for example, health data can be processed for secondary use (eg for innovation, research, policy making, and personalised medial services) only for specific purposes established by the Regulation.[58] Moreover, data exchange must take place in a secure environment that guarantees an adequate protection for personal data. Specific measures are then established for particular cathegories of data, such as sensitive data, in relation to which anonymisation mechanisms can be implemented to facilitate data sharing.[59]

In addition, and more importantly for the purposes of the present chapter, data spaces must respect existing competition law provisions. On this point, the Staff Working Document on Data Spaces merely states that data spaces shall comply with Articles 102, Article 101 TFEU and the related Guidelines for Horizontal Cooperation Agreements,[60] as well as the Block Exemption Regulations (BERs).[61] Similarly, the Data Act provides that the implementation of its provisions shall

[53] Bodenkamp (n 49).

[54] Staff Working Document on Data Spaces, 4.

[55] ibid.

[56] Data Act, Explanatory Memorandum,13.

[57] Regulation (EU) 2016/679 of the European Parliament and of the Council of 27 April 2016 on the protection of natural persons with regard to the processing of personal data and on the free movement of such data, and repealing Directive 95/46/EC (GDPR).

[58] 'Questions and Answers – EU Health: European Health Data Space (EHDS)' (European Commission, 3 May 2022), ec.europa.eu/commission/presscorner/detail/en/qanda_22_2712&gt.

[59] See 'Avicenna Alliance' (Avicenna-alliance.com, 2022), avicenna-alliance.com/latest-news/news/key-conclusions-of-the-workshops-on-common-european-data-spaces.

[60] European Commission, 'Communication from the Commission Guidelines on the applicability of Article 101 of the Treaty on the Functioning of the European Union to horizontal cooperation agreements' (2011/C 11/01) ('Horizontal Guidelines'). As well-known, the Guidelines are intended to assist market participants in self-assessing whether an agreement restricts competition and, if so, whether it fulfils the criteria for an exemption.

[61] Commission Regulations (EU) No 1218/2010 ('Specialisation Block Exemption Regulation') and Commission Regulations (EU) No 1217/2010 ('Research & Development Block Exemption Regulation').

not prejudice the application of the competition rules, or restrict it in a manner contrary to the Treaty.[62] However, neither the Staff Working Document on Data Spaces nor the Data Act analyse what anticompetitive issues might arise, or what measures should be taken to prevent possible competitors involved in the data spaces initiative from colluding. Based on these premises, section 5 builds on the main competition law issues that may result from data sharing initiatives in general to discuss potential competition law concerns that data spaces may generate.

4. Case Study: The Common European Health Data Space

The health sector is at the centre of a recent Regulation for the creation of a European Health Data Space (EHDS).[63] Given the crucial role that data play in the health system, made even more evident by the Covid-19 pandemic, the EU has made the creation of such domain-specific data space a priority.

To unlock the full potential of health data,[64] the EHDS first aims to allow individuals to easily access and control their own electronic health data (EHD) to better support health care delivery (primary use of EHD); second, it enables researchers, innovators, policymakers and regulators to re-use relevant EHD[65] to promote better diagnoses, treatment, and well-being for individuals, as well as to lead to better and more informed policies (secondary use of EHD).[66]

Certainly, the EHDS is in full compliance with current data protection regulation, and is designed to complement the rights and protections already provided by the GDPR, so that its goals can be effectively achieved. Indeed, the implementation of data access and transmission rights promoted by the GDPR is hampered by a lack of interoperability in the health sector, due to differences in local, regional, and national standards and specifications.[67] Such differences prevent the cross-border exchange of data. In addition, they prevent manufacturers of digital health products and providers of digital health services from entering the market.[68] Moreover, the majority of EHD cannot be made available for purposes other than those for which they have been collected, thereby limiting their secondary use.[69]

To promote interoperability and to strengthen individuals' right to data portability in the health sector the Proposal establishes essential requirements for health

[62] Data Act, Preamble, Recital 116.

[63] European Commission, 'Proposal for a Regulation of the European Parliament and of the Council on the European Health Data Space' COM(2022) 197 final ('the EHDS Proposal').

[64] Commission, 'A European Health Data Space: harnessing the power of health data for people, patients and innovation' (Communication) COM(2022) 196 final.

[65] Such as health records, genomics data, patient registries, etc.

[66] EHDS Proposal, 1–3.

[67] ibid, 3–8.

[68] ibid, 7.

[69] ibid, Recital 39.

record systems used to store and share individuals' EHD.[70] As for the secondary use of data, the EHDS Proposal complements the DGA by creating a genuine right to secondary use of public sector data and the Data Act by introducing specific rules for the portability of EHD.[71]

To summarise, the EHDS Proposal on the one hand gives people more control over their data through the electronic health record (EHR) mechanism; on the other hand, it provides greater security for their data through the introduction of health authorities, which are tasked with ensuring the implementation of natural persons' rights in relation to their data. Furthermore, the intention of the EHDS to create a coherent and efficient framework for the secondary use of individuals' health data would grant innovators, public institutions, and industry access to large amounts of high-quality health data. Access to those data is regulated through the abovementioned permission-based approach. This mechanism is intended to ensure greater control and security of shared data. However, at the same time, it may prove to be too cumbersome and thus hinder rather than facilitate data sharing and access. Indeed, the EHDS proposal sets a long list of data access applications requirements that must be complied with,[72] that could risk making the process of accessing data too time-consuming and inefficient. Also, according to Article 34, EHD can be processed for activities of public interest, education, and scientific research related to the health sector. It would therefore appear that not only institutions and public bodies will have access to the EHD, but also researchers and private parties, provided that data processing is carried out for the purposes set out in the said Article. If this is the case, it is not clear whether the access mechanisms are the same or whether they differ according to the public and private nature of the accessing entity. In addition, it is worth noting that Member States do not all have access to the same level of digital infrastructure,[73] and therefore the various authorities may not be equipped equally.[74] Furthermore, it is not clear how the EHDS Proposal in general would interact with other relevant cross-sectoral disciplines, such as intellectual property. What happens if the information to which access is requested is, for instance, protected by know-how? The Proposal merely states that where data is made available for secondary use, 'all measures necessary to preserve the confidentiality of IP rights and trade secrets shall be taken'.[75] Which are those measures? How can data be made available while preserving confidentiality provided by trade secret protection?

[70] ibid, 4.

[71] ibid.

[72] ibid, Art 35.

[73] See R van Kessel and others, 'The European Health Data Space Fails to Bridge Digital Divides' (2022) *BMJ*.

[74] 'The European Health Data Space Proposal of the European Commission' (*Twobirds.com*, 2022), www.twobirds.com/en/insights/2022/germany/the-european-health-data-space-proposal-of-the-european-commission.

[75] EHDS Proposal, Art 33.

As far as competition rules are concerned, the framework is certainly not clearer. The Proposal provides that any fee charged by health data access organisations or data owners must be transparent, proportionate, justified, and shall not restrict competition.[76] More in general, it also provides that the measures included in the EHDS Proposal should not be used to restrict competition in a manner contrary to Articles 101 and 102 TFEU.[77] Such meagre indications do not seem sufficient, given that health data pools[78] may represent a vehicle for anticompetitive conducts. Indeed, although it is true that, generally, research-based alliances do not raise particular competition law issues, and thus fall outside Article 101(1),[79] they may nevertheless generate anticompetitive concerns if the parties to the agreement 'have market power on the existing markets and/or competition with respect to innovation is appreciably reduced'.[80] Contractual arrangements based on the exchange of research data may strengthen the market position of the strongest party in a research consortium, thereby creating oligopolistic situations to the detriment of competition and innovation in the considered sector.[81] Moreover, research and development agreements can be exploited as a tool to establish a disguised cartel, ie to fix prices, limit output or allocate the market.[82]

5. Anticompetitive Risks of Data Sharing Agreements: Applications and Shortcomings of Article 101 TFEU

5.1. Data Spaces and Information Exchange

One of the greatest risks of data spaces both in general terms (section 3), as well as in the case under investigation (section 4), is that potential competitors participating in the initiative may use data spaces as a tool to exchange sensitive information or data, thereby increasing the risk of anticompetitive behaviour.

As mentioned, in general terms data sharing and data pooling agreements are often pro-competitive, as they enhance access to data and thus enable a greater exploitation of the innovative potential of said data.[83] Moreover, 'pooling of data

[76] ibid, Art 42.

[77] ibid, Recital 75.

[78] Defined as an aggregation of large health datasets belonging to different research actors who share them to foster scientific progress. See Schneider (n 19) 54.

[79] In particular, the Horizontal Guidelines states that research-based agreements between competitors generally do not generate competition law issues and are considered *per se* lawful (para 130). See also G Schneider, *Health Data Pools under European Data Protection and Competition Law: Health as a Digital Business* (Springer International Publishing 2022) 255.

[80] Horizontal Guidelines, para 133.

[81] Schneider (n 79) 232.

[82] ibid, 262. See also Horizontal Guidelines, para 128.

[83] Cremer and others (n 16) 9.

of the same type or of complementary data resources may enable firms to develop new or better products or services or to train algorithms on a broader, more meaningful basis'.[84]

However, such arrangements may also give rise to anticompetitive risks. The anticompetitive outcome will depend on, among other things, the market position of the parties involved, the type of data being shared, and the form of the agreement.[85] For example, data sharing and data pooling agreements regarding sensitive information, such as current and future prices, marketing strategies, and future products, will probably fall under Article 101(1) TFEU. In addition, through the exchange of data firms can increase their market power and thus their ability to hamper competition.[86]

In the Horizontal Guidelines of 2011, the Commission establishes general principles on the competitive assessment of information exchange between companies active in the same market. Accordingly, 'the exchange of strategic information can facilitate coordination (that is to say, alignment) of companies' competitive behaviour and result in restrictive effects on competition'.[87] In particular, information about prices and quantities is the most strategic, followed by information about costs and demand.[88] In addition to the type of information exchanged, other factors should be taken into account when assessing the effects of the agreement on competition, including its duration, the individualised or aggregated nature of the information exchanged, the age of the data, the frequency of the exchange, the public or non-public nature of the information or whether the exchange of information is public or confidential.[89]

Moreover, data sharing could have anticompetitive foreclosure effects on the market in which the exchange occurs.[90] This may happen when the information being exchanged is highly strategic for competition and covers a significant part of the relevant market.[91] Firms remaining outside the exchange system may suffer a significant competitive disadvantage.[92] As a remedy, parties could therefore be forced to grant access to the pool on fair, reasonable, and non-discriminatory (FRAND) terms, similarly to what happens in the case of patent pools.[93] However, assessing data pool agreements under the rules set for the analysis of standard

[84] ibid. See also H Richter and P Slowinski, 'The Data Sharing Economy: On the Emergence of New Intermediaries' (2018) 50 *IIC* 6–9.

[85] ibid.

[86] Lundqvist (n 17) 146.

[87] Horizontal Guidelines, para 2.2.

[88] ibid, Recital 86.

[89] ibid, Recital 76. See also I Graef, T Tombal and A de Streel, 'Limits and Enablers of Data Sharing: An Analytical Framework for EU Competition, Data Protection and Consumer Law' (2019) TILEC Discussion Paper, Tilburg University.

[90] Schneider (n 79) 281. See also S Schubert and FH Dayan, 'When Is Data Pooling Anticompetitive?' (Lexology, 2022), www.lexology.com/library/detail.aspx?g=40bb6970-8419-4f78-90aa-a9e160c61ef7.

[91] Horizontal Guidelines, paras 70–71.

[92] ibid.

[93] Cremer and others (n 16) 51.

essential patents (SEPs) does not take into account some of the specificities of such agreements.[94]

These concerns are even more compelling given the plan to develop EU data spaces. Indeed, when it comes to cooperation, it is not surprising that competition problems arise.[95] It is no coincidence that the Staff Working Document on Data Spaces states that they should operate in full compliance with the existing competition rules. However, it does not provide specific indications as to what measures should be taken to avoid potential illicit sharing. Even though so far little is known about how data spaces will be structured – save for the EHDS – it is crucial that certainty about the applicability of the competition law framework to these types of collaborations is increased, to foster the growth of data sharing initiatives such as that on data spaces. To this extent, the revised Horizontal Guidelines,[96] adopted by the Commission on 1 June 2023, represents an important starting point to help in addressing competition law issues arising from data sharing and data pooling practices, and also with regard to data spaces.

Against this backdrop, section 5.2 first provides a general overview of the process that led to the revision of the Horizontal Guidelines. Next, it discusses the new chapter on information exchange introduced in the revised version of the Guidelines. Then, the analysis shifts to the data spaces and, in particular, the anticompetitive issues that might arise from data sharing among actors involved in the pool. Finally, it comments on how the new Guidelines can be used to address those issues.

5.2. The Proposed Amendments to the Horizontal Guidelines and their Application to Data Spaces

While policy makers encourage data sharing and data pooling practices in all relevant sectors, there are many uncertainties about the applicability of the current competition rules to such agreements.[97] In the public consultation conducted between November 2019 and February 2020, many stakeholders pointed out that the section of the Horizontal Cooperation Guidelines on the competitive assessment of the information exchange does not provide enough criteria to evaluate data sharing and data pooling agreements.[98] In particular, there is a lack of criteria

[94] Zoboli (n 24) 686.

[95] Zingales (n 18) 13.

[96] European Commission, Annex to the Communication from the Commission, Approval of the content of a draft for a Communication from the Commission Guidelines on the applicability of Article 101 of the Treaty on the Functioning of the European Union to horizontal co-operation agreements, Brussels, (1 June 2023) C(2023) 3445 final (the Revised Horizontal Guidelines).

[97] G Schneider, 'Data Sharing for Collaborative Research under Art. 101 TFEU: Lessons from the Proposed Regulations for Data Markets' (2021) 17 *European Competition Journal* 567.

[98] 'Factual Summary of the Contributions Received During the Public Consultation on the Evaluation of the Two Block Exemption Regulations and the Guidelines on Horizontal Cooperation Agreements',

and guidance for the assessment of the size of a data pool or market share of those sharing data (ie how to define whether a data pool or data holders have a significant market share so that they would be subject to an obligation to grant access to such data?), and for the definition of the relevant market in these cases.[99] In addition, according to stakeholders, the Horizontal Guidelines do not provide specific guidance on horizontal cooperation agreements between companies without market power relating to non-commercial data.[100] In other words, they do not specify that such agreements do not raise particular anticompetitive concerns, nor do they provide a safe harbour or a *de minimis* market threshold for such types of arrangements. This lack of guidance does not allow SMEs to take full advantage of the innovative potential of data. Another issue is the lack of up-to-date examples on the nature of information exchanges that are likely to raise anticompetitive concerns, including data pooling, as well as on how an information exchange agreement can be deemed to be anticompetitive on the basis of the level of aggregation of information, the age of data, and the frequency of the exchange.[101]

Against this backdrop, the new version of the Horizontal Guidelines first provides clarification of the various forms of information exchanges, including different types of data sharing.[102] Accordingly, the term 'information' comprises raw data, pre-processed data, pre-manipulated data, as well as any other any other type – including non-digital data – of information.[103] An 'exchange of information', for the purposes of the Guidelines, covers physical information sharing and data sharing between actual or potential competitors, where the term 'data sharing' is interpreted broadly to include all possible forms and models underlying the access and transfer of data between companies, including data pools.[104] Then, the revised draft of the Horizontal Guidelines provides additional guidance to undertakings and association on the nature of the information exchanged to facilitate the self-assessment under Article 101(1).[105] Relevant concepts relate to the definitions of commercially sensitive information, genuinely public information or data, aggregated/individualised information and data, and the age of the information.

On closer inspection, the main changes introduced by the revised Horizontal Guidelines that may be particularly relevant for data spaces concern the section on the nature of the information and characteristics of the exchange. Probably, most of the data exchanged within and across data spaces will be of a public nature. The so-called 'genuinely public information' does not raise particular problems

2019 (Ec.europa.eu, 2022), ec.europa.eu/competition/consultations/2019_hbers/HBERs_consultation_summary.pdf.

[99] 'Evaluation Support Study on the EU Competition Rules Applicable to Horizontal Cooperation Agreements in the HBERs and the Guidelines. Final Report' (European Commission 2018) 107.

[100] ibid, 106.

[101] ibid, 109.

[102] Revised Horizontal Guidelines, para 6.1.

[103] ibid.

[104] ibid.

[105] ibid, para 6.2.3.

from a competitive point of view. It includes data that are equally accessible by the public, without it becoming more costly for customers and firms not participating in the exchange to access them. However, if competitors engage in an additional information exchange, other than sharing publicly available information (such as those published by regulators), there could be potential collusive effects on the market.[106] Moreover, as anticipated, data sharing may facilitate the exchange of sensitive information. For instance, health data pools may involve the sharing of competitively relevant scientific health data. The flow of information generated by the pool may strengthen the market position of each of the research actors involved, generating concentrated situations in the market and ultimately benefitting the strongest parties in the research consortium.[107]

In essence, data spaces involve a flow of information about a sector, which therefore requires the implementation of specific precautions to avoid illicit sharing (eg with 'Chinese walls', so that strategic information can only be exchanged between companies that do not compete with each other). With regard to information exchange between competitors, the new section 6.2.4.4. contains important guidance on measures to be taken to limit and/or control how data are used to prevent anticompetitive outcomes. In particular, such measures would prevent the exchange of commercially sensitive information from influencing a competitor's market behaviour.[108] In this context, one could mention the tool of 'clean teams' – namely secure environment in which selected employees and consultants can receive competitively sensitive information while continuing to comply with competition law – which is an instrument already known and particularly used in the case of merger and acquisition (M&A) transactions, even though they were explicitly foreseen in EU acts for the first time in the revised Horizontal Guidelines.[109] Clean teams could also be used in the case of data spaces and, more generally, whenever we have a pool of data and this may facilitate the exchange of sensitive information. The idea behind the updated version of the Horizontal Guidelines is to identify an independent third party to manage the data pool, subject to confidentiality rules on the sensitive information received by other participants.[110] Participants in the data pool would only have access to their own information and to the aggregated information of other participants. Furthermore,

[106] ibid.

[107] Schneider (n 79) 231–33.

[108] Revised Horizontal Guidelines, para 6.2.4.4.

[109] In this sense, the Revised Horizontal Guidelines, para 6.2.4.4, point 407, reads: 'Undertakings can, for instance, use "clean teams" or trustees to receive and process information. A clean team generally refers to a restricted group of individuals within an undertaking who are not involved in the undertaking's commercial operations and are bound by strict confidentiality protocols with regard to the commercially sensitive information. A trustee is an independent third party that provides services to the undertaking. A clean team or trustee can also be used for the purpose of implementing other forms of horizontal cooperation agreements, to ensure that the information provided for the purposes of such cooperation is exchanged exclusively on a need-to-know basis and in an aggregated manner'.

[110] Revised Horizontal Guidelines, para 6.2.4.4.

the implementation of specific technical and practical measures would prevent participants in the data pool from having access to sensitive information about other participants.[111]

Another potential issue is the risk of exclusion of a player from the market if they are excluded from the sectoral data space. As outlined in section 6.2.2.2 of the Revised Horizontal Guidelines, anticompetitive foreclosure on the same market where the exchange takes place can occur 'in data-sharing initiatives, where the data shared is of strategic importance, covers a large share of the market and competitors' access to the shared data is prevented'. Assuming that the information exchanged is strategic to competition and covers a significant part of the relevant market – but does not entail a risk of collusion – some form of open membership or access to the data pool would limit the risk of anti-competitive foreclosure. Therefore, access conditions to data spaces represent an important element to be evaluated in assessing possible foreclosure outcomes.

To this extent, FRAND rules could be established to grant access to data spaces. As widely known, FRAND terms originally refer to patent licensing in the context of SEPs: to stem the risk of abuse by SEP holders undertakings are generally committed to license the pooled technology to interested parties on FRAND terms. However, scholars have recently started to discuss the applicability of the FRAND principle also to data exchange agreements and, in particular, data pooling. Moreover, the Commission considered the possibility of establishing a framework based on fair, reasonable and non-discriminatory conditions for determining remuneration in the context of B2B data sharing.[112] More recently, the Data Act provides that whenever a data controller is obliged to make that available to a recipient,[113] such access should be based on reasonable, non-discriminatory, and transparent conditions[114] to ensure consistency of data sharing practices in the internal market, including across sectors, and to encourage and promote fair data sharing practices even in areas where no such right to data access is provided.[115] When data spaces involve competitively relevant data, the imposition of FRAND terms would prevent smaller undertakings from being excluded from the market.[116] At the same time, they would represent the basis to calculate remuneration whenever data access is granted upon the payment of a fee. Certainly, this approach may encounter many limits. Ultimately, there is no general consensus among jurisdictions on the exact definition of FRAND terms. With particular reference to data sharing, the landscape is fragmented and there is still uncertainty on the applicability of FRAND principles to data sharing and data pooling.[117]

[111] ibid, para 6.2.4.4.

[112] Zoboli (n 24) 686.

[113] That is, in the circumstances referred to in Art 5 of the Data Act.

[114] Data Act, Art 8.

[115] ibid, Recital 42.

[116] This is the case when certain data are relevant to enter a particular market.

[117] This also because the mechanisms of data sharing, data pooling, and SEPs present many differences. On the point see Richter and Slowinski (n 84) 20–21.

However, data spaces may represent an opportunity for the Commission to establish a common framework of principles on the applicability of FRAND terms to data sharing realm.

6. Concluding Remarks

The first part of this chapter highlighted the key role that an increase of data circulation among private players may play within the current economy. Sharing data is crucial to creating new products and developing new services. In this context, the European data spaces seem ideal. They promote sector-wide data sharing by increasing the control of companies and individuals over their data – overcoming current legal and technical barriers to the voluntary sharing of data and tackling the issue of lack of trust through the development of common rules for use and access of data that are fair, practical and clear. In addition, data spaces address the issue of lack of sectoral initiative by promoting and increasing the sharing and use of data within the EU and also across relevant sectors. This is especially relevant for those sectors, such as health, where there is an urgent need for data access and use to face current and future challenges.

In particular, the EHDS Proposal aims to unleash the power of the health data economy by ensuring a consistent and efficient framework for data access and re-use for secondary use purposes; empowering individuals to control their own data; ensuring interoperability and security of health data; and fostering a single market for digital health services and products.[118]

Beyond the features of each sector, what emerges is the fundamental role that the public sector will play in this ambitious project.[119] More importantly, the success of the initiative would seem to largely depend – again – on voluntary data sharing actions.[120]

At the structural level, data spaces need to be complemented by policies and measures that take into account the specificities of each sector. Moreover, by their very nature – public-driven and sectoral – data spaces raise specific complexities from the perspective of competition law. In this regard, the Staff Working Document (SWD) on Data Spaces merely states that data spaces must comply with existing competition rules, particularly the Horizontal Cooperation Guidelines. But, at present, there are no mechanisms in place to prevent potential anticompetitive behaviours. Certainly, collaborations or agreements between competitors,

[118] 'A European Health Data Space: harnessing the power of health data for people, patients and innovation' (Communication) COM(2022) 196 final.

[119] Zingales (n 18) 14.

[120] ibid. See also Staff Working Document on Data Spaces, 2 (specifying that 'apart from data sharing obligations set out in Union or Member States legislation, in the common European data spaces data will be made available on a voluntary basis and can be reused against compensation, including remuneration, or for free, depending on the data holder's decision').

which include data sharing, should be evaluated *ex post*, on a case-by-case basis. However, greater clarity on the information that may raise competition concerns would provide greater certainty for all actors and promote the success of the initiative. From this perspective, the revised Horizontal Guidelines may be important starting point to help addressing those issues, offering important guidance for interested stakeholders.

In conclusion, data spaces are undoubtedly an important initiative at European level, as they help to compensate the lack of cross-sectoral data sharing, and the case study on Health Data Spaces confirms such a positive assessment. However, the preliminary advancement of *ad hoc* regulation for data spaces, the application uncertainties, and the lack of activity of data spaces make it difficult to verify (yet) whether they are indeed a silver bullet for the EU data economy. In order to be so, it must certainly be ensured that they do not become a vehicle for collusion between competitors, and such a risk should have specifically been taken into account when structuring each data space.

7

Algorithmic Transparency in Rankings

Balancing Intellectual Property Rights and Disclosures in the EU and India

PRATIKSHA ASHOK

1. Introduction

In the digital economy, algorithms are the new air – they are everywhere, essential for survival online. Every keystroke, every search, and every step on the web is algorithmically controlled. Algorithms are a sequence of instructions to solve a problem and take decisions. Online platforms use algorithms in their operations, from ranking search results to processing payment portals. Though executed by machines, these algorithms are created by humans and awarded intellectual property protection. In modern online transactions, algorithms are integral to any online platform's business model and provide a competitive advantage.

One of the ways that algorithms impact consumer choice and affect decision-making is by ranking products and services on the platform. Consumers tend to choose the products first listed or ranked higher over others. As platforms became aware of this consumer behaviour, they began manipulating the appearance of listing by either favouring their products or selling the top listings to the highest bidder, thereby affecting competition in the market. In the quest to protect consumers, legislators call for transparent information to consumers. One of the ways to achieve this transparency is algorithmic transparency. Algorithmic transparency refers to the disclosure of factors that influence algorithms to those affected by these algorithms.

In the EU, to achieve this balance between providing information and the protection of intellectual property of businesses in rankings, the Fairness and Transparency (P2B) Regulation[1] introduced algorithmic transparency between

[1] Regulation 2019/1150/EU on promoting fairness and transparency for business users of online intermediation services (PE/56/2019/REV/1) [2019] OJ L186/57.

platforms and business users. This Regulation was supplemented by the Ranking Guidelines,[2] which serve as a guide to platforms when disclosing the main parameters that the algorithm considers to create rankings. The Regulation and the Guidelines attempt to create a level playing field amongst all the competitors in the market. The Modernisation Directive also included a similar provision about ranking transparency in its Unfair Commercial Practices Directive (UCPD) amendment.[3]

Similarly, in India, the Consumer Protection (E-Commerce) Rules[4] state that platforms must be transparent about the main parameters used by the algorithm in ranking products and services. The Indian Consumer Protection (E-Commerce) Rules are comprehensive and cover all marketplaces, being very technology-neutral. The EU and Indian legislation focus on algorithmic transparency in relation to rankings. Algorithmic transparency seeks to balance protecting users' rights and businesses' intellectual property rights. With the provision of transparent information about algorithms, consumers can make rational decisions without disclosure of the algorithm, which is an integral part of a platform's business model.

In the situation where algorithmic transparency achieves a balance between competitive advantage and information disclosures, could it be applied in other aspects of the platform business? This chapter discusses whether a similar algorithmic transparency standard can be called for in providing information to consumers about the parameters that create personalised content online. Drawing parallels with the ranking transparency model, the main parameters provided to consumers could also be provided where content is personalised.

2. Algorithms

Algorithms are like the nuclei in our brains. A nucleus in the brain receives data from the organs and processes and transmits it back.[5] Algorithms work similarly. Data is received and processed by the algorithm, and information is output. If there are issues with the brain, the inputs are processed incorrectly, the actions may not be correct, and the organs may not function properly.[6] Algorithms are programmed to react in a certain way – ie to produce a specific result if met with a

[2] Guidelines on ranking transparency pursuant to Regulation (EU) 2019/1150 of the European Parliament and of the Council (2020/C 424/01).

[3] Directive 2005/29/EC concerning unfair business-to-consumer commercial practices in the internal market and amending Council Directive 84/450/EEC, Directives 97/7/EC, 98/27/EC and 2002/65/EC of the European Parliament and of the Council and Regulation (EC) No 2006/2004 of the European Parliament and of the Council ('Unfair Commercial Practices Directive') [2005] OJ L149/22.

[4] Referred to in this chapter as the 'Consumer Protection (E-Commerce) Rules 2020'.

[5] Y Kobayashi, K Oshima, and I Tasaki, 'Analysis of Afferent and Efferent Systems in the Muscle Nerve of the Toad and Cat' (1952) 117 *Journal of Physiology* 152.

[6] A Gautam, 'Afferent and Efferent Impulses' in J Vonk and T Shackelford (eds), *Encyclopedia of Animal Cognition and Behavior* (Springer International Publishing 2017), available at link.springer.com/10.1007/978-3-319-47829-6_1255-1.

certain data set. However, if the algorithm is programmed incorrectly, it may lead to issues. Unlike the brain, the reason for algorithm issues can be traced to the creation of algorithms. Humans create algorithms for humans and use data inputs from humans.

In the online world, algorithms are sets of instructions designed in a well-defined manner to deal with computational issues. The widespread availability of increasingly large volumes of data and the increasing computing power needed to process it has meant more complex algorithms. Platforms of all sizes and styles of operation use algorithms to run the business and increase efficiency.[7] In addition to performing business processes, algorithms also improve efficiency, innovation, and consumer relations by being automated and by being a computation process rather than a human one.[8]

3. Algorithmic Transparency

Algorithmic transparency is a misnomer. It does not refer to the transparency of the algorithm used by businesses to process data collected. It refers to the transparency data points used by the algorithm. Algorithmic transparency is the principle that the factors that influence the decisions made by algorithms should be visible, or transparent, to the people who use, regulate, and are affected by systems that employ those algorithms.[9] Current research in the EU and India is focused on algorithmic transparency in relation to rankings.

Gestalt theory states that organisms perceive entire patterns or configurations, not merely individual components, ie the whole is more than the sum of its parts.[10] The aggregation of information on platforms assists in succinctly providing the information to consumers. Consumers perceive the veracity of a product or a service based on the average rating provided or when a specific product is placed

[7] C Codagnone and B Martens, 'Scoping the Sharing Economy: Origins, Definitions, Impact and Regulatory Issues', JRC Technical Reports – Institute for Prospective Technological Studies Digital Economy Working Paper 01/2016.

[8] H-W Micklitz and P Przemyslaw, 'Algorithms in the Service of the Civil Society' (2019) 8 *Journal of European Consumer and Market Law* 1; N Delgado, 'Algorithmic Transparency: Where Law Meets Technology' (College of Europe, Bruges Campus); F Di Porto and M Zuppetta, 'Co-Regulating Algorithmic Disclosure for Digital Platforms' (2021) 40 *Policy and Society* 272; V Lukovic, 'Information Asymmetries in Algorithms at Digital Platforms: Motivations to Participate and EU Regulatory Approach' [2021] 5th International Scientific Conference – EMAN 2021 – Economics and Management: How to Cope With Disrupted Times 167; 'Algorithms: How They Can Reduce Competition and Harm Consumers' (Competition & Markets Authority 2021); G Di Toro, 'Algorithmic Transparency Between Legal and Technical Issues' (Department of Business and Management and Computer Science Chair of Business Cyberlaw, LUISS).

[9] N Diakopoulos and M Koliska, 'Algorithmic Transparency in the News Media' (2017) 5 *Digital Journalism* 809.

[10] B Smith (ed), 'An Essay in Philosophy' in *Foundations of Gestalt Theory* 108.

higher than another.[11] Thus, the consumer is met with a list of products/services that a platform believes would best suit consumers, based on relevance.[12]

Existing literature explains the lack of information transparency about rankings as a regulatory challenge. The call for transparent information on platforms includes information about the parties, reputation criteria, and an expanded range of products and rankings.[13] Ranking issues were exacerbated when certain platforms placed their own products and services above those of their competitors.[14] The Exploratory Study conducted in the EU found that enhanced transparency about rankings increased consumers' trust and confidence in online platforms' decision-making.[15] While the Study shows that increased

[11] Consumers, Health, Agriculture and Food Executive Agency, 'Behavioural Study on the Transparency of Online Platforms' (Publications Office 2018) 2016 85 04 46; A Ghose, PG Ipeirotis and B Li, 'Examining the Impact of Ranking on Consumer Behaviour and Search Engine Revenue' (2014) 60 *Management Science* 1632; V Hatzopoulos, *The Collaborative Economy and EU Law* (Hart Publishing 2018) 11–12; N Golrezaei and others, 'Learning Product Rankings Robust to Fake Users' (2022) 71 *Operations Research* 1171; D Brouwer, 'A Non-Discrimination Principle for Rankings in App Stores' (2020) 9 *Internet Policy Review*.

[12] S Saumya and others, 'Ranking Online Consumer Reviews' (2018) 29 *Electronic Commerce Research and Applications* 78; Regulation (EU) 2019/1150 of the European Parliament and of the Council of 20 June 2019 on promoting fairness and transparency for business users of online intermediation services (2019) OJ L186/57 ('the P2B Regulation'); RM Ursu, 'The Power of Rankings: Quantifying the Effect of Rankings on Online Consumer Search and Purchase Decisions' (2018) 37 *Marketing Science* 530; C Twigg-Flesner (ed), *Research Handbook on EU Consumer and Contract Law* (Edward Elgar Publishing 2016) 228; A Ghose and PG Ipeirotis, 'Designing Novel Review Ranking Systems: Predicting the Usefulness and Impact of Reviews', *Proceedings of the ninth international conference on Electronic commerce – ICEC' 07* (ACM Press 2007); A Ghose and PG Ipeirotis, 'Estimating the Helpfulness and Economic Impact of Product Reviews: Mining Text and Reviewer Characteristics' (2011) 23 *IEEE Transactions on Knowledge and Data Engineering* 1498.

[13] C Busch and others, 'The Rise of the Platform Economy: A New Challenge for EU Consumer Law?' (2016) 5 *Journal of European Consumer and Market Law* 3; G Beltrà, 'Collaborative Economy – BEUC Position', BEUC The European Consumer Organisation – The Consumer Voice in Europe 5; K Nemeth and J Morais Carvalho, 'Current Challenges for Consumer Law' (2019) *Journal of European Consumer and Market Law* 3; G Straetmans, 'Misleading Practices, the Consumer Information Model and Consumer Protection' (2016) *Journal of European Consumer and Market Law* 5; 'Ensuring Consumer Protection in the Platform Economy', (BEUC The European Consumer Organisation 2018) BEUC-X-2018-080; Codagnone and Martens (n 7) 8; SAJN Nikolina, 'Modernisation of EU Consumer Protection Rules – A New Deal for Consumers', Briefing – EU Legislation in Progress 11; 'Online Platforms and the Digital Single Market' (House of Lords Select Committee on European Union) 10th Report of Session 2015–16; N Davidson, M Finck, and J Infranca (eds), *The Cambridge Handbook of the Law of the Sharing Economy* (Cambridge University Press 2018), doi.org/10.1017/9781108255882, 434.

[14] *XYZ v Alphabet Inc, Google LLC, Google Ireland Limited, Google India Private Limited, Google India Digital Services Private Limited* Competition Commission of India Case No 07 of 2020; *AT39740 Google Shopping* 8; S-T Kuiper and F ten Have, 'Google Shopping: Self-Preferencing Is a Form of Abuse of Dominance' *Lexology* (2 December 2021); J Persch, 'Google Shopping: The General Court Takes Its Position' *Kluwer Competition Law Blog* (15 November 2021); S Choudhary, 'Competition Commission of India Orders Google Inquiry after News Publishers Complain' *The Economic Times* (7 January 2022); A Kalra, 'India Antitrust Probe Finds Google Abused Android Dominance, Report Shows' *Reuters* (20 September 2021) 5.

[15] European Commission – Directorate General for Justice and Consumers and others, 'Final Report: Exploratory Study of Consumer Issues in Online Peer-to-Peer Platform Markets' (Publications Office 2017) 23.

transparency would increase trust in the platform, the counterfactual is that insufficient transparency could lead to consumers losing faith and dropping out of the platform.

The Market Study in India highlights similar concerns about the lack of clarity on rankings. The Study highlighted the problem that ranking criteria were too opaque. The rankings were created based on clickthrough rates, consumer ratings and reviews, price, reputation, and advertisements. The Market Study recommends that the main parameters of rankings and remuneration for rankings be disclosed.[16] In order to tackle issues of rankings in the EU and India, specific regulations concerning the transparency of information used to create rankings have been enacted.[17]

In order to balance the protection of intellectual property rights of platforms and the provision of information to protect consumers, regulations call for the disclosure of the main parameters used to create the rankings.[18] This balance is achieved when businesses do not disclose sensitive information regarding their business practices and the algorithms that run their platform, while at the same time providing information to consumers regarding the data collected and fed into the algorithm that may affect their decision-making.

Algorithmic transparency is only one of the tools which could be used to achieve the balance of protecting businesses' intellectual property rights and disclosures and information provided to consumers. Other avenues of platform regulation and algorithms would face severe blowback from stakeholders, and such regulation could affect their business practices. China calls for a blanket disclosure of algorithmic transparency in various fields. At the same time, the US provides a lighter regulatory touch by making businesses accountable for their algorithmic decisions. Algorithmic transparency is the current tool available to achieve this balance. With this tool, this chapter investigates whether algorithmic transparency can be employed in other aspects of algorithmic usage.

[16] 'Market Study on E-Commerce In India- Key Findings and Observations' (Competition Commission of India 2020) 12; BI De los Santos and S Koulayev, 'Optimizing Click-through in Online Rankings for Partially Anonymous Consumers' (2011) *SSRN Electronic Journal* 7.

[17] Regulation 2019/1150/EU on promoting fairness and transparency for business users of online intermediation services [2019] OJ L186/57; Consumer Protection (E-Commerce) Rules, 2020.

[18] N Delgado, 'Algorithmic Transparency: Where Law Meets Technology' (College of Europe, Bruges Campus) 20–25; C Simsek, 'Algorithmic Transparency in the EU' (Science Po- School of Public Affairs); European Parliament, Directorate General for Parliamentary Research Services, 'A Governance Framework for Algorithmic Accountability and Transparency' (Publications Office 2019) 7; G Di Toro, 'Algorithmic Transparency Between Legal and Technical Issues' (Department of Business and Management and Computer Science Chair of Business Cyberlaw, LUISS). Algorithmic transparency can be understood as the principle that the factors that influence the decisions made by algorithms should be visible or transparent to the people who use, regulate, and are affected by systems that employ those algorithms: J Goldenfein, 'Algorithmic Transparency and Decision-Making Accountability: Thoughts for Buying Machine Learning Algorithms' in Office of the Victorian Information Commissioner (ed), *Closer to the Machine: Technical, Social, and Legal Aspects of AI* (2019) 13.

4. Research Question and Methodology

This chapter investigates whether algorithmic transparency can be expanded to other aspects of algorithmic usage online. It uses an analytical approach to lay out the development of the legislation that have attempted to balance the provision of information and intellectual property protection. A comparative research method is adopted to compare the multijurisdictional approaches of the EU and India. This comparison is not to state whether one system is better – but to look at algorithmic transparency with a critical magnifying glass.

This chapter is structured to first look at the use of algorithms in rankings on platforms. The research then delves into the need for algorithmic transparency and the justifications that call for the balance of intellectual property and disclosures. The chapter further provides a detailed analysis of the legislation concerning disclosures of ranking algorithms in the EU and India and a comparative analysis. Rankings are discussed using two examples of platforms, Uber and Airbnb, as these platforms are becoming synonymous with ride-sharing and accommodation-sharing across the globe. Perspectives from other nations are examined to provide reasoning to expand the limitations of algorithmic discrimination from rankings to other avenues of algorithmic usage.

5. Rankings

5.1. Introduction to Rankings

Products and services are ranked in the physical world, ranging from everyday purchases like toothpaste to occasional purchases like computers.[19] This ranking can be on various bases – for example, the toothpaste ranked highest in teeth whitening may not be the same toothpaste that is ranked highest in terms of flavour. The terms of conditions considered for ranking are integral to understanding the basis of the ranking system in order to identify the best toothpaste in the market (for consumers' needs).[20]

Rankings are omnipresent online as well.[21] Search results are ranked in a particular manner, usually based on relevance but also modified based on price (high to low, low to high), proximity (closest or farthest), or relevance to the searched

[19] Showing that ranking is present in everyday transactions too. MR Solomon and others (eds), *Consumer Behaviour: A European Perspective* (3rd edn, Financial Times/Prentice Hall 2006) 98.

[20] SP Choudary, MW Van Alstyne and GG Parker, 'Platforms and Blockchain Will Transform Logistics' 5, 72; RB Khodaparasti, A Aboulfazli, and R Isakhajelou, 'Ranking the Most Effective Marketing Mix Elements on the Sales of Javid Darb Company Products: An AHP Technique' (2015) 8 *Journal of International Studies* 164; Solomon and others (n 19) 98.

[21] MC Compagnucci and others (eds), *Legal Tech and the New Sharing Economy* (Springer Singapore 2020) 127.

terms. Platforms rely on the intellect of algorithms to decide which search result, product, or service is ranked higher or lower based on the conditions selected.[22] For example, Airbnb properties (and hosts) or Oyo Rooms are ranked when consumers search for accommodations in a specific location. The criteria can be changed based on the various parameters; however, a default ranking occurs on relevance to the search terms.[23]

5.2. Two Parts of Rankings

Rankings consist of a two-step process: aggregating the information and applying algorithms to list the products and services in a specific manner.

The aggregation of information is the first step to ranking. Aggregation involves compiling information to prepare the database for algorithmic processing.[24] The aggregation process compiles data points and aggregates them (mathematical average) to provide aggregated information. For example, a 4.5-star rating (out of 5 stars) shown to consumers is an aggregate rating, created by aggregating ratings where individual ratings can be between 1 and 5.[25]

Algorithms form the second part of the creation of the rankings. Algorithms are specific instructions that use aggregated information to list the products in a specific manner.[26] Algorithms are unique to the platforms and form a part of their intellectual property.[27] For example, after aggregating the ratings, those products, and services with a 4.5-star rating (based on a single data point) may be placed higher than products with an aggregate 3-star rating.

[22] R Botsman, *Who Can You Trust? How Technology Brought Us Together and Why It Might Drive Us Apart* (Penguin Group 2017) 104. The author refers to online systems as 'magic', as the army of human beings, many of them single-minded 'maths nerds', involved in their operation are not seen. These 'magical occurrences' are known to be the work of algorithms. AJ Ravenelle, *Hustle and Gig: Struggling and Surviving in the Sharing Economy* (University of California Press 2019) 54; YA Arbel, 'Reputation Failure: The Limits of Market Discipline in Consumer Markets' (2019) *Wake Forest Law Review* 1239. Identical platforms can be ranked differently on different platforms, based on various conditions.

[23] Airbnb Terms of Service, perma.cc/TG7Y-44G3; Lukovic (n 8) 169.

[24] Note that aggregation of information to create rankings is different from ranking aggregation, which is the process of combining multiple ranked lists into a single ranking. J Ding and others, 'A New Hierarchical Ranking Aggregation Method' (2018) 453 *Information Sciences* 168; X Li, X Wang, and G Xiao, 'A Comparative Study of Rank Aggregation Methods for Partial and Top Ranked Lists in Genomic Applications' (2019) 20 *Briefings in Bioinformatics* 178.

[25] This can be a point-based system or a star-based system. Some online platforms also use emoticons to help the user describe their feeling of the product or service. C Busch and others, 'The Rise of the Platform Economy: A New Challenge for EU Consumer Law?' (2016) 5 *Journal of European Consumer and Market Law* 3 state that aggregation of R&R is one of the data points that are used to create a ranking system.

[26] A Fradkin, 'A Simulation Approach to Designing Digital Matching Platforms' (2019) *SSRN Electronic Journal* 5, 24.

[27] 'Algorithms: How They Can Reduce Competition and Harm Consumers' (n 8) 5; Delgado (n 18) 7; European Parliament – Directorate General for Parliamentary Research Services (n 18) 9; LC Reillier and B Rellier, *Platform Strategy: How to Unlock the Power of Communities and Networks to Grow Your Business* (Routledge 2017).

Rankings list products and services based on aggregating consumers' preferences, where aggregated data is processed through algorithms.[28] If the data input into the algorithm is incorrect, the output will reflect the errors, ie if aggregation is skewed in any manner, ranking is also skewed.[29] For example, fake reviews and incorrect platform information cause errors to creep into aggregation. Skewed aggregation leads to a skewed listing of products (as aggregation leads to the listing), reflecting incorrect consumer preference (which may skew consumer decision-making).[30] Rankings will also be skewed if certain products and services are paid for and placed higher in the ranking list than other similar products and services.[31] Thus, incorrect information in the system creates a domino effect – incorrect information leads to incorrect aggregation and a skewed ranking.

5.3. Legislative Protection

In the EU, the P2B Regulation, the Ranking Guidelines, and the Modernisation Directive amending the UCPD state that the main parameters that create a ranking system must be disclosed.[32] In India, provisions of ranking transparency are enacted under the Consumer Protection(E-Commerce) Rules.[33]

[28] G Charness and M Rabin, 'Understanding Social Preferences with Simple Tests' (2002) 117 *Quarterly Journal of Economics* 817; E Fehr and U Fischbacher, 'Why Social Preferences Matter – The Impact of Non-Selfish Motives on Competition, Cooperation and Incentives' (2002) *The Economic Journal* 1; JP Carpenter, 'Endogenous Social Preferences' (2005) 37 *Review of Radical Political Economics* 63; LC Reillier and B Rellier, *Platform Strategy: How to Unlock the Power of Communities and Networks to Grow Your Business* (Routledge 2017) 98.

[29] F Long and Y Liu, 'Fake Sales and Ranking Algorithms in Online Retail Marketplace with Sponsored Advertising' (2022) *SSRN Electronic Journal* 10.

[30] V Hatzopoulos, *The Collaborative Economy and EU Law* (Hart Publishing 2018) 12; Consumers, Health, Agriculture and Food Executive Agency (n 11) 85; C Jin, L Yang, and K Hosanagar, 'To Brush or Not to Brush: Product Rankings, Consumer Search, and Fake Orders' (2023) 34 *Information Systems Research.*

[31] V Hatzopoulos, *The Collaborative Economy and EU Law* (Hart Publishing 2018) 40. 'Commission Staff Working Document – Impact Assessment – Proposal for a Regulation of the European Parliament and of the Council on Promoting Fairness and Transparency for Business Users of Online Intermediation Services' (Hart Publishing 2016) 4; Opinion of the European Economic and Social Committee on 'Proposal for a Regulation of the European Parliament and of the Council on Promoting Fairness and Transparency for Business Users of Online Intermediation Services' (COM(2018) 238 Final – 2018/0112 (COD)) 6; J Kraemer and O Zierke, 'Paying for Prominence: The Effect of Sponsored Rankings on the Incentives to Invest in the Quality of Free Content on Dominant Online Platforms' (2020) *SSRN Electronic Journal* 6.

[32] P2B Regulation (n 12); Commission Notice – Guidelines on ranking transparency pursuant to Regulation (EU) 2019/1150 of the European Parliament and of the Council [2020] OJ C424/1; Directive (EU) 2019/2161 of the European Parliament and of the Council of 27 November 2019 amending Council Directive 93/13/EEC and Directives 98/6/EC, 2005/29/EC and 2011/83/EU of the European Parliament and of the Council as regards the better enforcement and modernisation of Union consumer protection rules [2019] OJ L328/7 ('Modernisation Directive'); Directive 2005/29/EC of the European Parliament and of the Council of 11 May 2005 concerning unfair business-to-consumer commercial practices in the internal market and amending Council Directive 84/450/EEC, Directives 97/7/EC, 98/27/EC and 2002/65/EC of the European Parliament and of the Council and Regulation (EC) No 2006/2004 of the European Parliament and of the Council [2005] OJ L149/22 ('Unfair Commercial Practices Directive – UCPD').

[33] Consumer Protection (E-Commerce) Rules, 2020, Rule 5(3)(f) – Liabilities of marketplace e-commerce entities.

5.3.1. *European Union*

a. Fairness and Transparency Regulation and the Guidelines on Rankings

In the EU, the P2B Regulation deals with ranking transparency between providers and service providers.[34] The Regulation states that providers of online intermediation services (platforms) are to set out in their terms and conditions the main parameters determining rankings and the reasons for the relative importance of those main parameters over other parameters.[35] This parameter description aims to improve predictability and help businesses improve the presentation of their products and services or a characteristic of those products and services.[36]

The Regulation also states that where direct or indirect remuneration service providers influence rankings, a detailed description of the effects of the remuneration on rankings is to be provided.[37] Specific products and services state that they are advertisements, ie they may not be the product or service searched for, but they are an advertisement paid for by the product/service provider to be ranked first in the search results displayed to consumers.[38] Further, when platforms have altered the rankings or delisted any service providers, the service providers must be notified of this alteration.[39]

[34] P2B Regulation (n 12) Art 2(8) – Ranking; C Busch, 'Towards a "New Approach" for the Platform Ecosystem – A European Standard for Fairness in Platform-to-Business Relations' (2017) 6 *Journal of European Consumer and Market Law* 227; C Busch, 'The P2B Regulation (EU) 2019/1150: Towards a "Procedural Turn" in EU Platform Regulation?' (2020) 9 *Journal of European Consumer and Market Law* 133.

[35] P2B Regulation (n 12) Art 5(1); C Twigg-Flesner, 'The EU's Proposals for Regulating B2B Relationships on Online Platforms – Transparency, Fairness and Beyond' (2018) 7 *Journal of European Consumer and Market Law* 222; R Senigaglia, C Irti, and A Bernes (eds), *Privacy and Data Protection in Software Services* (Springer Singapore 2022) 215; K Eisele, 'Promoting Fairness and Transparency in the Online Platform Environment' Briefing – Initial Appraisal of a European Commission Impact Assessment 8; D Brouwer, 'A Non-Discrimination Principle for Rankings in App Stores' (2020) 9 *Internet Policy Review*.

[36] P2B Regulation (n 12), Recitals 24, 25, 26, Art 5(5); C Twigg-Flesner, 'The EU's Proposals for Regulating B2B Relationships on Online Platforms – Transparency, Fairness and Beyond' (2018) *Journal of European Consumer and Market Law* 4.

[37] P2B Regulation (n 12) Art 5(3); 'Proposal for a Regulation on Promoting Fairness and Transparency for Business Users of Online Intermediation Services' COM(2018) 238 final 2018/0112 (COD).

[38] Brouwer (n 35) 12; I Graef, 'Differentiated Treatment in Platform-to-Business Relations: EU Competition Law and Economic Dependence' (2019) 38 *Yearbook of European Law* 448; M Cian, 'Online Platforms as Gatekeepers to the Digital World – A Preliminary Issue on Business Freedom, Competition and the Need for a Special Market Regulation' (2018) 5 *Journal of European Consumer and Market Law* 2; Hatzopoulos (n 31) 11–12; N Davidson, M Finck, and J Infranca (eds), *The Cambridge Handbook of the Law of the Sharing Economy* (Cambridge University Press 2018) 441–442 441–42, ch 32 (G Smorto, 'The Protection of the Weaker Parties in the Platform Economy'; G Compiani and others, 'Online Search and Product Rankings: A Double Index Approach' (2021) *SSRN Electronic Journal* 6.

[39] 'Position Paper on Ranking Transparency Guidelines' SME United (2020) 2; 'European Commission's New Guidelines on Ranking Transparency Pursuant to Regulation 2019/1150 on Promoting Fairness and Transparency for P2B Relationships', Uria Menendez (2020) 3; I Graef, 'Algorithms and Fairness: What Role for Competition Law in Targeting Price Discrimination towards Ends Consumers' (2018) 24 *Columbia Journal of European Law* 493; M Inglese, *Regulating the Collaborative Economy in the European Union Digital Single Market* (Springer International Publishing 2019) 107; Brouwer (n 35) 5–6.

The Regulation seeks fairness and transparency without requiring platforms to disclose algorithms or information that could deceive consumers by manipulating search results.[40] Intellectual property rights protect the algorithm that conducts business operations.[41] Thus, providers are not required to disclose the detailed functioning of their ranking mechanisms, including algorithms.

In light of the Regulation, the Commission developed further Guidelines to assist intermediation services in applying the ranking transparency requirements and optimising the presentation of the main parameters to the service providers.[42] For example, Airbnb, in its terms of service, provides ranking transparency.[43] The terms of service also state that Airbnb may allow hosts to promote their listings in the search or elsewhere on Airbnb by paying an additional fee.[44]

As stated, aggregation and rating are two different yet related processes. For example, Uber does not provide such a ranking of its users. The platform's operational structure does not call for rankings as it matches drivers and riders and does not provide a ranking of the closest drivers. The Privacy Notice of Uber provides transparency in terms of ratings which contribute to the average rating (aggregation).[45] This average rating, as they disclose, is created only with the ratings provided by the rider/driver, which is visible to the rider/driver.

Though the P2B Regulation applies to relationships between platforms and service providers, the Regulation is enacted keeping in mind the impact on consumers, consumer interests, and the prevention of consumer harm through manipulating rankings, thereby complementing EU consumer laws.[46]

b. Modernisation Directive and the UCPD

The Modernisation Directive amended the UCPD to incorporate the P2B Regulation principles to provide ranking transparency for consumers.[47] The

[40] P2B Regulation (n 12) Art 5(6) – Ranking; R Ducato and A Strowel, *Legal Design Perspectives: Theoretical and Practical Insights from the Field*, 167.

[41] P2B Regulation (n 12) Recital 27 and Art 5(6) – Ranking; Directive 2016/943/EU on the protection of undisclosed know-how and business information (trade secrets) against their unlawful acquisition, use and disclosure [2016] OJ L157/1.

[42] Regulation 2019/1150/EU on promoting fairness and transparency for business users of online intermediation services [2019] OJ L186/57 (Fairness and Transparency Regulation), Recital 28, Art 5(7) – Ranking; Guidelines on ranking transparency pursuant to Regulation (EU) 2019/1150 of the European Parliament and of the Council; 'Position Paper on Ranking Transparency Guidelines' (n 39) 2; 'European Commission's New Guidelines' (n 39) 3.

[43] Airbnb Terms of Service (n 23) Clause 6 – Managing Your Listings; A Fradkin, 'Search, Matching, and the Role of Digital Marketplace Design in Enabling Trade: Evidence from Airbnb' [2017] *SSRN Electronic Journal* 7.

[44] P2B Regulation (n 12) Art 7 – Differentiated treatment; 'Consumer Protection (E-Commerce) Rules, 2020' (n 5) Rule 5(4) – Liabilities of marketplace e-commerce entities.

[45] Uber Legal – India perma.cc/TQ3U-N2ZZ, Uber Legal – Belgium perma.cc/AW5E-6S8J; PA Albinsson and BY Perera (eds), *The Rise of the Sharing Economy – Exploring the Challenges and Opportunities of Collaborative Consumption* (Bloomsbury 2018) 276.

[46] P2B Regulation (n 12) Art 5(6) – Ranking; Guidelines on ranking transparency pursuant to Regulation (EU) 2019/1150 of the European Parliament and of the Council, Guidelines 6, 25, 76, 84.

[47] Modernisation Directive (n 32) Recitals 18, 19, 29, 21, 22, 23, and 26, and Art 3 – Amendments to Directive 2005/29/EC. Graef (n 39) 495.

Modernisation Directive introduced the definition of ranking in the UCPD, broadening ranking transparency to traders irrespective of the technological means used for presentation, organisation or communication.[48]

Consumers will have to be informed of the main parameters determining the ranking of products in searches and the relative importance of those parameters. The provision for misleading omissions that are considered unfair commercial practices under the UCPD has been amended to include ranking information as material information. The absence of transparent ranking information is a misleading omission and an unfair commercial practice.[49]

Further, the UCPD is amended to state that providing search results to consumers without clearly disclosing any paid advertisement or payment specifically for achieving a higher ranking of products within the search results shall be considered an unfair commercial practice.[50] The underlying idea is that many consumers are guided by the order indicated by the search engine. They assume that the ranking is determined by the relevance of the product or service searched for unless it is made clear that the ranking is affected by paid placements.[51]

5.3.2. *India*

a. Consumer Protection (E-Commerce) Rules

India's ranking is defined under the Consumer Protection (E-commerce) Rules.[52] The Rules also define e-commerce entities and categorise marketplace e-commerce entities and inventory e-commerce entities.[53] A marketplace e-commerce entity is an e-commerce entity that provides an information technology platform on a digital or electronic network to facilitate transactions between buyers and sellers.[54] Platforms are marketplace e-commerce entities because they facilitate e-commerce transactions between service providers and consumers.[55]

[48] UCPD (n 32) Art 2(m) – Ranking. 'Ranking' means the relative prominence given to products, as presented, organised or communicated by the trader, irrespective of the technological means used for such presentation, organisation or communication.

[49] 'Communication from the Commission – A New Deal for Consumers' (2018) COM(2018) 183 final 6; Nikolina (n 13) 3; B Rodriguez Galindo, 'Developments in EU Consumer Law: The New Consumer Agenda, Legislative Changes and Policy Initiatives' 24; C Schmon and P Gautier, 'Proposal for a Better Enforcement and Modernisation of EU Consumer Protection Rules – "Omnibus Directive" – The BEVC Review' 3.

[50] UCPD (n 32), Annex 1 – Commercial practices which are in all circumstances considered unfair – 11(a).

[51] BM Loos Marco, 'The Modernization of European Consumer Law: A Pig in a Poke?' (2019) *European Review of Private Law* 123. Nikolina (n 13) 3; Galindo (n 49) 7; Schmon and Gautier (n 49) 3.

[52] Consumer Protection (E-Commerce) Rules 2020, Rule 3(j) – Ranking.

[53] Consumer Protection (E-Commerce) Rules 2020, Rule 3(b) – E-Commerce Entity, Rule 3(f) – Inventory E-Commerce Entity, Rule 3(g) – Marketplace E-Commerce Entity.

[54] Consumer Protection (E-Commerce) Rules 2020, Rule 2(g) – Marketplace E-Commerce Entity, Rule 3(k) – Seller, Section 2(7) of the Consumer Protection Act 2019 – shall include any service provider.

[55] Consumer Protection (E-Commerce) Rules 2020, Rule 3(b) –E-Commerce Entity, Rule 3(f) – Inventory E-Commerce Entity.

The Rules specify the liabilities of the marketplace-e-commerce entities (platforms). The liabilities of platforms include the provision of an explanation of the main parameters which, individually or collectively, are most significant in determining the ranking of products or sellers on its platforms. The relative importance of those main parameters is to be made readily and publicly available.[56] These Rules are a leap for consumer protection and e-commerce legislation in India. They place the burden of ranking transparency on platforms and protect consumers by calling for explanations of the main parameters used to create rankings.

5.4. Ranking Transparency Market Mechanism

Airbnb and Uber are examples of two platforms that operate in both jurisdictions, unlike other platforms, for example, Ola (similar to Uber), which operates only in India, or Vaimoo (bike-sharing), which operates only in the EU. Uber and Airbnb have become synonymous with ride-sharing and accommodation-sharing, respectively. Uber's business model connects the riders with their drivers and does not rank them in the location. On the other hand, Airbnb lists properties based on the criteria provided. Though these two platforms are collaborative economy platforms, the following section highlights the differential interpretation and implementation of legislation.

5.4.1. Airbnb

In its terms of service, Airbnb provides a section on ranking transparency.[57] This transparency is present in its terms of service for European and non-European users.

The terms of service also state that Airbnb may allow hosts to promote their listings in search or elsewhere on the Airbnb Platform by paying an additional fee. This provision illustrates the differential treatment.[58] These provisions state the various data points collected and used to create rankings. The terms and services state that the search parameters based on the requirements of consumers, listing characteristics provided by the host, previous experience of prior guests, host requirements, and guest preferences are the main parameters considered to generate rankings shown to consumers. These parameters are only the main parameters

[56] Consumer Protection (E-Commerce) Rules 2020, Rule 5(3)(f) – Liabilities of Marketplace E-Commerce Entities.

[57] Airbnb Terms of Service (n 23) Clause 6 – Managing Your Listings; A Fradkin, 'Search, Matching, and the Role of Digital Marketplace Design in Enabling Trade: Evidence from Airbnb' (2017) *SSRN Electronic Journal.*

[58] Fairness and Transparency Regulation (n 42) Art 7; Consumer Protection (E-Commerce) Rules 2020, Rule 5(4).

and do not represent other non-main parameters or the relative importance of one of these parameters over another.

5.4.2. Uber

As stated, aggregation and rating are two different yet related processes. Uber does not provide rankings of its drivers or riders. The platform's operational structure does not call for rankings, as it matches drivers and riders based on the distance between the driver and the rider. The Privacy Notice of Uber provides transparency in terms of ratings which contribute to the average rating (aggregation).[59] This average rating, as they disclose, is created only using the ratings provided by the rider/driver, which are visible to the rider/driver. These aggregate ratings are calculated using the rating between 1 and 5 provided by the driver to the rider and vice versa. These aggregate ratings are visible to the potential riders and drivers while requesting a ride-share and viewing the aggregate rating.

Furthermore, Uber's privacy and rankings policy applies to all aspects of the company. The privacy policy applies to ride-sharing applications and other Uber products, including Uber Eats. Uber Eats aggregates and ranks the restaurants that it services. The above-mentioned privacy notice is the same for Uber, the ride-sharing application, and Uber Eats. Though Uber Eats provides rankings, it does not disclose the main parameters used for ranking. Thus, Uber in the EU is not compliant with the ranking transparency provisions under the P2B Regulation and the UCPD. Similarly, Uber's ride-sharing application in India complies with Consumer Protection (E-Commerce) Rules. However, Uber Eats is not, as it engages in the ranking of restaurants but does not disclose the main paraments of rankings.

6. The Delicate Balancing Act between Disclosures and Protecting Intellectual Property Rights of Businesses

Knowledge is power, and providing this power to service providers could lead to misuse. If the service providers know that the ranking algorithm favours listings with a particular amenity, they may either obtain that amenity or lie about having that amenity – leading to manipulating the aggregation and the ranking (click-bait), causing consumer deception.[60] For example, hosts on Airbnb might focus on

[59] Uber Legal – India perma.cc/TQ3U-N2ZZ; Uber Legal – Belgium perma.cc/AW5E-6S8J; Albinsson and Perera (n 45) 276.

[60] Codagnone and Martens (n 13) 8.

the main paraments that help them achieve a favourable ranking and not on other aspects of their treatment of consumers.[61]

Critics might argue that algorithmic transparency is not the only way to regulate platforms. Regulation of platforms and their algorithmic usage, standardisation, or even self-regulation of platforms could achieve similar objectives. However, the provision of information seeks to achieve balance while maintaining the interests of all stakeholders. Regulating algorithmic and business interests would not be welcome by platforms, thus creating an unhealthy platform environment for users.

Furthermore, consumers have limited information consumption capacity.[62] In addition to the information required to be processed while transacting on platforms, consumers are provided supplementary information about rankings and the use of their data, which may lead to an information overload.[63] The provisions in the P2B Regulation and the UCPD, and the Consumer Protection (Rules) achieve a delicate balance between the disclosures and providing transparent information to consumers while at the same time not disclosing essential aspects of the algorithm. The ranking transparency requirement requires the disclosure of the information used by the algorithm. This chapter argues that the requirement achieves the balance of protecting the IPR of businesses while providing disclosures to consumers on two prongs.

Firstly, the ranking transparency requirement does not require the disclosure of the algorithm or the working of the algorithm. The algorithm, when written down and applied, achieves copyright protection and trade secret protection as a part of the essential workings of the business model.[64] Second, the requirement also does not specify the disclosures, if any, of the weightage of each data point collected, the ways in which the data points are used, or if one parameter is more important than another. Consumers are only provided with the information that their data is collected to generate ranking, advertised as a benefit of providing their data.

As stated in section 2, algorithmic transparency is a misnomer as it does not refer to the transparency of the algorithm used by businesses but, rather, to the transparency of information collected that feeds into the algorithm. The data input is thus provided as a part of disclosures and transparency requirements while, at the same time, not stepping on the IPR protection of businesses.

[61] A Fradkin and others, 'Bias and Reciprocity in Online Reviews: Evidence From Field Experiments on Airbnb', *Proceedings of the Sixteenth ACM Conference on Economics and Computation – EC' 15* (ACM Press 2015) 24; M Inglese, *Regulating the Collaborative Economy in the European Union Digital Single Market* (Springer International Publishing 2019) 107.

[62] Ghose and Ipeirotis (n 12) 12; Consumers, Health, Agriculture and Food Executive Agency (n 11) 7; Solomon and others (n 19) 3.

[63] Assuming that all the consumers are rational consumers who take decisions based on the information provided to them.

[64] MJ Ryan, 'Secret Algorithms, IP Rights, and the Public Interest' (2020) 21 *Nevda Law Journal* 61; TR Moore, 'Trade Secrets and Algorithms as Barriers to Social Justice' (Center for Democracy and Technology, August 2017) 9.

7. Taking Algorithmic Transparency Forward?

Algorithmic transparency is a tool used in various sectors in countries across the globe. Nations are working towards algorithmic transparency in multiple aspects of the digital world.

In China, the Cyberspace Administration of China, the Ministry of Industry and Information Technology, the Ministry of Public Security, and the State Administration of Market Supervision and Administration jointly promulgated the Provisions on the Administration of Algorithm Recommendation for Internet Information Services (Algorithmic Recommendation Services).[65] The Provisions contain several mandatory requirements for the providers of the Algorithm Recommendation Services, including establishing and improving the feature databases used to identify illegal and undesirable information; not using an algorithm to falsely register accounts or illegal trading accounts, or manipulate user accounts or false likes, comments, retweets; and not using an algorithm to interfere with the presentation of information or conduct any act that affects online public opinion or evades supervision or administration, such as information blocking, excessive recommendations, manipulation of rankings or search results sorting, control of hot search or selection. From the provisions, algorithmic transparency is not limited to rankings but includes a broad spectrum of algorithmic recommendations to be provided transparently to consumers.

Similarly, the Algorithmic Accountability Act in the US was introduced because automated decision-making was becoming pervasive, making critical decisions about Americans' health, finances, housing, educational opportunities, and more.[66] The Act is not limited to algorithmic accountability in rankings and includes various sectors of automated decision-making. The Algorithmic Accountability Act requires companies to assess the impacts of the automated systems they use and sell, creates new accountability standards about when and how automated systems are used, and empowers consumers to make informed choices about the automation of critical decisions.

Countries across the globe are accepting algorithmic transparency in various aspects of operations of online platforms. The disclosures of main parameters, as provided in the EU and India, could be used as one of the tools to enable further information disclosures to consumers, balancing intellectual property rights (IPR) and consumer rights. Consider the example of the personalisation of products and services online. Personalisation online began with the growth of information technology. Companies like IBM, HP, Wipro, and Infosys created certain products personalised for home and office use and personalised software products

[65] Provisions on the Management of Algorithmic Recommendations in Internet Information Services 2022 State Internet Information Office, Ministry of Public Security of the People's Republic of China (No 9, March 2022).

[66] Algorithmic Accountability Act 2019 (OLL19293, 116th Congress, 1st Session).

for companies for specific purposes.[67] On platforms, too, products and services can be personalised. On platforms, this personalisation occurs using algorithms applied to collected consumer data.[68] For example, the algorithm can personalise the advertisements viewed by individuals to show certain products previously searched.

Personalisation benefits consumers as the algorithms use predictive intelligence using consumer behaviours and preferences to deliver better-personalised goods and services.[69] For example, personalised education services could tailor-make content for their users based on time spent, performance, and exercises.[70] The reason that personalisation can succeed is that no consumer likes to feel like just another statistic.[71] Personalised interactions with the platforms can create a personalised trust that retains existing consumers and attracts new consumers.[72]

Personalisation is similar to rankings provided by platforms as they rely on data collected from consumers; businesses collect, store, and process the data; algorithms are used to process this data; the provision of the information from the data collected impacts consumer decision-making. As algorithmic transparency is chosen to balance IPR and consumer rights, various platforms' operations use similar processes.

8. Conclusion

This chapter discusses algorithmic transparency in rankings as provided under legislative policies in the EU and India. Algorithmic transparency is one of the tools that enable a balance between the IPRs of platforms, and disclosures and provision of information to consumers. By examining perspectives from China and the US, the EU and India could consider provisions to enable consumers to receive and platforms to provide similar information in other sectors of operations of algorithms.

This chapter does not argue that algorithmic transparency is a perfect tool but, rather, that it is one of the tools aiding in achieving a balance between the IPR of businesses while disclosing information regarding the data used by algorithms by platforms. Using this tool, information regarding other platforms' operations could also be provided to consumers. Algorithmic transparency in any form has a long road ahead, with algorithmic usage likely to become ubiquitous.

[67] A Sundararajan, *The Sharing Economy: The End of Employment and the Rise of Crowd Based Capitalism* (MIT Press 2016) 43.

[68] Albinsson and Perera (n 45) 50.

[69] Sundararajan (n 67) 84.

[70] Albinsson and Perera (n 45) 111 and 120.

[71] 'Insights – How Personalization Builds Trust and Loyalty' (*Kobe Digital*, 24 October 2020).

[72] R Botsman, *Who Can You Trust? How Technology Brought Us Together and Why It Might Drive Us Apart* (Penguin Group) 28.

8

Regulating Digital Platforms

Intermediary Liability and Content Moderation in Copyright Enforcement

SUBHASHISH GUPTA AND SNEHA MEHTA

1. Introduction

Copyright deals with protection of an idea that is expressed in a tangible form. Works which are copyrighted include books, music, visual art, and software programs among others.[1] Also only the tangible form, be it physical or digital, is copyrighted, but not the idea. New interpretations of a copyrighted work can be produced, but not an exact copy of the original, which has raised legal issues in the past. The production of a creative work is often costly. Authors may take years to write a book, so they need to be adequately compensated for the effort. The compensation comes from the sales of the book that has been created. If unauthorised copies were available from another source at a lower price than the sale price of the original, then the author would lose money. Consequently, prospective authors would be wary of writing books if they feared copying. This would lead to lower supply of books. Therefore, preventing copying by enforcing copyrights protects the author's revenues and maintains the incentives for authors.

The barrier to obtaining copyright is quite low. Works that are original and observable can be copyrighted. This could potentially include an email, conversations on WhatsApp, and reviews on TripAdvisor. Just forwarding a message without the permission of the rights holder lead to copyright infringement. In response, there are exceptions in copyright law that originate from the Berne Convention that governments have incorporated in their national legislation from time to time.

Varian characterises copyrights in terms of height, width, and length.[2] 'Height' is the degree of novelty of the work to qualify for copyright protection. With

[1] See 'Copyright in the Digital Era: Country studies in Enquiries into Intellectual Property's Economic Impact' (OECD 2015).

[2] HR Varian, 'Copying and Copyright' (2005) 19(2) *Journal of Economic Perspectives* 121.

copyright the barrier is very low compared to other types of IPRs. 'Width' refers to the extent of the copyright and is synonymous with scope. For example, for a book, one may be allowed to copy a few pages with the benefit of exceptions and limitations (such as private copying exception). 'Length' refers to the time period that the work is under copyright protection.

Typically, there are large fixed costs of creating a piece of work but the costs of copying are relatively low.[3] Obviously, this is a simplification. The cost of creating a work will depend on the type of work and the relative efficiency of the creator. However, the cost of copying is usually lower than the cost of producing it. In particular, in the digital age, for some products it is possible to make exact copies at zero marginal cost. This development led to the formation of the World Intellectual Property Organization (WIPO) Performances and Phonograms Treaty (WPPT) and the WIPO Copyright Treaty (WCT). The relative ease of copying makes determining the optimal length of copyright difficult. The longer a piece of work is under copyright, the more valuable the protection is. The author of the work can reap revenues from the sale of the work for longer periods of time and will thus be incentivised to create works. However, the consumers of this work would have to pay to enjoy the work and some will have to forego the pleasure if they deem the price to be too high. So the optimal length must balance the social cost of too little copyright protection such that creators are not sufficiently incentivised to produce works, with that of too much protection where a large number cannot enjoy the work. Too few works to enjoy vs works too few can enjoy.

The above analysis assumes that authors can charge only one price for their work to all customers. This neglects opportunities for price discrimination. Obviously a creator or business that is in charge of production could increase profits through offering different prices and degrees of protection. Of course a firm may choose not to prosecute or prosecute only under certain circumstances, effectively choosing the extent of the copyright. It can also price discriminate across different market segments and across time (intertemporal price discrimination), which would also reduce welfare costs. Market segmentation is widely accepted practice; for example, textbooks are often sold in India for a fraction of their price in richer countries. Of course the publisher has to find a way to avoid arbitrage. Richer country customers may be able to buy in the country which offers lower prices. Worse, businesses may spring up that buy in poorer countries and sell in rich countries.

The advent of the digital economy has made such practices easier. It is now possible to tailor prices and other characteristics to individual customers. A fair amount of shopping is done online for items like groceries, household items, and electronics, and travel-related purchases (eg flights and hotel reservations). These platforms thus have considerable information about each customer, which they can use to estimate the price a customer is willing to pay for a particular product.

[3] WM Landes and RA Posner, 'An Economic Analysis of Copyright Law' (1989) 18(2) *Journal of Legal Studies* 325.

Consequently, the platform is able to capture more of the consumer surplus, through personalised pricing. Intertemporal price discrimination refers to the practice of charging a high price initially for a certain time period followed by a lower price later. It is a standard practice of publishers to print a hard cover edition of a new book by a best-selling author and sell it at a high price, and then later introduce a paperback edition which is sold at a lower price. Both types of discrimination improves consumer welfare, in the sense that consumers who would not be able to afford a book can now do so at the expense of those customers residing in richer segments or those who are willing to pay a premium to consume the work early. Digitisation is bane and a boon at the same time. It allows copying to become much easier but allows for a variety of price discrimination tactics. It also allows firms to provide works on rent or to use a subscription model.

Another issue with length is how to value the stream of earnings that come with selling the product across time. One should estimate the present value of the income stream. The further into the future income is realised, the lower is its present value. Thus very long patent protections may be pointless. The other point is that a creator typically has a fixed life. Going beyond the expected life span for patent protection may have little incentive effect. Of course one can argue that the selling and distribution of creative works is now the business of commercial corporations which are immortal. Consequently, they would value patents that are indefinitely long.

The link between profits of businesses in the creative field and their payments to creators incentivising creators to produce work is unclear. Do stringent copyright laws and enforcement lead to higher profits for such businesses which translates into higher payments for artists and consequently more creative output? Nadel suggests that present marketing methods and business models promote the creation of superstars.[4] They do little for ordinary musicians who may have released a couple of albums and who mostly survive on their income from live performances. Indeed, overall output in terms of variety may be suppressed and only those artists whom the executives think will become popular will do so.

The advent of the digital world has had a profound impact on copyright. The cost of copying depends on the object to be copied and the technology available. In the past, copying a book would be quite painful because it had to be done by hand. Once the printing press was introduced it became much easier to copy printed works. Some items cannot be copied at all. A painting can be copied by a forger or one can make prints, but it will not be the same as the original. The emergence of digital technologies has been a boon for copying, particularly in the realm of music.

A detour into the theory of public goods in the field of economics will illuminate the discussion. Unlike private goods (ie things we usually buy in the market),

[4] MS Nadel, 'How current copyright law discourages creative output: The overlooked impact of marketing' (2004) 19(2) *Berkeley Technology Law Journal*785.

public goods have two characteristics. They are nonrival and nonexcludable. 'Nonrival' means that consumption by one person does not affect consumption by another. The use of a bridge to cross a river by one person does not mean that another person cannot also use the same bridge. This would not be true for private goods. Two individuals cannot both eat the entirety of one bar of chocolate. 'Nonexcludable' means that it is technologically impossible to prevent a person from consuming a good. Usually, access to commonly owned property like the sea is nonexcludable. A pure public good will have both characteristics. Street lights would be a good example.

It is possible for goods to have only one of the characteristics. In particular a good may be nonrival but excludable. An example would be a song on Spotify. Letting another person listen to the same song that you have listened to would not reduce your listening pleasure. However, it is possible for Spotify not to allow access to the song to a non-paying subscriber. Note that the extra cost of letting another person listen to the same song is close to zero. So it would make sense to allow this to happen since Spotify does not lose anything and the consumer gains. It would increase economic efficiency and maximise welfare.

The situation with copyrights is the same. Many of the goods that enjoy copyright protection are nonrival but excludable. Excludability is a function of the copying technology. It would once have been fiendishly difficult to copy a book but Xerox machines made it easy. Digital technologies have achieved the same feat with a whole host of products, notably music. Copyright laws also reinforce excludability. They make it legally harder to copy. In a sense, there is an inverse relationship between the technology for excludability and the strength of copyright laws. The easier it is to copy the more stringent copyright laws need to be. Note that to maximise social welfare it would be appropriate to allow anyone to copy for free once the product has been produced. So one could argue that digital technologies have made many products approximate public goods, which are usually not provided by the market. One does not usually come across private providers of public highways or national police forces. So the copyright system is trying to mimic the market for the delivery of public goods. Experience with such attempts in the arena of other such public goods, such as infrastructure, suggests that it will be unsatisfactory.

At first glance, the relationship between copyright and competition law would seem to be antagonistic. Competition law, generally, tries to prevent monopolisation or abuses of monopoly power, while copyright, artificially, creates a monopoly so that a creator may enjoy the fruits of their labour. The intention of both, however, is to enhance consumer welfare.[5] Without copyright many products may not exist and without a competition law consumers will typically be overcharged. So the two

[5] See A Katz 'Copyright and Competition Policy' in R Towse and C Handeke (eds), *Handbook on the Digital Creative Economy* (Edward Elgar 2013). Also see G Colangelo, 'Enforcing copyright through antitrust? The strange case of news publishers against digital platforms' (2022) 10(1) *Journal of Antitrust Enforcement* 133.

should work harmoniously, though they rarely do. There is a tendency in India to use copyright protection to indulge in anticompetitive behaviour. The competition authority typically does not challenge this behaviour. At any rate, the Intellectual Property Act is out of the ambit of the Competition Act. Nevertheless the authority could be a bit more proactive in preventing copyright misuse.[6]

In the Indian context it is important to discuss the link between copyright and development.[7] Multilateral agencies and foreign governments often emphasise the importance of protection of intellectual property and copyright for achieving economic development.[8] The evidence on this link is scanty. Some of the poorest countries have some of the strongest intellectual property protection. It might be easy to copy a song or a book but it is very difficult to copy an electric vehicle, or an airplane, or a computer chip. Thus the emphasis on copyright protection is more about protecting revenues and less about development. Then the question arises: what do the alleged infringers want to copy that the righholders author and create? It would mostly be off-the-shelf computer utilities and some movies and music. The numbers are likely to be rather low. Given low literacy in English, the number of people in India watching English movies, listening to English songs, and using pirated software is likely to be small. It is also naive to assume that all those using a pirated version of the product would actually buy a copy at full price if copyright was strictly enforced. However, India does have a stake in copyright protection. It is an exporter of cultural products and proprietary software, and Indian movies and music earn a fair amount of revenue from international sales. Also, domestic producers of music are among those most affected by piracy. So a more nuanced approach is called for. Copyright clauses and high prices make it very difficult to use academic books, journal papers, and computer software for academic purposes. Surely, that drags down development. The design of the copyright system should serve the interests of the country. The length of the copyright and its width (scope) should promote economic development.

There are broader social issues at stake that are pertinent to India. One of them is free speech. Online social media platforms are often used to spew hatred and false information, and so public authorities are naturally inclined to control them. At the same time, too much control could reduce free speech. Copyright law could be used by authorities to curb free speech. If forwarding a WhatsApp message amounts to copyright violation then India is a nation of violators. This also brings up the issue of user generated content (UGC). A complementary problem is that of indirect liability, which we will discuss later. It is often easier to go after platforms

[6] R Hanna, 'Misusing Antitrust: The Search for Functional Copyright Misuse Standards' (1994) 46(2) *Stanford Law Review* 401.

[7] See WG Park, 'The Copyright Dilemma, Copyright Systems, Innovation and Economic Development' (2010) 64(1) *Journal of International Affairs* 53. Also look at T Papadopoulos, 'Copyright Law and Competition Policy: International Aspects' (2002) 9(2) *Agenda: A Journal of Policy Analysis and Reform* 113.

[8] RL Okediji, 'The Limits of International Copyright Exceptions for Developing Countries' (2020) 21 *Vanderbilt Journal of Entertainment and Technology* 689.

rather than individuals. Thus, copyright law, innovation, and free speech combine to form a heady concoction. Throw in the need to maintain public order in the mixture, and it becomes volatile.

2. Intermediary Liability

Intermediary liability has been a subject matter of debate among law and policy makers for over four decades. Its introduction dates back to the early 1990s, which witnessed dramatic developments in the digital world with the arrival of Web 2.0. With the commercialisation of the internet, it bought about a paradigmatic shift in social and economic behaviour. The internet slowly became irreplaceable and was no longer a fragile new means of communication that could easily be smothered in the cradle by overzealous enforcement of laws and regulations applicable to brick-and-mortar businesses. The open nature of these platforms, where no prior control was exercised, made these intermediaries the target of litigation for the behaviour of their users.

During the inception stage the definition of an 'intermediary' was similar in jurisdictions across the world. Over the years, with the rapid growth and evolution in technology and consumption by end users, the term intermediary has been revisited and the legislators have now expanded it to specific subsets of internet service providers, distinguishing them with 'active' and 'passive' status. This redefining is an outcome of intermediaries increasing their engagement with the content they 'host' on their 'platforms', which expanded their responsibility for that content. Even though the legislators have aimed to provide a sustainable framework, the intermediary liability regime remains arguably the single largest legal structure that may affect how our markets react to technological changes.

There is a fair amount of literature on the economics of intermediary liability and more recently on platform liability.[9] Frosio[10] says that one of the approaches to intermediary liability 'is associated with … the utilitarian approach to law in general' and quotes Kraakman[11] to develop the concept of a gatekeeper, who he compares with bartenders and accountants. This concept should be distinguished from the 'gatekeeper' concept in the Digital Markets Act.[12] There the concept is akin to the essential facilities doctrine in regulation. Here it means someone who is held responsible for preventing wrongdoing.

[9] See Y Lefouli and L Maido, 'The Economics of Platform Liability' (2022) 53 *European Journal of Law and Economics* 319.

[10] GF Frosio, 'Why Keep a Dog and Bark Yourself? From Intermediary Liability to Responsibility' (2018) 26(1) *International Journal of Law and Information Technology* 1.

[11] RH Kraakman, 'Gatekeepers: The Anatomy of a Third-Party Enforcement Strategy' (1986) 2(1) *Journal of Law, Economics and Organization* 53.

[12] Regulation (EU) 2022/1925 of the European Parliament and of the Council of 14 September 2022 on contestable and fair markets in the digital sector and amending Directives (EU) 2019/1937 and (EU) 2020/1828 (Digital Markets Act) [2022] OJ L265/1.

> [s]uccessful gatekeeping is likely to require (1) serious misconduct that practicable penalties cannot deter; (2) missing or inadequate private gatekeeping incentives; (3) gatekeepers who can and will prevent misconduct reliably, regardless of the preferences and market alternatives of wrongdoers; and (4) gatekeepers whom legal rules can induce to detect misconduct at reasonable cost.

Frosio remarks that these principles can be adopted for online intermediaries and platforms. The main issue is whether online intermediaries can or should be liable for 'misconduct' that takes place on their platforms. One could take a moral stance and say that it is the perpetrators who should be held liable and not the owners of the platform. One could, however, take a more practical view and say that the important objective is to reduce the objectionable behaviour. Given the costs of going after individual wrongdoers and that they are unlikely to be able to afford large amounts it would be easier to put the liability on the intermediary, particularly when it can stop misconduct quite easily.

The effects of making intermediaries liable are multifaceted.[13] The immediate effect is to impose an additional cost on the intermediary. Now the intermediary has to set side some resources to fight lawsuits. In addition the intermediary may change its behaviour when it comes to allowing users to interact on the platform. It would be reasonable to err on the side of caution and reduce the number of transactions, which may lead to reduced competition and increased prices, which in turn may lead to changes in the market structure.

3. Intermediary Liability in India

3.1. Introduction

In India, the Information Technology Act, 2000 ('IT Act') alone does not take the precedence over the subject matter on defining intermediary liability. In order to determine the jurisprudence of intermediary liability subjected to copyright infringement in India, there is always a harmonised construction of relevant provisions of the Indian Copyright Act, 1957 ('Copyright Act') in with the IT Act.

Indian legislators have filled in the gaps in its intermediary liability regime by predominantly learning from the US Digital Millennium Copyright Act (DMCA) with a blend of multiple common law doctrines of secondary liability, and the E-commerce Directive in the EU. This illustrates that India's position has always been in a transitional phase. In retrospect, the IT Act achieved a balance between shielding intermediaries from excessive liability and requiring them to take the necessary steps to deal with illegal and harmful content.

[13] Y Lefouli and L Madio, 'The Economics of Platform Liability', CESifo Working Paper No 8919 (2021), Available at SSRN: https://ssrn.com/abstract=3798940.

The participatory/or social online platforms now offer users an unrestricted open place to explore, stream, and download material as technology and the internet continue to advance. A variety of work was and is being shared and created online including literary, artistic, and dramatic works which are to be treated with the basic principles of copyright. The alarming surge of such copyright infringements in the digital platforms exhibited an inadequate framework to protect the intellectual property rights of the users. It was the European Union which took cognisance of this issue through modernising its copyright regime. The new Copyright Directive now mandates the intermediaries to have better equipped 'content recognition technologies' and advance filtering mechanism. A paradigm shift was being observed from the notice and take down mechanism. There was a growing agreement in jurisdictions around the world to bring in a more proactive auto filter which would make the intermediaries more accountable. The outcome of such a pressing need to create a stringent framework on intermediaries led to the adoption of the Indian Intermediary Guidelines and the Digital Media Ethics Code, 2021 ('Intermediary Rules, 2021'). The guideline has an immense pertinence to the Indian legal regime. However, even though it had an uncanny resemblance to what was adopted in more mature jurisdiction (like the EU), it provided a standard which was unique and innovative, given its own legal and cultural landscape.

Even in the past decade and the changes bought in for the intermediaries have pushed the boundaries of creating a framework preserving the rights of various stakeholders. However, there still exists the uncertainty subject to the scope within which the intermediaries should function. In order to continue addressing the issue of intermediary liability but with a broader and more consistent approach, India is all set to replace the existing IT Act with the new and important Digital India Act. The Act has been stated to be India's attempt to depart from the long-standing concept of intermediaries. It has been classified to be an overly ambitious framework that would now include e-commerce and fact-checking portals as well as standards for contemporary technologies, such as blockchain and metaverse.

3.2. Evolution of Intermediary Reforms in India: Information Technology Act, 2000

In 1996, the United Commissions on International Trade Law (UNCITRAL) adopted a model law on e- commerce and digital intermediaries. The model law provided a framework which was applicable to alternatives to paper-based method of communication and storage of information. The objective was to ensure there was uniformity in the laws of various cyber nations. The outcome of this mandate and the need to boost the functioning of the IT industries was the adoption of the IT Act. During this period, India was making its transition into an economy which was witnessing a remarkable growth in e-transactions. The legislation provided an umbrella framework which addressed various issues subjected to e-contracts, cybercrime, governance structure, and intermediaries. It gave an equal status to an online agreement as one would give to an agreement in a physical environment.

During its inception, the objective of incorporating a section on intermediaries was only limited to its broad objectives. It was the highly criticised judgment of *Avnish Bajaj v State*,[14] where a CEO of bazee.com (now eBay.in) faced imprisonment for a Multimedia Messaging Service (MMS) video of students in a sexual position circulating on his website, which made the legislators realise the slippery ground on which the intermediaries stood. It provided a door to hold the intermediaries liable for the content posted on their platforms. The loopholes and the hurdles in the IT Act were now in particular making efficient enforcement difficult. This led to the Amendment to the IT Act in 2008.

Before the Amendment there was no legislative framework for adequately handling issues of liability arising out of the activities hosted in the digital arena. It redefined the definition of intermediaries under Section 2(W)[15] and introduced guidelines to claim safe harbour under Section 79 of the IT Act. Section 79 ensured that the intermediary receives safe harbour protection as long it does not initiate the transmission, select the transmission receiver, or select or modify the information contained in the transmission, and that it observes 'due diligence' while discharging its duties. Even though the IT Act provided for safe harbour prior to the amendment, it only applied to network service providers as opposed to the amendment in 2008, which provided safe harbour to all intermediaries and for all kind of liabilities. However, adopting a one-size-fits-all approach, it neither fitted all kind of intermediaries nor did it fit all the wrongs. Another improvement in the amendment was the section referring to a 'actual knowledge' and not just a 'mere knowledge' providing a better definite induction of scope of their liability. The amended Section 79 devised a two-part strategy: (i) an actual knowledge as triggering event for an intermediary and (ii) the intermediary to act upon a notification. Further, in the absence of clarity on the term 'due diligence' the first Intermediary Guidelines and Rules, 2011 ('Intermediary Rules, 2011') were introduced, giving detailed procedural aspects to be followed by the intermediaries in order to claim safe harbour.[16] It is however important to acknowledge that beside the statutory provisions, Indian courts have played a significant role giving judicial pronouncements interpreting the safe harbour provisions and rights and liabilities of the intermediaries.

[14] *Avnish Bajaj v State* [2008]150 DLT 765.

[15] The new definition of intermediaries covered a wide range of intermediaries. It now included telecom service providers, network service providers, internet service providers, web hosting service providers, search engines, online payment sites, online-auction sites, online market places and cyber cafes. This meant it also covered the e-commerce websites under it. The old definition under Art 2(w) of the Information and Technology Act 2000 was narrow and provided limited protection under the law to 'network service providers'.

[16] See Intermediary Rules, 2021, Rule 3. Its silent features included (i) the need to inform the users of the computer resource not to transmit any information that among other things is harmful, obscene or defamatory; (ii) the requirement to 'act within 36 hours' of receiving knowledge of the transmission of any prohibited information; and (iii) the requirement to disable information that is contradictory to the Intermediary Law.

With social media now being a primary communication tool, there was a need to have 'well-intended' rules that bought clarity to the responsibilities of intermediaries. Indian legislators introduced the Intermediary Rules, 2021 (which replaced the Intermediary Rules, 2011) to provide a harmonious, soft-touch oversight mechanism concerning social media platforms (including digital media and over-the-top platforms).[17]

4. User Generated Platforms and the Intermediary Rules, 2021

4.1. Navigating the Digital Landscape

The rapid expansion and advancement of the internet has brought about a multitude of intricate legal issues concerning intermediary liability. The emergence of novel modes of online expression and communication, facilitated by the inherently open nature of the internet, has exposed regulatory inadequacies in the existing legal framework. The landscape of the digital environment has transformed significantly since the adoption of safe harbour provisions in India. The outdated nature of safe harbour provisions was being exploited by intermediaries to evade responsibility for willful infringements. The necessity of mitigating the mounting challenges engendered by user generated platforms prompted the adoption of a novel regulatory framework, culminating in the enactment of the Intermediary Rules, 2021.

The Indian Intermediary Rules, introduced in early 2021, regulate social media platforms, digital news media, and online streaming services operating in India. It provides a legal framework for online content moderation and combat issues concerning misinformation, fake news, and online harassment. Before the introduction of the Indian Intermediary Rules, user generated platforms, ie Facebook, Twitter, YouTube etc, were regulated and defined as intermediaries under Section 79 of the IT Act. Consequently, they were absolved of any liability for user generated content or communication on the condition that they exercised reasonable diligence and adhered to specific obligations, such as expeditiously complying with takedown directives issued by the relevant government or its authorised agency. However, it was observed by the policymakers that over time user generated platforms had formed a unique character as a platform and were moving away from being mere hosts of user generated content. The outcome of the evolving nature of platforms demonstrated the need to broaden the accountability measures for such intermediaries. Thus, the ultimate objective of the Indian Intermediary Rules,

[17] Special Correspondent, 'Govt announces new social media rules to curb its misuse', *The Hindu* (New Delhi, 25 February 2021) www.thehindu.com/news/national/govt-announces-new-social-media-rules/article33931290.ece.

2021 was to broaden the accountability of such intermediaries and mandate them to exercise vigilant oversight over the content uploaded on their platform.

However, opinions on these guidelines are divided between two extreme ideologies. There is an ongoing debate on whether one should focus on ensuring access to protected content online or impose obligations that may curtail freedom of speech and expression. Some argue that the guidelines may overly rely on algorithmic societies to enforce laws, which could potentially lead to censorship.

4.2. Section 79 Safe Harbour to Hardship: Key Provisions of the Intermediary Rules, 2021

The definition of intermediaries has been altered by the Intermediary Rules, 2021, dividing them into two categories: Social Media Intermediaries (SMI) and Significant Social Media Intermediaries (SSMI). Depending on their size and number of subscribers, each subset has distinct obligations assigned to it. SMIs are defined as platforms with at least 5 million registered Indian users[18] and SSMIs are defined as platforms with more than 5 million registered users.[19] The guidelines, however, go one step further whereby any intermediary by the order of the government would have to comply with the obligations imposed on SSMIs if it satisfies the threshold of a 'material risk of harm'. The arbitrary nature of a government discretion demonstrates the discriminatory nature of enforcing compliance.

Furthermore, an important change has been introduced in the form of due diligence and redressal mechanisms. In contrast to the due diligence guidelines set out in the Intermediary Guidelines, 2011, the new and reformed measures for intermediaries to claim safe harbour are much more comprehensive. The intermediaries are scrutinised in detail and are deemed to have a 'nanny-like approach' to users. Nevertheless, the comprehensive due diligence and redressal mechanism has been well-received as it establishes a defined structure for intermediaries to follow. It provides an oversight mechanism to ensure that the decisions of platforms are watertight. The requirement to have an internal complaints procedure has been put in place, whereby the SMIs and SSMIs are required to establish a grievance redressal mechanism to handle user complaints, which is to be made available to users 24 hours a day, seven days a week, and such complaints are to be acknowledged and resolved within a timeframe of 15 days. SSMIs additionally need to hire experts.[20] Each of their roles is divided to ensure (i) the grievances of the users have been addressed along with compliance with the due diligence and other

[18] See Intermediary Rules, 2021, Rule 2(w).
[19] See Intermediary Rules, 2021, Rule 2(v).
[20] See Intermediary Rules, 2021, Rule 4(a), (b), (c). It mandates that a significant social media intermediary (SSMIs) must appoint an Indian national as Chief Compliance Officer, a Nodal Officer, and a Resident grievance officer.

responsibilities as provided under Act and Rules; and (ii) to be in constant coordination with law enforcement agencies, 24 hours a day, seven days a week, and if needed furnish reasons for the disposal of complaints and the process followed.[21] In addition to the above, the rule mandates identifying the 'first originator' of the information. This means that the platforms will have to break end-to-end encryption, which was formerly one of the key backbones of their service and a guarantee provided under the terms of service agreement to the user.

One of the significant debates, however, was that the regime was creating a far too complex bridge for smaller platforms to traverse without attracting liability. SSMIs additionally need to hire experts.[22] With a lack of resources to comply with such strict regulatory regimes, an uneven playing field is endorsed, reducing the democratic and horizontal construct of platforms in the digital arena.[23] Taking a broader view, the Intermediary Rules, 2021 have established a standard for the global conversation about moving beyond the outdated safe harbour regime. They have demonstrated that online intermediaries, particularly large platforms, have the capability to implement stricter measures. Ultimately, these platforms have social and economic responsibilities to ensure that prohibited content is not promoted.

5. Intersection of Copyright and IT Act

5.1. Introduction

In the context of online copyright infringement, the Indian Copyright Act and intermediary liability are interconnected. Intermediaries such as internet service providers, social media platforms, and search engines are required to remove infringing content from their platforms once they receive notice from the copyright owner, as defined under Section 51 of the Copyright Act. The Copyright Act of 1957 did not have a specific provision addressing the liability of intermediaries. Consequently, there was no safe harbour provision under the Act to protect intermediaries from claims of copyright infringement. Intermediaries could be held liable under Section 51(a)(ii) for secondary copyright infringement. Section 51(a)(ii) provides that if any person permits any place to be used for communication of work to the public for profit and where such communication constitutes a copyright infringement then that person will be held liable for the infringement which takes place. This means that even if an intermediary is only providing a platform for communication of work, they may still be held liable for infringement under

[21] See Intermediary Rules, 2021, Rule 4(a), (b), (c).

[22] See Intermediary Rules, 2021, Rule 4(a), (b), (c). It mandates that a significant social media intermediary (SSMIs) must appoint an Indian national as Chief Compliance Officer, a Nodal Officer, and a Resident grievance officer.

[23] See Intermediary Rules, 2021, Rule 4(a), (b), (c).

the Copyright Act. Online service providers are especially susceptible to falling under the purview of Section 51(a)(ii) as information is typically stored on their servers to be transmitted to various locations. This storage and transmission of information on the intermediary's servers can be considered 'providing a place', which would make the intermediary liable under the section.

For a safe harbour subjected to copyright infringement, Section 81 under the IT Act consisted of a non-obstante clause that overrides other laws, excluding the Copyright Act and Patent Act. This confusion on the applicability of Section 79 for copyright issues was further highlighted in the *Myspace*[24] decision. In *Myspace*, the plaintiff contended that the defendants, by making available copyrighted audio and video files uploaded by their user without any licence, had indulged in secondary copyright infringement. The plaintiff argued on basis of Section 51 of the Copyright Act which makes an entity liable for secondary infringement if it was 'aware' or had reasonable grounds for believing there was infringement happening on its place.[25] The defendant was however trying to take protection under Section 79 of the IT Act, which protected intermediaries and revoked the safe harbour on the basis of whether the platform had 'actual knowledge' of the infringement on its platform. The court stated that Section 79 of the IT Act provides intermediaries with certain protections but does not curtail the rights of a copyright owner under the Copyright Act. It sets up minimum standards for intermediaries to avoid liability but does not provide blanket immunity from liability. The single-judge bench of Delhi Court held that Section 79 on reading with Section 81 of the IT Act does not apply to copyright infringements.[26]

On the other hand, the Madras High Court in *Vodaphone* held that Section 79 applied to copyright infringement as well.[27] However, the *Myspace* judgment led to the discussion that wording of Section 81 only spoke about 'exercising any right' under copyright, and merely providing safe harbour does not prevent one from exercising any right. It was then rectified when the division bench appeal set aside the earlier decision of the single bench, holding that Section 79 is also applicable to copyright infringements *(Myspace II)*.[28]

The cause of the irregularity in the above judgments was due to the absence of the safe harbour under the Copyright Act to protect the claims of copyright infringement. The defence to avoid such liability was provided if the person was

[24] *Super Cassettes Industries Ltd v Myspace* ('*Myspace*') [2011] (48) PTC 49 (Del).

[25] See Indian Copyright Act (1957), Section 51.

[26] *Myspace* (n 24). The court stated that 'conjoint reading of Section 79 and Section 81 makes it amply clear that the proviso to Section 81 prevents any provisions of IT Act to act as restriction on exercising of the rights by the copyright owner. This makes it clear when read the Section 81 which provides for the overriding effect of the IT act over other laws' (para 63).

[27] *Vodafone India Ltd v R K Productions* [2013] (54) PTC 149 (Mad). The court argues: 'It is not the function of the ISP to check each and every URL being accessed by every customer and each and every website is accessed by every customer. The function of the ISP does not include the exercise of any editorial control over any of the websites. The ISP has no concern or control with the content of any website'.

[28] *My Space Inc v Super Cassettes Industries Ltd ('Myspace II')* [2016] FAO(OS) 540/2011, C.M. APPL.20174/2011, 13919 and 17996/2015.

not aware or did not have reasonable grounds for believing the communication to the public would lead to a copyright infringement. But *Myspace* judgment made the legislators aware of a lacuna by not having intermediary safe harbour specifically under the copyright regime. In response, the Copyright (Amendment) Act, 2012 was enacted. It embodied a version of safe harbour under Section 52 protecting intermediaries involved in transient and incidental storage of work done purely during the process of electronic transmission or communication to the public[29] and protecting intermediaries involved in transient and incidental storage of work providing electronic links, access, or integration under certain conditions.[30] This provision adopted a notice and takedown scheme similar to that of the DMCA. Furthermore, it introduced a 'put back' provision similar to the one under DMCA.[31] The provision also integrated the 'fair dealing' concept, which provides a comprehensive list of acts as exceptions to infringement. However, it is essential to indicate that the terms 'fair use' and 'fair dealing' are not synonyms since their meaning and scope are defined by different legal systems. Fair dealing in India is subject to certain conditions, such as the amount and whether the portion used is substantial, the purpose and character of the use, and the effect of the use on the potential market for, or value of, the copyrighted work. In determining whether a particular use of a copyrighted work is fair, the court may consider all relevant factors, including the nature of the work, the amount and substantiality of the portion used, and the effect of the use on the potential market for or value of the copyrighted work. The concept is interpreted narrowly. The burden of proving a use of copyrighted work is fair rests with the user, and the courts have taken a cautious approach in interpreting this concept. The above provisions further lay down the procedures to be followed by the intermediaries if they were to be protected for violations under the Copyright Act.[32]

However, the probable conclusion of safe harbour applicability for copyright infringement in this vertical regime can be drawn from the *Myspace II* decision, wherein Section 79 of the IT acts as an additional layer of protection which commences when the secondary infringement and absence of fair dealing have been established under the Copyright Act. And that the general safe harbour (under Section 79 of the IT Act) applies over and above the copyright safe harbour (Section 52 of the Copyright Act). The relationship between the Copyright Act and the IT Act in India presents challenges due to the considerable similarities between them, raising questions about the reasons for their enactment. However, courts in India have favoured a harmonious interpretation of the provisions in order to reconcile the existence of the two acts. While this approach resolves issues related

[29] See Indian Copyright Amendment Act, 2012, Section 52(1)(b).

[30] See Indian Copyright Amendment Act, 2012, Section 52(1) (c). It gave immunity to the intermediaries provided (i) the right-holder had not prohibited the provision of such link access or integration or (ii) if they had reasonable grounds for believing that storage was not infringing.

[31] See Indian Copyright Rules, 2013, Rule 75. It gives the right-holder a window of 21 days to file a suit, failing which the intermediary was to restore the removed content.

[32] See Indian Copyright Rules (2013), Rule 75.

to the operation of the two sections, there are inconsistencies in their application due to their overlapping scopes. Harmonious reading aims to reduce contradictions and establish consistency by extending requirements, such as the need for a court order before taking down content by an intermediary, and upholding the condition of actual knowledge for both acts. Following the prescribed obligations under Section 52(1)(c) would shield an intermediary from infringement under the Copyright Act, while Section 79 applies to a broader range of intermediaries in general. Despite these efforts, the road ahead for intermediaries in India remains uncertain.

5.2. Intermediary Guideline, 2021 and its Implication for Copyright Infringements

The broad spectrum of the Intermediary Rules, 2021 mandates obligations under the intermediary user agreements and privacy policy to inform users not to do any acts or have information that infringes copyright[33] and also establishes an elaborate Notice and Takedown regime. The takedown requirement as per the Intermediary Rules, 2021 reinstates the requirement to remove content on receiving 'actual knowledge' with the additional duty of care which is time nuanced. But in contrast the vertical regime, which involves the IT Act and the Copyright Act, makes 'actual knowledge' in copyright infringement fulfilled when a notice is set in motion by the right-holder. However, the court in *Myspace II* while reading along with the judgment in *Shreya Singhal v Union of India*,[34] did not want to create a copyright exception to Section 79, which would lead to over-complying with takedown notices thereby affecting the freedom of speech of the users.

The Intermediary Rules, 2021 are moving from 'did not know' to 'ought to know' as the standard, creating a general monitoring obligation on these algorithmic heroes to ensure copyright enforcement. The Intermediary Rules, 2021 limits the role of online intermediaries as arbitrators of truth by being under the supervision of law enforcement agencies. It maximises transparency by having a right to information portal, wherein a user and a copyright owner are to be notified before removal of content and will have an opportunity to contest the complaint and track it same step by step. The guidelines further mandate that digital platforms must remove any content that violates copyright within 36 hours of receiving a complaint from the copyright owner or their authorised representative. Additionally, digital platforms must have systems in place to prevent repeat infringements and provide copyright owners with a process to file counter-notices in situations where content was taken down incorrectly. In the event that a person or entity believes their copyright has been violated by content on a digital platform,

[33] See Intermediary Rules, 2021, Rule 3(1)(b)(iv).
[34] *Shreya Singhal v Union of India* [2015] WP (crl.) No 167 of 2012.

they can submit a complaint to the platform's designated grievance officer. If the platform fails to respond within the specified time frame, or the complainant is unsatisfied with the action taken, they have the option to file a complaint with the Indian Copyright Office or pursue legal action against the infringing party.

It is however essential to understand that the Intermediary Rules, 2021, do not supersede the current copyright laws and regulations in India. The Indian Copyright Act of 1957 and its associated rules still apply, and digital platforms are obligated to adhere to both the laws and the Intermediary Guidelines.

6. User Generated Content

Like a lot of terms bandied about when it comes to the digital world, the meaning of 'User Generated Content' (UGC) is not readily apparent. The term 'content' refers to anything that is digitised and is available for consumption. It could be in written form, video or music, or any combination of the three or more. Typically, it should provide some sort of entertainment or information. A computer program would not be considered content. 'Generated' simply means created. The term 'user' is the most confusing. It probably refers to computer users, which would nowadays include almost everybody. At one level, it seems to distinguish between content produced professionally from the amateurish output that ordinary people produce. The OECD calls it 'User Created Content (UCC)' and it provides a definition that quotes Wikipedia, itself a UGC.

It is easier to list items that would qualify as UGC. It would include blogs and vlogs, photos and images, videos, educational content, and chats on WhatsApp and Twitter, among others. In the context of copyright the first issue is that most creators are not interested in earning money from their creation. Such users will turn down payment, as profit is not the primary motive. Indeed, the urge for creation seems to be derived from sharing, whether with friends or closed community groups, or the world in general. So, the creators do not want anything like copyright protection that would interfere with sharing. A complementary urge seems to be achieving popularity. Of course, it is possible that some creators would eventually want to earn money from their creations (monetise) and are merely distributing content for free until their audience reaches the requisite size.

Social media sites such as Facebook, Instagram, TikTok, Twitter, YouTube, WhatsApp, and travel-related sites such as MakeMyTrip are some of the highly popular websites in India.

7. Conclusion

One of the pressing issues in regulating UGC platforms is striking a balance between the freedom to conduct business and the responsibility to protect the public by maintaining a safe browsing and content consumption ecosystem on their platforms. Strict copyright enforcement can have a significant impact on UGC platforms both in terms of legal and financial costs including an ability to provide a platform for user generated content. Copyright enforcement measures often result in UGC platforms resorting to automatic filtration tools, biased content removal practices, restricted content sharing policies, limited innovation, and heightened legal liability. Additionally, there is a detrimental economic impact when User Generated Content platforms are compelled to allocate resources towards more complex content moderation systems, face loss of revenue due to automatic filtering tools removing excess content, and, significantly, face the risk of reduced user engagement due to apprehensions about overly strict policies. These factors may ultimately curtail the platform's desire to innovate or introduce new features in order to avoid any liability. Nonetheless, these platforms have presented legal policymakers with sufficient evidence to demonstrate that they possess a narrowly focused economic perspective and have deliberately neglected to implement measures to address the rising copyright issues that exist on their platforms. They frequently utilise the justification of promoting innovation and enabling users to freely share content as a defence for their inaction.

The extent of intermediary liability in India remains uncertain. The dual approach of the Copyright Act and the IT Act has left numerous issues unresolved. Even though the courts in India have provided substantial jurisprudence in interpreting the overall scope of intermediary liability there are still open-ended questions and a wide gap with effective implementation of both the Copyright Act and the IT Act.

The enhanced technological capacity of intermediaries has resulted in an increase in their obligations. With social media now being a primary tool, there is a need to have 'well-intended' rules that brings clarity on the responsibilities of these intermediaries. Given the history of adopting and learning from more mature jurisdictions, the Indian Intermediary Rules, 2021 has provided the international community a good example of how to provide a framework which is more innovative and presents viable solutions. However, it is crucial to note that the courts will still be relied upon to provide the necessary guidance concerning intermediary liability.

With India moving towards a full-fledged digital economy and witnessing new issues like the metaverse, crypto, Deepfakes, and artificial intelligence, it is all set to revamp its issues subjected to intermediary liability by introducing the Digital India Act, 2023 which will replace the Information Technology Act, 2000. The Digital India Act, which is presently being discussed by policymakers, is considered to be India's bold initiative to redefine the regulation of the digital realm.

9

Challenges to Competition and Innovation in Digital Markets

*Insights from Latin American Cases**

JUAN DAVID GUTIÉRREZ AND MANUEL ABARCA

1. Introduction

'With regards to digital markets, all the competition authorities of the world are in the same boat', said Frédéric Jenny, Chairman of the OECD's Competition Committee, at the 2019 *Latin American and Caribbean Competition Forum.*[1] In recent years, antitrust agencies from Africa, Asia, Europe, and Oceania have published reports, guidelines, and statements about competition challenges associated with digital economies. Some of these agencies have also enforced competition laws in cases of collusion, abuse of dominance, and mergers.[2] Additionally, recent reforms introduced in Europe, such as the Digital Markets Act (DMA) (2022) and Section 19a of the German competition law (2021) in the European Union, provide authorities new *ex ante* remedies and tools to deal with large digital platforms.

* The authors wish to thank the attendants of ASCOLA's 2020 annual conference and of the #COMIPinDigiMarkts2022 – Competition & IP in digital markets conference for their kind questions. We also wish to thank Friso Bostoen and Kalpana Tyagi for their insightful feedback on an earlier version of this manuscript.

[1] JD Gutiérrez Rodríguez, 'Retos de la competencia en los mercados digitales latinoamericanos' (*Derecho y Políticas de Libre Competencia en América Latina*, 4 October 2019), www.lalibrecompetencia.com/2019/10/03/retos-de-la-competencia-en-los-mercados-digitales-latinoamericanos.

[2] Antitrust cases and reports on digital platforms have been published by authorities in Australia, Canada, China, Egypt, the European Union, France, Germany, India, Indonesia, Japan, Kenya, Mauritius, Nigeria, Russia, South Africa, Sweden, Netherlands, Pakistan, Philippines, United Kingdom, United States of America and Zimbabwe, among others. For a list of reports on digital markets, see Stigler Center, 'World Reports on Digital Markets' (*The University of Chicago Booth School of Business*, 15 May 2019), www.chicagobooth.edu/research/stigler/events/antitrust-competition-conference/world-reports-on-digital-markets. For lists of cases, see Annexes B and D of World Bank, 'Antitrust and Digital Platforms: An Analysis of Global Patterns and Approaches by Competition Authorities' (World Bank 2021), hdl.handle.net/10986/36364.

What about Latin America and the Caribbean (LAC)? Is the region really in the same boat? This chapter examines the challenges to competition and innovation in digital markets identified by LAC's antitrust agencies. For the purposes of this chapter, we understand 'digital platform' as 'an economic agent with a business model that permits interactions and exchanges of information, goods, and/or services between multiple types of users, which can be producers, consumers, or a community, through digital means'.[3] Furthermore, the terms 'digital market' and 'digital economy' refer to markets and economic activities in which digital platforms are involved.[4]

This chapter examines the decisions of LAC's antirust agencies in competition law enforcement processes (antitrust and mergers) and competition advocacy activities (reports and opinions in regulatory processes) that assess digital markets. LAC's competition laws do not include, up to date, special provisions for digital markets as it occurs in other jurisdictions, such as Germany, nor there are regulatory tools such as the ones established by the DMA for the European Union. Even though LAC's legislators have not responded to the digital developments, the practice of the courts and the competition authorities do reflect and consider this emerging trend. Hence, this chapter focuses entirely on how the agencies and tribunals have addressed competition concerns about digital markets on a case-by-case approach.[5]

The research traced the enforcement and competition advocacy activities of 29 national competition authorities in 23 LAC countries (see Appendix to this chapter).[6] This chapter reports that, between 2015 and 2022, over half of these countries decided cases and/or issued reports that examined digital markets. While antitrust enforcement activities in digital markets have been exceptional, several antitrust agencies of the region have also addressed these issues in merger control and their advocacy processes. The latter has not been limited to the publication of market studies or reports; antitrust agencies have also contributed to regulatory processes with opinions about regulatory proposals associated with the digital markets.

[3] World Bank (n 2) 8.

[4] ibid.

[5] For a short essay on why Latin America should continue with a case-by-case approach, instead of adopting *ex ante* regulations, see M Abdala, A Lombardi and L Quesada, 'Latin America's Digital Markets: Competition or Regulation?' in J Peña and M Calliari (eds), *Competition Law in Latin America: A Practical Guide* (2nd edn, Kluwer Law International 2022).

[6] The chapter does not include supranational jurisdictions such as the Andean Community, the Common Market of the South, the Caribbean Community, nor the Central American Integration System. However, it is pertinent to mention that in September 2020 a lawsuit was filed before the General Secretariat of the Andean Community against Facebook, Google, Amazon, and Apple which alleged that the companies supposedly incurred in abuse of a collective dominant position in the Andean region. However, as at November 2023 the General Secretariat has to date not decided to start a formal investigation.

The chapter identifies decisions and activities from 13 jurisdictions during the period 2015–22. The research includes over 90 cases of antitrust enforcement processes (Argentina, Brazil, Mexico, Uruguay), merger control procedures (Argentina, Brazil, Colombia, Chile, Ecuador, Mexico), and competition advocacy activities (Brazil, Colombia, Costa Rica, Dominican Republic, Ecuador, El Salvador, Mexico, Panama, Paraguay, Peru, Uruguay).

This chapter is organised in four sections, in addition to this introduction. First, section 2 explains the methodology that was adopted to answer the research questions and then provides a context of Latin America's antitrust systems. Section 3 presents the main results related to the enforcement and competition advocacy activities by the LAC's competition authorities regarding digital platform markets. Section 4 discusses the main challenges to competition and innovation as identified in case law associated with digital markets. Section 5 concludes with a summary of the main findings of the chapter and suggests future avenues for research.

2. Research Design and Context

2.1. Methodology

This research follows a comparative case study approach.[7] The unit of analysis is LAC's national jurisdictions and the period of analysis between 2015 and 2022. Furthermore, each enforcement or competition advocacy activity linked with digital markets conducted by these competition authorities in each jurisdiction may be considered sub-units of analysis of this research. The research traced the antitrust enforcement and competition advocacy activities of 29 national competition authorities in 23 LAC countries (see Appendix to this chapter). Key data sources are the decisions, reports, and opinions published by LAC's competition authorities. The qualitative data was collected, processed, and triangulated for descriptive purposes. Over 90 cases of antitrust enforcement, merger control, and competition advocacy in 13 LAC countries were identified and analysed. More specifically, this chapter is based on a novel database that identifies 92 processes and reports, 70 closed or published cases, and 22 ongoing cases, that directly deal with digital markets in Latin America.[8]

[7] We follow Gerring who defines 'case study' as the 'intensive study of a single case or a small number of cases which draws on observational data and promises to shed light on a larger population of cases'. J Gerring, *Case Study Research: Principles and Practices* (2nd edn, Cambridge University Press 2017) 28.

[8] The complete list of cases in digital markets that were identified and analysed in this research is available at JD Gutiérrez and M Abarca, 'Database of Latin American Antitrust Cases in Digital Markets, 2015–2022 (v.1)' (Research Gate, 11 March 2023) www.researchgate.net/publication/369170142_Database_of_Latin_American_Antitrust_Cases_in_Digital_Markets_2015-2022.

2.2. Overview of LAC's Antitrust Systems

Most of the national competition laws of the region were enacted between the second half of the twentieth century and the beginning of the twenty-first century.[9] The beginning of the twenty-first century saw substantial reforms to the pre-existing established antitrust national systems.[10]

Currently, there are 29 national antitrust authorities (agencies and tribunals) in 23 LAC jurisdictions. Whereas 24 of these agencies are empowered to enforce competition laws across all the markets, five of them, namely the Utilities Regulation and Competition Authority (The Bahamas), *Superintendencia de Telecomunicaciones* (Costa Rica), *Instituto Federal de Telecomunicaciones* (Mexico), *Organismo Supervisor de Inversión Privada en Telecomunicaciones* (Peru), and *Instituto Dominicano de las Telecomunicaciones* (Dominican Republic) are limited by their statutes to the telecommunications sector.

The enforcement of competition laws in LAC is characterised by at least three features.[11] First, public enforcement prevails over private enforcement. Second, most of the proceedings have an administrative and/or civil nature, while in few jurisdictions antitrust breaches have a criminal nature. Third, competition agencies that decide cases are part of the executive branch of public power and most have the dual rule of prosecuting and adjudicating, except for Chile, Jamaica, and Panama, where the agencies are authorised to investigate but for enforcement, they must file a lawsuit before the courts.

LAC's antitrust systems have different degrees of maturity, and the enforcement of the laws is not uniform. The group of countries with more than two decades of uninterrupted enforcement of competition laws includes Argentina, Brazil, Chile, Colombia, Costa Rica, Jamaica, Mexico, Panama, and Peru. The rest of the jurisdictions recently enacted their laws and are still building their enforcement capabilities.[12] Furthermore, as Figure 9.1 illustrates, antitrust enforcement

[9] LAC's jurisdictions with antitrust laws: Argentina, Barbados, Bolivia, Brazil, Chile, Colombia, Costa Rica, Curaçao, Dominican Republic, Ecuador, El Salvador, Guyana, Honduras, Jamaica, Mexico, Nicaragua, Panama, Paraguay, Peru, Uruguay, Trinidad and Tobago, and Venezuela. The competition law of the Bahamas only covers telecommunication markets. The hydrocarbons law of Guatemala establishes that certain conducts amount to anticompetitive agreements, but the country does not have a comprehensive antitrust system. Aruba's competition law was issued in July 2020, but it has entered into force partially and its agency is still being set up. JD Gutiérrez, 'Aruba se une al club de la competencia: Fue lanzada la "Aruba Fair Trade Authority"', (*Derecho y Políticas de Libre Competencia en América Latina*, 6 June 2023), lalibrecompetencia.com/2023/06/06/aruba-se-une-al-club-de-la-competencia-fue-lanzada-la-aruba-fair-trade-authority.

[10] JD Gutiérrez, 'Derecho de La Competencia En América Latina y El Caribe: Evolución y Principales Retos', *Anuario de Derecho de la Competencia* (La Ley 2021); A Palacios and JD Gutiérrez, 'Histories of Competition Law in Latin America' in J Peña and M Calliari (eds), *Competition Law in Latin America: A Practical Guide* (2nd edn, Kluwer Law International 2022).

[11] For a detailed account of the main characteristics of competition laws in Latin America, refer to Gutiérrez (n 10).

[12] For an overview of the history of LAC's antitrust enforcement systems, see Palacios and Gutiérrez (n 10).

is concentrated in few jurisdictions: Brazil, Colombia, Mexico, Peru and Chile, account for 84 per cent of the cartel sanctions imposed in LAC between 2000 and 2020:

Figure 9.1 Number of cartel sanctions in LAC per jurisdiction (2000–2020)

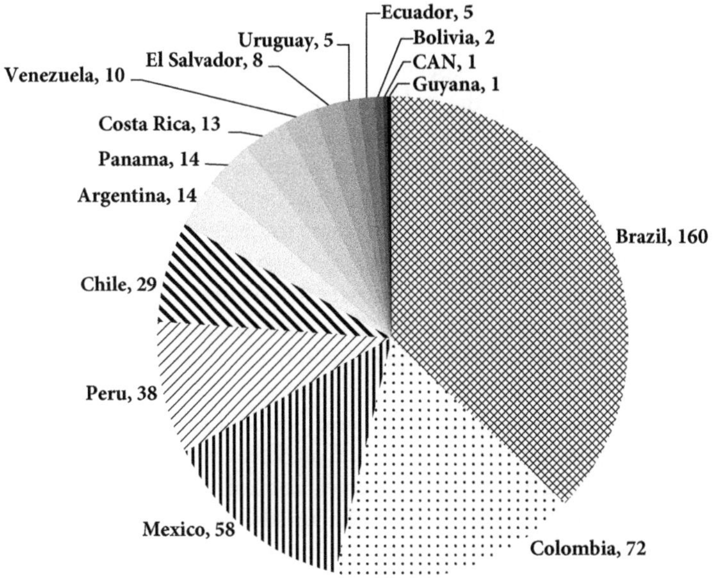

Source: Elaborated by the authors based on JD Gutiérrez, 'Chapter 28: South America' in P Whelan (ed), *Research Handbook on Cartels* (Edward Elgar Publishing 2023); M Martínez and others, 'Fixing Markets, Not Prices: Policy Options to Tackle Economic Cartels in Latin America and the Caribbean' (The World Bank 2021) 161436, documentos.bancomundial.org/es/publication/documents-reports/documentdetail/148021625810668365/fixing-markets-not-prices-policy-options-to-tackle-economic-cartels-in-latin-america-and-the-caribbean.

The next section of the chapter presents the main findings on how the Latin American authorities have addressed competition concerns on digital markets. The study includes three main types of activities carried out by the agencies regarding digital markets: investigation of anticompetitive practices, merger control, and competition advocacy (market assessments and competition assessments of regulatory projects).

3. Enforcement of Antitrust Laws in LAC's Digital Markets

Although extensive research has been carried out on the enforcement of antitrust laws in digital markets in North America, Europe, and Asia, the scholarship about

LAC is scarce. The most comprehensive paper on the case of LAC published to date is a background note prepared by the OECD's Secretariat for the 2019 *Latin American and Caribbean Competition Forum*. This OECD report was complemented by contributions from delegations of Brazil,[13] Colombia,[14] Ecuador,[15] and Mexico.[16] The contributions of these competition authorities describe their enforcement, merger, and advocacy activities in digital platform markets.

Research about competition enforcement and advocacy in digital platform markets of Latin America is nascent. This chapter contributes to fill this gap in the literature by surveying the enforcement and competition advocacy activities carried out by the competition authorities of the region. This first subsection presents descriptive statistics about these activities. The OECD reported that 'competition authorities Latin America and the Caribbean have dealt with very few enforcement cases involving digital platforms to date'.[17] Our research confirmed this finding: only Argentina, Brazil, Chile, Mexico, and Uruguay have conducted and finalised antitrust investigations in cases that involve digital markets. In other words, between 2015 and 2022, only 22 per cent of LAC's jurisdictions studied in this research (five out of 23) adopted definitive decisions in antitrust cases in digital markets.

However, we also found that in the same period, LAC's competition authorities assessed a significant number of digital markets cases in their merger control processes and advocacy activities. Merger control cases that involve digital markets were assessed in 43 per cent of the jurisdictions with mandatory merger control[18] (six out of 14). The jurisdictions that dealt with digital merger cases were Argentina, Brazil, Colombia, Chile, Ecuador, and Mexico.[19]

[13] OECD, 'Session III: Practical Approaches to Assessing Digital Platform Markets for Competition Law Enforcement – Contribution from Brazil' (Organisation for Economic Co-operation and Development (OECD) 2019) JT03451421, one.oecd.org/document/DAF/COMP/LACF(2019)21/en/pdf.

[14] OECD, 'Session III: Practical Approaches to Assessing Digital Platform Markets for Competition Law Enforcement – Contribution from Colombia' (Organisation for Economic Co-operation and Development (OECD) 2019) JT03451360, one.oecd.org/document/DAF/COMP/LACF(2019)10/en/pdf.

[15] OECD, 'Session III: Practical Approaches to Assessing Digital Platform Markets for Competition Law Enforcement – Contribution from Ecuador' (Organisation for Economic Co-operation and Development (OECD) 2019) JT03451358, one.oecd.org/document/DAF/COMP/LACF(2019)8/en/pdf.

[16] OECD, 'Session III: Practical Approaches to Assessing Digital Platform Markets for Competition Law Enforcement – Contribution from Mexico' (Organisation for Economic Co-operation and Development (OECD) 2019) JT03451728, one.oecd.org/document/DAF/COMP/LACF(2019)6/en/pdf.

[17] OECD, 'Practical Approaches to Assessing Digital Platform Markets for Competition Law Enforcement – Background Note' (Organisation for Economic Co-operation and Development (OECD) 2019) JT034501958, one.oecd.org/document/DAF/COMP/LACF(2019)4/en/pdf.

[18] The jurisdictions with merger control laws that are mandatory, fully operative and that cover all the economy (not just specific sectors) are the following: Argentina, Barbados, Brazil, Chile, Colombia, Costa Rica, Ecuador, El Salvador, Honduras, Mexico, Nicaragua, Paraguay, and Uruguay. Peru's new *ex ante* merger control, that includes all its economic sectors, entered into force only until June 2021. In the case of Bolivia, Dominican Republic, and Panama merger control is reserved for specific sectors.

[19] The FNE of Chile recently updated its merger guidelines by including digital topics that had been previously analysed by its case law. More specifically, the FNE included in its 2021 Horizontal Merger Guidelines a new chapter on digital platforms and digital markets which aimed at adding factors that could differ from the traditional merger analysis. This chapter includes guidelines on the

Competition advocacy reports, market studies and competition assessments of regulatory projects related to digital markets were published in 48 per cent of LAC's jurisdictions studied in this chapter (11 out of 23).[20] These are Brazil, Colombia, Costa Rica, Dominican Republic, Ecuador, El Salvador, Mexico, Panama, Paraguay, Peru, and Uruguay. Furthermore, the explicit prioritisation of a 'digital antitrust agenda' by the competition agencies of Colombia, El Salvador, Mexico, and Peru may render additional cases soon.[21]

In sum, between 2015 and 2022, 57 per cent of LAC's jurisdictions examined in this chapter (13 out of 23) decided antitrust cases and/or merger cases and/or published competition advocacy reports directly related to digital markets. The three most common markets or sectors analysed by these authorities were ride-hailing apps, e-commerce, and over-the-top (OTT) media services. Table 9.1 summarises a total of 70 cases (antirust and merger enforcement) and advocacy reports or opinions that have been decided and/or published by 13 of LAC's competition authorities with respect to digital markets during the period 2015–2022.[22] The table also lists the markets or sectors addressed by the authorities in its cases or reports.

The 13 LAC countries where enforcement and/or competition advocacy activities linked with digital markets were identified, share the following four characteristics: (i) most of them are among the biggest economies of LAC; (ii) eight of them (62 per cent) are located in South America; and (iii) eight of them (62 per cent) have been active for more than two decades; and (iv) the competition authorities that have decided antitrust cases (Argentina, Brazil, Chile, and Mexico) are in the top five largest economies of LAC (except for Uruguay).

Which jurisdictions do not have cases related to digital markets? The competition authorities from Barbados, Bolivia, Curaçao, Honduras, Jamaica, Guyana,

definition of the relevant market (addressing the inclusion of one or both sides of the market in the analysis), theories of harm (including the elimination of potential competitors and degradation of privacy), networks effects, tipping, and exclusory and exploitative risks regarding the use of data. FNE, 'Guía Para El Análisis de Operaciones de Concentración Horizontales', www.fne.gob.cl/wp-content/uploads/2021/05/Guia-para-el-Analisis-de-Operaciones-de-Concentracion-Horizontales-mayo-VF.pdf.

[20] All of LAC's competition laws explicitly grant a competition advocacy function to the agencies. However, not all legislations explicitly grant agencies the powers to conduct competition assessments of regulatory projects: only 21 out of 29 (72%) national antitrust agencies have this role.

[21] COFECE, 'Repensar La Competencia En La Economía Digital' (Comisión Federal de Competencia Económica (COFECE) 2018) www.cofece.mx/estudios-de-promocion-de-la-competencia-repensar-la-competencia-en-la-economia-digital; INDECOPI, 'Agenda Digital' (Instituto Nacional de Defensa de la Competencia y de la Protección de la Propiedad Intelectual (Indecopi) 2018) www.indecopi.gob.pe/documents/1902049/3742118/Agenda+digital+16.05.2018.pdf/4f28e644-deed-b4d9-b4b4-e4eeb-6ff09f0; SIC, 'Regulación y Competencia En Economías Colaborativas' (Superintendencia de Industria y Comercio (SIC) – Grupo de Estudios Económicos 2018) 19, www.sic.gov.co/sites/default/files/files/Proteccion_Competencia/Estudios_Economicos/Documentos_elaborados_Grupo_Estudios_Economicos/Economias_Colaborativas_GEE_final.pdf; OECD, 'Digital Platforms and Competition in Mexico' (Organisation for Economic Co-operation and Development (OECD) 2018) www.oecd.org/daf/competition/eng-digital-platforms-and-competition-in-mexico.pdf.

[22] Table 9.1 does not include 21 ongoing processes that have not been finalised to date.

Table 9.1 Antitrust enforcement and competition advocacy activities associated with digital markets in LAC (2015–2022)

Country / Authority	Advocacy opinion or market study	Antitrust decision	Merger decision	Markets or sectors involved
Argentina	0	1	1	OTT platforms, operative systems
Brazil	3	12	5	Internet search engines, e-commerce, ride-hailing apps, delivery apps, tourism, services, mobile apps, OTT platforms, automotive industry data-sharing apps
Colombia	7	0	3	Ride-hailing apps, e-commerce, sharing economy, hosting services, digital identification services, tourism services through apps, food delivery services, digital real estate
Costa Rica	4	0	0	Ride-hailing apps
Chile	0	3	9	E-commerce, OTT platforms, maritime transportation apps, automotive apps, ride-hailing apps, online gaming
Dominican Republic	3	0	0	Digital services, ride-hailing apps
Ecuador	4	0	1	Operative systems, ride-hailing apps, delivery apps
El Salvador	2	0	0	Ride-hailing apps, e-commerce
Mexico	3	1	2	E-commerce, search results, social networks, clouds, delivery apps
Panama	1	0	0	Ride-hailing apps
Paraguay	1	0	0	Ride-hailing apps
Peru	1	0	0	E-commerce, sharing economy
Uruguay	1	1	0	E-commerce, ride-hailing apps
Total	30	19	21	
Average per activity	2.3	1.5	1.6	

Source: Based on empirical analysis by the authors. The cases and activities summarised in this table are based on the database of Gutiérrez and Abarca (JD Gutiérrez and M Abarca, 'Database of Latin American Antitrust Cases in Digital Markets, 2015–2022 (v.1)' (Research Gate, 11 March 2023) www.researchgate.net/publication/369170142_Database_of_Latin_American_Antitrust_Cases_in_Digital_Markets_2015-2022).

Nicaragua, The Bahamas, Trinidad and Tobago, and Venezuela. These jurisdictions account for 43 per cent of LAC's jurisdictions with competition laws (10 out of 23) and share three common features: (i) they are relatively small economies (seven of these countries had the lowest GDP of the region);[23] (ii) six of them are in the Caribbean or Central America (except for Bolivia, Guyana, and Venezuela) and, (iii) most of the competition authorities have been active for less than two decades (except for Jamaica and Venezuela). One caveat: while most of these jurisdictions are 'developing countries', they are not poor: in terms of GDP (2021), four of them are classified as 'high income', two as 'upper middle income' and four as 'lower middle income' countries.[24]

While most of the cases and reports were issued in experienced competition authorities that operate in LAC's largest economies, the research also revealed that small economies with less experienced agencies also assessed digital markets. For example, Paraguay has less than a decade of experience enforcing competition laws and has one of the smallest economies of South America, but its competition agency issued a competition advocacy report on ride-hailing apps. Furthermore, Uruguay not only issued an advocacy opinion about a regulatory project on ride-hailing apps, but it also investigated a unilateral conduct in the sector of e-commerce platforms.

Finally, some of LAC's countries already had case law regarding payments markets which are pertinent for the digital markets cases. In fact, key concepts like 'two-sided markets' and 'network effects' that first appeared in cases of payment platforms seem to influence how the concepts are invoked in the case of digital platforms. Decisions from the competition agencies of Argentina, Chile, and Peru appear to follow this path.

4. Challenges to Competition and Innovation in Digital Markets: What the Cases Tell

The reports from competition agencies of Brazil, Colombia, Ecuador, and Mexico published by the OECD identified different types of challenges raised by digital platforms in LAC's markets. For example, the reports mention enforcement challenges such as: defining relevant markets in multi-sided markets; determining the existence of market power and assessing network externalities in multi-sided markets (MSPs); and assessing vertical restraints, such as price discrimination. This section discusses these topics and other concerns analysed by LAC's competition authorities in key case law related to merger control and the intersection between data protection and competition law.

[23] See World Bank data: data.worldbank.org/indicator/NY.GDP.MKTP.CD.

[24] Venezuela is currently not classified by the World Bank due to lack of updated national accounts statistics. See World Bank data: datahelpdesk.worldbank.org/knowledgebase/articles/906519-world-bank-country-and-lending-groups.

4.1. Merger Cases Involving Delivery Services Apps

Delivery services apps have emerged in the last few years as direct competition against the traditional supermarket segment. Due to the notification of merger transactions, LAC's competition authorities have analysed the dynamics between both segments in their national markets. This section analyses merger decisions in Chile, Mexico, and Colombia that examined transactions which included delivery services apps.

The first case reviewed is the failed merger of *Walmart – Cornershop* and the completed acquisition of the latter by Uber. In 2018, Walmart announced the acquisition of Cornershop in Chile and in Mexico. In Chile, Walmart participated in the supermarkets sector and in e-commerce, while Cornershop was a Chilean-based grocery and supermarket mobile delivery application (app) with presence in some LAC countries. The merger was approved by the Chilean competition agency, the *Fiscalía Nacional Económica* (FNE) on 11 January 2019. In a three-page decision, the FNE explained that the merger included activities associated with the 'brick and mortar' supermarket segment and digital markets, which included both e-commerce and mobile apps. However, the agency claimed that to evaluate the transaction 'it was not necessary a precise definition of the relevant market to conclude that in different scenarios of analysis there would be no risks that could significantly lessen competition'.[25]

The FNE analysed potential vertical and horizontal effects of the *Walmart – Cornershop* merger and discarded the argument that competition could be significantly and negatively affected. The FNE acknowledged the innovative character of the delivery services apps market, the growth of the market, the entry and expansion of new actors, and the low barriers to market entry. The agency also concluded that the online supermarket delivery market was still in its incipient stage and that sales via e-platforms were low in comparison to the total sales level of Chilean supermarkets.[26]

In contrast, the merger was blocked by the Mexican competition authority, the *Comisión Federal de Competencia* (COFECE). The first difference with the Chilean case was that Mexican competition agency issued a lengthy 91-page decision that examined in detail the relevant markets and the potential effects of the proposed transaction. The second difference between the two decisions was that COFECE defined narrow product and geographic relevant markets.

The COFECE considered that Cornershop operated in a two-sided market, where it had two types of clients: 'final consumers' who purchased through its mobile app or webpage, and undertakings that used the platform to offer goods and services.[27] The relevant market of the merger was defined as 'the logistics

[25] *Walmart – Cornershop merger* [2019] Fiscalía Nacional Económica (FNE) F161-2018 2.

[26] ibid.

[27] *Walmart – Cornershop merger* [2019] Comisión Federal de Competencia (COFECE) COT-032-2019 20–21. COFECE also acknowledged that both parties to the transaction participated in the

service of exhibition, purchase and immediate delivery of products offered by self-service stores and price clubs through internet pages and applications for mobile devices to end users'.[28] The agency added that this relevant market had two sides: 'the logistics service of product exhibition through webpages and mobiles apps and immediate purchase to businesses' and 'the logistics services of purchase and immediate delivery of produces offered by businesses … through webpages and mobiles apps to final users …'.[29] Moreover, the agency also narrowed the geographical market to eight individual cities in which both the parties operated, namely, Ciudad de México, Monterrey, Guadalajara, León, Querétaro, Puebla, Cancún, and Toluca.

The COFECE found that if the transaction was approved, in five of the cities Cornershop would be the only remaining app.[30] In addition, there existed diverse barriers of entry for new entrants, namely, sunk costs, associated with financial requirements and activities required to build customer trust; developing a distribution network for 'immediate purchase and delivery' (including the algorithmic technology required to operate it); the need to reach certain volume of clients and transactions to generate economies of scale and network effects (impaired by switching costs faced by users, which are exacerbated by the incumbent's data advantage for targeted advertising); the need to obtain authorisations from intellectual property holders to use third-party brands in advertisements; the sunk costs associated with advertisements; and the existence of exclusivity agreement between the incumbent and some businesses. Additionally, the agency claimed that the merger could generate vertical risks, such as input foreclosure and self-preferencing.

The parties offered four behavioural remedies: (1) offering third parties free and non-discriminatory access to the platform; (2) refraining from using information from Walmart's competitors to offer exclusive benefits; (3) amending the 'terms and conditions' of Cornershop's platform (the scope of the proposed reform was redacted in COFECE's decision); and (4) amending Cornershop's by-laws (the scope of proposed reform was also redacted). However, the competition authority concluded that proposed remedies were ineffective to: (1) 'ensure the risk that Walmart, directly or indirectly, could unduly displace competitors on the Cornershop platform …';[31] (2) prevent 'the risk that Cornershop could impede access to the platform to Walmart's competitors';[32] and (3) guarantee that Walmart would not use the information collected through Cornershop's platform to privilege certain undertakings.[33] In sum, COFECE concluded that the parties'

market of advertisement through webpages, but that the merger had a very low probability of affecting competition in that segment.

[28] ibid, 28.

[29] ibid, 31.

[30] ibid, 37.

[31] ibid, 79.

[32] ibid, 83.

[33] ibid, 86.

proposal 'did not correct the risks detected in the transaction' and the merger was blocked.[34] Following COFECE's prohibition decision, the parties abandoned the transaction.

In 2019, Uber announced the acquisition of Cornershop in Chile and Mexico. In Chile, the merger was approved after an in-depth investigation. By and large, the Chilean competition authority held that the segment for supermarket online sales was 'still incipient'.[35] The agency argued that, although it was a fast-developing market, online sales did not have enough share of the total supermarket sales level (in fact, in the case of the supermarket chain with the highest sales level, these sales only represented 3.6 per cent).

In this context, according to the agency's analysis, the market, structurally, would not be able to generate a *tipping point*. The agency argued that this scenario was likely to occur in markets with significant economies of scale, economies, as well as indirect network effects. Moreover, the presence of disruptive innovation projects in markets with strong network effects would generate that firms should compete to win the totality of the market. However, in the supermarket delivery app market, innovation processes would be more progressive than disruptive, and there would be limits to economies of scale and scope, while networks effects would be conditioned by the scale of users necessary to compete in the market. At the same time, the supermarket side of the market would be concentrated, with only four main players that had bargaining power that would allow them to better negotiate the terms of the app. In parallel, the Covid-19 pandemic crisis produced a demand shock regarding delivery apps, that would explain the acceleration of innovation processes for supermarkets. Specifically, firms were anticipated to respond with 'new services, the adoption of new technologies, and delivery and logistics systems for the commercialization of products, due to the relative importance that e-commerce has acquired over other sales channels during this period'.[36]

In Mexico, the merger was also cleared by the competition agency.[37] The public version of the approval resolution, a four-page decision, contains no further analysis of anticompetitive risks. However, according to a brief text published by the Mexican competition authority, since other actual and potential firms could exercise competitive pressure on the groceries segment, the loss of a potential competitor would not be relevant and bundling strategies would not be profitable.[38]

The most recent merger case involving delivery services apps was decided by the Colombian competition authority, the *Superintendencia de Industria y*

[34] ibid, 90.

[35] *Cornershop – Uber merger (Approval Report)* [2020] Fiscalía Nacional Económica (FNE) F217-2019.

[36] ibid, 27.

[37] *Cornershop – Uber merger* [2021] Comisión Federal de Competencia (COFECE) CNT-111-2019.

[38] COFECE, 'Concentración Uber-Cornershop' (Comisión Federal de Competencia (COFECE) 2021) www.cofece.mx/wp-content/uploads/2021/02/art-Uber-cornershop-03febrero2021.pdf.

Comercio (SIC). The transaction involved the Colombian companies CMR (the owner of the food delivery platform), Domicilios.Com, and COME YA (the owner of iFood Colombia). The competition agency described the digital platforms of both undertakings as a 'marketplace application' and therefore analysed it as a two-sided market with network externalities. The SIC cited case law from the European Commission to describe the basic characteristics of digital platforms, and academic papers from US and European scholars. As with the *Uber – Cornershop* merger in Chile, the Colombian agency also considered the effects of the Covid-19 pandemic, particularly because lockdowns and public health restrictions boosted the demand for food delivery services, favouring marketplace platforms.[39]

The relevant product market for the *Domicilios.Com – iFood merger* was defined by the SIC as 'delivery services of prepared food through marketplace applications', thereby excluding other types of food delivery services, including services operated through webpages or apps owned by restaurants. The main reason for limiting the relevant product market were the specific characteristics of marketplace platforms, particularly being multi-sided markets and its network effects. Additionally, in contrast to the other decisions of their Latin American peers, the Colombian agency concluded that the geographic dimension was national, not local, given that the business strategy of the platforms was national and that there were low barriers of entry and exit at the local and national level.[40]

To calculate the market share of the participants, the agency considered four different measures per platform: the number of active users; the number of total sessions; the number of processed orders; and the monetary value of total sales. However, the agency considered that the last two measures were more reliable indicators than the first two. The SIC acknowledged that the market was already 'highly concentrated' before the merger but that the combined market share of the merged entity was lower than the one of the market leaders. Then, after applying different concentration and dominance indexes, the agency concluded that the merger 'does not produce big risks of restrictions to competition given that the merged entity can exercise greater competitive pressure towards the leader'.[41]

Moreover, the agency analysed the potential horizontal effects, namely unilateral as well as coordinated effects. However, these effects were mitigated due to factors such as the fact that the market is dynamic, none of the participants has market power, low barriers to entry, the existence of potential competitors, and the low stability of market shares in the recent history of the market. Hence, the agency unconditionally cleared the merger and did not request remedies from the parties.[42]

[39] Domicilios.com – *IFOOD merger* [2021] Superintendencia de Industria y Comercio (SIC) Res No 10291 of 2021.

[40] ibid.

[41] ibid, 32.

[42] ibid.

4.2. Intersections between Competition and Personal Data Protection

Digital markets are data driven, meaning that the business models of these markets depend on the constant collection of great volumes of detailed information about users, transactions, prices, stock, and other information that is pertinent to offering personalised products and services. The intersection between competition law and data protection law seems inevitable in this realm.

Data protection and privacy rights is still a nascent topic in most LAC's countries, except for Mexico and Colombia. However, several countries have recently issued data protection and privacy statutes or are currently discussing bills, and the enforcement of pre-existing legislations appears to be increasing. The rise of data protection rights and laws in the region generates both situations of tension and complementarity with antitrust laws.

In Chile, a discussion regarding competition and data protection occurred in the *Uber – Cornershop* merger case.[43] When the Chilean competition agency started an in-depth investigation, one of the preliminary risks detected consisted of exploitative risks regarding the use of users' data. The FNE held that 'the group of several services in one sole platform could increase the ability of the merged entity to ask for an increased amount of data to its users, that could result in a deterioration of the terms and conditions of access to the services'.[44] Note the similar terms in the German Facebook case.[45]

However, when the merger was approved, the Chilean competition agency dismissed these risks. In general, the FNE held that data would not be the main input to the operation of apps in the market, unlike other data-related platform business models (for example, search engines or social networks). The agency argued that it was likely that the data would be used to increase the quality of the products or services offered.[46] In this context, users would be able to change platforms if there was a degradation of privacy policies.

On the other side of the Andes, the Argentinean competition authority, *Comisión Nacional de Defensa de la Competencia* (CNDC), started an investigation against WhatsApp following the update of its terms and conditions regarding the use of data and its combination with other integrated platforms, like Facebook and Instagram. The CNDC proposed the adoption of interim measures, including suspending the application of the new terms of services. The authority identified the following as exploitative risks:

[43] See section 4.1.

[44] *Cornershop – Uber merger (Resolution to proceed to Phase II)* [2020] Fiscalía Nacional Económica (FNE) F217-2019 [24].

[45] Richard Tepper, 'Definición de Mercados y Plataformas Digitales' (Capítulo de América Latina de la Academic Society for Competition Law – ASCOLA, 2020) www.youtube.com/watch?v=LOWiB9X1zYU, 08:41.

[46] *Cornershop – Uber merger (Approval Report)* (n 37).

> (i) the unreasonable and excessive collection of data (required or obtained) of users of these platforms, (ii) the absence of real options for users of these platforms to limit the treatment of their data outside the platform on which the data was required or obtained, and (iii) the subordination of the messaging service use of WhatsApp to the acceptance of the actualization of the service's conditions and the company's privacy policy.[47]

This interim measure was upheld by a local appeal court in 2022 and the process is ongoing before the competition authority.

Finally, in Colombia a recent merger showcased the intersections between competition and data protection law. Three of the biggest commercial banks in Colombia informed the Financial Superintendence (FS), which reviews mergers in its sector, of a transaction that aimed at creating a new company that would provide digital identification services. The FS requested an opinion about the transaction from the *Superintendencia de Industria y Comercio* (SIC). In its opinion, the SIC considered that the merger's effects would not be horizontal (there would be no structural changes in the market of financial services) but, rather, vertical. The SIC argued that the merger would create a new market, 'applications for digital identification and online authentication' and the joint post-merger market share of the merged entity would be 100 per cent – in other words, a complete monopoly.[48]

The Colombian competition agency, which applies a 'significant lessening of competition test' in merger control, claimed that the position of the new company as solo provider of these services could create opportunities for abuse of dominance, aggravated by the fact that new entrants would have a low probability of success in the absence of interoperability with the dominant firm's platform.[49] The SIC proposed to the FS four types of remedies which in turn were adopted by the financial regulator in its final decision. First, a remedy associated with the new company's corporate governance structure: guarantee the independence of the directors of the company from its owners. Second, compliance with the data protection laws and competition laws (especially regarding discrimination and tying). Third, to send periodic reports to the SIC about sales, cost structures and number of users. Finally, a behavioural remedy, ensuring 'interoperability' and 'data portability' that would offer potential user migration to other platforms without additional costs. This last remedy was conditioned on the fact that the new company had prior authorisation from data subjects to transfer their information

[47] CNDC, 'Dictamen Firma Conjunta Número IF-2021-42671970-APN-CNDC#MDP' (Comisión Nacional de Defensa de la Competencia (CNDC) 2021) 56, www.argentina.gob.ar/sites/default/files/2017/02/cond_1767.pdf.

[48] *Bancolombia, Banco Davivienda and Banco de Bogotá merger* [2020] Superintendencia de Industria y Comercio (SIC) Res No 21069 of 2020.

[49] L Alfonso Miranda, JD Gutiérrez and S Natalia Barrera, *El Control de Las Concentraciones Empresariales en Colombia* (Grupo Editorial Ibañez – Universidad Javeriana 2014).

to third parties, given that such authorisation is mandatory under the data protection laws.[50]

5. Conclusions

This chapter examined over 90 cases adopted by LAC's antirust agencies in their competition law enforcement processes (*ex ante* and *ex post*) and competition advocacy activities (market studies and opinions in regulatory processes). The chapter reports that, between 2015 and 2022, 57 per cent of LAC's jurisdictions that have national competition laws and operational competition authorities have decided cases or issued advocacy reports associated with digital markets.

Most cases dealt by LAC's competition authorities focus on *ex ante* tools: merger control and competition advocacy. In other words, *ex ante* interventions are more common than *ex post* interventions. Moreover, the biggest economies with experienced authorities were more likely to conduct antitrust cases that involved digital markets.

The substantive challenges to competition and innovation in digital markets addressed by LAC's antitrust agencies are analogous to the ones detected by their peers in other continents. Moreover, the substantive analysis by LAC's authorities is not homogeneous due to the characteristics of local markets and the institutional trajectories of the authorities.

However, LAC's competition authorities have faced a special issue regarding the entry of new digital actors in traditional markets, in terms of whether the emergence of new digital actors can exercise competitive pressure to traditional markets. For example, e-commerce to brick-and-mortar retail, ride-hailing apps to private transport, OTT to paid TV, and online delivery to traditional delivery markets. In this regard, most competition authorities have held, in terms of enforcement, whether lack of regulation can lead to anticompetitive conduct, and, in terms of advocacy, whether the absence of regulation can lead to competitive advantage in favour of new digital actors. In general, LAC's authorities have insisted in their role as competition agencies, and not as regulators. In this context, competition authorities have issued opinions of the competitive impact of new regulations or have developed new proposals.

In sum, while LAC's competition authorities may not be in the same boat as their peers in other continents, but they are certainly in the same sea. While the recent developments on other jurisdictions, especially Europe and the USA, can influence both substantive analysis and future regulatory proposals, LAC case law has developed and adapted itself to address local problems that can be analysed from a competition law perspective. In this regard, this chapter has tried to systematise LAC's competition authorities' response to local competition and innovation challenges.

[50] *Bancolombia, Banco Davivienda and Banco de Bogotá merger* (n 48).

Appendix – National Antitrust Authorities in Latin America

Argentina	Comisión Nacional de Defensa de la Competencia (CNDC) www.argentina.gob.ar/defensadelacompetencia
Bahamas (The)	Utilities Regulation and Competition Authority (URCA) www.urcabahamas.bs
Barbados	Fair Trading Commission www.ftc.gov.bb
Bolivia	Autoridad de Fiscalización de Empresas www.autoridadempresas.gob.bo
Brazil	Conselho Administrativo de Defesa Econômica (CADE) www.cade.gov.br
Brazil	Secretary for Competition Advocacy and Competitiveness (SEAE) of the Ministry of Finance www.gov.br/economia/pt-br/acesso-a-informacao/institucional/quem-e-quem/secretaria-especial-de-produtividade-emprego-e-competitividade/secretaria-de-advocacia-da-concorrencia-e-competitividade
Chile	Fiscalía Nacional Económica (FNE) www.fne.cl
Chile	Tribunal de Defensa de la Libre Competencia www.tdlc.cl
Colombia	Superintendencia de Industria y Comercio (SIC) www.sic.gov.co
Costa Rica	Comisión para Promover la Competencia (COPROCOM) www.coprocom.go.cr
Costa Rica	Superintendencia de Telecomunicaciones (SUTEL) www.sutel.go.cr
Curaçao	Fair Trade Authority Curaçao (FTAC) ftac.cw/en
Dominican Republic	Comisión Nacional de Defensa de la Competencia procompetencia.gov.do
Dominican Republic	Instituto Dominicano de las Telecomunicaciones (INDOTEL) indotel.gob.do
Ecuador	Superintendencia de Control del Poder de Mercado www.scpm.gob.ec

El Salvador	Superintendencia de Competencia www.sc.gob.sv
Guyana	Competition and Consumer Affairs Commission of Guyana ccac.gov.gy
Honduras	Comisión para la Defensa y Promoción de la Competencia www.cdpc.hn/index.html
Jamaica	Fair Trading Commission jftc.gov.jm
Mexico	Comisión Federal de Competencia Económica (COFECE) www.cofece.mx/cofece/index.php
Mexico	Instituto Federal de Telecomunicaciones (IFT) www.ift.org.mx
Nicaragua	ProCompetencia procompetencia.gob.ni
Panama	Autoridad de la Protección al Consumidor y Defensa de la Competencia www.autoridaddelconsumidor.gob.pa
Paraguay	Comisión Nacional de Competencia www.mic.gov.py/mic/site/comercio/conacom.php
Peru	Instituto Nacional de Defensa de la Competencia y de la Protección de la Propiedad Intelectual (Indecopi) www.indecopi.gob.pe
Peru	Organismo Supervisor de Inversión Privada en Telecomunicaciones (OSIPTEL) www.osiptel.gob.pe
Uruguay	Comisión de Promoción y Defensa de la Competencia www.mef.gub.uy/578/5/areas/defensa-de-la-competencia---uruguay.html
Trinidad and Tobago	Trinidad and Tobago Fair Trading Commission (TTFTC) (from February 2020 the agency became fully operational) tftc.org
Venezuela	Superintendencia Antimonopolio (web page currently not available and since 2015 it seems that it ceased to operate)

10

Regulation of the Digital Markets in the UK, US and the EU

Context, Criteria, Containment, *and Beyond*

MEHMET BILAL UNVER

It is widely acknowledged there is a need for *ex ante* regulation to cope with the competition and consumer harms arising from the digital markets. This chapter investigates the policy approaches of the EU, the UK, and the US from the viewpoint of 'economic regulation' based on a three-step analysis aiming to explore; what products and services are encompassed within the *context* of policy approach; what *criteria* are followed to designate the behaviours that need to be addressed; and what tools and remedies are *contain*ed to address such behaviours. Policy approaches are thereby reviewed to clarify how far each approach fits the principles of economic regulation. In conclusion, it is found that such principles are echoed to varying degrees within each policy approach. While reasonable peculiarities are visible within the meaning of *context*, for example based on the 'core platform services' (EU), 'digital businesses' (UK), and 'covered platforms' (US) respectively, the *criteria* to define undesirable market behaviours and ensuing remedies under *containment* pose unpredictabilities, particularly in the EU and the US approaches. Regulatory design and structure proposed in the UK approach with its substantiated links across the underlying three *chains* tips the balance to this policy framework. After all, it is concluded that unsubstantiated links within and across such chains particularly in the EU and US approaches contrast with a coherent economic regulation model and need reconsideration.

1. Introduction: Background Information

It is widely acknowledged that there is a need for *ex ante* regulation to cope with the competition and consumer harms arising from the digital markets. To respond to such harms, various regulatory measures were adopted or proposed in the EU, the UK, and the US in the recent years. Such *ex ante* measures are aimed to address actual or potential market failures, for example 'killer acquisitions', self-preferencing, combining data from different lines of services without users' consent, using discriminatory interfaces, and restricting interoperability with business users, given the shortcomings of the competition law and the rising concerns about entrenched market power of global tech giants.[1] Often being echoed with the so-called tech giants or GAFAM (Google, Amazon, Facebook, Apple, and Microsoft), it remains to be seen to what extent regulation of digital markets serves or fits the principles of economic regulation under the policy approaches across the globe.

Seeking answer to this question, this chapter takes 'economic regulation' as the baseline to explore and compare such policy approaches. In this field, leading scholarly work and debate surround different theories that are driven by the notion of the 'free market economy' and how to regulate its excessive forms and consequences, for example anticompetitive practices, unpredicted externalities, and inefficiencies.[2] Albeit with the presumption that the best *de facto* regulator is the market itself, the quest to find out how to best serve society distilled 'utilitarian' approach, which justifies limiting economic freedom in order to improve social welfare.[3] Regulation, according to this view, is only justified where private forms of market failure correction, such as private law remedies, are more costly or less effective than regulatory intervention.[4] Economic regulation largely builds on this utilitarian basis permitting distributive models and wide-ranging tools and remedies, for example to facilitate new entrants.

Resembling competition law, economic regulation starts from the premise that free markets are beneficial to society and has, so far, confined its intervention to cases where markets may not work as expected, particularly because of market failures, for example in the case of excessive usage of market power.[5] Following this approach, market failures are acknowledged to constitute the natural boundaries

[1] See OECD (Organisation for Economic Co-operation and Development), *Ex ante regulation of digital markets* (OECD Competition Committee Discussion Paper, 2021) 9–12, www.oecd.org/daf/competition/ex-ante-regulation-and-competition-in-digital-markets.htm. See also Centre on Regulation in Europe (CERRE), *Digital Markets Act: Making economic regulation of platforms fit for the digital age* (2020) 16; J Crémer, Y-A de Montjoye and H Schweitzer, *Competition policy for the digital era* (prepared for the European Commission, 2019) 10 and 52, ec.europa.eu/competition/publications/reports/kd0419345enn.pdf; Digital Competition Expert Panel, *Unlocking digital competition: Report of the Digital Competition Expert Panel* (Furman Report) (2019) 58–64, www.gov.uk/government/publications/unlocking-digital-competition-report-of-the-digital-competition-expert-panel; C Booth and S Center, *Stigler Committee on Digital Platforms: Final Report* (2019) (Stigler Report) 80–92, www.chicagobooth.edu/-/media/research/stigler/pdfs/digital-platforms---committee-report---stigler-center.pdf.

[2] See WK Viscusi, JE Harrington, Jr, and DEM Sappington, *Economics of Regulation and Antitrust* (The MIT Press 2018) 458–74.

[3] See J Drexl, W Kerber, and R Podszun, *Competition Policy and the Economic Approach* (Edward Elgar 2011) 76.

[4] E Windholz and GA Hodge, 'Conceptualising Social and Economic Regulation: Implications and Economic Regulation: Implications for Modern Regulators and Regulatory Activity' (2012) 38 *Monash University Law Review* 212, 221.

[5] See I Lianos, 'Competition Law as a Form of Social Regulation' (2020) 65(1) *The Antitrust Bulletin* 3, 4–5, doi.org/10.1177/0003603X19898626.

of economic freedom,[6] representing the impetus throughout the last four decades shaping the economic regulation. Digital markets regulation would mean correcting excessive market conducts by setting out certain conditions for access and pricing, for which the notion of market failures becomes useful to draw policy lessons.

From this point of view, this chapter examines the policy approaches of the EU, UK, and US, against the widely acknowledged principles of economic regulation, drawing on market failures, if not being limited to this concept.[7] Regulatory structure and design (architecture) of each policy approach is analysed based on the chains of 'context', 'criteria', and 'containment' against which proposed measures are reviewed. This three-step analysis aims to explore what products and services are encompassed within the *context* of each policy approach; what *criteria* are followed to designate the behaviours that need to be addressed; and what tools and remedies are *contain*ed to address such behaviours. Each policy approach is then discussed to clarify how far the proposed/adopted measures fit the principles of economic regulation.

Overall, it is found that such principles are echoed to varying degrees within the framework of each policy approach. Albeit with reasonable peculiarities concerning the *context*, for example based on the 'core platform services' (EU), 'digital businesses' (UK), and 'covered platforms' (US), the *criteria* and the *containment* chains are found to pose unpredictabilities, particularly within the EU and the US policy frameworks. Conversely, a bottom-up policy is visible in the UK approach that well illustrates inter-connection of the so-called chains of economic regulation with lessened risk of unpredictability.

In conclusion, the coherent design of the so-called chains, including the substantiated links across them, tips the balance to the UK policy framework. After and above all, it is underlined that architectural elements within a digital markets regulation play a key role for a coherent and promising model of economic regulation entailing substantiated links within and across such chains. Given this, the chapter concludes that the existing policy approaches for digital markets regulation, particularly those in the EU and US, should be reconsidered from the proposed economic regulation viewpoint based on three-chain architecture.

2. Economic Regulation: Main Pillars and Contours

Regulations are a form of government intervention in markets and consist of requirements to achieve certain standards or purposes. It is systematic and

[6] Market failure can be defined as an ability of the market to deliver goods and services to consumers in an efficient manner, ie because unrestricted competition cannot be sustained in the industry in question (OECD, *Striking the right balance between competition and regulation: The key is learning from our mistakes* (OECD 2002) 4).

[7] This chapter however does not focus on every aspect of digital markets regulations. It reflects on the analysis of behavioural measures excluding the structural tools and remedies.

designed to solve a particular problem or produce a particular outcome.[8] To attain an identified set of outcomes a process is brought into place that involves a focused and sustainable attempt to change public behaviour based on the standards of which the purpose is called regulations.[9] This implies a process that commences with certain policy objectives and is run towards achievable goals via a toolset and instruments which draw the boundaries of 'regulation'.

Interventions of economic regulation may pursue different objectives, for example effective competition, consumer protection, encouraging green investment, and innovation.[10] Among these, ensuring effective competition represents the leading policy objective.[11] Given the widely accepted premise that market forces do not always guarantee that consumer utility and surplus is ensured, regulatory state intervention often targets market failures and aims to create competitive markets through economic regulation.[12]

While some form of regulation might be required to deal with market failures and inefficiencies, each situation needs to be assessed individually as regulation will not be efficient if it costs more than the harms that it seeks to address.[13] Such an approach also means pre-empting or minimizing any harm to the society that would otherwise result from the conflicting or overlapping rules, for example *ex ante* and *ex post* interventions. Overall, this requires a sound regulatory vision through which stakeholders should be driven towards achievable outcomes based on guiding principles. Such a regulatory approach would pre-empt or minimise any harm to the society that would otherwise result from the conflicts of interest or overlapping rules, for example between *ex ante* regulations and *ex post* competition law.

Ex ante interventions introduced by any economic regulation embody substantial policy choices, most likely to lead through asymmetrical regulation to a relatively swift transition to competition.[14] This makes dominant players first and foremost subject to *ex ante* obligations to achieve the policy objectives. Wholesale access and price regulations illustrate such economic regulations targeted at dominant players, for example undertakings having a certain market size and volume. Overall, policy makers should adhere to consistent pathways and regulations when addressing the inherent imbalances in the digital markets and achieving the

[8] Windholz and Hodge (n 4) 219.

[9] Windholz and Hodge (n 4) 217.

[10] See UK government, Department for Business, Energy and Industrial Strategy, 'Economic Regulation Policy Paper' (January 2022), www.gov.uk/government/publications/economic-regulation-policy.

[11] ibid; OECD, *The OECD Report on Regulatory Reform Synthesis* (OECD 1997) 33, www.oecd.org/gov/regulatory-policy/2391768.pdf. See also MB Unver, 'End(s) of the Harmonization in the European Union: Centrifuging or Engineering?' (2021) 11 *Journal of Information Policy* 582, 605.

[12] See P Humphreys, 'Europeanisation, Globalization and Policy Transfer' (2002) 8(2) *Convergence: The Journal of Research into New Media Technologies* (Special Issue on Telecommunications Regulation in Europe) 52, 57.

[13] OECD 2002 Report (n 6) 4.

[14] E Pitt, 'Competition Law Telecommunications' in I Walden and J Angel (eds), *Telecommunications Law* (Blackstone Press 2001) 265–68.

desired objectives of economic regulation, with particular respect to dealing with market failures and inefficiencies.[15]

3. Overview of Digital Markets and their Regulation

3.1. Major Characteristics of the Digital Markets

In technology markets, we witness a change of the dynamics of market economy, comprising not only the well-known aspects of a new economy, such as high fixed cost and low marginal cost of developing and selling intellectual property, network effects, and rapid and disruptive innovation,[16] but also the transformative features of Artificial Intelligence (AI) and big data analytics that facilitate novel ways of competition and innovation.

In fact, using AI algorithms to collect, label, and process data would cultivate new ways of competition and innovation, resulting in the traditional boundaries of digital markets being blurred. This is usually compounded by the indirect network effects exploiting platformisation of legacy digital markets and enabling an ecosystem in which various services, for example social networking platforms, search engines, and app stores as well as intermediation/hosting services such as home sharing, ride-sharing, and dating may be bundled with marginal or even zero profit in exchange for individuals foregoing control of their personal data.

Such ecosystem features reflect a digital landscape, altering the old economy markets from being mainly focused on marginal cost and efficiency to become data and innovation driven.[17] Digital hubs of services are ever fast evolving to such ecosystems whereby different technological inputs and drivers, for example the Internet of Things (IoT) and AI, are all combined and the old competition tools are improved, for example via extended market leverage, and multiplied with new techniques, for example zero pricing for consumers.

While critical mass platform services once represented a mutual interdependency between businesses and platforms during the early days of the platform economy, this dynamic has now shifted to a situation where the former depend on the latter. In particular, GAFAM constitute an example of the problem of a few platforms controlling data and gaining market power due to the data-driven business model.[18] Such dependency of business users is mainly driven and reinforced by structural advantages of GAFAM, being echoed with their position of

[15] For similar views, see also M Bauer and others, 'The EU Digital Markets Act: Assessing the Quality of Regulation' (ECIPE Policy Brief, No 2) (2022) 3–7, ecipe.org/publications/the-eu-digital-markets-act.

[16] Viscusi, Harrington, and Sappington (n 2) 379.

[17] B Lundqvist, 'Regulating Competition in the Digital Economy: With a Special Focus on Platforms' in B Lundqvist and MS Gal (eds), *Competition Law for the Digital Economy* (Edward Elgar 2019) 11.

[18] ibid.

'unavoidable trading partner'.[19] These features, including the 'winner takes all' impact, make the ecosystem leaders well-positioned to control the dynamics of market economy.[20]

Against this background, GAFAM (the big five) are regarded not just as individual companies engaged in mutual competition, but also as a 'corporate platform elite' utilising 'superplatforms' to control the gateways to digital markets.[21] Overall, the controlling powers of these ecosystems can overshadow the competitive process, although consumers would still benefit from the platformisation of digital markets having ecosystem features. Ezrachi and Stucke raise the concern whether a level playing field is at all possible in a world 'where entry is possible, but expansion will likely be controlled by super-platforms'.[22] All these concerns signify the widely accepted need to set a new agenda of economic regulation for digital markets.

3.2. 'Economic Regulation' of Digital Markets

All the above factors are leading up to a new era of *ex ante* regulation, as driven by the expert reports,[23] and opening a new chapter of economic regulation on top of the antitrust cases.

Economic regulation becomes more puzzled given the most encountered competition problems being topped up with the ecosystem features renovating old economy markets. Mainly because of the need for speed and effectiveness, *ex ante* regulation seems to signify a mainstream policy for the GAFAM and other big market players. As manifested by wide-ranging reports,[24] a globalised consensus concerning *ex ante* (economic) regulation of digital markets is becoming visible.[25]

As mentioned, policy makers are inspired by the competition law interventions so far against the actual and potential market failures in digital markets. These markets have repeatedly undergone competition law scrutiny and interventions

[19] See P Alexiadis and A de Streel, 'Designing an EU Intervention Standard for Digital Platforms' (EUI Working Paper RSCAS 2020/14) 6, ssrn.com/abstract=3544694.

[20] See also K Dasgupta and M Williams, 'The New Economics and Regulation of Digital Platforms: Lessons from the Old World of Regulation?' 2020 (ITS Online Event, Calgary, 14–17 June 2020) 10–11, www.econstor.eu/bitstream/10419/224850/1/Dasgupta-Williams.pdf.

[21] A Ezrachi and ME Stucke, *Virtual Competition: The Promise and Perils of the Algorithm-Driven Economy* (Harvard University Press 2016).

[22] ibid.

[23] See the Furman Report (n 1); the Stigler Report (n 1); Crémer, De Montjoye and Schweitzer (n 1). See also Australian Competition & Consumer Commission, 'Digital platforms inquiry' (Final Report, July 2019), www.accc.gov.au/publications/digital-platforms-inquiry-final-report.

[24] See n 1 and 23 above. Across the reports, there is a broad consensus that the core problem that *ex ante* regulation is aimed to address is the imbalance of bargaining power resulting from the dependency of business users on the services provided by the gatekeepers, eg GAFAM controlling access to consumers and, thus, markets (D Geradin, 'What Is a Digital Gatekeeper? Which Platforms Should Be Captured by the EC Proposal for a Digital Market Act?' (SSRN, 18 February 2021) 7, ssrn.com/abstract=3788152.

[25] See n 1 above.

particularly for the big players' strategic behaviours, for example combination of users' data from distinct lines of services in the same ecosystem;[26] self-preferencing in rankings;[27] creating unfair advantages to their own apps/services through exclusivity clauses/agreements;[28] using non-public data generated from business users in competition with them;[29] and putting the rival companies at a disadvantageous position against the consumers by charging unfair prices.[30]

Notwithstanding, competition law issues and problems do not fully represent the policy responses in dealing with the related concerns and issues, which extend to data portability, 'side loading' of third-party apps, price and performance transparency for ads, etc. Despite the fact that all these concerns result in a broad political consensus, the scope and aims of the adopted or proposed measures differ across countries, incorporating regulatory design and structure.

4. Policy Approaches to Regulation of Digital Markets

4.1. General Overview

Concerning digital markets regulation, the EU, UK, and US follow distinctive approaches and legislative schedules. The DMA, after being approved by the EU Council and Parliament, entered into force on 1 November 2022. The UK and the US lag at the parliamentary level, although their policy stance is clear with respect to the nature and limits of *ex ante* regulation.

The policy approaches in the EU, the UK, and the US are examined in the following subsections. Aims, scope, and tools of *ex ante* regulation under each policy approach are summarised first, which is then followed by a review of each approach with a focus on regulatory design and structure.

[26] See Bundeskartellamt *Facebook* decision, 6th Dec Div, B6-22/16, 6 February 2019, currently on appeal, www.bundeskartellamt.de/SharedDocs/Entscheidung/EN/Entscheidungen/Missbrauchsaufsicht/2019/B6-22-16.pdf%3F__blob%3DpublicationFile%26v%3D5. See also Bundeskartellamt, 'Bundeskartellamt prohibits Facebook from combining user data from different sources' (*News*, 7 February 2019), www.bundeskartellamt.de/SharedDocs/Meldung/EN/Pressemitteilungen/2019/07_02_2019_Facebook.html.

[27] See *Google and Alphabet v Commission (Google Shopping)* [2017] OJ C445/21, upheld in Case T-612/17 *Google and Alphabet v Commission* EU:T:2021:763.

[28] See *Google and Alphabet v Commission* (*Google Android*) [2018] OJ C445/21, upheld in Case T-604/18 *Google and Alphabet v Commission* EU:T:2021:763; *Google and Alphabet v Commission* (*Google Adsense*) [2019] OJ C 255, currently on appeal in Case T-334/19; *Google AdTech and Data Related Practices* (Cases COMP/AT. 40670) 22 June 2021 (Opening of Proceedings), 14 June 2023 (Statement of Objections).

[29] *Amazon Marketplace* (Case AT.40462) *and Amazon Buy Box* (Case AT.40703) Commission Decision C/2022/9442 [2023] OJ C 87.

[30] Competition and Markets Authority (CMA), 'Press release: CMA investigates Apple over suspected anti-competitive behaviour' (4 March 2021), www.gov.uk/cma-cases/investigation-into-apple-appstore.

4.2. The EU's DMA

The European journey of regulating digital markets has started with the Commission's DMA Proposal published in December 2020.[31] The DMA was published on 12 October 2022 and became applicable on 2 May 2023.[32] This Regulation aims to ensure 'contestable and fair markets in the digital sector across the Union where gatekeepers are present, to the benefit of business users and end users'.[33]

The DMA shapes out regulation of the digital markets based on the specified 'core platform services' (CPSs) as listed under Article 2.[34] This broad list of CPSs is followed by the thresholds to designate 'gatekeepers', as set out in Article 3. Designation of gatekeepers is of paramount importance for the overall structure and functionality of the DMA, as all the prohibitions and obligations build on this concept.

Article 5 of the DMA imposes a number of prohibitions and obligations on gatekeepers, for example to refrain from combining and cross-using personal data sourced from the relevant CPSs; prohibition of most-favoured-customer clauses; enabling uninstallation of preinstalled software; applying no requirements on offering or interoperating with the gatekeeper systems regarding supportive technical services. A similar set of obligations are placed under Article 6 of the DMA which, however, are not self-executive and need to be specified by the Commission.[35] The distinction between the obligations under Articles 5 and 6 signifies a peculiar set up, posing complexity and unpredictability.[36] Furthermore, in the case of systemic non-compliance the DMA enables the Commission to impose new remedies, meaning further restrictions, requirements and complexities might loom on the horizon.[37]

[31] European Commission, 'The Digital Markets Act: ensuring fair and open digital markets', ec.europa.eu/info/strategy/priorities-2019-2024/europe-fit-digital-age/digital-markets-act-ensuring-fair-and-open-digital-markets_en.

[32] See the Regulation (EU) 2022/1925 of the European Parliament and of the Council of 14 September 2022 on contestable and fair markets in the digital sector and amending Directives (EU) 2019/1937 and (EU) 2020/1828 [2022] OJ L 265 ('Digital Markets Act' or 'DMA'). See also European Commission, 'Competition Policy: Digital Markets Act (DMA)', competition-policy.ec.europa.eu/dma_en.

[33] See DMA, Art 1(1).

[34] According to Art 2(2) of the DMA, CPSs comprise (a) online intermediation services; (b) online search engines; (c) online social networking services; (d) video-sharing platform services; (e) number-independent interpersonal communications services; (f) operating systems; (g) web browsers; (h) virtual assistants; (i) cloud computing services; (j) online advertising services.

[35] Such obligations (susceptible of being further specified under Art 8) include, but are not limited to, prohibition of self-preferencing; refraining from combining personal data for the purpose of delivering targeted or micro-targeted advertising; enabling end users to switch between and subscribe to different software applications; enabling effective interoperability to the same operating system, hardware or software features.

[36] See P Akman, 'Regulating Competition in Digital Platform Markets: A Critical Assessment of the Framework and Approach of the EU Digital Markets Act' (2021) 10 (SSRN, 1 December 2021), ssrn.com/abstract=3978625.

[37] See DMA, Art 18(1).

Under the DMA, the EU Commission is empowered to determine new gatekeepers as well as to enlarge the list of the CPSs following Articles 17 and 19. Moreover, the Commission is entitled to open investigations and proceedings, for example in order to specify further remedies on gatekeepers in the case of non-compliance, or to keep those obligations up to date.[38] Last but not least, Article 9 sets out a 'suspension' process on an exceptional basis, for example for the reasons of economic viability of the gatekeeper operations, and Article 10 envisages the possibility of exemptions on the grounds of public health or public security.[39] Under both procedures, the burden of proof is on the gatekeeper.

Considering the obligations of Articles 5 and 6 apply quasi-automatically and Articles 9 and 10 leave limited room for exemption, a reversal of the burden of proof seems to be hardly possible.[40] While the principles of equal treatment, proportionality, and due process are emphasised under the DMA,[41] compliance with these principles does not guarantee a regulatory dialogue, as one would seek from the perspective of good regulatory practice.[42]

4.3. The UK Government's Response

In the UK, the regulatory process was stimulated by the Furman Report (March 2019),[43] which was followed by the market study conducted by the Competition and Market Authority (CMA) (July 2020)[44] and the CMA advice to the government[45] (December 2020). Another indicative key milestone was the UK government's consultation document titled 'A new pro-competition regime for the digital markets' (July 2021) proposing an *ex ante* regulatory regime for the digital markets.[46] Finally, the UK government issued its response in May 2022,[47] sending

[38] See DMA, Art 8(2) and 12(1).

[39] DMA, Art 10(1)–(3).

[40] Cabral and others, 'The EU Digital Markets Act: A Report from a Panel of Economic Experts' (prepared for the European Commission) (2021) 28, publications.jrc.ec.europa.eu/repository/handle/JRC122910.

[41] DMA, Art 7(1)(b).

[42] In a limited fashion, such a room can be argued to exist under Recital 65 and Art 8(3) with respect to re-evaluating the obligation(s) as to whether it is 'effective in achieving the objective of the relevant obligation in the specific circumstances of the gatekeeper'. Yet, lack of a broadly applicable provision incorporating reversed burden of proof and wide-ranging evidential tools can rebut this argument.

[43] See n 1 above.

[44] CMA, 'Online platforms and digital advertising market study' (1 July 2020) ('CMA market study'), www.gov.uk/cma-cases/online-platforms-and-digital-advertising-market-study.

[45] UK government, 'Press release: CMA advises government on new regulatory regime for tech giants' (8 December 2020) ('CMA advice'), www.gov.uk/government/news/cma-advises-government-on-new-regulatory-regime-for-tech-giants.

[46] UK government, Department for Digital, Culture, Media & Sport and Department for Business, Energy & Industrial Strategy, 'A new pro-competition regime for digital markets' (20 July 2021), www.gov.uk/government/consultations/a-new-pro-competition-regime-for-digital-markets.

[47] UK government, Department for Digital, Culture, Media & Sport and Department for Business, Energy & Industrial Strategy, 'Consultation outcome: A new pro-competition regime for

the message that they aim to regulate the digital markets in line with the Furman Report and the CMA market study.

According to the UK government's response, the Digital Markets Unit (DMU), a specialised unit established under the CMA in April 2021,[48] will implement the prospective pro-competition regime for digital markets. In this new *ex ante* regime, pro-competitive interventions (PCIs) are expected to target a small number of firms having substantial and entrenched market power that enables them to have Strategic Market Status (SMS). According to the UK government, possession of this market power should provide such firms with a 'strategic position' in at least one digital activity.[49] The government also indicated that there will be an exhaustive list of criteria to determine the SMS firms.[50] In addition, a minimum revenue threshold will be introduced by the government to clarify which firms are to be out of the scope of the SMS designation process.[51] It is made clear by the UK government that the DMU will be mandated to publish guidance explaining all the relevant steps and concepts.[52]

According to the UK policy approach, the DMU will set out the (bespoke) conduct requirements for the SMS firms based on specific categories. While the high-level objectives, namely 'fair trading', 'open choices', and 'trust and transparency', will inform the conduct requirements,[53] it is expected that the DMU will be empowered to remove or amend such requirements subsequent to the SMS designation. SMS firms will then have an opportunity to put forward evidence to establish that a particular conduct that would otherwise breach a conduct requirement would bring about benefits to consumers.[54] This 'exemption' process marks a stark distinction to the EU approach for the effective evidential process that would minimise the likely Type I and II errors.

It is underlined that the DMU remedies will be proportionate to address an 'adverse effect on competition' and 'will tackle the root causes of entrenched market power'.[55] In this regard, wide-ranging remedies, for example including not

digital markets' (6 May 2022) ('UK government response to consultation'), www.gov.uk/government/consultations/a-new-pro-competition-regime-for-digital-markets/outcome/a-new-pro-competition-regime-for-digital-markets-government-response-to-consultation.

[48] CMA, 'Collection: Digital Markets Unit' (7 April 2021), www.gov.uk/government/collections/digital-markets-unit.

[49] UK government response to consultation (n 47). This component of 'strategic position' has been introduced by the government in the period subsequent to the CMA's advice and particularly within the public consultation launched in July 2021, marking a distinction to the CMA's focus on addressing the sources of market power.

[50] UK government response to consultation (n 47).

[51] UK government response to consultation (n 47).

[52] UK government response to consultation (n 47).

[53] Under CMA market study, each objective, namely 'fair trade', 'open options', and 'trust and transparency' are corelated to and explained by a set of principles. According to the CMA, such principles need to be amended in line with evolving market conditions by the DMU to respond the complexities of the digital markets (CMA market study (n 44) 341–46, 357).

[54] UK government response to consultation (n 47).

[55] UK government response to consultation (n 47).

only interoperability between platforms and services but also ownership separation remedies, would be introduced, yet it is envisaged that the applicable remedies would follow a robust, evidence-based investigation through which any countervailing benefits should be considered along with any likely adverse impact.[56] According to the government's response, there will also be safeguards including consultation requirements and rights of appeal to prevent overzealous interventions, alongside the flexibility for trialling and iterating new remedies.[57]

In general, the UK approach is less ambitious in terms of specific obligations and more focused on the high-level objectives, principles, and investigative tools needed to achieve pro-competitive digital markets.

4.4. The US Bills

Four bipartisan bills proposed in June 2021 lay down the ground for *ex ante* regulation of digital markets in the US. Such bills include the proposed American Choice and Innovation Online (ACIO) Act,[58] Augmenting Compatibility and Competition by Enabling Service Switching (ACCESS) Act,[59] Ending Platform Monopolies Act (US Bill – HR3825),[60] and Platform Competition and Opportunity Act (US Bill – HR3826).[61] While the first two bills are concerned with conduct of the digital market players and behavioural remedies, the latter two are related to structural problems and remedies. Notwithstanding this, the criteria used to designate the 'covered platforms' under the four bills are common.[62] Below, two bills are examined with a view to fleshing out the US policy approach concerning the behavioural tools and remedies.

The proposed ACIO Act, which draws a general framework regarding discriminatory behaviours by 'covered platforms', sets out a wide range of prohibited conduct and remedies for these platforms.[63] The proposed ACCESS Act, on the

[56] UK government response to consultation (n 47).

[57] UK government response to consultation (n 47).

[58] American Choice and Innovation Online Act, HR 3816, 117th Cong, 1 (2021) (ACIO Act), www.congress.gov/bill/117th-congress/house-bill/3816/text?r=8&s=1.

[59] Augmenting Compatibility and Competition by Enabling Service Switching (ACCESS) Act, HR 3849, 117th Cong, 1 (2021) (ACCESS Act), www.congress.gov/bill/117th-congress/house-bill/3849.

[60] Ending Platform Monopolies Act, HR 3825, 117th Cong, 1 (2021), www.congress.gov/bill/117th-congress/house-bill/3825/text.

[61] Platform Competition and Opportunity Act, HR 3849, 117th Cong, 1 (2021), www.congress.gov/bill/117th-congress/house-bill/3826.

[62] See ACIO Act, s 2(d)(1) and s 2(g)(4)(B); ACCESS Act, s 2(d)(1) and s 2(g)(4)(B); Ending Platform Monopolies Act, s 5(5)(B) and s 6(a)(1)(A); Platform Competition and Opportunity Act, s 3(d) and s 4(a)(1)(A).

[63] Prohibitions under the proposed ACIO Act are of paramount importance for the functioning of this Act, which include but are not limited to, no advantaging the covered platform's own products/services over those of another business user; no discrimination among similarly situated business users; no restriction or impeding the capacity of a business user to access or interoperate with the same platform, operating system, hardware, and software features available to the covered platform; no tying; no use of non-public data obtained from or generated on the platform by the activities of a

other hand, includes data portability and interoperability-related obligations. Within this framework are set out the rules for the covered platforms to ensure a set of transparent, third-party-accessible interfaces enabling the secure transfer of data to users/business users[64] as well as to facilitate and maintain interoperability with competing businesses upon certain standards issued by the technical committee at the Federal Trade Commission (FTC).[65]

The proposed ACCESS Act's clear-cut structure and prescriptive norms[66] contrast with the general yet tailorable requirements, for example regarding non-discrimination, under the proposed ACIO Act. This latter approach is considered to be future-proof, enabling regulatory flexibility and limiting gaming[67] as well as including better and responsive interventions against the peculiarities of the covered platforms, for example based on their business models. Furthermore, the proposed ACIO Act provides the covered platforms with an 'affirmative defense' opportunity to be able to argue that the prohibitions should not apply to them, for example for the lack of harm.[68]

Among the policy approaches examined, the US approach can be distinguished as it enables both civil and administrative actions. The FTC is empowered to commence a civil action to recover a civil penalty and seek other appropriate reliefs before the court, as well as having general enforcement powers under the US bills.

5. Review of the EU, UK, and US Approaches

5.1. Structure of the Review: Analysis Based on *Context*, *Criteria*, and *Containment*

Below, this study attempts to make a deeper analysis from an architectural outlook concerning the existing policy approaches. It aims to conduct a three-step analysis for each policy approach, following the *chains* of economic regulation explained below.

business user or its customers to offer or support own products/services; no restricting or impeding a business user from accessing data generated on the platform by the activities of the business user or its customers preventing portability by the business user of such data; no restricting or impeding covered platform users from uninstalling software apps preinstalled; and no self-preferencing (ACIO Act, s 2(a) and 2(b)).

[64] ACCESS Act, ss 3 and 4.

[65] ACCESS Act, ss 3 and 4.

[66] See ECIPE Policy Brief (n 15) 14.

[67] The Tobin Center for Economic Policy, 'International coherence in digital platform regulation: an economic perspective on the US and EU proposals' (Policy Discussion Paper No 5, 2021) 15.

[68] See ACIO Act, s 2(c)).

Respectively, this three-step analysis examines:

- *Context*: What products and services are encompassed within the *context* of this policy approach?
- *Criteria:* What *criteria* are followed to designate the behaviours that need to be addressed?
- *Containment*: What tools and remedies are *contain*ed in the policy approach to address such behaviours?

Following this three-step analysis, this chapter aims to explore any gap or deficiency arising from the EU, the UK, and the US approaches from an architectural point of view. Figure 10.1 illustrates the baseline architectural design of the so-called chains with a view to revitalising a perspective of economic regulation for the digital markets. Based on the illustrative chains in Figure 10.1, this chapter investigates each policy approach with respect to not only the inner boundaries of the chains but also interlinks between them to make an overall analysis.

Figure 10.1 Chains of 'economic regulation'

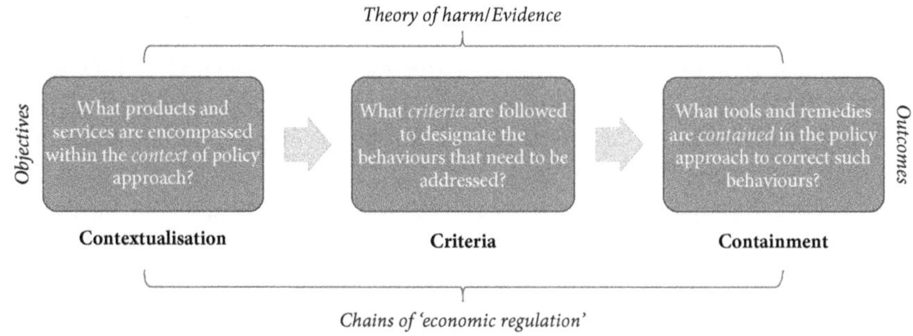

As demonstrated in Figure 10.1, policy *objectives* should be set at the outset of each policy framework. *Context* designates the covered products and services that are susceptible to economic regulation. *Theories of harm* underlie the *criteria* paving the way for regulation of any of the covered products or services. *Evidence* is sought to find out whether certain market conduct or imperfections need to be addressed under the policy objectives and principles. To that end, the regulator needs to rest on the *criteria* to find out any need for intervention to end the market failure(s). The process then proceeds with the *contain*ment of the remedies to achieve the policy *outcomes*. Under this last chain, *evidence* is again needed for a best design of the remedies responding to the market failure(s).

This suggests two implications: (i) the sequential chains of 'economic regulation' need to fit in a policy framework; and (ii) all the chains and their components need to be inter-connected for a well-functioning model of economic regulation. The following analysis of the policy approaches is based on this understanding of the 'economic regulation'.

5.2. Analysis of the EU's DMA

Context: Under the context of DMA, 11 different digital services called CPSs that are susceptible to *ex ante* regulation are listed, and this list can be expanded.[69] For instance, cloud computing services are listed as a CPS, whereas many types of the Internet of Things (IoT) services are not. Notwithstanding, if this vertical integration is seen as an advantage of existing market power towards an adjacent market, for example for the IoT services in question, the latter may qualify as a CPS when provided by a dominant cloud provider.

Likewise, new gatekeepers can be added into the list following an investigation under Article 17 even where the investigated service provider does not meet the quantitative thresholds required to be a gatekeeper.[70] Investigations and proceedings, for example, under Articles 17 and 19 can *feed back* regarding any need for new categories of CPSs, gatekeepers, and/or restricted practices. While such 'feedback' process would be a positive step forward, this can also be a source of unpredictability for the potential uncertainties, for example regarding the extent to which current obligations will be expanded, whether an implementing/delegated act or interim measure is required, and to what extent competition law interventions will be taken into account.

Arguably, lack of full clarity within the meaning of *context* is inevitable; however, this should not mean further engineering in a regulatory design. In fact, achieving predictability is best served by identifying the stepping stones and eliminating the stumbling blocks, thereby deterring a fragile model of regulation and discouraging the need for re-design or re-engineering of the regulatory model.

Criteria: 'Market contestability' and 'fairness' represent the key objectives of the DMA.[71] The DMA does not offer guiding principles as to how these objectives can be achieved, except with a few indicative parameters that can be derived from Article 12(5) and recitals 32 and 33. For instance, from the contractual 'imbalance' between the parties or the concept of 'proportionality' as frequently referred to under the Regulation, some applicable tests or criteria can, barely, be derived.[72] For potential criteria, reference can be made to the Article 12(5)(a)(i), which refers to 'creation or strengthening of entry/expansion barriers', suggesting this can create risks affecting contestability, reminiscent of legacy competition threats.[73] Likewise, some implications can be infused from Article 12(5)(a) which indicates

[69] See section 4.2.
[70] See section 4.2.
[71] See DMA, Art 1(1).
[72] See also Akman (n 36) 25.
[73] Arguably, the two goals of the DMA including contestability are not as far removed from competition law as the DMA's proposal itself would suggest, and both these objectives are best understood as part and parcel of competition policy (P Larouche and A de Streel, 'The European Digital Markets Act: A Revolution Grounded on Traditions' (2021) 12(7) *Journal of European Competition Law and Practice* 542, 544).

any gatekeeper 'prevent[ing] other operators from having the same access to a key input'[74] can harm contestability. This provision may pose a potential conflict with the *ex post* interventions, as it may phase out competition law tools or doctrines, for example 'essential facilities', if a pro-active implementation approach is pursued.

Overall, absence of clear-cut criteria may potentially result in some gaps and unpredictable consequences under the DMA. Recitals 32–34 and some relevant provisions, for example Article 12(5), in conjunction with the qualitative thresholds under Article 3(1), in a cumulative reading, allude to the quasi-structural entry barriers and the mechanisms of controlling access as a potential threat of unfairness and non-contestability. This guidance, however, does not mean sufficient signposts as to the market behaviours that need to be addressed and can compromise soundness of the applicable obligations.

Economic regulations target certain outcomes to reach out to a competitive market and subsist on a set of standards or criteria enabling predictability and sustainability. In the absence of these clear links and signposts, regulatory engineering as well as a regulatory vacuum would emerge, threatening the relevant markets and depleting the human resources with no or minimum benefit for the stakeholders as well as the end users. This potential threat arising from the absent *criteria* means unsubstantiated links between *context* and *containment* chains, as demonstrated in Figure 10.2, where the chain of 'criteria' is technically removed, and 'designation of gatekeepers' functions as the *de facto* new chain between 'context' and 'containment'. This situation, which represents an architectural deficiency, carries the potential for unpredictabilities.

Figure 10.2 Architectural design of the EU's DMA

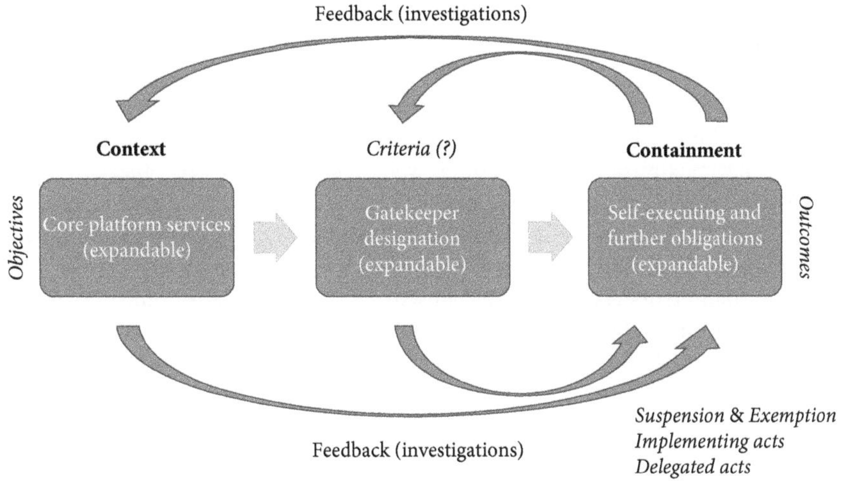

[74] See DMA, Art 12(5)(b)(ii).

On the positive side, investigations would enable two-way feedback process, as can be seen along the chains both expanding and stabilising the regulatory system. Whereas expansion would be seen in the short run, the feedback effect would tip the system to a more stabilised one in the long run. Both would feed into the regulatory system to filter out a better implementation, for example regarding designation of gatekeepers, newly prohibited practices, CPSs, and remedies. While a positive impact can arise based on the outputs of the feedback processes, all these are constrained with the regulatory design and structure. As a matter of fact, stabilisation can take a longer period than expected or may never take place. Positive feedback effect would thus be limited and/or outweighed by the negative effects, for example welfare losses and/or regulatory costs.

Containment: As the mainstream rule of the DMA, gatekeepers must comply with the Articles 5–7 obligations. While the Article 5 sets out the self-executing obligations, the obligations under Article 6 are formulated as 'susceptible of being further specified'.[75] These behavioural obligations are clearly inspired by the earlier antitrust case law.[76] Yet, the rationale behind the two different categories and the way they will be assumed by the gatekeepers requires some clarification, particularly in view of the distinct CPSs or business models for which a tailored regulatory treatment might be needed. It is unclear which obligations in Articles 5 and 6 will be applied to which CPSs and whether the market players can correctly self-select the right ones.[77] It appears that further obligations can thus be engineered, based on various reasons and scenarios, such as non-compliance under Articles 8(2) or 18(1) or updating the obligations under Article 12(1).

Given the wide regulatory discretion and the potential unpredictabilities within the meaning of 'containment' as well as 'context' and 'criteria', the overall framework of the DMA poses a clear risk of engineering and a likely regulatory vacuum. This would however contrast with the main pillars and principles of economic regulation.

Closely related to this, what outcomes are achievable is another key question posing an additional layer of unpredictability for the EU regulatory system. Given the fact that maximisation of consumer welfare is not the *de jure* objective of the DMA, the desirable end goals to be achieved by the envisaged measures are unclear although the leading concerns are visible. This situation means leaving some space for erroneous interventions, more explicitly Type I and II errors.

How such errors are to be internalised within the DMA system remains to be seen. Within the DMA structure, it seems that potential Type I errors can be partially corrected under Articles 9 and 10 which are concerned with 'suspension'

[75] Unlike the obligations under Arts 5 and 6, the obligations under Art 7 of the DMA are not imposed on all the gatekeepers but only those providing number-independent interpersonal communications services.

[76] Regarding the precedents of EU competition law that illustrate the footprints of the EU's DMA, see Akman (n 36) 5–6.

[77] Akman (n 36) 27.

and 'exemption' of the obligations respectively. Since such provisions allow reversal of obligations on an exceptional basis, they can hardly be invoked to smooth the functioning of the DMA and correct the Type I or II errors.[78] Overall, not only effectiveness of this kind of corrective approach but also and more importantly the DMS structure and design is questionable from the perspective of economic regulation.

5.3. Analysis of the UK Government's Response

Context: According to the policy approach proposed by the UK government, only activities whose core component is digital technologies will be covered. While the scope of the new regime will clearly be limited to 'digital activities', there is uncertainty as to the boundaries. On the other hand, the government have indicated that it will be working to develop a definition of such activities.[79]

At present, the UK position seems to be quite flexible within the meaning of 'context'. Marking a contrast to the EU's DMA, the UK policy approach does not aim to cover pre-listed products or services, which potentially results in a definitional gap. Notwithstanding, this uncertainty regarding the chain of context within the UK approach does not seem to create an unsurmountable problem. First, according to the CMA advice and the UK government response, only a small number of digital firms are likely to meet the SMS test.[80] Second, the CMA not only suggests a quite high threshold in terms of firms' size and revenue but also recommends that the DMU should initially prioritise the firms active in particular activities such as online marketplaces, app stores, social networks, web browsers, online search engines, operating systems, and cloud computing services.[81]

Criteria: The UK approach entails an asymmetrical regulatory system focused on SMS, for which the government aims to provide an exhaustive list of criteria, which accounts for the major global players. According to the UK government, the list of the criteria to define the SMS firms will be exhaustive. The CMA considers that the SMS position arises when users of the firm's products and services lack good alternatives and there is limited threat of entry or expansion by rivals.[82] In this regard, the five factors set out by the CMA would need to be taken into

[78] Crucially, the Type I errors would be more likely, given Arts 12 and 17–19 that give way to new gatekeeper obligations, designation of new gatekeepers, and CPSs.

[79] UK government response to consultation (n 47).

[80] Both the UK government and the CMA consider that a small number of operators should be covered by the new *ex ante* regime, although the government has not yet detailed its proposed criteria to designate the SMS firms under legislation. The CMA, on the other hand, recommend the DMU prioritises firms with annual UK revenue in excess of £1 billion, and particularly those which also have annual global revenue in excess of £25 billion (CMA advice (n 45) 32).

[81] CMA advice (n 45) 32.

[82] CMA advice (n 45) 28.

account, in particular to indicate whether a firm has a strategic position.[83] The cumulative impact of such factors can be understood to mean market behaviours that are likely to affect competition, ie raising entry costs or constraining the expansion of the smaller rivals, restricting interoperability, self-preferencing, and creating difficulties for third parties to advertise their own products and/or offer services. While a positive correlation between such market behaviours and the SMS presence can be signposted, this is of a less indicative nature in comparison to the EU approach since the UK policy, referring to such competition threats and using terminology of competition law, does not blacklist certain behaviours.

Furthermore, the UK approach relies on the guiding principles as well as the high-level objectives, ie fair trading, open choices, and trust and transparency, from the beginning. Although the extent to which the CMA market study and advice will be transposed in legislation and reflected into practice is uncertain,[84] well rooted and principles-based regulatory regime in the UK would mitigate this uncertainty.[85]

Against this background, the concept of 'conduct requirements', as will be operationalised for the SMS players, would establish and effectuate the principles for economic regulation. It is envisaged that conduct requirements will eventually shape the way SMS market players should behave as per their respective business model. Given examples of such requirements include the following:

- requiring SMS firms not to apply discriminatory terms, conditions, or policies to certain users or categories of users, compared to equivalent transactions,
- preventing bundling or tying the provision of its other products or services by making access to them conditional on the use of the relevant designated activity and
- providing clear, relevant, accurate, and accessible information to users.[86]

One could argue such conduct requirements would as equally determine the criteria to correct the market behaviours as they mean obligations for them. This

[83] With regard to the SMS, the CMA point out the conditions when: (i) a firm has achieved very significant size or scale in an activity, for example where certain products are regularly used by a very high proportion of the population or where the value of transactions facilitated by a specific product is large; (ii) the firm is an important access point to customers (a gateway) for a diverse range of other businesses or the activity is an important input for a diverse range of other businesses; (iii) the firm can use the activity to extend market power from one activity into a range of other activities and/or has developed an 'ecosystem' of products which protects a firm's market power; (iv) the firm can use the activity to determine the rules of the game, within the firm's own ecosystem and also in practice for a wider range of market participants; or (v) the activity has significant impacts on markets that may have broader social or cultural importance. (See CMA advice (n 45) 31).

[84] See also n 53 above.

[85] Regarding the UK history and principles of economic regulation, see UK government, Department for Business, Innovation and Skills (BIS), 'The Principles for Economic Regulation' (April 2011), www.gov.uk/government/publications/principles-for-economic-regulation. Relying on the same principles for many utility sectors (Economic Regulation Policy Paper (n 10)) the UK government's response does not differ concerning digital markets.

[86] UK government response to consultation (n 47).

argument has some merit considering these requirements would function as guiding principles as well as have a prohibitive and obligatory nature. However, the fact that there will be some categories based on distinct business models would mitigate any uncertainty while suggesting the chains of the UK system are well inter-connected and can eliminate potential unpredictabilities.

In the UK, the DMU is expected to have fully-fledged powers in the course of design of the remedies, whereby no default obligation or remedy is placed under the 'containment' chain.[87] Before this, an exemption process within the chain of 'criteria' is provided for the SMS firms to substantiate that their conduct that would otherwise breach a conduct requirement brings about benefits to consumers. This would not only enable a genuine regulatory dialogue including a (reversed) burden of proof but also reinforce the regulatory system, with a key check-balance mechanism minimising the likely Type I and II errors.

The UK approach, while being responsive to the need for experimentation, strengthens the regulatory system and structure to mitigate the risk of unpredictability. Overall, both inner boundaries of the 'criteria' and its links with other chains as well as the policy objectives within the UK's proposed approach feature a robust regulatory regime.

Containment: As far as the chain of containment is concerned, the UK approach is not prescriptive in its framework for the so-called 'pro-competitive interventions' (PCIs). PCIs mean a variety of remedies[88] to be imposed where an 'adverse effect on competition' can be demonstrated. According to the CMA, any intervention in this regard 'must result from a detailed assessment and understanding of competition concerns in a particular activity, and for this assessment to consider the potential effectiveness and proportionality of any intervention as well as any risks and possible unintended consequences'.[89]

It is envisaged that the DMU will have a broad discretion by which to specify and implement remedies in the overall process. The new regime is expected to mirror the Schedule 8 to the Enterprise Act 2002 in terms of remedy design powers.[90] On the other hand, the DMU's information-gathering powers seem to be more enhanced than those under the Competition Act and the Enterprise Act.[91] Besides, the proposed system entails regulatory experimentation, for example ranging from accepting binding undertakings to trialling and iterating new remedies, which all point towards a *bottom-up* approach.

[87] Regarding the CMA's exemplary five types of PCIs, see n 83 above.

[88] The CMA's advice refers to the *data-related interventions, interoperability and common standards, consumer choice and defaults interventions, obligations to provide access on fair and reasonable terms* and *separation remedies* as the five key PCIs and emphasises the need for the DMU to provide guidance for these (CMA advice (n 45) 43).

[89] CMA advice (n 45) 42.

[90] UK government response to consultation (n 47).

[91] Under the UK approach, the DMU will be able to apply civil penalties to named senior managers who fail to ensure that their firm complies with requests for information, alongside the director disqualification for regulatory breaches (UK government response to consultation (n 47)).

Distinctive aspects of the chains within the UK approach are illustrated in Figure 10.3. Although the UK model offers well-elaborated and inter-connected chains along with a promising system of economic regulation, inner boundaries of each chain would need to be fine-tuned, particularly regarding how the principles ought to be applied in achievement of the policy objectives. Having said that, in the legislative process it is advisable to further reflect on the CMA's suggestions, aiming at more settled inner boundaries.

Figure 10.3 Architectural design of the UK approach

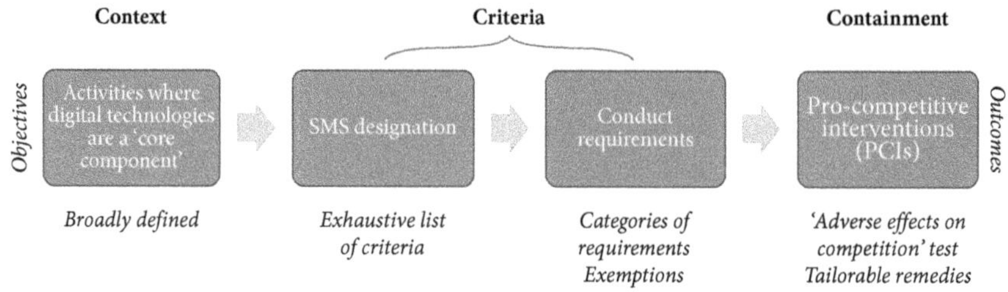

5.4. Analysis of the US Bills

Context: Within the 'context' of the four US bills are designated three categories of digital platforms. According to this rather narrower approach, 'online platform' is defined to mean:

> a website, online or mobile application, operating system, digital assistant, or online service that:
>
> - enables a user to generate content that can be viewed by other users on the platform or to interact with other content on the platform;
> - facilitates the offering, sale, purchase, payment, or shipping of goods or services, including software applications, between and among consumers or businesses not controlled by the platform; or
> - enables user searches or queries that access or display a large volume of information.[92]

The above list includes social media and music/video streaming, online intermediation services, and search engines, respectively. In this list, which is common across the bills, some of the platform services, ie number-independent interpersonal communications services, online advertisement, operating systems, web browsers, virtual assistants, and cloud computing do not appear to be included.[93] Although the definition of 'online platform' seems to allow new services to be included, this does not guarantee the predictability needed for economic regulation.

[92] ACIO Act, s 2(g)(10); ACCESS Act, s 5(12); Ending Platform Monopolies Act, s 5(10); Platform Competition and Opportunity Act, s 3(h).

[93] See also The Tobin Center (n 67) 8.

Criteria: Under the US approach, not every online platform but only those 'covered' within the statutory limits are subject to *ex ante* regulation. In this regard, online platforms which meet three specific 'criteria' are qualified as 'covered platforms' for a period of 10 years.[94]

While the first two criteria are quantitative in nature, the third criterion, the 'critical trading partner'[95] assessment, means a qualitative threshold, which is reminiscent of the EU approach. In practice as long as a digital platform meets the quantitative criteria it will most likely satisfy the threshold, given the lack of any indicator to test this concept.[96] This implies a less expansive and intrusive approach in comparison with the EU's DMA.

In terms of undesirable market behaviours, a distinction needs to be made between the proposed ACIO and ACCESS Acts. It should be underlined that the criteria to designate discriminatory/abusive market behaviours under the proposed ACIO Act are clearer given the listed prohibited conducts preceding any potential remedy. This proposed Act has similarities to the UK approach incorporating well-elaborated signposts functioning as the criteria.

Looking into the US approach, the thresholds applicable to the designation process would be considered within the initial phase of 'criteria' for their very indicative nature, as demonstrated in Figure 10.4. Hence, the ultimate functionality of this chain ('criteria') becomes complete when moving to the phase of 'prohibited conducts' under the proposed ACIO Act. This second phase, concerning the prohibited market conduct, is however absent in the proposed ACCESS Act, which poses a structural gap and deficiency. Overall, the two-pronged system of the US approach can be criticised, given the fragmented criteria that would give rise to complexity and unpredictability.

Containment: Moving to the chain of the 'containment', the remedies are of a mixed nature, given the two-pronged system design. Under the proposed ACIO Act, there exists a phase of 'prohibited conducts' which is followed by the compliance monitoring and remedy design, incorporating the judicial reliefs and sanctions. As in the UK approach, covered platforms' practices are first calibrated through the requirements of prohibited conducts, namely the so-called second phase of the criteria, and then scrutinised as to whether the required standards are respected under the 'containment'. Under the proposed ACCESS Act, covered platforms are directly subject to a set of obligations mainly focused on enhancing interoperability. Concerning this Act, which details interoperability obligations

[94] The period of 10 years during which designation lasts is much longer than others, namely the EU and the UK policies. The timespan for review is set as three years in the EU's DMA and five years in the UK government response.

[95] According to s 2(g)(6) of the proposed ACIO Act, 'critical trading partner' means a 'trading partner that has the ability to restrict or impede (A) the access of a business user to its users or customers; or (B) the access of a business user to a tool or service that it needs to effectively serve its users or customers'.

[96] The Tobin Center (n 67) 9.

Figure 10.4 Architectural design of the US approach

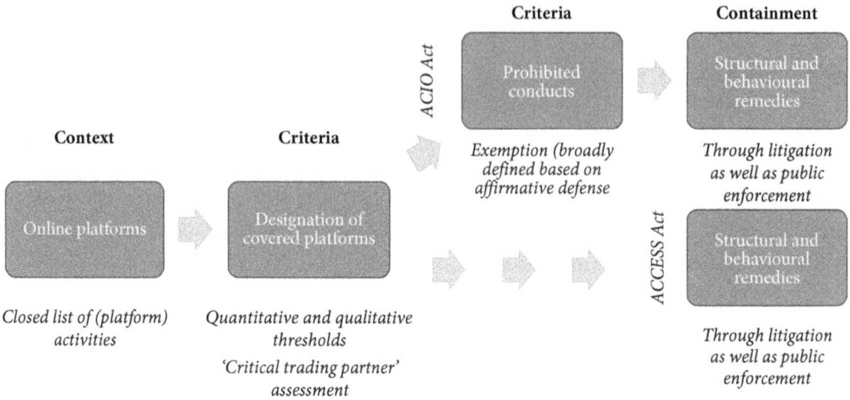

and exemptions, one can question what makes interoperability distinctive in terms of the policy objectives.[97]

Overall, the two-pronged US approach means structural complexity, considering that key signposts of the 'criteria' chain are bypassed moving towards the remedy design under the proposed ACCESS Act. This approach, in contrast with the ACIO Act, means absent well-elaborated inner boundaries as well as guiding principles and criteria under this chain. This refers to a situation, as in the EU's DMA, there is no substantiated link between the chains of 'context' and 'containment', when it comes to the proposed ACCESS Act. All the US bills nevertheless mark a distinction from the EU approach as they aim to effectuate regulatory dialogue with the stakeholders and include a reversal of the burden of proof, ie when the exemption is likely or review of the obligations is required.

6. Conclusion

6.1. Summary and Main Findings

Economic regulation means direct intervention into decisions by market players concerning market entry or exit, pricing, product features, etc to optimise the welfare gains, most often by mimicking a competitive market. The presence of policy objectives and achievable outcomes along with inter-connected chains of 'context', 'criteria', and 'containment', as discussed in this chapter, appear to be the

[97] For instance, according to the proposed ACCESS Act, s 6(c)(1): 'After designating an online platform as a covered platform, the Commission shall issue standards of interoperability specific to the covered platform.' This and other proposed measures under the ACCESS Act can be criticised given the directly applicable obligations based on interoperability standards and their implications.

key drivers for a well-functioning economic regulation. From this point of view, this study examines the policy approaches of the EU, UK, and US regarding regulation of digital markets, based on a three-step analysis embodying the so-called chains.

Inter-connection of these chains cuts across the regulatory design and structure to deal with the existing challenges of digital markets including market failures. These chains, when coherently designed and integrated to each other, can play a significant role in building up a sustainable and well-functioning model of economic regulation. This suggests a well-elaborated regulatory design – together with substantiated links and inner boundaries across the sequential chains – is key to a promising model of digital markets regulation.

However, in the EU case, as Figure 10.2 demonstrates, *cross links* and the *inner boundaries* of the chains are fraught with structural gaps and deficiencies. The former problem results from the absence of a chain (of criteria) between 'context' and 'containment', whereas the latter surfaces within the expansive regulatory approach, for example through designation of CPSs, gatekeepers, and newly prohibited practices and obligations, posing unpredictabilities. Lack of 'regulatory dialogue', 'reversed burden of proof', and 'guiding principles' should be noted as additional sources of concern, discrediting the high-level goals and intentions of the EU policy makers. The feedback effect as illustrated in Figure 10.2, although helpful to filter and find out the Type I and II errors, should not be expected to reverse this structural deficiency, overall.

The UK approach well represents a contrary situation, whereby one can witness a good combination of regulatory commitment and flexibility with a view to responding to market failures. This mainly stems from the policy objectives, milestones, and outcomes being linked to each other, along with well-established safeguards and checks and balances as well as guiding principles. In the proposed regime, all the chains appear to be flexibly set to enable adjustment of the conduct requirements and remedies in view of the business models. Although some uncertainties exist within the inner boundaries of the chains, eg regarding how to apply the principles under each high-level objective, the substantiated links across the chains and their overall coherency promise a good example of economic regulation model. To reinforce the proposed regulatory system with far more settled inner boundaries, the UK parliament should firmly reflect on the CMA advice and market study in the legislative process.

One can spot similarities between the UK and US policy approaches, particularly in view of the sequential and inter-connected chains of economic regulation. Except under the proposed ACCESS Act, no direct consequence is attributed to meeting the thresholds, and covered platforms are subjected to certain prohibitions to be followed by the tailorable remedies. Under the chain of 'criteria', a larger room is visible for the exemption based on the so-called 'affirmative defense', as in the UK approach. Yet, we do not know the extent to which there will be differentiation across the covered platforms concerning the prohibited conducts. This uncertainty needs to be underlined for the proposed ACCESS Act where substantiated links do not exist across the chains of 'context' and 'containment'. In fact, the direct link between such chains, namely meeting the thresholds of being a 'covered platform' and the obligations would cause a fragile structure and the likelihood of regulatory vacuum. With similarities to the EU approach, this situation would lead to unpredictability and potential in regulatory engineering.

6.2. Why Does the Compass of Economic Regulation Point to the UK?

Given the policy approaches of the EU, UK, and US, architectural elements in each approach altogether offers a comparative viewpoint as to digital markets regulation from the perspective of economic regulation manifested here, ie based on the chains of 'context', 'criteria', and 'containment'. From this point of view, one can trace the effective and robust system of the UK approach in its proposed regime based on coherent and inter-connected chains of economic regulation enabling a sufficient degree of predictability as well as flexibility. Lack of some details in this proposed system does not seem to create a significant gap or deficiency for the sound structure including a number of safeguards and also checks and balances, as well as guiding principles.

There are distinctive features of the UK approach that are noteworthy here. First and foremost, the UK approach rests on a principles-based regulatory regime and bottom-up approach, which signifies a coherent and systemic understanding of economic regulation. At this notion and structure lie the well-elaborated and designed chains of economic regulation, which needs to be highlighted as a core aspect of the UK approach. For instance, the test of 'adverse effect on competition' which should be met for the PCIs not only bridges the 'containment' to the previous chain of 'criteria' but also reinforces better economic regulation against market failures including structural problems. Closely related to this, one can derive that all the sequential links build on the thrust of creating competitive digital markets which can be identified as another significant aspect guiding the UK system towards achievable outcomes. Finally, under the proposed regime, wide-ranging tools and remedies are set out, demonstrating a commitment to apply the PCIs, although the flexibility through the regulatory system is also kept on with many details being left to the DMU. From this point of view, the UK approach can be deemed a successful example of combining regulatory commitment with regulatory flexibility.

The EU's DMA system embodies various gaps and unpredictabilities, which are closely related to the so-called chains lacking well-elaborated cross links and inner boundaries. This would arguably be diminished in time with the feedback effect based on the investigative tools and the implementing and delegated acts. However, the structure of the DMA does not allow enough room for regulatory experimentation that can effectively dissipate the concerns of regulatory engineering. Such concerns are less relevant in the US approach, which erects more signposts for the stakeholders and greater room for differentiation, if not equally across the two proposed acts. In this regard, the US stays in between the EU and UK. While the US policy approach – particularly looking into the proposed ACIO Act – has key similarities with that of the UK, the latter marks a more coherent and promising model given its bottom-up approach including the bespoke codes of conduct and trialling and iterating type novel remedies.

Overall, as the UK approach suggests, substantiated links within and across the chains would enable robust models of economic regulation, mitigating potential gaps and uncertainties. Without such an architecture as well as the guiding principles and outcomes, the intended results from a digital markets regulation would not be achieved as expected. Given this, the existing policy approaches for digital markets regulation, particularly those in the EU and US, should be reconsidered from the viewpoint of economic regulation based on the three-chain architecture manifested above.

11

Assessment of AI-enabled Price Discrimination under Competition Law in China

QIAN LI AND NIELS PHILIPSEN

1. Introduction

In digital markets, the rise of business models based on the collection and processing of consumer data allows undertakings to charge business customers and final consumers different prices for the same goods or services, offered at precisely the same time. Concentrated big data and accurate algorithms as analytical tools enable undertakings to predict each consumer's willingness to pay with increasing accuracy and thereby offer consumers personalised recommendations and tailored prices. In this context, concerns have arisen about the possibility and consequence of AI-enabled price discrimination (AIPD) as an abuse of dominance employed by dominant Big Techs in digital markets. The central question of this chapter is therefore whether and when AIPD amounts to an abuse of dominance under competition law, and how Chinese competition authorities respond to this challenge in digital markets.

From an economic perspective, AIPD is not always undesirable. In digital markets, AIPD makes economic sense as it can increase static efficiency, and under certain market conditions, it can promote dynamic efficiency as well as boost consumer welfare.[1] Nevertheless, it may create exclusionary and/or exploitative effects if Big Techs abuse their dominant market positions. Other than those based on efficiency, it may also trigger fairness and distributional concerns. Since the protection of competition on the merits and consumer welfare are the objective of Chinese Anti-Monopoly Law,[2] it makes sense for the intervention of competition law to tackle the concerns caused by anticompetitive AIPD.

[1] Q Li, N Philipsen, and C Cauffman, 'AI-enabled Price Discrimination as an Abuse of Dominance: A Law and Economics Analysis' (2023) *China-EU Law Journal*, Vol. 9, p. 51–72. (published online 27 April 2023), https://doi.org/10.1007/s12689-023-00099-z.

[2] *Anti-Monopoly Law of the People's Republic of China* [中华人民共和国反垄断法], promulgated on 30 August 2007, amended on 24 June 2022 and enacted on 1 August 2022 (AML); Art 1 AML.

In China, price discrimination falls within the scope of Chinese competition law and would be considered a possible abuse of dominance within the meaning of Article 22 of the Anti-Monopoly Law (AML).[3] To answer questions raised previously, when and whether AIPD amounts to an abuse of dominance under competition law requires competition authorities to assess AIPD carefully and make a trade-off between different considerations. The question of how Chinese competition authorities respond to this challenge in digital markets to achieve the goals of competition law will be examined in more detail in this chapter.

China seems to provide adequate possibilities in competition law to address concerns caused by anticompetitive AIPD, at least on paper. Article 22(1)(6) AML challenges the discriminatory treatment engaged in by a dominant undertaking, while Article 22(1)(1) AML prohibits abusive conduct which imposes unfairly high or low prices, without the conditions of Article 22(1)(6) AML being satisfied.[4] The Guidelines on the Platform Economy[5] and the Regulation of Algorithm Recommendations for Internet Information Services[6] also provide guidelines to tackle anticompetitive AIPD. The roadmap of this chapter is therefore as follows. After this introduction, section 2 qualifies AIPD as discriminatory treatment under Chinese competition law while section 3 evaluates AIPD as unfair pricing to address concerns caused by anticompetitive AIPD. Section 4 discusses AIPD as an algorithm recommendation service in digital markets. Then section 5 provides the path ahead to tackle anticompetitive AIPD in the digital era.

2. AIPD as Discriminatory Treatment

Anticompetitive AIPD may amount to differential treatment under Article 22(1)(6) AML when an undertaking with a dominant market position applies discriminatory treatments on trading prices or other trading conditions to their trading parties with equivalent conditions without any justifiable reasons.[7] In this section, we assume that the involved undertakings do indeed have dominant market positions and discuss how to qualify AIPD as discriminatory treatment under the AML.

[3] Art 22 AML.

[4] Art 22(1)(7) AML also provides the general prohibition of abusive conduct as determined by the Anti-monopoly Law Enforcement Agency under the State Council.

[5] *Anti-monopoly Guidelines of the Anti-monopoly Committee of the State Council on the Platform Economy* [国务院反垄断委员会关于平台经济领域的反垄断指南] ('Guidelines on the Platform Economy').

[6] Regulation of Algorithm Recommendations for Internet Information Services [互联网信息服务算法推荐管理规定] ('Administration Regulation of Algorithm Recommendations').

[7] Art 22(1)(6) AML.

2.1. Identifying 'Trading Parties' in Digital Markets

Article 22(1)(6) AML keeps silent as to whether 'trading parties' includes both industrial customers and final consumers. Since the legal text of the AML is mainly borrowed from the EU,[8] China may learn lessons from the EU. In the EU, Article 102(c) of the Treaty on the Functioning of the European Union (TFEU) prohibits dominant undertakings from 'applying dissimilar conditions to equivalent transactions with other trading parties' and further requires this conduct to 'thereby [place] them at a competitive disadvantage'. As such, scholars generally argue that 'trading parties' include industrial customers but exclude final consumers, since final consumers are not literally competing with each other. However, despite the settled EU case law considering only industrial customers as 'trading parties', those cases also do not require proof of 'placing them at a competitive disadvantage'.[9] In this sense, it is possible to include final consumers as 'trading parties' within the meaning of Article 102(c) TFEU.

When seeking arguments from literature, scholars usually compare the legal text of the AML with US and EU competition law and seek inspiration to understand terms in the AML such as 'trading parties'. For instance, Xu Guangyao argues that although price discrimination has two possible adverse consequences (one is to damage competition, mainly referring to the exclusion of competitors; the other is to exploit consumers, as some of them have to pay a higher price), competition law in the US, EU, and China does not directly focus on the interests of consumers but protects the interests of consumers by protecting competition.[10] In the US, the Robinson-Patman Act applies to both Type I price discrimination, which excludes the seller's competitors in upstream markets, and Type II price discrimination, which excludes some of the seller's customers and benefits others. In the EU, Article 102(c) TFEU seems to focus only on Type II price discrimination in the formulation of the legal text, but its case law is not limited to this. Article 102(c) TFEU is often applied in cases of Type I price discrimination, thus being substantially consistent with the understanding of US law. In China, Article 22 AML targets both two types of price discrimination on the ground of the formulation of Article 22(1)(6) AML.[11] According to Xu, final consumers are excluded from the protection of competition law as 'trading parties' when encountering price discrimination. However, it is possible that a large number of final consumers are

[8] See A Bradford and others, 'The Global Dominance of European Competition Law over U.S. Antitrust Law' (2019) 16 *Journal of Empirical Legal Studies* 731, 766.

[9] For example, see Case C-95/04 P *British Airways plc v Commission* EU:C:2007:166, paras 144–45. See also Case T-301/04 *Clearstream Banking AG and Clearstream International SA v Commission* EU:T:2009:317, para 194.

[10] G Xu [许光耀], 'Anti-Monopoly Analysis on Price Discrimination' [价格歧视行为的反垄断法分析] (2021) 11 *Law Science Magazine* [法学杂志], 21, 22.

[11] ibid.

subject to price discrimination in downstream markets and that these consumers thereby suffer losses, particularly in bilateral digital markets in which business-to-business and business-to-consumer relationships coexist.

The formulation of Article 22(1)(6) AML is rather clear as it prohibits dominant undertakings from 'applying discriminatory treatments on trading prices or other trading conditions to their trading parties with equivalent conditions without any justifiable reasons'. Unlike Article 102(c) TFEU, this formulation does not require the price discrimination in question conducted by the involved dominant undertaking to place other trading parties at a competitive disadvantage. As such, this provision covers both exclusionary price discrimination and exploitative price discrimination. Therefore, it makes sense to include both industrial customers and final consumers in Article 22(1)(6) AML and apply this provision to evaluate AIPD in digital markets.

This has been confirmed by a judicial interpretation by the Supreme People's Court, namely, the Provisions on Several Issues Concerning the Application of Law in Trial of Civil Dispute Cases Arising from Monopolistic Acts of 2012.[12] The AML Judicial Interpretation aims to properly adjudicate civil dispute cases arising from monopolistic acts, curb monopolistic acts, protect and promote fair competition in the market, and safeguard the interests of consumers and the public interests of society.[13]

Article 1 states that 'the civil dispute cases arising from monopolistic acts refer to the cases of natural persons, legal persons or other organisations who have suffered losses due to monopolistic acts as well as disputes arising from the contents of contracts, the constitution of trade associations, etc in violation of the AML. As such, natural persons who suffer losses due to monopolistic acts are eligible to bring lawsuits before the courts. According to Article 2 of the *AML Judicial Interpretation*, 'if the plaintiff files a civil lawsuit directly before the people's court, or files a civil lawsuit before the people's court after the decision of the AML Enforcement Agency has taken legal effect, and if the other conditions of admissibility stipulated by law are met, the people's court shall accept it'.[14] Therefore, if the interested legal persons and natural persons suffer losses due to monopolistic acts, they are entitled to file lawsuits before the court with other conditions being met.

There are cases in which final consumers directly file lawsuits against dominant undertakings according to the AML. In the *Tong Hua vs China Mobile Group Shanghai Co, Ltd*[15] case, the defendant in its standard contract promised to keep the plaintiff's mobile phone number active for a 90-day retention period, but terminated and cancelled it, and then used a number with a 60-day retention period to

[12] Provisions on Several Issues Concerning the Application of Law in Trial of Civil Dispute Cases Arising from Monopolistic Acts [关于审理因垄断行为引发的民事纠纷案件应用法律若干问题的规定] ('AML Judicial Interpretation').

[13] Preamble, AML Judicial Interpretation.

[14] Art 2, AML Judicial Interpretation.

[15] *Tong Hua v China Mobile Group Shanghai Co, Ltd* [2014] Civil Judgment, Second Instance, Shanghai High People's Court, no 105.

replace the original 90-day retention period number. The plaintiff claimed that this misbehaviour of the defendant was an abuse of market dominance in the form of refusal to trade and discriminatory treatment, which thereby caused losses to the plaintiff. The court in the first instance found that the defendant's conduct did not amount to an abuse of a dominant position and therefore dismissed the plaintiff's claim. Tong Hua appealed to the Shanghai High Court against the judgment of the first instance. The Shanghai High Court upheld the judgment of the first instance and dismissed the appellant Tong Hua's appeal request.

In the first instance, the court judged the eligibility of the plaintiff according to Article 1 of the AML Judicial Interpretation. This article indicates that civil monopoly dispute cases include two basic types: lawsuits arising from damages suffered as a result of monopolistic acts; and lawsuits arising from disputes over the content of contracts, the constitution of trade associations, etc, which violate the AML. In this case, the plaintiff suffered losses as a result of the defendant's monopolistic act, that is, abusing its dominance to terminate and cancel the mobile phone number involved in the case within the 90-day retention period, and replace it with a 60-day retention period. This has been confirmed by the court of appeal, the Shanghai High Court, which clarified that the appellant was actually claiming that he suffered losses due to the appellee's monopolistic behaviour abusing its dominant market position.

As indicated in this case, the court has confirmed the eligibility of natural persons who have suffered losses due to monopolistic acts to file lawsuits. Therefore, both industrial customers and final consumers are entitled to file lawsuits when they suffer losses caused by monopolistic behaviour by other undertakings. It is noteworthy that the burden of proof lies on the plaintiff to provide evidence regarding the loss caused by the defendant's monopolistic behaviour. Due to information asymmetry between final consumers and dominant undertakings, it is challenging for final consumers to take the burden of proof in digital markets, in particular since dominant undertakings are supported by a large volume of data and complicated algorithms. This to some extent explains why Tong Hua's claim was dismissed after two instances.

2.2. Identifying 'Equivalent Conditions' in Digital Markets

Article 22(1)(6) AML does not explicitly define the term 'equivalent conditions'. Nevertheless, the Provisions on Prohibiting Abuse of Dominant Market Position (hereinafter, the Provisions) are formulated according to the AML to prevent and curb abuse of dominance based on the enforcement experience and market reality.[16] Article 19 clarifies that 'equivalent conditions' refers to 'trading parties [having] no differences that substantively affect transactions between the trading

[16] Art 1, the Provisions.

parties in terms of transaction security, transaction cost, scale and capability, credit status, transaction process, duration of the transaction, and other respects'.[17]

Traditionally, scholars interpret 'equivalent conditions' in the manner that the goods or services provided by undertakings are of the same quality, condition, grade, model, etc.[18] In this sense, whether large wholesalers and retailers, supermarkets and retailers, are on the same competitive terms should be judged on a case-by-case basis in the relevant market.[19] Furthermore, according to Xu Guangyao, the 'same specification and quality of products' produced by the same seller generally have the same production costs, but this wording does not clearly cover transaction costs.[20] Even if two transactions involve products of the same grade and quality, prices may differ if their costs of sale (including advertising costs, transportation costs, etc) are different and this may not be considered price discrimination as long as the seller receives the same return from both buyers.[21]

As such, scholars argue that the 'equivalent conditions' of goods can be determined in terms of the physical characteristics of the goods and the transaction costs.[22] One factor is to compare the physical characteristics of goods purchased by different trading parties to the transaction, including elements such as the function, quality, quantity, and use of the goods, while the other is to examine the transaction costs paid to complete the purchase, including elements such as price paid, method of payment, level of taxes and fees, and transportation costs.[23] Regarding the 'equivalent transaction' for the provision of services, it is possible to compare events that significantly affect transaction costs during the particular time period in which the service is provided.[24]

Those factors are still applicable to assess AIPD in digital markets. This has been confirmed by the Guidelines on the Platform Economy, which (as mentioned above) have been developed according to the AML to prevent monopolistic conduct and protect fair market competition in the platform economy. The Platform Guidelines provide a similar definition to the one in the Interim Provisions, which states 'no differences between trading parties that substantively affect trading in trading security, trading cost, credit status, trading link, trading duration, and other respects'.[25]

[17] Art 19, the Provisions.

[18] See M Xu and Y Meng [徐孟洲,孟雁北], *The Competition Law* [竞争法], (3rd edn, China Renmin University Press 2018) 167. See also J Sun [孙晋], *Anti-monopoly Law-Institutions and Principles* [反垄断法-制度与原理] (Wuhan University Press 2010) 105.

[19] J Wu [吴炯], *Interpretation of the Anti-Monopoly Law of the People's Republic of China* [中华人民共和国反垄断法解读] (Beijing, China Industry and Commerce Press, 2007) 96.

[20] See n 10 above.

[21] See n 10 above.

[22] W Zhou [周围], 'Anti-Monopoly Regulation of Personalized Pricing Algorithms in the Age of Artificial Intelligence' [人工智能时代个性化定价算法的反垄断法规制] (2020) 74 *Wuhan University Journal* (Philosophy and Social Science Edition) [武汉大学学报(哲学社会科学版)] 108, 115.

[23] ibid.

[24] ibid.

[25] Art 7, Guidelines on the Platform Economy.

In digital markets, technological interoperability and market integration between online and offline markets has been achieved, but information asymmetry still exists between the two markets.[26] As a result, undertakings are able to take advantage of this asymmetry to personalise pricing for consumers who do not have relevant information or have high search costs. As such, the *Platform Guidelines* further clarify that 'the differences in privacy information, transaction history, individual preferences and consumption habits of the trading parties obtained by the platform during the transaction do not affect the determination of the equivalent conditions of trading parties'.[27]

The decisions made by the competition authorities can provide some clues to determine whether the discriminatory treatment is under equivalent conditions. In 2014, the Pizhou Branch of Xuzhou Tobacco Company ('Xuzhou Tobacco') was fined by the Jiangsu Administration for Industry and Commerce for abuse of dominance through discriminatory treatment.[28] Xuzhou Tobacco had a dominant market position in the Pizhou tobacco wholesale market and took advantage of its dominant market position to implement discriminatory treatment of the trading parties under equivalent conditions. Xuzhou Tobacco applied a customer management system of the tobacco industry to classify its cigarette retailers based on the dimensions of retail format, market type, and business scale, and supplied cigarettes to retailers through an automatic distribution mechanism. Three branches of Jinying Company and two branches of Huanlemai Company were direct-to-consumer retailers and were classified as 'KA' customers. They all signed the KA type of customer management service agreement with the same text and assumed the same rights and obligations as agreed in the agreement. However, Xuzhou Tobacco treated three branches of Jinying Company more favourably with regard to the frequency to order cigarettes and the quantity of 'the most popular cigarette' distributed through the online ordering system (xz-eb.js.tobacco.cn). As such, the trading parties as industrial customers were considered as being under equivalent conditions but encountered different treatment when making transactions.

The judgment of the court can also provide some inspiration to define trading parties under equivalent conditions. In the *Wang Xinyu v China Telecom Co, Ltd, Xuzhou Branch*[29] case, the plaintiff, Wang Xinyu, a student enrolled in the China University of Mining and Technology in 2012, claimed that the defendant, China Telecom applied discriminatory treatment to him regarding his mobile phone package compared with other users by abusing its dominance, but his claim was dismissed after the trial by the court. In 2013, the plaintiff had participated in the defendant's 'Tianyi Mobile "Top-up+Sign-up" 3G smartphone payment reduction

[26] See n 22 above.

[27] Art 7, Guidelines on the Platform Economy.

[28] Administrative Penalty on Abuse of Market Dominance by Pizhou Branch of Xuzhou Tobacco Company in Jiangsu Province [2014] Announcement of Competition Law Enforcement, no 18.

[29] *Wang Xinyu v China Telecom Co, Ltd Xuzhou Branch* [2014] Civil Judgment, First instance, Nanjing Intermediate People's Court, no 256.

promotion' and selected a package with minimum monthly price of RMB79, including 400 SMS messages, 300 minutes of calls, 820M of mobile internet data, 126 hours of broadband and 600 minutes of local calls within the campus group, and bought one mobile phone at a discounted price. In September 2014, the price and content of the same type of promotion launched by the defendant changed, with a minimum monthly price of RMB59 (with a monthly rebate of RMB10) for a package that included 140 minutes of calls, 3G internet data, 240 SMS messages, 600 minutes of local in-group calls, 220 hours of broadband, and a top-up bonus on the purchase of a mobile phone.

During September to November 2014, the plaintiff asked to extend the broadband hours in the original package to 300 hours per month to match the then newly launched package for the freshman class of 2014, but the defendant required the plaintiff to pay an RMB400 telephone fee before extending it, to which the plaintiff complied. However, in mid-October 2014, upon the plaintiff's inquiry at China Telecom's business office, the plaintiff became aware that users who were then using the RMB79 package with 120 hours broadband were not required to pay or top up any fees to extend their broadband hours to 300 hours per month, which was in line with the current RMB49 package, and this seemed unfair to the plaintiff. The plaintiff therefore asked the court to rule that the defendant must cease the monopolistic act of abusing its dominant market position to operate unduly differential treatment, change the content of the plaintiff's original RMB79 package to the RMB49 package sold in September 2014, and pay the plaintiff RMB60 for the overpayment of the package for the two months from September–November 2014.

The court held that the dispute was whether the defendant was an undertaking with a dominant market position and had committed an abuse of a dominant market position by applying differential treatment in terms of trading conditions, such as price, to trading parties under equivalent conditions, without justifiable reasons. The court defined the relevant market as the comprehensive telecommunication business service in the Xuzhou Campus of the China University of Mining and Technology. The court found that the proof provided by the plaintiff could not prove the defendant's dominant market position and its abusive conduct by discriminatory treatment.

When assessing whether the defendant conducted discriminatory treatment, the court interpreted that the counterparty to transactions under equivalent conditions, without a clear explanation in the law, generally refers to the counterparty who trades or prepares to trade with the undertaking at the same time and whose own conditions and needs are basically the same. In this case, when consumers plan to choose comprehensive telecommunications services, they can choose to accept the services of the defendant in this case, or they can choose the services provided by other undertakings. Furthermore, consumers can choose the package services and different price levels provided by undertakings such as the defendant, or they can choose billing services directly without choosing a package. Moreover, consumers can choose both the campus package involved in this case and other packages that are not targeted at students. As such, given the variety of packages available, the circumstances and needs of each consumer are not the same and the conditions cannot of course be the same, so the defendant cannot be a counterparty to all consumers under equivalent conditions, but only to those consumers who have all joined or intend to join the defendant's campus package at the same time.

From the evidence provided by the parties, the comprehensive telecommunications service operators, including the defendant, launch packages that are not identical in price and content to the previous packages every once in a while, with eligibility conditional upon the consumer not being enrolled in the previous package or after the expiry of the term of the previous package. When the plaintiff requested to change the package, the performance period of the plaintiff's package agreement had not expired, and the purchase subsidy paid by the defendant in advance had not been made up. If the agreement between the two parties had been cancelled or changed at this time, the interests of the two parties would be unbalanced and the interests of the defendant would be damaged. As such, during the period of its package agreement, the transaction conditions of the plaintiff and the counterparty who had signed up to the aforementioned packages, especially the September 2014 package, were not the same, and the two were not counterparties with the same conditions.

Therefore, according to the court, there were legitimate and lawful reasons for the defendant to adjust the price and content of its packages over time. The plaintiff and the consumers who joined the September 2014 package were not counterparties to the transaction under equivalent conditions, and the defendant's reduction of the price of the September 2014 package was not an abuse of a dominant market position in the form of price discrimination. This result leaves space for undertakings to set prices and conduct economic activities under their own autonomy.

2.3. Defining 'Discriminatory Treatment' in Digital Markets

Article 19 of the Provisions specifies the 'discriminatory treatment' in the form of (1) implementing different transaction prices, volumes, varieties, and quality grades; (2) implementing different volume-based discounts and other preferential conditions; (3) implementing different terms of payment and modes of delivery; (4) implementing different contents and terms of warranty, contents and terms of maintenance, supply of spare parts, technical guidance, and other after-sales service conditions.[30] In digital markets, Article 17 of the *Guidelines on the Platform Economy* articulates the factors to be considered when assessing discriminatory treatment, which include but are not limited to '(1) applying discriminatory transaction prices or other transaction conditions based on big data and algorithms and in accordance with the payment capacity, consumption preference and usage habits

[30] Art 19, the Provisions.

of the trading parties; (2) applying discriminatory standards, rules and algorithms; and (3) applying discriminatory payment terms and transaction methods'.[31]

According to scholars such as Xu Guangyao, 'discriminatory treatment' refers to the price conditions of the transaction as well as other conditions beyond the price, such as terms of transport, place of transaction, mode of delivery, mode of payment, etc, which creates the effects of price discrimination.[32] For instance, if a seller offers transport services to one buyer but not to another, the effect is the same as lowering the price for the former.[33] However, if the former buyer has to pay the full cost of transport, the rate of return to the seller from the two transactions is not different and is therefore not price discrimination.[34] Furthermore, scholars argue that price discrimination is the main form of discriminatory treatment, where a seller demands a different price from a buyer of the same grade or quality of goods, or where a buyer pays a different price to a seller who offers the same grade or quality of goods so that the difference in price paid by the seller to the buyer, or by the buyer to the seller leads to different trading opportunities and thereby has a direct impact on fair competition between them.[35]

Private enforcement can provide some inspiration to evaluate discriminatory treatment. Although the court judged the *Liu Quan v Beijing Sankuai Technology Co, Ltd* case[36] on the ground of tort law and did not deal with the plaintiff's claim based on the AML, the decision can provide some clues to assess equivalent transactions in digital markets. In the *Liu Quan v Beijing Sankuai* case, the plaintiff, Liu Quan ordered a set meal at 11.55am on 19 July 2018, through the Meituan food delivery platform operated by the defendant, Sankuai. At 12.08pm on the same day, a colleague of Liu Quan ordered the same set meal from the same restaurant on the platform. The delivery address was the same, but the delivery fee was 1 yuan less than Liu Quan's. The plaintiff, Liu Quan claimed that Sankuai took advantage of the industry monopoly and the technical means of 'exploiting consumers through Big Data' to offer discriminatory pricing, which violated Liu Quan's legitimate rights and infringed the relevant provisions of the AML.

The defendant disagreed with the alleged price discrimination and argued that the delivery fee of an order is not a fixed value, but a variable value based on a variety of factors in the business district where the restaurant is located at a certain time, such as the number of riders and the riders' willingness to take orders. The background platform log provided by Sankuai showed that the business district involved in Liu Quan's order began to rise sharply at 11.47am on the same day, and the delivery fee rose dynamically. After 11.57am, the sharp rise in orders ended and the delivery fee dynamic returned to a normal level. As such, Sankuai

[31] Art 7, Guidelines on the Platform Economy.
[32] See n 10 above.
[33] See n 10 above.
[34] See n 10 above.
[35] Sun [孙晋] (n 18) 105.
[36] *Liu Quan v Beijing Sankuai Technology Co, Ltd* [2019] Civil Judgment, first instance, People's Court of Furong District, Changsha City, Hunan Province, no 13515.

increased the delivery fee by one yuan. In addition, Liu Quan received compensation of 3.02 yuan for the 'on-time delivery' guarantee service purchased by Liu Quan, which also proved that his order on that day was in a state of 'explosion', and the order placed by Liu Quan was not placed at the same time as his colleague, so the delivery fee was not comparable.

The court judged this case based on tort liability law. The court held that, despite the two orders mentioned by Liu Quan being the same as far as the restaurant, product, and delivery address were concerned, the time of placing the orders was inconsistent. Sankuai dynamically adjusted the delivery fee according to the platform transaction volume, which was its own business behaviour and did not infringe Liu Quan's rights. As such, the court held that timing as a variable made the transactions inequivalent in this case and did not agree that dynamic pricing amounts to discriminatory treatment. Furthermore, despite Liu Quan claiming that the behaviour of Sankuai involved violations of the AML, the court stated that this issue did not fall within the scope of this court's review, and therefore did not deal with it.

In this case, we can observe that the court understands the mechanism of economic activities in digital markets by allowing the cost justifiable price differences during the transactions, which is in line with the essence of price discrimination in economics. In the meantime, we can also see the heavy burden of proof laid down on the plaintiff and the challenge to identify discriminatory treatment under equivalent transactions and prove the misconduct of the defendant in digital markets. In digital markets, transactions vary from each other, particularly with the support of big data and algorithms. Therefore, there are multiple factors to determine whether the involved transactions are equivalent. As such, a case-by-case analysis is necessary for the assessment of discriminatory treatment in equivalent transactions.

2.4. Objective Justification for Discriminatory Treatment in Digital Markets

The Provisions provide general guidance to apply objective justifications when assessing price discrimination, while the Guidelines on the Platform Economy specify this application, particularly in digital markets. According to Article 19 of the Provisions, the objective justification includes:

> (1) implementing different terms of the transaction on the basis of the actual needs of transaction counterparties and in compliance with the justified transaction habits and industry practices; (2) preferential promotion offers for the first transactions of new users within a reasonable period of time; (3) implementing random transactions based on fair, reasonable and non-discriminatory platform rules; and (4) other reasons that can justify the acts.[37]

[37] Art 19, the Provisions.

In digital markets, the Platform Guidelines add one more justified reason when 'implementing random trading under the rules of fairness, rationality, and non-discrimination'.[38] Furthermore, regarding 'preferential promotion offers within a reasonable period of time', the Platform Guidelines require preferential promotion offers 'to new users' rather than limit them in the 'first transactions to new users'.[39]

When evaluating the objective justification, there are factors the competition authorities should take into account. Article 22 of the Provisions stipulates seven factors, which are:

> (1) whether the conduct in question is prescribed in laws and regulations; (2) the impact of the conduct in question on security and cybersecurity; (3) the impact of the conduct in question on economic operational efficiency and economic development; (4) whether the conduct in question is required for the regular business operation of the undertakings and the realization of its regular efficiency; (5) the impact of the conduct in question on undertakings' business development, future investment and innovation; (6) whether the conduct in question can benefit the transaction counterparties or consumers; (7) the impact of the conduct in question on social public interests.[40]

Indeed, since those factors are ambiguous, objective justifications should be considered on a case-by-case basis.

In the *Xuzhou Tobacco* case, the competition authorities found no objective justification for the discriminatory treatment exercised by Xuzhou Tobacco.[41] On the one hand, the supply policy of the tobacco industry per se could not justify the discriminatory treatment. Even if it is justifiable, the principle of fairness was deviated as to Xuzhou Tobacco treating 'KA' customers differently, specifically through manually restricting the quantity of 'the most popular cigarette' distributed to branches of Huanlemai Company through the online ordering system. On the other hand, the claim that Jinying Company should be treated favourably due to its strong business ability and large sales volume of cigarettes in history was also untenable, since Jinying Company was controlled by Xuzhou Tobacco and the large sales volume was more dependent on the supply preference of Xuzhou Tobacco, rather than its business ability and market competitiveness.

However, as shown in the *Wang Xinyu v China Telecom*[42] case, undertakings are entitled to adjust the price and content of products and services over time based on actual needs. The full service telecommunications service operators, including the defendant, may launch packages that are not identical in price and content to the previous packages every once in a while, the inclusion of which is conditional upon the consumer not being enrolled in the previous package or the expiry of

[38] Art 17, Guidelines on the Platform Economy.
[39] Art 17, Guidelines on the Platform Economy.
[40] Art 20, the Provisions.
[41] Administrative Penalty on Abuse of Market Dominance by Pizhou Branch of Xuzhou Tobacco Company in Jiangsu Province [2014] Announcement of Competition Law Enforcement, no 18.
[42] *Wang Xinyu v China Telecom Co, Ltd Xuzhou Branch* [2014] Civil Judgment, First instance, Nanjing Intermediate People's Court, no 256.

the term of the previous package. Since the performance period of the plaintiff's package agreement had not expired, and the purchase subsidy paid by the defendant in advance had not been made up, the interests of the two parties would be unbalanced and the interests of the defendant would be damaged if the agreement between the two parties was cancelled or changed before its termination. As such, undertakings enjoy the freedom to adjust the products and services based on social needs and the market reality. This provides evidence for Article 19(1) Interim Provisions as 'implementing different terms of the transaction based on the actual needs of transaction counterparties and in compliance with the justified transaction habits and industry practices'.

3. AIPD as Unfair Pricing

Article 22(1)(1) AML may provide an alternative to tackle AIPD as unfair pricing. In digital markets, the specific evaluation of 'unfair pricing' and its 'objective justification' should be clarified to seek the possibilities to tackle AIPD.

3.1. Defining Unfair Pricing in Digital Markets

Article 22(1)(1) AML prohibits undertakings with a dominant market position from selling products at unfairly high prices or buying products at unfairly low prices.[43] The undertakings involved are assumed to hold dominant market conditions in the relevant market. The abuse of dominance (in the manner of 'unfair pricing') may lead to exclusionary or exploitative effects, since the stronger the market power, the stronger the possibilities of undertakings to hinder market competition. As such, it is important to determine whether the price is 'unfair' and whether it can be justified by the involved undertaking.

To determine whether the pricing is 'unfair', the Provisions provide guidance for the specific assessment. Article 14 Provisions clarify the factors to be considered in the determination of 'unfairly high price' or 'unfairly low price': (1) whether the selling price or purchasing price is significantly higher or lower than the price of the same or comparable goods sold or bought by other undertakings under the same or similar market conditions; (2) whether the selling or purchasing price is significantly higher or lower than the price of the goods sold or bought by the same undertaking in other regions with the same or similar market conditions; (3) whether the selling price is increased or the purchasing price is decreased beyond the reasonable range when the cost is stable; (4) whether the rate of price increase for goods sold is significantly higher than the rate of cost increase or the

[43] Art 22(1), AML.

rate of price reduction for goods purchased is significantly higher than the rate of cost reduction for the counterparty; and (5) other relevant factors that need to be considered.

From this provision, two approaches to determine whether the pricing is 'unfair' can be summarised. One approach is to compare the selling or purchasing pricing with the same or comparable goods, which includes (1) goods sold or bought by other undertakings under the same or similar market conditions, and (2) goods sold or bought by the same undertaking in other regions with the same or similar market conditions. The other approach is to compare the rate of price increase or the price decrease with the change range of the cost, which includes (1) the cost change rate of the involved undertaking itself, and (2) the cost change rate of the counterparties. As such, if industrial customers and final consumers find the price unfair, they can either compare the price in question with the comparable goods or compare the price change rate with the cost change rate.

The abovementioned two approaches to determine unfair pricing, which seem aimed at traditional offline markets, are also applicable in digital markets; however, the characteristics of the digital economy need to be taken into account. This has been confirmed by the Guidelines on the Platform Economy. Article 12 clarifies the factors to be considered to analyse unfair pricing in digital markets: (1) whether the price is significantly higher or lower than the price of the equivalent kind or comparable products of other similar undertakings under the equivalent or similar market conditions; (2) whether the price is significantly higher or lower than the price of the equivalent kind or comparable products of undertakings in the field of platform economy under the equivalent or similar market conditions; (3) whether an undertaking in the field of the platform economy raises selling price or reduces purchasing price beyond the reasonable range when the cost is stable; and (4) whether the prices of products sold by an undertaking in the field of the platform economy are raised significantly at a rate higher than the cost increasing rate, or the prices of products purchased are decreased significantly at a rate lower than the cost reducing rate.[44] In addition, considering the innovative characteristics of the digital markets, when determining the equivalent or similar market conditions, platform type, business model, trading links, cost structure, specific trading conditions, and other factors may be considered in general.[45]

3.2. Objective Justification for Unfair Pricing in Digital Markets

Considering the rapidly changing markets and the possibilities for market intervention, it is wise to provide options for dominant undertakings to justify their

[44] Art 12, Guidelines on the Platform Economy.
[45] Art 12, Guidelines on the Platform Economy.

behaviour. The AML is silent regarding the justification for unfair pricing. The Provisions provide basic principles to evaluate whether misbehaviour can be justified. Article 22 of the Provisions articulates that when determining 'unfair' and 'unjustified reasons', the competition authorities are to consider the following factors: (1) whether the relevant behaviours are prescribed in laws and regulations; (2) the impact of the relevant behaviours on security and cybersecurity; (3) the impact of the relevant behaviours on economic efficiency and economic development; (4) whether the relevant behaviours are required for undertakings' reasonable economic activities and realisation of reasonable benefits; (5) the impact of the relevant behaviours on undertakings' economic development, future investment, and innovation; (6) whether the relevant behaviours can benefit the trading parties or consumers; (7) the impact of the relevant behaviours on social public interests.[46]

As such, the Provisions leave space for undertakings to justify their activities. If the pricing is allowed in other laws and regulations, it can be justified, indeed. For the economic factors, the competition authorities should consider whether the pricing in question can improve economic efficiency and economic development; whether the pricing is required for undertakings' reasonable economic activities to make reasonable profits; whether the pricing serves for undertakings' economic development, future investment, and innovation; and whether it can benefit trading parties or consumers. For other considerations, whether the behaviour can be justified by social public interests seems ambiguous and requires multiple pieces of evidence for proof. These factors to be taken into account apply in both traditional markets and digital markets since they are the same transactional relationships in essence despite the different trading forms online and offline.

4. AIPD as an Algorithm Recommendation Service

In digital markets, there are also rules to tackle AIPD in specific industries, for instance, the Regulation of Algorithm Recommendations, jointly issued by the Cyberspace Administration of China, Ministry of Industry & Information Technology, Ministry of Public Security, and State Administration for Market Regulation (SAMR) to regulate algorithm-based recommendations for Internet information services, safeguard national security and public interests, protect the legal rights and interests of citizens, legal persons, and other organisations, and boost the sound and orderly development of Internet information services.[47] Article 2 applies to the provision of internet information services by applying recommendation algorithm technology within the territory of the People's Republic of China, unless otherwise provided for by laws or administrative regulations.[48]

[46] Art 20, the Provisions.
[47] Art 1, Regulation of Algorithm Recommendations.
[48] Art 2(1), Regulation of Algorithm Recommendations.

More specifically, 'applying recommendation algorithm technology' refers to applying generation and synthesis, personalised recommendations, sorting and filtering, scheduling decisions, and other algorithm technologies to provide information to users.[49] AIPD relies on big data analysis and algorithm-based personalised recommendations in pricing to estimate consumers' willingness to pay, which is supported by algorithm-based technology and may fall within the scope of this Regulation.

Article 21 articulates that algorithm-recommended service providers which sell goods or provide services to consumers must protect consumers' rights to fair transactions and must not use algorithms to commit unreasonable differential treatment and other illegal acts in respect of transaction prices and other transaction conditions based on their preferences, transaction practices, and other characteristics.[50] On the one hand, consumers are entitled to fair transactions when receiving goods or services from algorithm-recommended service providers. Those undertakings are not allowed to trade with consumers against their willingness despite the information advantage of algorithm-recommended service providers.

On the other hand, algorithm-recommended service providers are prohibited from unjustified discriminatory treatment in pricing based on consumers' preferences, transaction practices, and other characteristics. As we know, AIPD is to provide different consumers prices at (or close to) their personalised willingness to pay on the basis of consumers' personal characteristics. As long as undertakings have some element of market power in digital markets, they are able to exploit consumers by analysing consumers' personal information and offering personalised recommendations accordingly.

As such, this provision offers theoretical possibilities to tackle AIPD and protect consumers in digital markets. The Regulation of Algorithm Recommendations can capture algorithm-recommended services employed by both dominant and non-dominant undertakings, which serves as a supplement to the application of the AML to address concerns caused by AIPD.

5. Path Ahead to Tackle Anticompetitive AIPD

Although there have been no established cases of anticompetitive AIPD in China, China seems to provide adequate possibilities in competition law to address concerns caused by anticompetitive AIPD, at least on paper. If the alleged AIPD conducted by a dominant undertaking falls within the scope of Article 22 AML, the dominant undertaking is subject to sanctions including a cease-and-desist order, confiscating illegal gains and/or a fine of 1–10 per cent of the turnover in

[49] Art 2(2), Regulation of Algorithm Recommendations.
[50] Art 21, Regulation of Algorithm Recommendations.

the previous business year. Moreover, according to Article 54 AML, the undertaking in question can offer commitments to eliminate the anticompetitive effects so that the competition authorities have the discretion to decide the suspension of the investigation. The SAMR is also empowered to deal with concerns caused by AIPD on the legal basis of the Regulation of Algorithm Recommendations. Whether those measures are effective to address concerns caused by AIPD requires further analysis and should be further examined in practice.

Since AIPD takes place in both dominant and non-dominant markets, China also established regulatory frameworks to tackle it based on rules beyond competition law. Rules beyond competition law deal with the collection and use of consumers' personal information, as well as with automated decision-making and algorithm-based recommendation services based on collected consumer information. These rules limit the ways in which undertakings can accurately estimate consumers' willingness to pay and may therefore reduce the possibilities for AIPD. A discussion of rules beyond competition law is beyond the scope of this chapter but may also require further analysis, particularly from the perspective of effectiveness.

12

US Competition Law in Digital Markets

ALLEN P GRUNES AND ROSA L BAUM

1. Introduction

United States antitrust officials have taken more than two decades to travel up the learning curve on applying competition law to digital markets. The story chronicles how, after successfully challenging Microsoft's monopolisation of the operating system market, the US settled into a period of relative inactivity as the current crop of tech firms emerged, achieved dominance in their core markets, and took steps to limit or exclude competition. Only recently have the US Department of Justice (DOJ) and the Federal Trade Commission (FTC) again begun to take significant enforcement action in this sector.

For its part, the United States Congress has held extensive hearings on competition in the high-tech sector. A lengthy report emerged in 2022 from these hearings. Elected officials introduced bills dealing with issues such as self-preferencing by the largest tech firms, the rules of the Google and Apple app stores, data portability and interoperability, and the impact of digital services on journalism. However, no laws were enacted other than minor legislation revising merger filing fees and helping state attorneys general maintain antitrust cases in venues they select. The prospect for substantive legislation on digital issues, which appeared promising early in the Biden Administration, has faded.

1.1. The Microsoft Case

More than 20 years ago, the DC Circuit's decision in *Microsoft* laid a framework for the analysis of anticompetitive conduct by a dominant digital company.[1] It was an attempt to balance, on the one hand, deference to tech firms in terms of their design choices as they create new products and improve existing products. On the other hand, the case concerned the application of antitrust to a zero-price product

[1] *United States v Microsoft, Corp*, 253 F 3d 34 (DC Cir 2001).

(the internet browser), network effects and barriers to entry (the 'application barrier to entry') and, above all, the importance of scale to digital competition.

Liability was based not on self-preferencing, but on conduct intended to prevent Microsoft's would-be rival, Netscape, from achieving the scale necessary to compete or displace Microsoft's operating system monopoly. The conduct included, among other things, investing hundreds of millions of dollars in Internet Explorer (Microsoft's browser) and then giving it away for free; licensing agreements which prevented computer manufacturers from changing the initial boot up sequence or desktop; and preferential contracts with internet access providers and content providers in return for exclusive or preferential distribution and promotion of Internet Explorer. In the words of Bill Gates, Microsoft sought to 'cut off [Netscape's] air supply'.[2] Ultimately, the circuit court agreed with the DOJ that Microsoft's design features and various contractual terms with third parties were deployed to exclude Netscape rather than to benefit Windows users.[3]

As Senator Richard Blumenthal and Professor Tim Wu have pointed out, the beneficiaries of *Microsoft* were start-ups that have grown to be behemoths in their own right. While in a certain sense ironic, Blumenthal and Wu regard it as a feature of the innovation cycle:

> But this is how the innovation cycle works: It creates room for saplings to grow into giants, but then prevents the new giants from squashing the next generation of saplings. (Microsoft was itself, in the early 1980s, the beneficiary of another antitrust case, against IBM, the computing colossus of its time.)[4]

The *Microsoft* decision did not emerge from nothing. It can be viewed as an update for the digital world of a United States Supreme Court (SCOTUS) case from half a century earlier, *Lorain Journal Co v United States*, 342 US 143 (1951). In *Lorain Journal*, a newspaper refused to deal with advertisers who chose to advertise on a radio station that had entered the local market. The newspaper's owners perceived the radio station to be a competitive threat. The conduct at issue was an effort to starve the radio station of advertisers or other revenue sources – similar to what Microsoft tried to do. Interestingly, newspapers and radio stations, like an operating system, are also two-sided markets with network effects. These features magnify growth: as the number of readers or listeners grows, the medium becomes more attractive to advertisers. As revenue increases, so does quality, which brings in more listeners. But the same features also aggravate decline and show why 'cutting off the air supply' of a new competitor can be such an effective anticompetitive strategy. Importantly, digital platforms have an advantage that traditional media do not: their geographic and commercial expanse. Their reach 'exacerbates

[2] A Gavil and H First, *The Microsoft Antitrust Cases: Competition Policy for the Twenty-first Century* (MIT Press 2014) 64.

[3] *Microsoft* (n 1) 51–80.

[4] R Blumenthal and T Wu, 'What the Microsoft Case Taught Us', *New York Times* (18 May 2018), www.nytimes.com/2018/05/18/opinion/microsoft-antitrust-case.html.

their influence over commerce and creates higher barriers to entry and expansion for entrants and smaller competitors'.[5]

1.2. The Decline of Enforcement after Microsoft

Microsoft was a landmark case. But then, US enforcement of the Sherman Act Section 2 in the tech sector came to a virtual standstill for almost two decades. As Blumenthal and Wu observed:

> Unfortunately, ever since the *Microsoft* case there has been remarkably little oversight of the technology sector, despite the obvious signs of corporate consolidation and outsize market power. Enforcement of the antimonopoly laws has fallen: Between 1970 and 1999, the United States brought about 15 monopoly cases each year; between 2000 and 2014 that number went down to just three.[6]

The poster child was perhaps the FTC's 2011–13 investigation of allegations made against Google that the company was anticompetitively promoting its own vertical properties through alterations of its search results page. The end result: only two limited 'voluntary commitments'. Google agreed 'voluntarily' (meaning without a consent decree) to discontinue the practice of 'scraping' the content of competing websites and threatening to delist these rivals entirely from its search results when they protested the misappropriation of their content. It also agreed to remove certain restrictions on the ability of advertisers to simultaneously advertise on Google and competing search engines, or to 'multihome'.[7] In 2015, portions of an internal FTC staff memorandum were accidentally released and published. The memorandum recommended bringing a case against Google. But the Commission ultimately voted not to bring an action. In failing to act, the Commission arguably 'misread the evidence in front of them and left much of the digital future in Google's hands'.[8]

Likewise, large tech firms have acquired hundreds of companies without challenge and often without any in-depth merger review. While many of these acquisitions were likely harmless, a number were not.

One problematic transaction was Google's 2007 acquisition of the leading internet advertising server, DoubleClick. In its statement allowing the Google/DoubleClick deal, the FTC majority described swaths of the digital ad market as 'relatively nascent, dynamic and highly fragmented', adding that other big

[5] S Salop, *Dominant Digital Platforms: Is Antitrust Up to the Task?* (2021) 130 *Yale Law Journal* 563, 571.

[6] ibid.

[7] Letter from David Drummond, Google Senior Vice President of Corporate Development and CLO, to Hon Jon Leibowitz, FTC Chairman (2012); Statement of the FTC Regarding Google's Search Practices In the Matter of Google Inc., FTC File Number 111-0163 (2013).

[8] L Nylen, 'How Washington Fumbled the Future', *Politico* (16 March 2021), www.politico.com/news/2021/03/16/google-files-ftc-antitrust-investigation-475573.

companies 'appear to be well positioned to compete vigorously against Google'.[9] The majority also opined that Google and DoubleClick did not meaningfully compete with each other: Google was prominent in search and search advertising, although it was moving into the business where DoubleClick made its living, namely display ads on websites and video ads.[10]

Commissioner Pamela Jones Harbour registered the lone dissent. She noted that the majority ignored the critical data in their analysis of the merger: 'If advertisers and publishers have to channel their online advertising through Google/DoubleClick in order to access the best dataset that supports targeted advertising, will any other firms have the ability or incentive to compete meaningfully in this market?'[11] Commissioner Harbour was right. Following the DoubleClick acquisition, Google built up its ad technology business with a string of other acquisitions. It bought start-ups that made software for publishers, advertisers, and mobile ads, including AdMob in 2009, Invite Media in 2010, and AdMeld in 2011.

Facebook's 2014 acquisition of WhatsApp was another problematic acquisition, spotlighting the importance of privacy as a facet of non-price competition. WhatsApp did not sell advertising space or collect troves of personal data from its users. It charged a nominal fee and promised not to collect names, emails, addresses, or other contact information from its users' mobile address book or contact lists, other than mobile phone numbers. In contrast, Facebook harvested users' data to target them with advertisements. Thus, before the merger, consumers could choose between two popular texting apps with different price/privacy trade-offs. While the European Commission ultimately fined Facebook for providing incorrect information during the Commission's review of the merger, the FTC did not challenge the merger.

What explains the drop-off in enforcement? Among the arguments often heard is that competition in the digital era is dynamic rather than static; that this competition is 'for the market' (in the sense of creating whole new markets or industries) rather than 'in the market'; that such competition can be expected to result in just one or a few large firms; and that the drivers of innovation are not as well understood as, say, the economics of price. All of which imply that antitrust regimes should tread carefully, lest they make errors in enforcement decisions and inadvertently slow down the pace of innovation. Other arguments include the argument that there are few entry barriers in digital markets (including the familiar 'competition is one click away' argument).

At least in part because the US is the home of many of the large tech firms, these arguments have resonated. Of course, the tech firms have not hesitated to

[9] Statement of the FTC Concerning Google/Doubleclick, File No 071-0170 (2007) 13.

[10] See generally ibid.

[11] Dissenting Statement of Comm'r Harbour In the Matter of Google/Doubleclick, File No. 071-170 (2007) 8.

reinforce the arguments through many and varied avenues, including aggressive lobbying and contributions to like-minded institutions and individuals. As an example, Bloomberg has reported that Alphabet, Meta, Apple, and Amazon and their trade groups spent hundreds of millions of dollars in lobbying and advertising to defeat recent legislative proposals. This advertising campaign argued, among other things, that the bills would destroy Google Search and Amazon Prime and disrupt the global economy.[12]

Digital platforms have been able to frame US policy discussions to focus on the benefits their products provide consumers and the services they deliver. The discourse has thus been about technology development and innovation. Comparatively, in the European Union (EU), scrutiny has expanded to look at the effect of the technology and spurred the EU to become the leader in regulation development.

1.3. New Learning

The year 2019 saw three major policy reports on digital markets in the UK,[13] the EU,[14] and the US.[15] The reports have many points in common. All see digital markets as conferring great consumer benefits but also raising significant competitive issues. All identify similar economic drivers in digital platform markets including strong (global) economies of scale and scope, substantial network effects, the crucial importance of data, and the influence of consumer behavioural biases. All find that digital platform markets have a tendency towards tipping and concentration and towards the creation of ecosystems within which market power may be extended across markets. And all consider government actions to address competition concerns to have been insufficient and recommend strengthened antitrust enforcement and perhaps also regulation.[16]

Tellingly, the EU and UK reports were prepared at the direction of governmental officials while the US report was not. The latter was conducted under the auspices of the Stigler Center of the University of Chicago. The authors of the US report included several former antitrust enforcement officials but it was not an official report, and the US government did not adopt its recommendations.

[12] E Birnbaum, *Big Tech Divided and Conquered to Block Key Bipartisan Bills*, Bloomberg (20 December 2022), www.bloomberg.com/news/articles/2022-12-20/big-tech-divided-and-conquered-to-block-key-bipartisan-bills#xj4y7vzkg.

[13] J Furman and others, *Unlocking Digital Competition: Report of the Digital Competition Expert Panel* (The Crown 2019).

[14] J Crémer and others, *Competition Policy for the Digital Era* (European Commission 2019).

[15] F Scott Morton and others, *Committee for the Study of Digital Platforms Market Structure and Antitrust Subcommittee Report* (George Stigler Center for the Study of the Economy and the State, the University of Chicago Booth School of Business 2019) ('the Scott Morton Report').

[16] See S Ennis and A Fletcher, *Developing International Perspectives on Digital Competition Policy* (2020) Center for Competition Policy and Norwich Business School, University of East Anglia.

Thus, while 2019 was a pivotal year for thinking about digital markets, it also reflected a difference in the development of policy in the EU and UK, on the one hand, and the US on the other.

2. Overview of Current US Domestic Legal Landscape

2.1. Obstacles: The Chicago School of Economics and the Consumer Welfare Standard

Starting in the 1970s, Chicago School of Economics theories revolutionised US antitrust law. The exact contours of what this school of thought champions are hotly disputed, but its origins lie in steadfast commitment to libertarianism and nonintervention. Those who professed the theory maintained that markets, without government intervention, would work themselves out. This theory drew a convincing comparison to the inconsistent and haphazard US antitrust enforcement of the 1960s.[17] See, for example, *United States v Topco Assocs*, 405 US 596, 609 n 10 (1972) (applying the 'per se rule' to a competitively harmless joint venture, on the premise that the rule of reason would 'leave courts free to ramble through the wilds of economic theory in order to maintain a flexible approach').

However, the Chicago School's inability to account for modern developments in economics and an ever-morphing economy capitalising on innovation, networks, and strategic behaviour – aspects of the economy that are only heightened in the digital market arena – has led to its obsolescence.[18] Entrenched by corporate incentives – and their influence over conservative institutions and the judiciary – to maintain the status quo thereby benefiting from anticompetitive markets, the School did not adopt modern economic tools. Its default – that if conduct cannot be proven to be anticompetitive it does not warrant government intervention – has made it a creature of the twentieth century.[19]

It was during this time that the US also adopted the consumer welfare standard. The overall stated goal of this standard 'is to encourage markets in which output, measured by quantity, quality, or innovation, is as large as possible consistent with sustainable competition'.[20]

Similarly, the consumer welfare standard has come under attack by various academics and advocacy organisations. Criticisms include that the standard is

[17] H Hovenkamp and F Scott Morton, 'Framing the Chicago School of Antitrust Analysis' (2020) 168 *University of Pennsylvania Law Review* 1843, 1843–44, 1848.
[18] ibid, 1844.
[19] ibid, 1850.
[20] H Hovenkamp, 'Is Antitrust's Consumer Welfare Principle Imperiled?' (2019) 45 *Journal of Corporation Law* 101, 103.

inconsistent with the US antitrust legislative history;[21] that its application has led to a high degree of concentration in many industries and systematic underenforcement of the antitrust laws;[22] and that it is difficult to apply in zero-price markets, multisided markets, and to acquisitions of early stage competitors. These criticisms are particularly relevant to digital markets, which often have these features.

The current heads of the FTC, Lina Khan, and the DOJ Antitrust Division, Jonathan Kanter, have both publicly criticised the consumer welfare standard. Assistant Attorney General Kanter has expressly advocated for replacing the standard with an analysis that would reach harm to the competitive process. Similarly, Chair Khan has called for a 'holistic' approach to antitrust enforcement. The most succinct criticism has come from Professor Wu, who until recently served on the National Economic Council as Special Assistant to the President for Technology and Competition Policy. Professor Wu posited that the consumer welfare standard was essentially made up out of whole cloth by two University of Chicago professors, Aaron Director and Robert Bork.[23] And in 2021, President Biden argued that this view of antitrust was a 'failed' experiment.[24]

Notwithstanding these criticisms, it is unlikely that the US will drop the consumer welfare standard. Respected academics, such as Professor Herbert Hovenkamp, have defended the consumer welfare standard. Professor Hovenkamp has suggested that replacing 'consumer welfare' with 'harm to the competitive process' would replace a relatively objective standard with one that is essentially amorphous and without content. The argument embraces the notion that consumer welfare, whatever its weaknesses, at least has the virtues of being predictable for businesses (so they can conform their conduct) and enforceable by courts. Discarding predictability, in Professor Hovenkamp's view, would be to return to the days when antitrust decisions were largely discretionary and incoherent.[25]

This lack of enforcement is consequential. 'Underenforcement is likely to be costlier than previously thought because among other things, market power of large technology platforms is more enduring.'[26] Entrants to digital markets 'find it difficult to overcome the high barriers to take on digital platform incumbents', and

[21] See C Bogus, 'The New Road to Serfdom: The Curse of Bigness and the Failure of Antitrust' (2015) 49 *University of Michigan Journal of Law Reform* 1, 46–51.

[22] See H Boushey and H Knudsen, *The Importance of Competition for the American Economy* (Council of Economic Advisors 2021), www.whitehouse.gov/cea/written-materials/2021/07/09/the-importance-of-competition-for-the-american-economy.

[23] See T Wu, *The Curse of Bigness: Antitrust in the New Gilded Age* (Columbia Global Reports 2018) 83–92.

[24] *Remarks by President Biden at Signing of an Executive Order Promoting Competition in the American Economy*, The White House (9 July 2021), www.whitehouse.gov/briefing-room/speeches-remarks/2021/07/09/remarks-by-president-biden-at-signing-of-an-executive-order-promoting-competition-in-the-american-economy.

[25] Hovenkamp (n 20) 104–08; see also J Kirkwood, 'Tech Giant Exclusion' (2022) 74 *Florida Law Review* 63, 95–101 (arguing fundamental goals of antitrust law should not be altered and antitrust enforcement actions should be evaluated by impact on consumer welfare and supplier welfare).

[26] Scott Morton Report, 73–74.

'[n]o matter how dynamic the technology, an entrant will not unseat a monopolist if the monopolist is permitted to buy the dynamic entrant for a share of monopoly profits'.[27] Economic forces are unlikely to come to the rescue, as both merging parties benefit from the transaction. It is the public that loses.[28]

2.2. Statutory Blind Spots

Another shortcoming of US antitrust law is the minimum revenue (turnover) threshold of pre-merger review. The 1976 Hart-Scott-Rodino Antitrust Improvements Act established the country's pre-merger notification program. As relevant to our discussion of digital markets, the Act exempts from review transactions valued at less than $50 million, as adjusted.[29] Technology mergers often fall under this threshold and thus are rarely reviewed or challenged.[30] This twilight zone increasingly benefits digital platforms as they hold asymmetrical knowledge regarding their small competitors and can acquire them without triggering review.

This enforcement blind-spot compounds with large tech platforms' ability to combine financial and data resources.[31] Digital platforms have 'both the incentive and the ability … to outspend, out-invest, or to acquire incumbents or new competitors'.[32] Platforms have also taken to creating 'kill zones' around themselves.[33] Creating essentially a buffer zone of sorts around their markets, platforms 'acquire any potential competitors, dissuading others from entering, and thus preventing innovation from serving as the competitive threat that is traditionally believed to keep monopoly incumbents on their toes'.[34] As one venture capitalist explained, '[w]e don't touch anything that comes too close to Facebook, Google or Amazon'.[35] This startup investing avoidance of sub-industries – social platforms (Facebook), internet software (Google), and online retail (Amazon) – is visible in market trends. Since 2009, these areas have fared poorly when compared to the larger markets.[36] Studies on this trajectory suggest that these large tech platforms dampen innovation.[37]

[27] ibid, 81.

[28] ibid, 60, 81.

[29] See T Wollman, 'Stealth Consolidation: Evidence from an Amendment to the Hart-Scott-Rodino Act' (2019) 1(1) *American Economic Review: Insights* 77. This review threshold resulted from a 2000 amendment increasing the cutoff. From 1976 to 2000, the threshold was $10 million. For a sense of perspective, this change precipitated an abrupt 70% decline in pre-merger notification. ibid.

[30] Scott Morton Report, 67 n 137.

[31] ibid, 54.

[32] ibid.

[33] ibid.

[34] SK Kamepalli and others, 'Kill Zone' (2021), ssrn.com/abstract=3555915.

[35] E Dwoskin, 'Facebook's Willingness to Copy Rivals' Apps Seen as Hurting Innovation', *Washington Post* (10 August 2017), www.washingtonpost.com/business/economy/facebooks-willingness-to-copy-rivals-apps-seen-as-hurting-innovation/2017/08/10/ea7188ea-7df6-11e7-a669-b400c5c7e1cc_story.html.

[36] Scott Morton Report, 56.

[37] ibid.

Facebook has even harnessed the ability to spot nascent competitors through its acquisition of a mobile phone monitoring application, Onavo.[38] A December 2013 internal slide deck noted: 'With our acquisition of Onavo, we now have insight into the most popular apps. We should use that to also help us make strategic acquisitions.'[39] Facebook seemingly used Onavo to generate internal 'Early Bird' reports for Facebook executives, which focused on 'apps that are gaining prominence in the mobile eco-system in a rate or manner which makes them stand out', and therefore to identify acquisition targets, including WhatsApp.[40]

2.3. US Supreme Court Decisions

US Supreme Court decisions have further complicated antitrust enforcement, expanding the industries and conduct that have become, for all practical purposes, exempt from antitrust scrutiny.

US antitrust agencies first confronted allegations that high-tech firms were violating the Sherman Act, the US's seminal law protecting against unlawful restraints and monopolisation, amidst a fever of excitement surrounding the promise of the expanding internet and increasing access to connectivity.[41] Scholars posited that 'innovation efficiencies are the principal form of economic efficiency which ought to be protected and promoted by laws designed to maintain a competition process'.[42] This light-touch approach is perfectly captured by Richard Posner's closing in *Antitrust in the New Economy*: '[T]he byword of a prudent enforcement agency and a sensible court will be: caution.'[43]

While *Microsoft* is rightfully lauded as being ahead of its time in anticipating the dangers digital platforms may pose to competition, and still stands as a blueprint for modern antitrust challenges to big tech, aspects of the case have arguably negatively impacted efforts to take on big tech.[44] Critically, the court dodged the applicability of the per se rule to the government's claim that Microsoft tied Internet Explorer and Windows and thus violated the Sherman Act.[45] While the court's move likely did not affect the outcome in the case itself, it arguably broke with the Supreme Court's holding in *Jefferson Parish Hospital District No 2 v Hyde*, 466 US

[38] See D Seetharaman and B Morris, 'Facebook's Onavo Gives Social-Media Firm Inside Peek at Rivals' Users', *Wall Street Journal* (13 August 2017), www.wsj.com/articles/facebooks-onavo-gives-social-media-firm-inside-peek-at-rivals-users-1502622003.

[39] First Amended Complaint, *FTC v Facebook Inc*, No 1:20-cv-03590-JEB (filed 19 August 2021).

[40] ibid.

[41] See R Allensworth, 'Antitrust's High-Tech Exceptionalism' (2021) 130 *Yale Law Journal* 588, 593–95.

[42] J Flynn, 'Antitrust Policy, Innovative Efficiencies, and the Suppression of Technology' (1998) 66 *Antitrust Law Journal* 487, 509.

[43] R Posner (2001) 68 *Antitrust Law Journal* 925, 943.

[44] Allensworth (n 41) 597.

[45] *Microsoft* (n 1) 84.

2 (1984), in which the Court held that ties meeting several economic criteria were per se unlawful. The *Microsoft* Court reasoned that applying a per se analysis to software serving as a platform for third-party applications created 'undue risks of error and of deterring welfare-enhancing innovation'[46] and declined to opine on Microsoft's claims regarding the benefits from Application Programming Interface (API) integration, noting instead that 'judicial "experience" provide[d] little basis' for believing that these packages were conclusively unreasonable.[47] Thus, the court went on to explain that 'the nature of the platform software market affirmatively suggests that per se rules might stunt valuable innovation'.[48] '[T]he decision to break with binding precedent, invoking the innovative qualities of the defendant enshrined in case law a powerful idea: as a dynamic sector of the economy, the high-tech industry can claim special dispensation.'[49]

The US's special treatment of the tech sector expanded with the Supreme Court's decision in *Verizon Communications Inc v Law Offices of Curtis V Trinko, LLP*.[50] Trinko sued Verizon under the 1996 Telecommunications Act and the Sherman Act, Section 2, claiming that Verizon was discriminating against its rivals by refusing to supply them with network connections.[51] Rather than require that Verizon prove it had a legitimate justification to not deal with a telecom competitor,[52] Justice Antonin Scalia's majority opinion held that Verizon did not have such a duty – a conclusion he reasoned safeguarded the 'incentive to innovate'.[53] Justice Scalia went on to emphasise that US law has been 'very cautious in recognizing' situations where refusals to deal with rivals is anticompetitive 'because of the uncertain virtue of forced sharing and the difficulty of identifying and remedying anticompetitive conduct'.[54] With this determination, 'Justice Scalia ignored the fact that the balance between incentivizing innovation by limiting a competitor's duty to share its success with rivals and incentivizing innovation by condemning a dominant firm's exclusionary conduct had already been struck under the Court's duty-to-deal cases'.[55]

And one of the largest set-backs to antitrust enforcement came in *Ohio v American Express Co* ('*Amex*').[56] In 2010, the DOJ and various states claimed that American Express, Visa, and MasterCard 'anti-steering' provisions – contract provisions that prohibited merchants from attempting to steer customers away from high fees charged by the credit card companies – had anticompetitive effects.

[46] ibid, 89–90.
[47] ibid, 90–91.
[48] ibid, 92.
[49] Allensworth (n 41) 598–99.
[50] *Verizon Communications Inc v Law Offices of Curtis V Trinko, LLP*, 540 US 398 (2004).
[51] ibid, 404–05.
[52] The US Supreme Court's line of 'duty-to-deal' cases established that 'monopolists can be held liable for refusing to deal with their competitors without a legitimate justification'. Allensworth (n 41) 599.
[53] *Trinko* (n 50) 407; see also Allensworth (n 41) 600.
[54] *Trinko* (n 50) 408.
[55] Allensworth (n 41) 600.
[56] *Ohio v American Express Co*, 138 S Ct 2274 (2018) ('*Amex*').

The costs placed on merchants for accepting these cards created a vicious cycle and a dysfunctional market dynamic. Merchants were forced to increase prices on the goods to account for these fees, arguably harming both credit card users and those customers from lower income classes who are more likely to pay with cash. However, because of the rewards – even minimal ones – offered by the credit cards to users, those customers who are able to, continue to swipe their cards. Visa and MasterCard settled with the DOJ and dropped the provisions from their contracts,[57] but American Express litigated the question.

Much of the focus in the *Amex* litigation rested on market definition. American Express – like Google, Amazon, Facebook, Twitter, and many other large digital platforms – operates a two-sided market, creating 'an interdependent network ecosystem'.[58] Regrettably, the decision in *Amex* was based on the notion that vertical restraints almost always enhance efficiency and almost never harm competition – a conclusion that has been called into question.[59] This perspective represents something of the simplifying formalism that other countries are moving away from, and is a critical assumption to examine in the realm of digital markets.

In a 5-4 decision written by Justice Clarence Thomas, the Supreme Court concluded that the DOJ had not carried its burden to show anticompetitive effects.[60] Instead of recognising direct evidence of anticompetitive, actual fee increases derivative of this practice, the Court held that the government had to show that the net price – to include that paid by the merchant and the potentially negative price (essentially a benefit) paid/received by the cardholder – in the two-sided market had increased. Relying on the increasing volume of credit card usage, the majority 'characterized the Amex fee increase as competition on the merits because it could support larger user rewards'.[61] Although the majority stated that the decision is limited to 'transaction platforms' where the buyer and seller are connected, the case reaffirms the centrality of market definition in antitrust cases.

Of the 2019 reports, only that of the US grapples with the *Amex* decision, perhaps reflecting the fact that it presents a uniquely American problem. That report recognises that although direct evidence of competitive effects is often superior to going through the exercise of product market definition, the Supreme Court in the *Amex* case went in the opposite direction. Thus, US law appears to maintain the arguably incoherent position that a plaintiff in a vertical restraint case 'may not rely on direct proof of harm to competition'.[62]

[57] Final Judgment as to Defendants MasterCard International Incorporated and Visa Inc, No CV-10-4496 (EDNY July 20, 2011).

[58] Salop (n 5) 570.

[59] Scott Morton Report, 77.

[60] *Amex* (n 56) 2290.

[61] ibid, 574.

[62] Allen Grunes, 'Developing International Perspectives on Market Definition in Digital Markets' (2020) American Antitrust Institute 6, www.antitrustinstitute.org/wp-content/uploads/2020/06/Grunes1.pdf.

Amex's impact is borne out in *United States v Sabre Corp*, 452 F Supp 3d 97 (D Del 2020), vacated, No 20-1767, 2020 WL 4915824 (3d Cir July 20, 2020),[63] a merger that was unsuccessfully challenged in the US but ultimately blocked in the UK.[64] Sabre, a digital platform aggregator for airline schedules, fares, and seat availability, sought to acquire Farelogix, a software company for airline technology. Judge Stark made factual findings that Farelogix assisted airlines' efforts to lower distribution costs through bypassing entities like Sabre and other global distribution systems and even noted that 'Sabre and Farelogix view each other as competitors'.[65] However, relying on *Amex*, Judge Stark determined that as a matter of law, the two entities could not compete because Sabre is a two-sided platform and Farelogix operates on only one side of the platform.[66]

Therefore, '[c]ontrary to the rule that antitrust law protects competition, not competitors, *Amex* protects competitors that have platform business models at the expense of competition on either side of the platform'.[67]

2.4. Recent Governmental Affirmative Steps

Antitrust policy and enforcement has not been completely dormant. For example, on 9 July 2021, President Biden issued an Executive Order on Promoting Competition in the American Economy. This executive order encompasses 72 initiatives addressing competition matters spanning the American economy. It adopts a whole-of-government approach to antitrust enforcement, enlisting agencies outside of the DOJ and FTC to use their statutory authority to analyse anticompetitive implications of transactions they review or conduct in the various markets they oversee.[68] Additionally, the appointment of Lina Khan to head the FTC, along with the confirmation of a third Democratic commissioner in mid-2022, led many observers to anticipate, correctly, that the FTC has a plan of action to make enforcement in the realm of digital platforms a priority.[69]

Following a loss in court, the FTC dropped its challenge to Meta Platforms, Inc's acquisition of Within Unlimited.[70] The FTC had alleged that Meta was attempting to illegally acquire Within Unlimited's fitness app and substantially lessen competition, or tend to create a monopoly, in the virtual reality market for

[63] *United States v Sabre Corp*, 452 F Supp 3d 97 (D Del 2020), vacated, No 20-1767, 2020 WL 4915824 (3d Cir July 20, 2020).

[64] The Third Circuit vacated the trial court's decision as moot after Sabre terminated its proposed acquisition.

[65] *Sabre Corp* (n 63) 131.

[66] ibid, 136.

[67] R Stutz, 'We've Seen Enough: It Is Time to Abandon Amex and Start Over on Two-Sided Markets', American Antitrust Institute, www.antitrustinstitute.org/wp-content/uploads/2020/04/Amex-Commentary-4.21.20-Final.pdf.

[68] Exec Order No 14036, § 2 (2021).

[69] C Kang, 'Lina Khan, a Big Tech Critic, Tries Answering Her Own Detractors', *New York Times* (9 June 2022), www.nytimes.com/2022/06/09/technology/lina-khan-ftc.html.

[70] See Complaint, *FTC v Meta Platforms, Inc, et al*, No 221-0040, 3:22-cv-04325 (DDC July 27, 2022).

fitness apps.[71] The FTC argued that, as the seller of the most widely used virtual reality headset and a key player in the virtual reality app world, Meta's acquisition, rather than entry as a competitor, would likely stifle competition and dampen innovation. While this is undoubtedly a loss for the FTC, the court affirmed the continued validity of the 'potential competition' doctrine. The case does, however, highlight the difficulty of applying that doctrine. Merger analysis is a predictive game, and proof that a potential entrant would have entered the market but for the merger adds to the difficulty. The Sherman Act Section 2 has advantages in this regard. It allows agencies to look back at completed mergers, including those of nascent competitors, and its causation requirement is less exacting. Thus, the latter gives enforcement agencies a more concrete basis on which to challenge acquisitions which, in hindsight, cemented a firm's dominance.[72]

One such example of these lawsuits is the Biden Administration's challenge, filed in 2023, to Google's conduct in the ad tech industry. In January 2023, the DOJ, along with eight states, filed suit against Google, alleging that Google had 'corrupted legitimate competition in the ad tech industry by engaging in a systematic campaign to seize control of the wide swath of high-tech tools used by publishers, advertisers and brokers to facilitate digital advertising'.[73] The DOJ is asking that Google be required to divest much of its suite of ad technology products.[74] The complaint also singles out Google's acquisition of DoubleClick as anticompetitive. As of the writing of this chapter, the FTC and 17 state attorneys general have also recently sued Amazon, alleging that the online retail and technology company is a monopolist that uses a set of interlocking anticompetitive and unfair strategies to illegally maintain its monopoly power.

And while 2022 ended with a lack of congressional action to update US competition laws, enforcers did not end the year empty-handed. The Consolidated Appropriations Act of 2023, a $1.7 trillion end-of-the-year spending package, included antitrust elements. For example, the bill included the Merger Filing Fee Modernization Act which, while not targeting the issues faced by digital markets, will have an impact on some of the players. The act updates the merger filing fees for the first time since 2001 by lowering fees on smaller acquisitions and raising them substantially for the larger mergers. This additional revenue is expected to be used to fund antitrust enforcement.[75] Furthermore, Congress allotted an additional $85 million to the antitrust enforcement agencies: $50 million to the FTC and $35 million to the DOJ's Antitrust Division.[76]

[71] ibid, para 1.

[72] See A Grunes, 'Mergers as Monopolization' (2023) *Competition Policy International.*

[73] Complaint, *United States, et al, v Google LLC*, No 1:23-cv-00108 (ED Va Jan 24, 2023); see also D McCabe and N Grant, 'US Accuses Google of Abusing Monopoly in Ad Technology', *New York Times* (24 January 2022), www.nytimes.com/2023/01/24/technology/google-ads-lawsuit.html.

[74] See Complaint, *United States v Google LLC* (n 73).

[75] Klobuchar Bipartisan Legislation to Restructure Merger Fees, Strengthen Antitrust Enforcement Passes Congress (2022), www.klobuchar.senate.gov/public/index.cfm/news-releases?ID=D059DD97-DDB5-4C89-90DA-CFF3E203ACDA.

[76] E Cortellessa, 'Schumer Kills Bill Big Tech Feared Most, But Boosts Budgets of Agencies Targeting Them', *Politico* (22 December 22, 2022), time.com/6243256/schumer-kills-antitrust-big-tech-bills.

Moreover, federal entities are not the only actors in the US domestic arena. While the scope of this chapter does not stretch to encompass a comprehensive review of relevant state provisions that directly or indirectly address some of these competition issues, many state attorneys general and a number of state legislatures have been active players.[77] In addition to direct antitrust provisions, some states are opening different avenues to disrupt big tech. For example, select states – California, Colorado, and Virginia – have taken a leading role on incorporating consumer rights to data portability, a key aspect of control over data that also has antitrust implications in digital markets.

3. US Regulatory and Legislative Changes

3.1. The DMA and its US Corollary

Other chapters in this volume provide a thorough analysis of the nuances and intricacies of the European Union's Digital Markets Act (DMA),[78] and so there is no need to repeat or undertake any such analysis in this chapter. However, the DMA is likely to impact the US.

In theory, the DMA only applies within the European Economic Area. However, some affected firms ('gatekeepers') may be forced to, or prefer to, align their business models with the DMA globally to avoid the extra costs of managing diverging lines of effort.[79] While we cannot comprehensively anticipate the full extent of the DMA's impact on major tech platforms, it is likely that various features of the DMA will result in worldwide compliant features.[80] For example, the DMA's interoperability requirements[81] may become the global standard simply because it will be burdensome for platforms to operate differing application programming interfaces (APIs). And the provisions mandating transparency in pricing for advertisers[82] may decrease the benefits for the platforms to be opaque regarding this data and may lead to US actors reaping the same benefit.[83] Comparatively, questions remain surrounding, for example, a

[77] See K Arcieri, 'States Seen as Next Battlefield for Big Tech Antitrust Cases', *S&P Global* (4 October 2022), bit.ly/3GrYvVH (noting 'state levers' in California, Texas, New York, and Colorado in the antitrust arena).

[78] Regulation 2022/1925 of the European Parliament and of the Council of 14 September 2022 on contestable and fair markets in the digital sector and amending Directives 2019/1937 and 2020/1828 (Digital Markets Act) [2022] OJ L265/1 (DMA).

[79] See, eg, 'The Brussels Effect: The Rise of a Regulatory Superstate in Europe', Lecture by Anu Bradford (18 January 2012).

[80] See 'Diving in the Digital Markets Act (DMA): Implementation and Implications', Lecture by Gene Kimmelman, Harvard Kennedy School (11 October 2022).

[81] DMA, Art 6.

[82] ibid, Art 5.

[83] See 'The EU Digital Markets Act and its Implications for the United States', Lecture by Jacques Cremer, LeadershIP (28 September 2022).

platform's ability to harvest data from customers in the US to target customers in the EU in ways the DMA does not allow within the EU.[84]

Lawmakers in the US have contemplated a bill in the spirit of the DMA: The American Innovation and Choice Online Act (the 'Klobuchar Bill').[85] The legislation is, as its core, a digital platform non-discrimination act. Among other provisions, the Klobuchar Bill contains rules, like the DMA, prohibiting platforms from engaging in conduct such as harmful self-preferencing by gatekeeper platforms that control key chokepoints of digital markets; unfairly limiting the availability of competing products from other merchants on the platform; restricting or impeding a competitor from accessing or interoperating with the platform, operating system, or hardware or software features; restricting a user's ability to install or uninstall software; and rigging search or ranking functionalities.[86] Also similar to the DMA, the Klobuchar Bill applies to only certain actors in this space – specifically, major business lines of the largest gatekeeping tech companies. Covered entities are those online platforms which, including other qualifications: have the ability to restrict or materially impede access between a business and its customers or a tool or service (a 'critical trading partner'); have more than 50 million monthly active users in the US or 1 billion worldwide; have more than 100,000 active US business users; and record net annual sales or market capitalisation of more than $550 billion.[87]

A distinguishing feature of the Klobuchar Bill is its inclusion of affirmative defences. Under the Klobuchar Bill, defendants retain affirmative defences such as establishing that relevant conduct 'has not resulted in and would not result in material harm to competition' of that the conduct was:

> narrowly tailored, could not be achieved through less discriminatory means, was nonpretextual, and was reasonably necessary to (i) prevent a violation of, or comply with, Federal or State law; (ii) protect safety, user privacy, the security of non-public data, or the security of the platform; or (iii) maintain or substantially enhance the core functionality of the covered platform.[88]

But like other antitrust legislative proposals in the US, hearings and debate on this bill to date have not yielded concrete action. While the bill was approved by the Senate Judiciary Committee with bipartisan support, it went no further.[89] However, it is likely to be re-introduced and thus we may not have seen the last of this effort.

[84] ibid.
[85] See American Innovation and Choice Platform Act of 2022, S 2992, 117th Cong (2022).
[86] ibid.
[87] ibid, section 2(a)(5).
[88] ibid, section 3(b).
[89] E Cortellessa, 'Schumer Kills Bill Big Tech Feared Most, but Boosts Budgets of Agencies Targeting Them', *Politico* (22 December 2022), time.com/6243256/schumer-kills-antitrust-big-tech-bills.

3.2. The Broader US Landscape

Often discussed simultaneously with the Klobuchar Bill, the Open App Markets Act seeks to eliminate anticompetitive conduct by application store operators and open applications markets to facilitate more expansive user choice and competition. It would prohibit a covered entity from: (1) requiring that a developer use an in-application payment system owned or operated by the entity as a condition of distribution or accessibility; (2) mandating that pricing conditions on its platform be equal or more favourable to users than on any other application platform; or (3) engaging in punitive actions against a developer for using or offering different terms or conditions through another in-application payment system or application store.[90] And like the Klobuchar Bill, the Open App Markets Act was approved by the Senate Judiciary Committee but has not been brought to a vote on the Senate Floor.

Various other bills take aim at different problems specifically identified in the digital platforms space. For example, the Platform Competition and Opportunity Act focuses on mergers, prohibiting any acquisition by companies that operate a covered platform, unless the merging parties can prove by clear and convincing evidence that: (1) the acquisition is valued at less than $50 million, (2) the target company does not compete with the platform's operator or does not present a nascent or potential competitive threat, or (3) the acquisition would not enhance the platform operator's market position or its ability to maintain such a market position as a critical trading partner platform.[91] The Ending Platform Monopolies Act[92] imposes vertical structural separation on covered platforms and the Augmenting Compatibility and Competition by Enabling Service Switching Act[93] requires covered platforms permit interoperability from potential competitors or businesses. None of these bills appear likely to move forward.

The Journalism Competition and Protection Act (JCPA) is a particularly striking and timely proposal.[94] As digital platforms have skyrocketed in reach and success, the news industry has collapsed at an unprecedented scale. Many JCPA advocates explain that this proposed legislation would combat digital platforms' role in that crash. The legislation, some explain, is 'motivated by a single, fiery accusation: Google and Facebook are "free-riding" off the news'.[95] These critics point a finger at this free-riding, positing that it, more than anything else, 'has driven journalism into financial collapse'.[96]

[90] Open Markets Act, S 2710, 117th Cong (2022).
[91] Platform Competition and Opportunity Act, S 3197, 117th Cong (2021).
[92] Ending Platform Monopolies Act, HR 3825, 117th Cong (2021).
[93] Augmenting Compatibility and Competition by Enabling Service Switching (ACCESS) Act, HR 3849, 117th Cong (2021).
[94] Journalism Competition and Protection Act, S 673, 117th Cong (2022).
[95] B Wofford, 'Facebook Freeloads Off Newspapers. This Plan Might Stop It', *Wired* (30 September 2022), www.wired.com/story/facebook-freeloads-off-newspapers-this-plan-might-stop-it.
[96] ibid.

The JCPA carves out an exemption allowing news publishers to collectively bargain with digital platforms to negotiate platform payments to the publishers for the news they provide – essentially, revenue sharing in exchange for posting news content. While this proposal has bipartisan support and even backing from tech giants like Microsoft, it has not passed Congress.[97] Notably, Australia experienced the same resistance from major big tech players on a similar bill but it moved forward with the bill's enactment. While Facebook temporarily wiped its news feed from Australian Facebook, it ultimately complied. And now, Australian news outlets' collective bargaining has yielded hundreds of millions of dollars.[98]

But even the consideration of this legislation, its significant backing, and the acknowledgment of the critical risks of letting competition law lag, have promisingly broadened the discussion in the US. And Chair Khan and AAG Kanter have indicated that their 'goal is to stretch the uses of antitrust law beyond the ways it has been applied for decades, including against the biggest tech companies'.[99]

4. Conclusion

The outlook for a substantial update to US competition law to meet the challenges of digital markets is uncertain. But the expanded focus on competition and a growing understanding of how it impacts varying aspects of US policy give the authors of this chapter hope for long-term action.

A report from the US House of Representatives published in 2022 hints at alignment as it highlights the same concerns regarding big tech that spurred the DMA. The report condemns big tech's efforts to harness monopoly power to act as gatekeepers and to undermine potential competition.[100] Furthermore, there is bipartisan support for efforts such as reforming the burden of proof in merger challenges, passing a data portability standard, and recognising that direct proof of market power supplants the need to define a market.[101] Other recommendations include removing the monopoly power requirement for exclusionary conduct by big tech firms.[102]

[97] ibid.

[98] ibid.

[99] D McCabe, 'Why Losing to Meta in Court May Still be a Win for Regulators', *New York Times* (7 December 2022), www.nytimes.com/2022/12/07/technology/meta-vr-antitrust-ftc.html.

[100] *Investigation of Competition in Digital Markets* (2022) Subcommittee on Antitrust, Commercial, and Administrative Law of the Committee on the Judiciary of the House of Representatives, www.govinfo.gov/content/pkg/CPRT-117HPRT47832/pdf/CPRT-117HPRT47832.pdf.

[101] Rep Ken Buck, *The Third Way* (2022) Subcommittee on Antitrust, Commercial, and Administrative Law of the Committee on the Judiciary of the House of Representatives, buck.house.gov/sites/evo-subsites/buck-evo.house.gov/files/wysiwyg_uploaded/Buck%20Report.pdf.

[102] See Kirkwood (n 25).

Additionally, the implementation and impact of the DMA may make regulation in the US easier. It may even present an opportunity for digital platforms to cede to regulation but champion a different approach in the US.[103]

Clearly, consensus on policy has not emerged. But there has been better coordination across borders on mergers. Likewise, in dealing with single-firm conduct, there is reason to believe that each jurisdiction has been playing to its strengths: regulation in the EU; agency enforcement, including the possibility of break-up, in the US.

[103] For example, the UK's approach will likely track more generalised legal standards and will include, among other provisions, empowering the Competition and Markets Authority to launch market analyses and investigations. The legislation is expected to advance company-specific interventions within a flexible and participatory regulatory process that emphasises adoption of behavioural norms. See G Kimmelman, 'How the UK's Proposed Digital Regulation Will Add to Europe's Lead in Tech Platform Oversight' (forthcoming 2023).

PART III

Summary

13

Content, Competition, and Data

Ex ante *Regulation to Make Digital Markets Contestable*

KALPANA TYAGI

1. Introduction

The rise and the success of the GAFAM (ie Google, Apple, Facebook, Amazon, and Microsoft) is unprecedented. The digital startups created a new type of economy, called a truly digital economy, from the very beginning. In this 'perennial wave of creative destruction', one saw many waves of start-ups, where only the fittest survived. What are the criteria that determined their fitness to survive? This includes many parameters – such as foresighted strategic decisions (consider for instance, Google's early acquisitions of DoubleClick and YouTube), innovative business models, and scientific innovations. The innovations introduced by these digital conglomerates merit appreciation. Innovation laws, most notably intellectual property law, and competition law offer an important impetus to this innovation, by offering the right and balanced set of incentives for firms to innovate. Competition authorities early on recognised that in these markets the competition is 'for' the markets, and not 'in' the markets.[1] Taking note of the industry-specific dynamics, authorities in the EU, the US, and many other antitrust authorities worldwide, erred on the side of non-intervention, and unconditionally allowed many oligopolistic mergers, and sometimes, even mergers-to-monopoly.[2] Intellectual property laws also offered substantial innovation incentives for an unrelenting growth of the platform economy. Finding that too strict a platform liability framework may hinder the growth of the digital economy, the US and the EU offered platforms immunity to grow and develop, without being anxious about the nature and the type of content available on their platforms. In the US,

[1] K Tyagi, 'Promoting Competition in Innovation through Merger Control in the ICT Sector: A Comparative and Interdisciplinary Study' (Springer 2019) 20.

[2] Tyagi (n 1); see ch 18 'Big Data and Merger Control' therein.

this immunity took the form of Section 230 of the Communications Decency Act. The Act, part of Title V of the US 1996 Telecommunications Act, offers platforms, whether a small blogger or a big social networking platform, such as Facebook, protection from legal liability for infringing content uploaded by users on their platforms. The EU equivalent of this legislative provision was the E-Commerce Directive. It is said that this immunity framework was so instrumental to the growth of the internet, and perhaps the Silicon Valley (where all of GAFAM is based), that Section 230 may be referred to as 'the twenty-six words that created the internet'.[3]

Over time the digital platforms evolved – both in terms of their ability to process data to gather meaningful insights as well as offering more targeted and curated content that can effectively meet the needs of upcoming generations, particularly the younger generations with 'shorter attention spans'. Sophisticated technology, and augmented platforms not only effectively cater to these diminishing attention spans, they also contribute to these retreating attention spans. On a positive note, platforms have evolved from the standard 'text-based communication' format to a more visually and sensory-augmented format. As Facebook becomes more established amongst the older generation, the likes of Snapchap and TikTok – with their short and catchy videos and augmented-reality-driven content – gain traction amongst the younger audience.[4] From a behavioural and psychological perspective, whether platforms have contributed to contracting attention span may be an interesting area of research. From a competition law perspective, what remains centre stage are the instances of anti-competitive conduct, and abuse of power by the digital incumbents that began to emerge once the markets started tipping to certain platforms and standards. Certain segments of the digital economy also started showing signs of maturity. Regulatory and enforcement experience with the platform economy indicated that the time had now come to somehow *ex ante* regulate these platforms. There is also a dimension of industrial policy to this debate. However, as this book concentrates on the competition and regulatory dimension, the contributions to this book concentrate only on competition and regulation-related aspects of the discussion.

In light of the centrality of digitalisation for future growth, in February 2020, the European Commission's Communication, 'Shaping Europe's Digital Future' recognised the need for well-rounded 'Digital Services Act' rules. This package did follow a few months later, on 15 December 2020. The DSA rules package comprises of the Digital Services Act (DSA), and the Digital Markets Act (DMA). While the DSA seeks to update the 2000 E-Commerce Directive, the DMA

[3] J Kosseff, *The Twenty-Six Words That Created the Internet* (Cornell University Press 2019).

[4] Australian Competition and Consumer Commission, 'Analysis of and reference to Sensor Tower Data in Australian Competition & Consumer Commission, Digital Platforms Services Inquiry, Interim Report 6: Report on Social Media Services' (March 2023) 8, www.accc.gov.au/system/files/Digital%20platforms%20services%20inquiry%20-%20Interim%20report%206%20-%20Report%20on%20social%20media%20services_0.pdf (ACCC Analysis (2023)).

offers an *ex ante* regulatory framework to make digital markets fair and contestable. In the EU, in addition, an increasingly fragmented approach amongst the Member States – such as the more stringent obligations to curb illegal content and hate speech in the national German Network Enforcement Act (Gesetz zur Verbessurng der Rechtsdurchsetzung in sozialen Netzwerken) the French Avia law and the Austrian Anti-Hate Speech Law (Kommunikationsplattformen-Gesetz) – gave way to substantial uncertainty amongst platforms (small and big alike) as regards the applicable legal framework.[5] Overall, the time was ripe to update the 2000 E-Commerce Directive, and adapt the intermediary liability framework to ensure that it is fit for, and works in, the digital age. The DSA coupled with the DMA forms part of the overarching framework of the 'Digital Services Act' rules.

The EU is not alone in the race to tame these gatekeepers. Other jurisdictions, likewise, are pursuing a similar objective. Whereas the European Commission concentrates on a closed list of 'core platform services that meet the gatekeeper threshold', in the US, four bi-partisan bills aimed at regulating large online platforms, introduced on 11 July 2021, refer to 'covered online platforms', and the UK's Competition and Markets Authority (CMA) refers to 'firms with strategic market status (SMS)'.[6] Are these differences merely semantic or will they influence the enforcement and ground implementation of these legislative measures? Can they somehow overburden the incumbent platforms with regulatory checks and balances, and thereby, diminish their incentives to innovate? Will they indeed make the markets 'contestable', as understood in the economic literature?[7] Contributions to this book from across six jurisdictions worldwide bring forth these emerging approaches to the regulation of the digital economy. Notably, contributions by Andriychuk, Unver, Gupta and Mehta, Zoboli and Corrado, Ashok, Mazur, and Baum in this volume bring out different facets of the emerging platform regulation in these jurisdictions. While the EU, the UK, India, and China have some concrete regulatory framework in place, the US takes a step forward and two cautious steps backward in this regulatory race. Interestingly, while the Latin America countries (LAC), as discussed by Abarca and Guiterrez, are yet to introduce a regulatory framework; the practice of LAC's competition authorities indicates a trend, that may at some point in time, crystalise into a regulatory framework.

The thread that weaves all the contributions in this book together is a comparative approach by the authors to understand the challenges that plague the digital economy and how different legal instruments (namely, competition, consumer, intellectual property, data protection, and privacy) have been adeptly utilised to

[5] I Buri and J van Hoboken, 'The Digital Services Act (DSA) proposal: a critical overview' Discussion Paper: Digital Services Act (DSA) Observatory and Institute for Information Law (IViR), University of Amsterdam (28 October 2021), 6.

[6] T Tombal, 'Ensuring contestability and fairness in digital markets through regulation: A comparative analysis of the EU, UK and US approaches' (2022) 18(3) *European Competition Journal* 468.

[7] WJ Baumol, JC Panzar, and RD Willig, *Contestable Markets and the Theory of Industry Structure* (Harcourt Brace Jovanovich 1982).

tame these digital gatekeepers. Considering that competition issues cannot be seen in isolation, the authors, accordingly, also explore the intellectual property and consumer law framework across the book. This approach is also evident in the two simultaneous legislative proposals – namely the Digital Markets Act (DMA) and the Digital Services Act (DSA).[8] Whereas the DMA promises to enhance competition and fairness in the internal market, the DSA seeks to ensure a safe digital environment, where the promises of the Charter of Fundamental Rights will be respected.[9] A fine reading of the DMA indicates a positive correlation between competition and innovation.[10] Is this new and emerging approach that promotes fair markets, a march away from the long accepted Schumpeterian thinking in the digital markets, whereby monopoly rents are considered to be an incentive that lead to each new disruptive wave of creative destruction?[11] What is the nature of this new regulatory set-up? Does it complement or does it compete with the EU competition law? The wave towards this quasi-regulatory approach first surfaced with the 2019 Report by Schweitzer et al, wherein the experts referred to the emergence of an ecosystem-based competition in the platform economy.[12] The Furman Report for the UK's Competition and Markets Authority went a step further and called for the establishment of a Digital Markets Unit.[13] If the choice of a legal basis is any indicator, the DMA and the DSA are an evident move towards a more regulatory approach. Article 10(2) and recitals 4, 5, and 10 DMA indicate that it is not a regular piece of competition law legislation.[14] The Commission's choice of Article 114 of the Treaty on the Functioning of the European Union (TFEU) as the legal basis, and not Article 103 TFEU, indicates a march towards regulatory competition.[15]

2. Interplay between Data, Content, and Competition

This regulatory overlap between different areas of law is the result of the interplay between the so-called free content, and the data that platforms gather from its users. The rise of big data meant that platforms can now gather large amounts of

[8] See Andriychuk (ch 3 in this volume) and Unver (ch 10 in this volume) for more on the DMA.

[9] A de Streel and P Larouche, 'The European Digital Markets Act Proposal: How To Improve A Regulatory Revolution' (2021) 2 *Concurrences* 46.

[10] P Larouche and A de Streel, 'The European Digital Markets Act: A Revolution Grounded on Traditions' (2021) 12(7) *Journal of European Competition Law & Practice* 542.

[11] Tyagi (n 1).

[12] Kommission Wettbewerbsrecht 4.0 (2019), www.bmwk.de/Redaktion/DE/Artikel/Wirtschaft/kommission-wettbewerbsrecht-4-0.html.

[13] *Unlocking digital competition – Report of the Digital Competition Expert Panel* (2019) ('Furman Report').

[14] R Podszun, P Bongartz, and S Langstein, 'The Digital Markets Act: Moving from Competition Law to Regulation for Large Gatekeepers' (2021) 2 *EuCML* 60.

[15] O Andriychuk, 'Shaping the New Modality of the Digital Markets: The Impact of the DSA/DMA Proposals on Inter-Platform Competition' (2021) 44(3) *World Competition* 261.

data, and make meaningful interpretations from them. As an example, when a user types in the keyword 'healthy and organic food supplements', the platform knows that the user is looking for food supplements that are healthy and organic. This offers the possibility to offer personalised recommendations, and micro-target each user. If search results show an exact match, the user is more likely to click on them, and make a positive purchase decision. In other words, what first seemed free (meaning content), is after all, not all that free! It has long been recognised in marketing that when something is free, then the consumer is the product. Platforms facilitate this possibility to make personalised recommendations, and make every individual a product through targeted, contextual and behavioural advertising. There are many concerns relating to targeted behavioural advertising. Platforms use data and behavioural insights to 'nudge' users to act in a manner that may not be in the best of their interests.[16] These are the 'dark patterns' of the platforms, whereby the design of the platform causes customer confusion, such that their preferences are not decided based on their real interests – rather, the choices are driven by the design of the platform.[17]

Central to this nudging is the role of data. Data helps platforms make meaningful interpretations about user behaviour, and offer personalized recommendations. Thus, to triangulate the novel regulatory challenges presented by the digital economy, the Commission complemented its Digital Services Act proposal, with the Data Governance Act. The Data Act aims to increase the resilience of data by making it reusable across sectors. Here, the proposal also eyes the introduction of competition across the data value chain through 'personal data sharing intermediaries'. Corrado and Zoboli in their chapter in this volume accordingly look at data spaces and evaluate the effectiveness of this proposal.

What is the thread that weaves content and competition on the platforms? Why is it important to look at the two together for the design of a suitable *ex ante* Regulatory framework to make digital markets more contestable? Further, what is contestability – is it the same as competition, or is it different? Does 'contestability' in the DMA carry the same (or even similar) connotation as Baumol's 1982 classic work, 'Contestable Markets and the Theory of Industrial Structure'?

Regulation of the digital markets must be distinguished from the typical utility-kind regulation, such as the one seen in natural monopolies like electricity. The 'intermediation power' to select digital platforms requires consideration of a higher order public interest, such as that not captured by Article 102 TFEU, and to bridge this gap, the DMA seems to 'slide into a regime of public utility regulation'.[18] Regulating platforms calls for a more 'pro-competitive regulatory approach'.[19] Such a regulatory approach eyes the following two-fold objectives: first,

[16] ACCC Analysis (n 4) 137.

[17] ibid, 146.

[18] H Schweitzer, 'The Art to Make Gatekeeper Positions Contestable and the Challenge to Know What Is Fair: A Discussion of the Digital Markets Act Proposal' (2021) 3 *Zeit für europäisches Privatrecht* 503.

[19] A Bonatti and others, 'More Competitive Search Through Regulation', 8.

lowering barriers to market entry, and second, facilitating factors that encourage multi-homing by users.[20] What are the reasons that motivate such an approach? Digital platforms are multi-sided platforms (MSPs), whereby users on one side of the platform are generally offered either free or subsidised goods and services. The other side of the platform makes a monetary payment. The platform acts like a gatekeeper, or an infrastructure superhighway, which brings these users together by solving the coordination problem. In that respect, these platforms play a very important role, as they facilitate transactions that would otherwise not take place. 'Size, business model, and connection capacity' are but some important indicators of a gatekeeper.[21] In the process of facilitating transactions, these platforms also gain access to valuable data, ie information about the habits, tastes, and preferences of the platform users. This access to data offers these platforms a potent power to offer personalised recommendations and services. The digital networks work like an endless loop, wherein they make customised offers that are to the customer's liking. Finding relevant search results, the users turn back to the platform to further meet their needs, and in the process offer even more data. Schumpeter's 'wave of creative destruction' may find limited effect in this endless digital loop, as market entry barriers (principally, access to data and algorithms) limit the prospect of successful market entry. Contractual restrictions can go a long way in erecting barriers to market entry. Android, for instance, uses contractual restrictions to limit competition.[22]

However, data is not the sole enabler of competition. Access to data needs to be seen in relation to the algorithms. Therefore, over-regulation, too, may stifle competition. Algorithms are oftentimes protected by proprietary intellectual property rights (IPRs). IPRs encourage innovation as they ensure that innovators can profit from innovation. Copyright for instance plays a very important role in the digital economy, as all creators, following an original creation of the work (be it a poem, a story or any other work), automatically benefit from copyright protection.[23] In this respect, the IPRs resolve the incentives problem by offering intangible proprietary rights to make the innovation and creativity non-rival and non-excludable.[24] Even though *prima facie* copyright (a form of intellectual property) and competition law may seem to go in different directions, there is a common thread that binds them together, which is 'to enhance consumer welfare'.[25]

While it is evident from the foregoing that data, and its related aspects, may exhibit anticompetitive effects, the case of algorithms may be somewhat different. Incentives to innovate must be kept into consideration in order to balance the different interests of access vis-à-vis innovation.

[20] ibid.
[21] N Dunne, 'Platforms as Regulators', 20.
[22] Bonatti and others (n 19) 9.
[23] Berne Convention, Art 2 and Art 5.
[24] Gupta and Mehta (ch 8 in this volume) 144.
[25] ibid 144. See also the references therein.

3. Concluding Thoughts and Further Research

The discussion in this book makes it amply clear that in light of the special nature of the platform economy, contestability of the markets calls for recurring *ex ante* regulatory oversight. In the *Google Shopping* and *Google Android* cases, the Commission, following a long investigation, imposed an exhaustive range of remedies.[26] While a few years may be a short time frame to assess the effectiveness of these remedies, from what emerges, at the moment at least, it seems that these remedies have so far neither affected Google's position of dominance nor facilitated any competing market entries.[27] This means that some kind of *ex ante* regulatory framework is a *sine qua non* to facilitate the contestability of the digital markets.

An important related question is then the nature, intensity, and frequency of this regulatory intervention. Should this intervention be detailed and prescriptive? Alternatively, should the intervention be more abstract? Anticompetitive behaviour, and questionable business models notwithstanding, it is abundantly clear that these platforms have significantly contributed to the recent fast-paced developments in the converged digital economy.

In its attempt to tame in the digital intermediaries, the EU has taken a well-integrated approach touching upon distinct facets of law. In its 2020 Communication on 'Shaping Europe's Digital Future', while introducing the key action plan for a European Data Strategy (comprising of a legislative framework for data governance, and potential Data Act) as well as the Digital Services Act package (comprising of the Digital Services Act and the Digital Markets Act), the Commission was of the opinion that:[28]

> [C]ompetition policy alone cannot address all the systematic problems that may arise in the platform economy. Based on the single market logic, additional rules may be needed to ensure contestability, fairness and innovation and the possibility of market entry, as well as public interests that go beyond competition or economic considerations.

The DMA (part of the DSA package) was first proposed in December 2020. The urgency of the situation, such as irreversible competitive harms once the relevant markets tipped to a certain standard, prompted a swift action from the legislature, and the DMA entered force in November 2022. The basis of the proposed legislation is Article 114 TFEU. In September 2022, the European Parliament, and the

[26] *Google Shopping* (AT. 39740) Commission Decision, available here: competition-cases.ec.europa.eu/cases/AT.39740. Decision of the General Court in Google Shopping (T-612/17) available here: curia.europa.eu/juris/liste.jsf?num=T-612/17. *Google Android* (AT. 40099) Commission Decision, available here: competition-cases.ec.europa.eu/cases/AT.40099. Decision of the General Court in Google Android (in Case T-604/18) available here: curia.europa.eu/juris/document/document.jsf?text=&docid=265421&pageIndex=0&doclang=en&mode=lst&dir=&occ=first&part=1&cid=2637.

[27] Bonatti and others (n 19) 3.

[28] Communication from the Commission to the European Parliament, the Council, the European Economic and Social Committee and the Committee of the Regions, 'Shaping Europe's digital future', eur-lex.europa.eu/legal-content/en/TXT/?uri=CELEX%3A52020DC0067.

Council of the EU stamped the DMA with their seal of approval. The gatekeepers will have until 6 March 2024 to comply with the requirements of the Act.

It is not easy to place the DMA on the legal spectrum. While being closely similar to and aligned with EU competition law, it remains dissimilar to the core competition law framework. To understand what the DMA is all about, one must look into the structure, the contents, and approach to decipher the exact nature of the DMA. The DMA enforcement framework takes a wide approach taking into account competition, consumer, and data protection law.[29] The DMA refers to a list of closed-ended core platform services (CPS). These include the following eight categories: online B2C intermediation services, which includes marketplaces, such as (1) the Apple App Store and Google Play Store; (2) online search engines, such as the Google search engine; (3) online social networks, such as Facebook; (4) video-sharing platform services, such as YouTube; (5) number-independent interpersonal communication services, such as Skype; (6) cloud computing Services, such as Amazon Web Services (AWS); (7) operating systems, such as Apple iOS; and (8) advertising services, such as Google ad exchange. The list in a certain sense also reflects and relates to current or already complete antitrust investigations by the Commission under Article 101 and 102 TFEU. What is common to all these CPS are that they share certain industry-specific features that make them susceptible to market failure. These include the enduring market power of these platforms and insurmountable barriers to market entry for potential entrants.[30]

The DMA promises to make the digital markets contestable. This goal is not pursued in isolation by the DMA. Other EU regulatory frameworks complement and sustain this objective of the DMA. The Platform-to-Business Regulation (P2BR), the General Data Protection Regulation (GDPR), the Audio Visual Media Services Directive (AVMS Directive), and the European Electronic Communications Code (EECC) are key complements to the DSA package.[31] The DMA also develops, and builds upon the 2020 EU Platform to Business Regulation (EPBR). The P2B Regulation entered force in July 2019, and became effective from 12 July 2020. The Regulation is a part of the Commission's larger EU Digital Single Market Strategy. As stated in Article 1(2), the P2B Regulation is applicable to online intermediation services and online search engines, that are either established in the European Union (EU), or that 'offer goods or services to consumers located in the Union'.[32]

The DMA respects the fundamental principles of the EU law, namely, the obligations imposed under its framework should relate to and help attain its

[29] B Beems, 'The DMA in the broader regulatory landscape of the EU: An Institutional Perspective' (2022) *European Competition Journal* 25.

[30] cf chs 1, 3, and 12 in this volume.

[31] A de Streel and P Larouche, 'The European Digital Markets Act proposal: How to improve a regulatory revolution' (2021) *Concurrences*.

[32] Article 1(2) Subject matter and scope, Regulation (EU) 2019/1150 of the European Parliament and of the Council of 20 June 2019 on promoting fairness and transparency for business users of online intermediation services [2019] OJ L186/57.

objectives, and second, the principle of proportionality.[33] The principle of proportionality requires that the regulatory requirements should be necessary and must not exceed what are required to meet the goal, ie the underlying objective.

This book contributes to the existing literature by offering a normative basis for regulation of digital platforms. It also brings to light the non-price dimensions of competition, and interdependences between different areas of law in light of the rise of non-price competition in the platform economy.

Remedial design in the DMA (in the EU), and other regulatory frameworks applicable in other jurisdictions, and an analysis of whether they are efficient and effective can form the basis for further follow-on research.

Further research may also explore whether the time is now ripe to inch towards polycentricism in competition and regulation; a vision that takes additional non-price considerations into account, and one that transcends the narrow confines of the relevant product and geographic markets.

[33] de Streel and Larouche (n 29) 47.

INDEX

www.ingramcontent.com/pod-product-compliance
Ingram Content Group UK Ltd.
Pitfield, Milton Keynes, MK11 3LW, UK
UKHW021238300926
15471UKWH00013B/509